**Gale ECCO Print Editions**

Relive history with *Eighteenth Century Collections Online*, now available in print for the independent historian and collector. This series includes the most significant English-language and foreign-language works printed in Great Britain during the eighteenth century, and is organized in seven different subject areas including literature and language; medicine, science, and technology; and religion and philosophy. The collection also includes thousands of important works from the Americas.

The eighteenth century has been called "The Age of Enlightenment." It was a period of rapid advance in print culture and publishing, in world exploration, and in the rapid growth of science and technology – all of which had a profound impact on the political and cultural landscape. At the end of the century the American Revolution, French Revolution and Industrial Revolution, perhaps three of the most significant events in modern history, set in motion developments that eventually dominated world political, economic, and social life.

In a groundbreaking effort, Gale initiated a revolution of its own: digitization of epic proportions to preserve these invaluable works in the largest online archive of its kind. Contributions from major world libraries constitute over 175,000 original printed works. Scanned images of the actual pages, rather than transcriptions, recreate the works ***as they first appeared.***

Now for the first time, these high-quality digital scans of original works are available via print-on-demand, making them readily accessible to libraries, students, independent scholars, and readers of all ages.

For our initial release we have created seven robust collections to form one the world's most comprehensive catalogs of 18$^{th}$ century works.

*Initial Gale ECCO Print Editions collections include:*

> ***History and Geography***
> Rich in titles on English life and social history, this collection spans the world as it was known to eighteenth-century historians and explorers. Titles include a wealth of travel accounts and diaries, histories of nations from throughout the world, and maps and charts of a world that was still being discovered. Students of the War of American Independence will find fascinating accounts from the British side of conflict.

***Social Science***

Delve into what it was like to live during the eighteenth century by reading the first-hand accounts of everyday people, including city dwellers and farmers, businessmen and bankers, artisans and merchants, artists and their patrons, politicians and their constituents. Original texts make the American, French, and Industrial revolutions vividly contemporary.

***Medicine, Science and Technology***

Medical theory and practice of the 1700s developed rapidly, as is evidenced by the extensive collection, which includes descriptions of diseases, their conditions, and treatments. Books on science and technology, agriculture, military technology, natural philosophy, even cookbooks, are all contained here.

***Literature and Language***

Western literary study flows out of eighteenth-century works by Alexander Pope, Daniel Defoe, Henry Fielding, Frances Burney, Denis Diderot, Johann Gottfried Herder, Johann Wolfgang von Goethe, and others. Experience the birth of the modern novel, or compare the development of language using dictionaries and grammar discourses.

***Religion and Philosophy***

The Age of Enlightenment profoundly enriched religious and philosophical understanding and continues to influence present-day thinking. Works collected here include masterpieces by David Hume, Immanuel Kant, and Jean-Jacques Rousseau, as well as religious sermons and moral debates on the issues of the day, such as the slave trade. The Age of Reason saw conflict between Protestantism and Catholicism transformed into one between faith and logic -- a debate that continues in the twenty-first century.

***Law and Reference***

This collection reveals the history of English common law and Empire law in a vastly changing world of British expansion. Dominating the legal field is the *Commentaries of the Law of England* by Sir William Blackstone, which first appeared in 1765. Reference works such as almanacs and catalogues continue to educate us by revealing the day-to-day workings of society.

***Fine Arts***

The eighteenth-century fascination with Greek and Roman antiquity followed the systematic excavation of the ruins at Pompeii and Herculaneum in southern Italy; and after 1750 a neoclassical style dominated all artistic fields. The titles here trace developments in mostly English-language works on painting, sculpture, architecture, music, theater, and other disciplines. Instructional works on musical instruments, catalogs of art objects, comic operas, and more are also included.

# The works of Mr. Nathaniel Lee, in two volumes. Volume 2 of 2

Nathaniel Lee

biblioLife
old books. new life.

# THE
# WORKS
## OF
# Mr. *Nathaniel Lee*,

## VOLUME *the* SECOND.

CONTAINING,

| | |
|---|---|
| CÆSAR BORGIA | OEDIPUS. |
| LUCIUS BRUTUS | DUKE *of* GUISE. |
| CONSTANTINE | MASSACRE *of* PARIS |

*There in a Den, remov'd from Human Eyes,*
*Posseſt with Muſe, the Brain-ſick Poet lyes.*
*Too miſerably wretched to be nam'd,*
*For Plays, for Heroes, and for Paſſion fam'd*
*Thoughtleſs he Raves his ſleepleſs Hours away,*
*In Chains all Night, in Darkneſs all the Day.*
*And if he gets ſome Intervals from Pain,*
*The Fit returns, he foams, and bites his Chain,*
*His Eye-balls rowl, and he grows Mad again*

*LONDON*:
Printed for RICHARD WELLINGTON, at the *Dolphin* and *Crown* in St. *Paul*'s Church-Yard. MDCCXIII.

# CÆSAR BORGIA;

SON OF

Pope *ALEXANDER* VI.

A

# TRAGEDY.

Written by *NAT. LEE.*

*LONDON*,

Printed for *Rich. Wellington*, at the *Dolphin* and *Crown* at the West End of St. *Paul's Church-Yard*, 1712.

# PROLOGUE, Written by Mr. *Dryden.*

*TH' unhappy Man, who once has trail'd a Pen*
*Lives not to please himself but other Men,*
*Is always drudging, wasts his Life and Blood,*
*Yet only eats and drinks what you Think good:*
*What Praise soe're the Poetry deserve,*
*Yet every Fool can bid the Poet starve.*
*That fumbling Letcher to revenge is bent,*
*Because he thinks himself or Whore is meant:*
*Name but a Cuckold, all the City swarms*
*From* Leaden-Hall *to* Ludgate *is in Arms.*
*Were there no fear of* Antichrist *or* France,
*In the blest Times poor Poets live by chance.*
*Either you come not here, or as you grace*
*Some old Acquaintance, drop into the place,*
*Careless and qualmish with a yawning Face.*
*You sleep o're Wit, and by my troth you may,*
*Most of you Talents lye another Way.*
*You love to hear of some prodigious Tale.*
*The Bell that toll'd alone, or* Irish *Whale.*
*News is your Food, and you enough provide,*
*Both for your selves and all the World beside:*
*One Theatre there is of vast resort*
*Which whileome of Requests was call'd the Court.*
*But now the great* Exchange *of News 'tis hight,*
*And full of hum and buzz from Noon till Night:*
*Up stairs and down you run as for a Race,*
*And each Man wears three Nations in his Face,*
*So big you look, tho' Claret you retrench,*
*That arm'd with bottled Ale, you huff the* French:
*But all your Entertainment still is fed*
*By Villains, in your own dull Island bred.*
*Would you return to us, we dare ingage*
*To show you better Rogues upon the Stage:*
*You know no Poison but plain Rats-bane here,*
*Death's more refin'd, and better bred elsewhere.*
*They have a civil way in* Italy
*By smelling a Perfume to make you dye*
*A Trick would make you lay your Snuff-box by.*
*Murder's a Trade----------so known and practis'd there,*
*That 'tis Infallible as is the Chair----------*
*But mark their Feasts, you shall behold such Pranks*
*The Pope says Grace, but 'tis the Devil gives Thanks.*

# Dramatis Personæ.

| | | |
|---|---|---|
| *Cæsar Borgia*, *Palante* Duke of *Gandia*. | Sons of *Alexander* the Sixth. | Mr. *Betterton*. Mr. *Williams*. |
| *Machiavel*, | Secretary of *Florence*. | Mr. *Smith*. |
| *Paul Orsino*, | Head of the *Factions* against *Borgia*. | Mr. *Gillow*. |
| *Ascanio Sforza*, | A Buffoon Cardinal. | Mr. *Lee*. |
| *Vitellizzo*, | Chief of the *Vitelli*. | Mr. *Percival*. |
| *Enna*, | | |
| *Ange*, | | |
| Cardinals, *&c.* | | |
| *Bellamira*, | Daughter of *Orsino*. | Mrs. *Lee*. |
| *Adorna*, | Her Kinswoman and Confident. | Mrs. *Price*. |
| Attendants, *&c.* | | |

*The Scene* Rome.

CÆSAR

# CÆSAR BORGIA.

## ACT I. SCENE I.

*Scene is a Chamber of State, at distance are discovered little* American *Boys with Boxes of Jewels in their hands; on each side of the Stage, from the flat Scene to the Chamber, long* Indian *Screnes are spread at their full length.*

*Enter* Alonzo, *and* Don Michael.

*D. Mich.* ARE these the Presents, sayst thou, of the
New Cardinal *Ascanio Sforza*? (late
*Al.* They are; he offers thus to *Machiavel*,
And thinks that Gold may bribe him to betray
The Duke *Valentinois* But, *Michael*, tell me
What does the World report of this Creation,
Does it not rail, and grin, and bite the Pope?
*D. Mich.* Has it not Reason? For, betwixt our selves,
Would any Man in his high Dignity
So vilely sell the Glories of the Church?
Twelve Cardinals at once created!
*Ascanio* first, because he bids him most,
A fine effeminate Villain, bred in Brothels,
Senseless, illiterate, the Jear of *Rome*,
A blot to the whole See! One fitter far
For Hospitals, that paints and patches up
A wretched Carcass worried in the Stews.
But, see! the gaudy Pageant moves this way:
How spruce he looks! and with a Pocket Glass
Surveys the gloating Image.
*Alonz.* All Luxury:
I heard, the night succeeding his Creation,
That he got drunk, and kiss'd the Prelates round
For joy—But, see he comes, retire and leave me
(*Ex.* D. Mich.

 *Enter*

*Enter* Ascanio Sforza.

*Ascan.* Well, *Borgia*, well! if I am not reveng'd!
Was there none else in *Rome*, but *Bellamira*?
Ah *Bella*, *Bella*, *Bella*, *Bellamira*!
I saw her first at Mass, as I remember,
Cherubin and Seraphin were nothing to her:
Oh such a skin full of alluring flesh!
Ah, such a ruddy, moist, and pouting Lip,
Such Dimples, and such Eyes! such melting Eyes,
Blacker than Sloes, and yet they sparkl'd fire,
Then such a way she had to roul 'em round;
As thus, and thus——a thousand amorous ways,
And wink and gloat, and turn 'em to the corners——

*Alonz.* My Noble Lord!

*Ascan.* My dear, my dear *Alonz.*!
Nay, let me greet thee. 'twas the Father's Custom.
But tell me, lovely, dear *Alonzo*, tell me:
Thou hast the softest fine Complexion for
A Lover; best take heed of walking late:
Tell me I say, or I will pinch thy Cheek?
Moves he this way, or does he teem alone
With some state Birth? if so, I'll wait agen.

*Alonz.* Whom does your Eminence intend?

*Ascan.* Thy Lord:
Whom should I mean, intend, or think of else
Thy Lord and mine. Well he's an Oracle! intend
Why Man, I dream of nothing else!

*Alonz.* But Wenches.

*Ascan.* O *Machiavel*! there, there's a word, a sound,
An Air, a blast, a Thunder clap of wit,
To rouse our Foggy thick-scull'd Cardinals:
I'll say no more, Would he were *Pope*,
Head of the Christian World, and I his Engine,
His particular member, to bring, to cast,
To throw, disperse, convey the warmest
Sprinklings of his benediction.

*Alonz.* My Lord, I humbly offer'd your Address,
While with an Eye, swift as the Sun and piercing,
He ran your Letter o're: and sure it stirr'd him
For strait he turn'd, and darting me, he ask'd

If the great Cardinal, meaning you, my Lord,
Which ſhews the deep reſpect he bears your Perſon,
Knew not that *Borgia* was his beſt of Friends.
*Borgia*, he cry'd again, to whom the Lords
Of *Florence* ſent me their Ambaſſadour
With promis'd aid againſt the Rebel *Orſino*.

*Aſcan.* Has he receiv'd——ſtay, I ſay, has he? here,
Open thy Fiſt, now gripe me faſt, and tell me.

*Alonz.* I durſt not name your Preſents,
But, bowing, ſoon retir'd, and plac'd 'em here,
That as he follows, he may view at once,
All your Magnificence——if ought of Earth
His Temper holds, this Lightning will diſſolve it:
But ſee! He comes, be pleas'd, Sir, to retire,
And you ſhall hear the Zeal with which I ſerve you.

*Enter* Machiavel.

*Mach.* Thus have I drawn the Platform of their Fates;
As oft I have beheld, by Maſters hands,
A Tale in painting admirably told,
Here a ſoft *Dido* ſtabb'd into the Breaſt,
A Hero there thrown headlong from a Window,
To meet her Lover wrack'd upon the Shore:
So have I form'd in more than Braſs or Marble,
The Deaths of thoſe whom I intend to huſh.
O, *Cæſar Borgia*! ſuch a Name and Nature!
That is my ſecond ſelf, a *Machiavel*!
A Prince! who, by the Vigor of his Brain,
Shall riſe to the old height of *Roman* Tyrants.

*Alonz.* He deeply thinks; nor dare I interrupt him,
Till he comes forward.

*Aſcan.* Peace, and give him way--O ſuch a Headpiece!

*Mach.* In all my ſtrict Enquiries, all the Humours
Which I have drain'd with more than Chymiſts Pains,
I have not found a Temper ſo compleat
To finiſh forth a Greatneſs as my *Cæſars*.
Firſt, he's a Baſtard, got in a Fit of Nature!
She ſhook him from her Nerves in a Convulſion.
His Father ſtampt the Bullion in a heat,
And taking from the Mint the fiery Ore,
His Image bleſt, and cry'd, it is my own

Yet more, a Priest begot him, and 'tis thought
That Earth is more oblig'd to Priests for Bodies,
Than Heav'n for Souls! nay, and a young Priest too,
Perhaps in the Embraces of a Nun,
Who ventur'd Life to clasp the lusty Joy.

*Ascan.* Oh, if a Man could but hear him now! Brain,
Alas, *Alonzo*, we are Stuff to him—— (all Brain;
Meer Entrails, but the Guts of Government,
Nothing to him—— hark——he goes on——.

*Mach.* Why, what a start of Nature is this Man
Whom by Ambition, not by Love I'll raise?
Therefore *Ascanio*'s new golden World,
I gravely take, for Ruin to the Bride,
To her old doting Father, Brothers, Uncles;
And the whole Race of *Orsin* and *Vitelli*
Is fixt by Fate and me. No more! the fleeting Air
May catch the sounds, and walls themselves have ears.

*Alonz.* My Lord! the Cardinal *Ascanio* [*coming forward*
Is planted to your Order. (*and bowing.*

*Mach.* Let him hear us——
Urge me no more,——for 'tis impossible

*Alonz.* My Lord, he thinks not so.
He says your Voice is as the Mouth of Heav'n
Stiles you a God, and in the extravagance
Of his unbounded admiration, swears
Nothing to you can be impossible.

*Mach.* Extravagance indeed!
Yet such extravagance expresses love,
And merits all my thanks: and had he mention'd
Ought but the ruin of my best of Friends,
I would with all the Wings of expedition
Have shot thro' a thousand bars to do him service.

*Alonz.* My Lord! he does not hint at *Borgia*'s ruin.

*Mach.* Does he not wish that I should break the Nuptials?
'Tis sure the Marriage I at first dislik'd,
I pierc'd the Charmer with a narrow Eye
And found how Wit and Beauty threatn'd in her,
With all the subtlest Graces, that might lull
Stubborn Ambition to inglorious Rest.
But Love already had perform'd his part,

And

And laid the warring *Borgia* at her Feet,
How then should I oppose his first Enjoyment,
Who was his Legate, and sollicited
The Parents of the beauteous *Bellamira*

*Alonz.* At least Sir, for the future, lay some Block
That may disturb the Progress of their Loves,
And since you have alledg'd 'tis for his Glory
This Marriage were undone, since it is done,
Let it be hurtful in the Consequence.

*Mach.* Thus I should prove indeed a Friend to *Florence*,
Who hate *Orsino's* Race: Nay, I should act
The truest part of Friendship to my *Borgia*,
Snatching this Soft'ner from his War-like Bosom,
And turning him new bent, for Arms and Glory——
Ha! What new Scene of Gallantry is this:
Whence, and from whom comes this Magnificence
And wherefore kneel these Offerers at my Feet?

*Alonza.* They are the Children of the new-found World,
The Forms of *Zemes*, call'd the *Indian* Gods.

*Mach.* Away with 'em, and bid 'em tell their Lord,
*Machiavel's* Virtue never shall be brib'd,
And for their Service give 'em twenty Crowns:
But if thou darest to rob 'em of a Spangle,
You know my Humour——never see me more.

*Alonz.* Doubt not my Lord, but I'll observe your Humour--
Come in, my Lord——I told you he would melt.
Sir, the great Cardinal. So——now they cringe,
What, and embrace too! Oh thou damn'd, damn'd World.
These will be heard and make your Statesmen smile,
When Orphans, Widows, and the crippled Souldiers
Are elbow'd off, and thrust away in Frowns. [*Exit with the Boys.*

*Mach.* My Lord, you make me wonder! Sure you'v been
In Love your self with old *Orsino's* Daughter!

*Ascan.* Lov'd her, my Lord! witness these falling Tears!
Why do you thaw my Nature with your Questions?
Witness bright Stars! Witness your golden Planets!
And all ye Woods, and all ye purling Streams,
And Birds and Flocks, and Grots, and Rocks, and Flow'rs!
Nay, Sir, I tell you, she was mine betroth'd,

If I could cast my Coat, which had been done.
For nothing tickles the present Pope like Gold,
Dazles him that he weeps Indulgences,
Forgives, absolves, all for Omnipotent Gold,
Dispenses Pardons sometimes in a Fury,
He sends his Bulls abroad that roar like Thunder:
When strait a Golden Calm
Come o're their Backs, and then they are still as Lambs:
Why should I hold you long amongst the rest,
That saw her *Borgia*, that unlucky Bastard,
Behold and lov'd her——I, my Lord, was ruin'd.

*Mach.* My Lord! I wish the Marriage may not prosper:
He's bent to enjoy her, and in that I sooth him:
For subtly offering once to bring him off,
I found pale Anger in his Face like Death,
Whereon I feign'd compliance, and have wrought
The Business to a head——But let time work,
And rest assur'd, that what so mean a Man
As *Machiavel* with honour can perform,
To pay you perfect Service shall be done.

*Ascan* My Lord! farewel --when I protest and swear,
Ev'n by the Altar of fair *Bellamira*,
My Life is yours. Believe I am your Servant,
Not a step further by my Robe! your Captive,
Your Eminence most humble Creature, Servant, Slave. [*Ex.*

*Mach.* I am ty'd for ever. Ascanio *walking.*
No dull Buffoon! thou walking lump of Lust,
Not to revenge thy ungor'd Appetite
Shall *Borgia* kill her: But for his own Renown.
He is my Champion Prince, *Italian* Tyrant,
Not form'd to languish in a Womans Arms.
Oh——'tis a fault, were I so fram'd for greatness,
E're I would amble in a Female Court,
And cringe, and skip, and play the Ladies Cripple,
I would be Gibbeted i'th' Common way,
For Crows and Daws to peck my Carrion Limbs.
But I must rouze him, and 'Ill do't by Death,
Ev'n by the bloody Death of her he doats on.

*Enter* Adorna.

Here's one Ingredient I must mix to make

The

The Portion Death——The Wretch is deep in Love
With *Borgia*'s Brother, the young Duke of *Gandia*,
That Way I make her ſure!

*Ador.* My Lord.

*Mach.* My dear *Adorna*,
How goes the Marriage forward? and how treats
The Gallant *Borgia*, great *Valentenois*,
*Romania*'s Duke his fair and Virgin Bride?

*Ador.* The Rites are to be ſolemniz'd this Morning;
Tho' *Bellamira* quite abhors the Marriage,
Who ſtill when *Borgia* humbly ſues for Love;
Anſwers him with Tears, and pays his Vows
With Ominous Weeping.

*Mach.* And how takes he that?

*Ador.* He walks and muſes deeply, ſpeaks to no Man,
But *Paul Orſino*, whoſe moſt watchful Wit
I fear deſcries where he has lockt her Heart;
With a bent Brow ſhe eyes the Duke of *Gandia*,
Salutes him not of Late: He came this Morning
Into her Chamber; dreadful was his Action,
Unworthy of my Blood, he thundred out;
But if the generous *Borgia* is refus'd,
Think not of *Gandia*, but of Blood and Death.

*Mach.* What inauſpicious Chance diſcover'd to him
A ſecret, which I thought Conceal'd from all,
But thee and me, and thoſe unhappy Lovers?

*Ador.* I cannot gueſs, he paus'd a while then ſigh'd,
And ſtarting up in fury charg'd her riſe:
Receive, he cry'd, receive him as a Husband
Whom the ſelected vertues of thy Sex
Can ne're deſerve, adorn thee like a Bride,
And meet him, tho' thy Treacherous heart is Mortgag'd,
Meet him at leaſt with well diſſembled Love,
Or by my hopes, I'll wreke my anger on thee,
With all the Torment that *Italian* Fury,
Could e'er invent for an Adulterous Wretch:
He cry'd I will, and after make thee nothing.

*Mach.* Haſte thee away! charm with thy utmoſt skill
The mourning *Ballamira*, to obey him:
The knot once ty'd, *Gandia* will ſoon diſpair.

Leave

Leave me to work him then: Millions to one
But I ſhall make him thine.

*Adr.* But did Duke of *Gandia* once proteſt?

*Mach.* Proteſt! He did proteſt, and ſwear, and vow.
Go, go, and haſte! for the day grows upon us. Ex. Adorna,
His Brother too! This Duke of *Gandia* bleeds,
For he is grown of late the *Romans* darling,
Warm'd in the very Boſom of the *Pope*,
And dearer than my *Borgia* to his Siſter,
The famous *Lucrece*, who can charm her Father
In all the heat of Excommunications,
When he throws Bulls, like Thunderbolts about him,
She like a *Venus* to his angry *Jove*
Moves with inceſtuous Fires, folds her white Arm
About his chafing Neck, ſtrokes his black Beard,
And ſmooths his furrow'd Cheeks to dimpled ſmiles,
The Brothers too enjoy'd her. O Heav'n, and Earth!
Not the firſt day, after ſuch infinite time
That Motion had th' irregular matter rowl'd
When all the wandring Atoms hit at laſt
Into this beauteous form, even when our Sires
Firſt mingled, was there ſuch a looſe of Nature,
Such a triumvirate of Lawleſs Lovers,
Such Rivals as out-do even *Lucian*'s Gods!
Ha! the *Orſini* here! and the *Vitelli*!
They move this way in murmuring *Cabals*,
Methinks Death darkens every Viſage there.
'Tis ſo——They are no more——Or this is true,
Or *Machiavel* knows nothing of Mankind. *Ex.* Mach.

*Enter* Orſino, Vittellozzo, Aſcanio, Adrian, Enna, Ange, *three Cardinals.* Oliveretto, Gravina.

*Vitel.* I ſay agen, I do not like the Marriage,
Were *Bellamira* mine, I'd ſell her off
For Gold, I'd merchandize her tender Beauty
With Infidels, and ſend her to the *Turk*,
Like an *Andomada*, to Gorge the Monſter,
Rather than to wed her to perfidious *Borgia*.

*Orſin* You are too violent.

*Vitel.* I think not ſo.
A drowning Man will graſp at any thing,
Nay ſink his Friend that leap'd among the Waves

To

To give him life, but you tho' in the gulph,
Ride on to Ruine, tho' your Friends call out.

*Ange.* Nay, though they point the Whirle-pool just be-
That would devour us all. [fore you,

*Adrian* Besides 'tis Impious,
Against all Right of Nature, Law of Reason,
To act the Tyrant o're a Daughters Will.

*Ascan.* She knows the Cruelties of *Cæsar Borgia*,
Has heard his Rapes and Murders! Mercy on me!
How did he use the poor *Venetian* Lady?
He forc'd her in a Wood, nay in a Ditch,
As I am credibly inform'd by those
That heard her squeak, in a Dry-Ditch deflowr'd her!
Add yet to this, my Lords, How, when the *French*,
At sacking of a Town, broke open Nunneries,
He truss'd at least 40 the pretty'st Rogues,
The Tenderest quaking things! never broke up'
All spotless Maids, like Buds never blown upon,
Nor touch'd even with the Tip of any Finger,
And kept them for his Letchery.

*Orsin.* Methinks my Lord *Ascanio*! my Lord *Millain*,
Or my Lord *Cardinal*, more Moderation
Would better fit a man of your Profession?
I would not come to the old Argument,
For then we clash: *Borgia* is now my Son;
Therefore I pray once more forbear to tax him;
The Theme is great and worthy that we mention,
*Romania*'s Duke and Nephew to the Pope.

*Ascan.* Prithee, old *Paul*: Prithee now be'n't so hot:
Good Reverend Gray-Beard: If you name his Greatness,
Pronounce him right, ev'n as his Holiness
Has own'd him to the World without a Blush,
His natural Son, his Nephew or his By-blow, that is,
In short old *Paul*, his down right Bastard.

*Orsin.* Without a blush· Should I stand up the Champion
Of absent *Borgia*, and unravel thee,
I tell thee, Priest, thou Scandal to the Altar,
Thy Front, thy Eyes, thy Lips, each part of thee
Would blush with Scarlet deeper than thy Robe.

*Ascan.* Peace Dotard peace.

I say

I ſay old ſtuttering *Paul*, thou'lt ha' the worſt on't:
Therefore peace, peace Dotard.

*Orſin.* Ha!

*Vitel.* Forbear: My Lord, Remember!

*Orſin.* How dares he thus provoke me?
Who knows, yet urges me, knows in his heart
How I have pierc'd into his deepeſt Thoughts,
Have had Intelligence of all his Vices,
Ev'n of his cloſeſt, darkeſt Deeds of Luſt,
And dar'ſt thou call me Dotard? Saucy Church-man!
Thou that gav'ſt Whores Indulgences for Sin;
So rank, that he frequents the common Stews;
For a new Face will give his ſcarlet Coat
To make the Strumpet fine.

*Oliv.* My Lord, Conſider where, to whom, of whom,
And what it is you utter?

*Orſin.* Place me, ſome Power,
Upon Saint *Peter*'s Vane, the very Ball,
And turn my Voice to Thunder, that I may
Lay open to the World the Helliſh Acts
Of this Contagious Prelate.

*Aſcan* Spit, ſpit thy Venom, nay, nay, let him out
Mark how he ſhakes now, by my Holy Dame [with't----
I have nettled him, Poor *Paul*——I Pity the old Fool—

Orſin *Aſcan.* Then Prieſt, let me demand thee,
Is not the Cupping-Glaſs that burns thy Luſt,
And draws thy riſing Gall to ſuch a Bliſter,
My Daughter's Scorn, and loathing of thy Perſon?
Ha! is't not that? I think I have ſtung you, Cardinal!
Worſe than the *Neapoli* Pox you gave
Our *Roman* Harlots———

*Aſcan.* Why how now, *Paul*, what doſt thou grow foul
Mouth'd now? by my Holy-Dame, had I a Sword
I'd firk thee, *Orſin*——I'd ſo Whip thee, *Paul*,
So flaw'g and ſcourge thee, thou ſhouldſt eat thy Words.
The Pox! why, how now? ha! the Pox i'faith!
The Pox to me! let me come at him——hah!

*Orſin.* Ha wilt thou fight?
So forward Prieſt! by Heaven I'll ſhave your Crown,
Stand back and let me mow this Poppy off;

Thi[s]

This rank red Weed that ſpoils the Churches Corn.

*Vitel* Did ever Fury run to ſuch a height!
Why, my Lord Cardinal, know you this place,
And how 'tis priviledg'd?

*Aſcan.* My Lord, I am ſilenc'd.
An eaſie Man made up of Patience. I!
No Gall in me! give me thy hand Old *Paul*:
Henceforth w'are Friends, and as a Friend I'll tell thee,
Ev'n from my Heart, I'll tell thee what I think:
Thou art bewitch't, Old *Paul*, beſotted, fool'd——;
This Son in-law of thine has ſeal'd thine Eyes,
And ſhortly I ſhall ſee thee walk the Streets
With a Dog and a Bell——nay——prithee be not angry;
For 'tis in love, I'll tell thee of a Dotage,
And ſo your ſervant noble *Vitellozzo*,
*Anga* and *Enna* yours——Farewel, my Lord,
And laſtly thine whoſe Neck is in the Nooſe,
Old Woodcock, *Orſin.* [*Exit* Cardinal.

D. *Gravin.* I am not us'd to fear,
But yet methought *Aſcanio*'s laſt Words
Were dreadful to my Ears.

*Orſin.* I have engag'd
My Daughter, Life and Honour, and all my Fortunes
For the Duke's Faith, and the Security
Of every Perſon here; why ſhould we doubt him?
Have we not ſeen his Labour in this Matter?
Four Thouſand Duckets, given us down in Hand,
With an Aſſurance of our former Pay,
Nay more, he binds himſelf not to conſtrain
Any one of us to appear in Perſon
Before him, but who pleaſes of himſelf:
Therefore let me intreat you clear your Brains,
Meet all this day together at the Marriage,
And pay him as he merits faithful Homage.

*Vitel.* There's ſomething here fore-bodes, in ſpite of
The Muſick that he makes, a harſh Concluſion.

*Orſin.* For ſhame no more! the very Fears of Children,
Becauſe he gives our Friends Allowances
And honours them with Charges, Governments,
Beyond their Qualities, we dread his Dealing,

And swear he means to draw our Faction from us.

*Vitel.* Henceforth say what you will, do what you please,
Since to your Interests I am link'd by Fate:
I will no more oppose your specious Reasons,
But instantly go wait upon the Duke. *Trumpets.*

*Orsin.* This day to add new Honours to the Marriage,
Our Son-in-law, the Duke *Valentinois*,
Receives the *Rose* before the Consistory,
A Grace which seldom is vouchsafed to Kings,
Indeed the greatest which the Sacred Head
Of the whole Christian World can give to Man,
The very highest Round of Human Glory.

Scene *draws, and shews the Consistory.* Borgia *comes forward, with the* Rose *carry'd before him in great Pomp. His Son* Seraphino *led by* Alonzo, Machiavel, *Attendants,* Ascanio, *and five* Cardinals, *&c.*

*Borg.* O *Machiavel*! was ever Pomp like this?
The Morning dawns with an unwonted Crimson;
The Flowr's more od'rous seem, the Garden Birds
Sing louder, and the laughing Sun ascends
The gaudy Earth with an unusual Brightness——
All Nature smiles, and the whole World is pleas'd,
Even all the World, but thy unhappy *Borgia*.

*Mach.* And why should he, whom every Man concludes
The Darling of the Times, whom bounteous Heav'n
Has Crown'd with Glory in successful Wars,
Whom it now doubly Crowns with Beauty too,
The brightest of her Sex, Why should he thwart
The whole Worlds Vogue, and think himself unhappy?

*Borg.* Yes *Machiavel*! Thou worthi'st of Mankind,
To thee I'll strip my Heart, that secret Bed,
With Vices, Virtues, every naked Thought,
And shew thee all the Mixture of a Man,
We are observ'd——Think me not over frail
Because I love: Were *Bellamira* dearer,
Her Father bleeds, and all the Rebel-Race;
I'll first insnare the Fools: Then preach Fate to 'em.

*Mach.* And let 'em know, just as the Cords are drawing,
None ought to offend his Prince, and after trust him.

*Borg.* My Lord *Orsino*! O forgive me, Heaven!

Who

Who have thus grosly fail'd to pay the Reverence
I owe the best of Fathers, best of Friends:
This Day, this glorious Day, for ever blest,
And never to be lost in *Times* dark Legend,
Crowns me your Son Thus then I bend my Knees,
Which are not us'd to kneel but at the Altar.
And O! permit me thus to kiss your Hand,
And pay the Eternal Vows of my Obedience.

*Orsin.* O rise, my Lord, all Duty is out done
With but one single bare Acknowledgment,
Yet for a satisfaction to this Company,
Say, do you love my Daughter *Bellamira*?

*Borg.* Ha! What says my Father? Do I live?
O Heaven! Why do you wound me with the Question?
Does the poor suff'ring Fair One Virtue love,
Who drinks the Brook, and eats what Nature yields,
Rather than feast in Courts with loss of Honour?
Do those, who on the Rack for Heav'n expire,
Love Angels, and Eternal Brightness there?
'Tis sure they do: And oh——'tis full as sure,
That *Cæsar Borgia* dies for *Bellamira*.

*Orsin.* No more, you Honour her and me too much:
Therefore this day I give her to your Arms
With all the pleasure of a proud old Father,
O'rejoy'd to see his Daughter match'd above him:
By Heav'n, my Eyes grow full, here all our discord
For ever end, all Jars betwixt the *Orsins*,
*Vitelli*, and the Duke of *Valentinois*,
Be bury'd ever in this strict Imbrace.

*Borg.* Since you will have it so, forgive my Duty;
Let me grow bold, and as a Friend imbrace you——

*Orsin.* See here, my Lord, for scarce can I distinguish,
Through the bright Joy that dazles my weak Sight,
*Oliverotto*, and the Duke *Graviana*,
When *Vitellozzo* comes to grace your Nuptials.
All on their Knees acknowledge you their Prince.

*Borg* My Equals all; Nor shall this Homage be,
I swear it shall not. Rise my Lords; your Arms.
Let me imbrace you round: By all things sacred,
I swear that none of you have been to blame,

Were you Confederates against my Arms?
You were: But *Borgia*'s infinite Ambition
Forc'd you against your Wills to let him know,
His head strong Youth, like a young fiery Horse,
Unless you kindly stop him in his speed,
Would hurl him from some Precipice to Ruin.
*Orsin.* See *Vitellozzo*! how he takes our Crimes
Upon himself.
*Borg.* Behold this Child, my Son!
I know not any thing the World calls precious,
Which in the darkness of my heart can match him,
But *Bellamira*. Take him *Vitellozzo*,
Take the dear Blood that trickles from my heart,
The very Strings that wind about my Life,
And let him for my part be Surety,
As beauteous *Bellamira* is for yours.
*Orsin.* Farewel, my Lord: With these Attendants here
I go to hast the Bride: and let my Life
Be answer for the little *Seraphino*. [*Ex.* Orsina Vitelli.
*Ascan* He has her now, that delicate bit of beauty
Which I reserved for my own Lechery.
He drills her from her old deluded Sire,
Hell and she melts! she melts into his Mouth:
But by my holy Dame I'll be reveng'd
On every part of him: His little Bastard,
Because he doats on him shall streight be mangled——
I'll do't I say: Yes by my holy Dame,
I will revenge my loss of Lechery——
Ha! what a Jerk was that? it grates my Bones,
Pray Heav'n it ben't a Spice, a little Tang
Of the *Neapolitan* Itch, O my holy Dame. [*Ex. with* Cardinals.
*Borg.* Now *Machiavel*, prepare to hear my Soul,
Hear to what softness and effeminate mourning
All my dear Victories at last are melted:
For I will tell thee though thou'lt scarce believe,
Since first I saw the Charming *Bellamira*,
The very Image of *Charlotta*'s scorn,
I have not had one hour of Free repose,
Ev'n when at last I have resolv'd to joyn
Our Hands and trust her with my tender Glory,

I've

I've ſtarted from my Bed, at midnight roſe,
And wander'd by the Moon· Then laid me down
Upon ſome dewy Bank, and ſlept till Morn.

*Mach.* Therefore there muſt be ſome ſtrange Circum
That firſt induc'd thoſe Fears,ſome dang'rous hint ſtance
For your ſuſpicions——

*Borg.* Yes *Machiavel*,
There is, there is a cauſe for my ſuſpicions.

*Mach.* Are your ſure of it?

*Borg.* Moſt ſure I am,
Sure as reſerv'dneſs does imply averſion:
Yet I, as if my Flames were Fire in Froſt,
The more ſhe cools, ſcorch, rage, and burns the more—

*Mach.* I gueſs your meaning, like *Charlotta*, ſhe
Has pawn'd her Heart---but 'tis confeſs'd you know him--

*Borg.* Ha! did I know the Name of him I dread?
What God in Arms ſhould ſave him from my Sword?
Here thou haſt rouz'd the Lion in my Heart,
*Italian* Spite, Revenge and blaſting Fury
Devours my Soul! all Mildneſs ſleeps like Death:
I boil like Drunkards Veins--Death! Hell and Vengeance!

*Mach.* Suppreſs this Fury——
Come! come! my Lord—— I find you are better skill'd
In Camps and Courts, and know not yet loves World.
She is reſerv'd you ſay, when you approach her,
Why, let her weep too: Was it ever known
A ſubtle Bride laugh'd on her wedding Day,
Or claſp'd her Lover in the Eye o'th' World?
I find you are unlearn'd! Sir--'tis their Trade,
The very Nature, Soul, and Life blood of 'em——
To whine and cry, and turn their heads away,
When their hearts dote on what they ſeem to ſcorn!

*Borg.* If it were ſo!

*Mach.* Why it was always ſo,
Is ſo, and will be ſo to the Worlds end!
Give me your hand, and take her on my word,
I have been bred in Courts, ſounded the humours
Even of all Women kind: Therefore adviſe you
Repair immediately to old *Orſino*,
Who with his Beauteous Daughter waits your Coming.

*Borg.* Could she be truly mine! the Wings of Winds
Would be too slow to waft me to her Arms!
*Mach.* Once more I say, she is and shall be yours,
Truly, religiously, devoutly yours——
Why all this thoughtless groundless Jealousy?
Let Manly Confidence and *Roman* Virtue
Master this Gothick Fury in your Blood.
*Borg.* By Arms! by all the Glories I have won!
Thou hast awak'd my Love, and Charm'd my fears.
*Charlotta!* O the very figure of her,
But sure the Beauteous Lines are softer here:
And now I find 'tis ruin to forgo her——
*Mach.* No more my Lord. 'Tis I that thus embark you
And if some starting Plank should flaw the Vessel
To your destruction---- I am ruin'd too----
Since all I have, or am, or ever would be,
Is to be yours, your sworn unbyass'd Friend.
*Borg.* Thou best of Men
Thou art my Oracle, my Heav'n, my Genius,
And as some God, shalt guide me through the World.
Let's go to the Conqust, tho' through Death we go,
Marriage and Death both new Experiments.
Methinks I see the Taper in the Window,
The busie Nurse unveils the weeping Maid,
And I must naked pass through Seas to reach her.
O fatal Marriage! O thou dismal Gulph!
Which like the *Hellespont* dost rore between
Me and my Joys. Is there no other way?
None, none, the Winds and the dash'd Rocks reply:
Why let 'em roar, and let the Billows swell;
Till the rack'd Orbs be with the Deluge drown'd.
'Tis fixt, I'll plunge, or perish, or enjoy her——
*Mach.* Justly resolv'd, nor let a few false Tears
Melt you again to an untimely mildness.
*Charlotta* thus deluded you in *France*,
Which render'd all you Court ridiculous:
Remember that, and the least the like disgrace
Should happen new, drag her if she refuses!
*Borg.* I will, my *Machiavel* --- O Arms! O Glory!
What an Eternal Rest would smear your Lustre.

Did

Did not this Spirit of Ambition fire me!
I'll tell her that the Lives of all her Race,
Are now within my Power.
*Mach.* Nay, threaten her!
*Borg.* I will do more than threaten,
Think not the dreadful *Cæsar* will be rows'd
To threaten only; that's a sleeping *Borgia*,
A loving, dreaming, Conscientious *Borgia*,
But when I wake there's always Execution———
*Mach.* It has been so.
*Borg.* And shall I swear again,
No *Machiavel*, she must be mine or dye,
Should she for Refuge to the Temple flie!
I'd after her; there if she scorns my flame,
To the Dumb Saints I will my Vows proclaim,
And in their View resolve the Glorious Game:
Upon the golden Shrines I'll lay her Head,
And ev'n the Altar make my Bridal Bed----[*Ex.* Ambo.

---

## ACT II. SCENE I.

*Enter* Orsino *and* Bellamira *in Mourning.*

*Orsi.* WHERE didst thou get the daring thus to move me!
By thy dead Mothers shrowd, not the first Night,
When in her Youthful arms I grasp'd her to me,
Was I so hot with Love as now with Rage,
Thou Young and Virgin Witch, thou new found Fury?
*Bella.* Ah! *Sir*, for I am afraid to call you Father,
Give me my Death. give to these trembling Breasts
A Thousand Wounds, or cut me Limb from Limb,
But do not look so dreadfully upon me———
Nor blast me with such Sounds. Oh pity me!
There's not one fatal Sentence, one dread VVord,
But runs like Iron through my freezing Blood.
What have I done? Ah, what is my Offence?
And tell me how, which way shall atone you?
*Orsin.* O, thou vile wretch! what is thy Offence?
Dost thou not know it? Exquisite dissembler!
Thou leading Sorc'ress! He-cat of thy Sex!

Subtleſt of all thy kind, that ever rowl'd
Their falſe deluding Eyes, and in their Glaſſes
Conjur'd for looks to cheat the ſimple World!
But to take all evaſion from thy Guilt,
Did I not charge thee, as thou fear'ſt my Curſe,
This very Morning to adorn thy ſelf
As one whom the Great Duke intends to honour
By making thee his Bride?

*Bell.* Alas! you did,
And I am come, Oh Heaven! and all you Powers
That pity Womans Weakneſs, I am come
My Lord as you commanded! and have vow'd,
Tho' Death attends my Nuptials, to obey you.

*Orſin.* Thou ly'ſt even in thy Heart, thou know'ſt thou ly'ſt.
Thou haſt maliciouſly, moſt groſly fail'd
In this Obedience. Say, declare, haſte, anſwer,
Thou moſt ungrateful Wretch, Ah, how unlike
Thy meek, thy Perfect bright and bleſſed Mother,
Is this a Habit for a glorious Bride?
Doſt thou thus meet the generous *Borgia*?
I know thy awkard Heart, thou mean'ſt by this
To tell the World, thou doſt not like thy Husband,
And daſh him at the Altar: But by Heav'n,
Whither thou, Murdereſs, now art ſending me,
This ſhall not ſerve thy Purpoſe. In this dreſs
That blaſts my Eyes and ſtrikes my Soul with ſadneſs,
I'll ſee the Prieſt for ever make you one.

*Bellam.* Ah! how have I deſerv'd this cruel Uſage?
Did ever Daughter yet obey like me?
Not ſhe who in the Dungeon fed her Father
With her own Milk, and by her Piety
Sav'd him from Death, can match my rigorous Virtue;
For I have done much more. Torn off my Breaſts,
My Breaſts, my very Heart, and flung it from me,
To feed the Tyrant *Duty* with my Blood.

*Orſin.* Call'ſt thou the lawful Impoſition of
A careful Father, that intends thee Honour,
Tyrannical and bloody? Rage reſume me,
Here, ſeeſt thou this? O would the gallant *Borgia*
Could fling thee from his Soul, as I from mine,

For

For 'tis Respect to him that saves thy Life;
Else by the Feaver that quite burns me up,
I'd ponyard thee, till all thy Robes were Crimson:
Yet since thou hast the Impudence to brave me,
And call thy Father Tyrant to his face,
I that have foster'd thee even from the Womb,
And bred thee in my Bosom, hear and tremble;
For I will curse thee till thy frighted Soul
Runs mad with Horrour, till thy Mother starts
From her cold Monument, to beg me cease,
Though all in vain.

*Bellam.* I cast me at your Feet;
I'm all Obedience: See, Sir, ——see me here
Groveling upon the Earth.

*Orsin.* Curs'd be the Night,
Ten Thousand Curses on that fatal Hour,
When my great Spirit trifled with thy Mother
For the Production of so false a Joy!

*Bellam.* O horrid blasting Breath!

*Orsin.* When I am dead,
My troubled Ghost shall nightly haunt thy Dreams.

*Bellam.* Ah, hold---I kiss your Feet, and hug your Knees.

*Orsin.* Though in thy Husbands Arms, I'll draw the Cur-
And stare thee into Frenzy, and thy Lord (tains.
I'll Charm so fast, thy Shrieks shall not awake him.

*Bellam.* Yet Sir, forbear; tread on me, trample me.

*Orsin.* And all the day, when other Spirits sleep,
I'll follow thee with Groans, and curse thee still.
Nay, when thou seek'st for Company to scape me,
I'll make thee scream. See there his Spirit stands.

*Bellam* Hear him not Heav'n!

*Orsin.* After thy first Imbrace,
May thy Lord loath thee; swear thou art no Virgin,
And cast thee off as a most leud Adulteress.

*Bellam.* If there be Saints or Angels · Oh I charge you---

*Orsin.* Or if thy Husband should by chance retain thee,
Heart burnings, Jealousies incite him still
To plague thee with a Thousand Hells on Earth,
And after end thee in some horrid manner.

*Bellam.* Ponyard me as you promis'd! Oh stab me!

*Orsin.*

*Orsin.* Eternal Barrenness shut up thy Womb,
If ought that's humane chance to raise thy Hopes,
May it be Monstrous at the curst Production,
And After-Birth, or some abhorr'd Conception.

*Enter Duke of* Gandia *in Mourning.*

*Bellam.* Y'have said enough! my Heart, my Spirits fail
And I have now my Wish without a Dagger. (me

*Orsin.* What now? another Mourner? Hell and Furies!
They both have plotted to undo my Honour.
Well—Duke of *Gandia*—but I'll call thee Bridegroom.

*Gand.* Ha! how's this? the beauteous *Bellarmira*
Upon the Earth. Help, help——my Lord, she's cold;
Your Daughter swoons.——

*Orsin.* I care not, let her Perish,
And thou, who hast seduc'd her, perish with her:
Swoon with her, sink with her, die both, and both be damn'd.
(*Ex.* Orsino.

*Gand.* Wake *Bellamira* from this Sleep of Death:
Life of *Palante*'s life! give me a Word,
See thou art Safe, clasp'd in thy *Gandia*'s Arms,
*Palante* holds thee. Say what Murderer
Offer'd this Cruelty, and I'll revenge thee!

*Bellam.* Where am I? ha! loose, loose me from your
Stand off, fly from me, fly, *Palante*, fly! (Arms,
For we must never, never meet agen
The *Poles* may sooner joyn: O I am lost,
By an inexorable Father ruin'd,
Cursed, blasted, and for thee, unhappy Prince,
Thou hast undone me, though not by thy Will,
For sure thou lov'st the wretched *Bellamira*
Yet by the consequence of this Affection,
Thou hast destroy'd my Peace of Mind for ever:
Thou hast been ruinous and mortal to me!
As Robbers, Ravishers, or Murderers!
Therefore be gone! fly from my Eyes for ever,
And never let me see *Palante* more.

*Gand.* I go for ever from you, as you charge me,
And for that purpose I did hither come,
But little thought that you would drive me thus:
I hop'd at least, that when I parted from you,

And

And bid you everlastingly farewel,
I hop'd, but oh those flattering hopes were vain!
That gentle *Bellamira* should have sigh'd
Or dropt a Tear, when I would take my leave
And never see her more.

*Bellam.* O Cruelty!
You rend the Plaister from the bleeding Wound.

*Gand.* An elder Brother calls you to his Bed,
And you perhaps will not be ravish'd thither:
O *Bellamira*! I had once those Vows
Which thy frail heart does now resign to *Borgia*.
But I have staid too long: Farewel for ever;
When I am gone, and thou for many years
Enjoy'st the Change thy Father forc'd thee to,
(For sure I cannot think it all thy doing!)
If happy *Cæsar Borgia* chance to fold thee
More closely in his Arms then was his Custom,
Say to thy Heart with a relenting Thought,
Thus, if our Fates had pleas'd, the wretched *Gandia*
Would thus have lov'd me. But no more farewel.
You're pleas'd to banish me- -and---- I'll obey. *Exit turns.*

*Bell.* Come back! come back! you shall not leave me thus
Let Fathers Curse, and Jealous Husbands Rage,
Love has a force that can surmount the World.

*Enter* Borgia.

If then 'tis destin'd that you must be gone,
And leave me to the Arms of Cruel *Borgia*——

*Borg.* Ha! but observe: there may be more in this.

*Bell.* If we two Lovers, whom for tenderness
The World can never match, must part for ever——

*Gand.* O, that for ever!

*Borg* It's Apparition all,
By Heav'n, a Dream, I swear, a very Dream.

*Bell.* Yet take, O take this dying farewel with thee!
And whomsoe're thy Passion shall Espouse,
Remember! O Remember this, and leave me:
No Man was ever so by Woman lov'd,
As thou *Palante* art by *Bellamira*.

*Gand.* Stop there, for to go on will give me Death.
O! thou hast utter'd Sounds of such a strain

As Nature cannot bear. like utmost Musick,
Which while it charms the Sense makes chill the Blood.
No more! for by my glimmering joys, I fear
Tho'lt sing my Soul to Everlasting Sleep!

*Borg.* Then let me wake you

*Bell.* O Heav'ns! we are undone!

*Borg.* Start not, nor weep not! beauteous *Bellamira*!
For there is nothing toward you, but well;
Fortune her self now smiles on your Design,
And Heav'n and Earth conspire to make you happy
These Mourning Habits on your Wedding Day,
Had chance not guided me to hear your Loves,
Would have betray'd the Secret——

*Gand.* O Brother! what must I expect? I know not
Whether I ought to hope or fear.

*Borg.* Hope all:
For curst is he that parts whom Heav'n has joyn'd:
I stand convinc'd that Love has made you one,
And may those Chaster Fires that warm your hearts,
Vie with the Stars for Immortality——

*Gand* Speak it again, again confirm this goodness,
For one so Noble sure this World contains not:
O! 'tis too little but to name him Noble,
For such a Soul aspires above the Clouds,
So great, Æthereal, and so God-like fram'd,
He must look down on Kings, such vast compassion,
Such an unheard Magnificence of Mercy
As we must both adore: Kneel, *Bellamira*,
For 'tis a God we talk with.

*Borg.* O you must not.
Methinks fair *Bellamira*, who still answers
With the accustom'd Language of her Tears,
Methinks you should have told me all this while;
Your Beauties were not doom'd for *Cæsar Borgia*.
'Tis true, I often fear'd by your reserv'dness,
Your Heart must be ingag'd——Or thou, *Palante*,
Had'st thou but told me when I woo'd her first,
How many sighs and sorrows, hadst thou sav'd me!
I would not then have launch'd, but yielded up
The Noble Fraight, this more than *Indian* Treasure,

An

And given thee all my interest in her Father.

*Gand.* Alas I fear'd!

*Borg.* I hold you Sir excus'd:
May you be happy as your Souls can wish;
But I must beg you from this place retire
For your own interest, *Orsino* here
Entreated me to wait him, and 'tis now
Upon this day, allotted for my Marriage,
Unfit to break the business of your Loves.
Yet doubt not, O most happy lovely Pair,
But Care and Time shall perfect all your Wishes.

*Gand.* Give me your Arms: I had design'd this Morning,
Made desperate with my Griefs, t'acquaint your Ear
With all the progress of my ruin'd passion.
I thought that you would storm, and use me ill,
And had design'd I know not what to forfeit
My life, rather than lose my *Bellamira*:
But you have so prevented me——

*Borg.* No more.
How, fairest *Bellamira*! not one word?
Am I ordain'd the Proxy of your Love,
Without the Breath of thanks?

*Bell.* The bounteous Heav'ns
Rain on your head whole Deluges of mercies,
For this great goodness! Hear me, oh ye Powers.
Hear me upon my Knees; where e're he goes.
Guard him with blessings! give him his own wishes:
If to the Wars he pass, Renown attend him,
And growing Conquest dwell upon his Arms;
Let him attain by a long course of Valour,
And gallant acts to the old *Roman* Greatness,
And when at last in Triumph he returns,
May all the sighing Virgins strow his way, (*Ex. with* Gandia.
And with new Garlands Crown his coming Glory.

*Enter* Machiavel.

*Mach.* Something's discover'd, and I guess the business!
My Lord, you're wanted, and the beauteous Bride.

*Borg.* I charge thee name her not upon thy Life.
Here, tear, tear off these unbecoming Garments,
Get me my Horse, and bid my Arms be ready,

Yes,

Yes, *Machiavel*, with to morrows dawn,
Thou shalt behold me in another Dreſs,
Breathing Defiance to theſe ſofter Wars
*Mach.* But why, Sir! why? how comes this ſudden
Why have you charg'd me that I ſhould not ſpeak (change!
Of *Bellamira*?
*Borg.* Cruel *Machiavel*!
Why doſt thou bring the fatal Charmer back,
Whom I would drive for ever from my Soul?
*Mach* This wondrous alteration of your humour,
Muſt ſure ariſe from ſome as wondrous cauſe.
Have you diſcover'd ought?
*Borg.* All, all's diſcover'd,
And ſuch an over ſight in thee, but where,
Where now is thy profound Sagacity?
Where all thy Depoſitions, Promiſes,
Warrants, Ingagements that ſhe ſhould be mine?
Chaſtly, religiouſly, devoutly mine?
*Mach* And is ſhe not?
*Borg.* By Heav'n quite oppoſite.
All that my boding heart preſag'd to thee
Before, has happen'd, happen'd in ſuch manner,
As quite out-went my own Imagination.
*Mach.* Who'ere he is that has ſupplanted you,
By your juſt Rage he was a ſecret Villain,
The cloſeſt Traytor that e're plotted miſchief,
And juſtly has deſerv'd the ſtab you gave him.
*Borg.* How, *Machiavel*? ha, didſt thou talk of ſtabbing?
*Mach.* I neither think, nor know what's your intention,
But that's your Countries Cuſtom in ſuch caſes:
Beſides, Sir, when I did diſcourſe you laſt,
You fell into Convulſions of Deſpair,
With mentioning the very name of Rival,
And thunder'd out whole Volleys of revenge.
*Borg.* True *Machiavel*: but could not think my Rival
Should prove my Brother.
*Mach.* Ha!
*Borg.* Raiſe, raiſe me Heaven,
Some other Man that dares to take her from me,
To ſnatch the only Beauty I can love,
And at the Altar too, from my imbraces,

If I not end him, though he were Imperial,
Ev'n in the middle of his Guards ———.

*Mach.* Your Brother!
And have you Confirmation that she loves him?

*Borg.* Why dost thou wonder? I both saw and heard,
Heard all his Vows, and her most passionate Answers:
She loves him. Yes, these cursed Remembrancers,
These Eyes have seen it. O! she dotes on him,
Feeds on his Looks——eyes him, as pregnant Women
Gaze at the precious thing their Souls are set on.

*Mach.* And you perhaps will bear it from a Brother
With all the meekness of an Anchorite,
A Man of quite another World! you'd best
Go to the Wars, be shot, and leave his Brother
The Heir of all, sole Darling of the Pope.

*Borg.* 'Tis certain, that I seem'd to appearance
Mild and relenting? begg'd 'em leave me here,
That I might think———.

*Mach.* Think! by your Holy Father,
You have no Blood, no Soul, nor Spirit left
The Genius of your House must blush at this;
A Brother! why, so much the more a Villain.

*Borg.* O *Machiavel*!

*Mach.* O Conscientious *Borgia*,
By all that's great, it is in him flat Incest,
There's for your Conscience, if you will have Conscience,
She was betroth'd yours by her Father's Will,
Publish'd to the World, and what else makes a Marriage?
And for a Brother thus to undermine you,
And carry it too? Are you *Italian* born?
Begot by one? O, make it not a Doubt,
I grieve, I groan, I am mad to see you thus!
What, to be made the Talk, the Jeer of *Rome*,
As once you were at *Paris* by *Cabrlotta*:
No——I'll revenge thee! cold as thou art and dead!
And may this Steel be sheath'd in *Machiavel*,
If that the treacherous Duke of *Gandia* scape me. (*Exiturus.*

*Borg.* Come back, I say, for what is to be done,
I'll act my self. Where was I? or where am I?
No *Machiavel*, thou know'st 'tis not my Conscience

Be-

That lets the Villain live: I think thou hast heard
The fatal Jars w'have had about my Sister:
For I remember, being in her Bath,
And by her Women told we were at VVords,
She ran in haste half naked to the *Pope*,
VVho came to part the Fray; and swore in fury,
VVith horrid Imprecations, who e're fell
By th'others Hands, he never would have Mercy
On the Surviver. This, my *Machiavel*,
Is *Borgia*'s Conscience—For to do a Murder,
And not be safe, is Drunkards Policy.

*Mach.* VVhat then is your intent?

*Borg.* To follow Nature:
For so do Flames that burn, and Seas that drown;
Yes, *Machiavel*, and care not what comes on't:
So when Security, and black Occasion
Point me to death, I will be rough as those,
And blood him, till he changes to a Ghost:
Yet since my Fathers threats bar present Murder,
I'll find a way to rack him.

*Mach.* Ha! you mend——
To take again your beauteous Prize; that is,
The lovely *Bellamira* still retains
Some holds about your Heart.

*Borg.* O, 'tis confess'd;
And howsoe're my Tongue has plaid the Braggart,
She Reigns more fully in my Soul than ever:
She Garrisons my Breast, and Mans against me
Even my own Rebel Thoughts, with thousand Graces,
Ten thousand Charms, and new discover'd Beauties.
O! hadst thou seen her when she lately blest me,
VVhat tears, VVhat looks, and languishings she darted;
Love bath'd himself in the distilling Balm.
And oh the subtle God has made his entrance
Quite through my Heart, he shouts and triumphs too,
And all his Cry is Death, or *Bellamira*.

*Mach* VVhy! this is like the Spirit of your Father.
You bring his graceful Vigour just before me,
Just, just as first he wore the triple Crown,

Just so he walk'd, just with that fiery Movement,
So sparkled too his Eyes! so glow'd his Cheeks
Nor fear *Palante*, when she's in your Arms,
When she perceives the fervour of your Passion
Panting upon her naked Breasts for Mercy
*Borg.* Sighing, as if my very Soul would burst,
And grasping, *Machiavel*, as if Death's Pangs were on me
*Mach* Now stealing to her Lips, dissolv'd in Tears,
And pressing close, but softly, to her Side,
Whispering, O why, why, gentle *Bellamira*!
Then with a sudden Start let loose your Love;
Grasp her as if you could no longer bear it
Clasp her all Night, and stifle her with Kisses:
O, there are thousand Ways!
*Borg.* Ten thousand thousand,
Millions, and infinite, yet add to those,
I'll try 'em all, nor shall a Drop of Mercy
Fall from my Eyes, though I beheld *Palante*
Dead at her Door O Expectation burns me!
O *Bellamira*! Heart! how she does inflame me?
*Mach* Then there's no need of warlike Preparations?
*Borg* Talk no more of War, for now my Theme's all [Love:
The War like Winter vanishes, 'tis gone,
And *Bellamira* with eternal Spring,
Drest in blue Heav'ns, and breathing Vernal Sweets,
Drops like a *Cherubin* in Smiles before me
*Mach* Oh, that the World could but behold you thus!
That *Bellamira* saw you in this Height
Of dazling Passion, and becoming Fury! [hurl'd,
*Borg* Thus, to a glorious Coast, through Tempests
We sail like him who sought the *Indian* World.
'Tis more, 'tis Paradise I go to prove,
And *Bellamira* is the Land of Love.
I have her in my View, and hark, she talks,
And see, about, like the first Maid she walks.
Fair as the Day when first the World began;
And I am doom'd to be the happy Man. [*Exeunt.*

## ACT III. SCENE I.

*Enter* Ascanio *and* Alonzo.

*Alonz.* MY Lord, this is an Act so newly horrid,
So ghastly a Contrivance of Revenge,
That Fiends themselves would start at the Proposal.
I to do this; I, who have bred him up!
Oh *Seraphino*! nurs'd thee in my Bosom,
To gash thy Cheeks, and tear out both thy Eyes!

*Ascan.* The Sums of Gold are order'd to be paid;
Half on your bare Consent. On Execution
The whole. *Alonzo*, thou hast no Compassion
When Interest comes in play: Don't I know,
At the Command of *Machiavel*, or *Borgia*,
Thou would'st not stick to poison ev'n the Pope?
Come, come, dissemble not thy Occupation,
Murder's thy Trade, and Death thy Livelihood,
Therefore perform this Act of spritely Vengeance,
And I'll create thee noble—— [turn,

*Alonz.* 'Tis sure, ere long, when I have serv'd their
That they will end me too, for fear of talking;
Therefore, my Lord, how-e'er my Conscience stings me,
For 'tis most true, I love the innocent Boy;
Send home the Gold——

*Ascan.* Thou shalt along with me;
I will not send, but pay it thee in Hand, [is that?
Full twenty thousand Crowns —— Why, what a Sum
Full twenty thousand Crowns!
Why, I will tell thee, there are Rogues in Orders,
*Monks, Fryars, Jesuits*, that would kill their Fathers,
Ravish their Mothers, eat their Brothers and Sisters,
For half the Sum. What, twenty thousand Crowns!
Away, away! Come, come, pull out his Eyes,
And make a *Cupid* of the little Bastard.
I swear thou shalt, what, twenty thousand Crowns!

*Alonz.* My Lord, I am charm'd.

*Enter* Machiavel *and* Adorni.

*Ascan.* My good Lord *Machiavel*.

*Mach.* My noble Lord,

Th

The humbleſt of your Servants — [*Ex*. Aſc. *and* Alon.
Now, my *Adorna*, now the time is coming,
When thou ſhalt rival even the Queen of Love,
For, by my Life, a Bridegroom like *Palante*
Might match an Empreſs — But he's thine, no more.
I've ſworn he's thine This Day, that gives his Brother
Thy beauteous Couſin, is the bleſt Fore-runner
Of my *Adorna*'s certain Happineſs.
*Ador.* Heav'n only knows the Iſſue of my Fate;
But did not Love and languiſhing Deſire
Tranſport me from my ſelf, I ſhould endeavour
To help the poor deſpairing *Bellamira*.
Not many Hours ago ſhe ran upon me
With Extaſies, even crying out for Joy,
In ſpite of Fate, *Palante* ſhall be mine,
Then told me all that you diſcours'd but now:
When on that Minute cruel *Borgia* enter'd
With old *Orſino*, who commanded her,
I'th' midſt of Prayers and Tears, and ſhrieking Sorrows,
Strait to attend her Husband to the Temple.
*Mach* Excellent! and how bears *Palante* this!
*Ador* So much the worſe, becauſe quite unexpected.
And while I told it in moſt moving Terms,
He ſtruck his Breaſt, and caſt his Eyes to Heav'n,
Enquir'd for you, then talk'd of Blood, and vaniſh'd.
*Mach* I have been, ever ſince I came to *Rome*,
A Confident to both I like the Method,
The *Machine* moves exactly to my Mind,
Sails like a Ship well ballaſt through the Air,
And ploughs the riſing Miſchiefs clear before me.
I've heard thee often talk of pretty Letters
That paſt between *Palante* and thy Couſin.
*Ador* I have 'em all in keeping, by her Order.
*Mach* Let me peruſe 'em.
*Ador.* Will you be ſecret then?
*Mach.* Away, and fear not, they ſhall make thy Fortune:
Soon as the Marriage Rites are paſt, we'll meet.
[*Exit* Adorna.
But lo, they come! The Duke of *Gandia* frowns,
I fear my *Cæſar*, and muſt watch their claſhing.

SCENE *draws, and discovers the Progress of a stately Marriage*; Ascanio, Adrian, Enna, *Cardinals, going before*, Orsino *following*: Bellamira *supported by two Virgins in white* Borgia *follow'd by* Vitellozzo, Alonzo, *&c.*

*Gand* Sir, I must speak with you.

*Borg* 'Tis inconvenient.

*Gand* 'Tis not our first of Jars. Remember *Lucrece*, Our Sister *Lucrece*, and be then perswaded Necessity requires your Ear.

*Borg* For what?

*Gand* If you dare walk aside with me, I'll tell you.

*Borg* After the Priest——

*Grand* No Sir —— before the Priest——
Fate hovers near us: you shall give me hearing.

*Borg.* What Boy! how say'st thou; shall!——

*Gand* Yes Sir, you shall.

*Borg.* No more, for fear we should be over-heard:
I'll instantly return, upon my Honour:
Let me but wait *Orsino* to the Gate,
And I'll attend thee, on my Word I will——
The Priest shall wait 'till thou have Satisfaction.

[*Exeunt all but* Mach. *and* Gan

*Mach.* What have you said, my Lord?

*Gand.* Forbear to know,
I think thou lov'st me, yet a Proof were well,
And since Occasion now demands a Trial,
Refuse not what my Friendship shall enjoin thee.

*Mach* 'Tis granted, though the Consequence be Dea

*Gand* Begone, this Moment leave me to my self.

*Mach* I apprehend Let me embrace you
Why shall I leave you? But my Word's ingag'd;
Call all those pow'rful Provocations up,
Your Wrongs, your most ignoble Injuries,
To steel your Arm, and die your Victory
In Blood: I go——because you grow impatient.
No more, but Conquest, Death, or *Bellamira*——
Yet I must watch you hereabouts For *Borgia*,
Though skill'd and gallant, yet may meet his Deat
And that I must prevent, for I'll allow no Stroke

To Chance, though my undaunted Hero dares all
That Man can dare ——

*Gand* Why comes he not?
know he's brave, renown'd in foreign Wars,
And to his Skill in Arms has such a Courage,
s makes a rash Man run upon his Ruin.
et in his Height of Fury I can dare him,
My Blood defies him mortally to Death.
es *Machiavel*, I'll take thy fatal Counsel,
The Word is Conquest, Death, or *Bellamira*.

*Enter* Borgia.

*Borg* So, Sir, you see I have obey'd your Summons.
You must be satisfy'd, though Beauty stays,
Though the Bride stays, though *Bellamira* stays.
That is, tho' Heav'n with all its waiting Glories
ops at your Call, and stands to give you hearing.

*Gand* Y'have us'd me basely.

*Borg* No.

*Gand.* I say you have,
ithout a Provocation.

*Borg* That were base
ded: When unprovok'd I do a Wrong,
y I, when justly urg'd, want due Revenge.

*Gand* You've falsify'd your Word, betray'd me basely,
Betray'd a Brother. O my Stars, a Brother!
at would have burst through all the Bars of Death,
d yielded all things to you, but his Love.
foolish Eyes! But these are your last Tears,
d I must mend your Course with Blood.

*Borg* He weeps!
s ever seen Hypocrisie like this?
hou young impudent and blooming Liar,
o, like our Curtesans, are early practis'd,
d in their Nonage taught the Arts of Vice.
I forgo my Temper——Is this all?
know I am in haste, and cannot brook
nger Conference.

*Gand* I know you cannot,
I shall force you. Yes, thou Tyrant Brother,
u that art fallen from all the Height of Glory,

To the low Practice of the worst of Slaves,
I will revenge the Honour thou hast lost.
Nor shalt thou pass to *Bellamira*'s Arms,
'Till through my Heart thou cutt'st thy horrid Way.
Draw then——

*Borg* I will not.

*Gand* By Revenge and Fury,
Thou shalt not pass but on my Rapier's Point.

*Borg* Think not, thou young Practitioner in Arms,
That all thy Force, tho' levell'd at me naked,
Should stop me, if I once resolv'd my Way.
But I am calm, and wish thee, for thy Safety,
To let me pass. Thou talk'st a while ago
Of *Lucrece* —— but no more of that —— my Father,
O, fear'd I not his Thunder which so oft
Has menac'd me if e'er I rose against thee,
Long, long ere this, had'st thou been Dust, even now;
For that Abuse which late thou gav'st my Ear,
For that abhorr'd Conception of my Sister,
For that damn'd Mention, by the lowest Hell,
And by the burning Fiends, thou should'st be Ashes.

*Gand* Blush not, nor purse thy threatning Brow, but
And dare not to despise the weakest Arm [draw,
That strikes with Justice Yes, upon thy Breast
Elate, and haughty as thou carry'st it,
I doubt not but my Sword shall write thee Traitor.

*Borg* No more O that I had
Some one renown'd, and winter'd as my self,
T' encounter like an Oak the rooting Storm!
But thou art weak, and to the Earth wilt bend,
With my least Blast, thy Head of Blossoms down.
If by thy Hand I fall (as who e'er div'd
So deep in Fate, but sometimes was deceiv'd?)
I do bequeath thee more than all my Dukedoms,
Far more indeed than Worlds, my beauteous Bride;
But if I conquer thee, and shew thee Mercy,
Never love more, nor after I am marry'd,
Dare for thy Soul to speak of *Bellamira*

*Gand* I thank thee, and accept the Terms with Joy,
Which Blood must ratifie. And here I swear,

If vanquish'd by thy Arm (though Death I hope,
Will, more than Oath, confirm the fatal Bargain)
For ever to renounce all Claim, and yield,
By my Eternal Absence, *Bellamira*.

*Borg.* Come on then: And let Love and Glory steel
Thy unflesh'd Arm. Think, on this Moment hangs
Thy whole Life's Joy, or worse than Death, Despair,
I would not win such Beauty without Blood:
But as the brave *Gonsalvo*, being shot,
Mov'd not at all, nor chang'd his mighty Look;
As if the Gallantry of such Demeanour
Could charm coy Victory to raise the Siege:
So would I with my Blood distilling down,
Answering her Tears, lead *Bellamira* on,
And woo her at the Altar with my Wounds.

*Gand.* No more.

*Borg.* Agreed. The Word is *Bellamira* ——

[*They fight*, Gandia *is wounded*.

Hold, hold *Palante*, for thou bleed'st.

*Gand.* A Scratch.

*Borg.* My Father cries out, save him on thy Life.

*Gand.* Guard well thy Life.

[*Fight again* Borgia *is wounded on the Arm, but disarms* Gan.

*Enter* Machiavel.

*Mach.* What means this Noise of Arms?
Why these Swords drawn? What now, my Lords,
Both wounded? [Borgia *throws* Gandia *his Sword*.
By Heav'n, I swear, you shall proceed no further.

*Borg.* 'Tis now too late to tell thee how we quarrell'd,
Look to his Wound. Soon as the Cure's perform'd,
I'll serve the Duke of *Gandia* with my Fortune.
But far from *Rome*, for he has agreed
Never to see my *Bellamira* more.
For me——I'll to the Temple.

*Mach.* My Lord, you bleed.

*Borg.* The Skin's but rac'd:
Would it were deep in the most mortal Part,
So *Bellamira*, when the Blood gush'd forth,
Would sink upon my Breast, and swear she lov'd me.
But that's too much to hope; whate'er is doom'd,

I swear this Night to grasp the conquer'd Prize:
Yes, yes, *Palante*, hear, and fly for ever;
All the white World of *Bellamira*'s Beauty
This Night I'll travel o'er, to feast my Love,
The little Glutton shall be gorg'd with Revels,
He shall be drunk with Spirits of Delight,
With all that amorous Wishes can inspire,
And all the Liberties of loose Desire [*Exit*.

*Gand.* I'll after him, and at the Altar end him.
Was't not enough to wound and vanquish me,
But he must triumph too? I rave and talk
I know not what, for he is generous,
And nobly merits what his Valour won:
Yes, happy *Borgia*, I will keep my Word;
And, since thus lost to all that I held dear,
Abandon this loath'd World

*Mach.* You must retire.

*Gand.* I will devote the sad Remains of Life
To the blest Company of holy Men!
Learn Contemplation, and, the Dregs of Life
Purg'd off, taste clearer and more sprightly Joys,
Partake their Transports in the brightest Visions,
See opening Heav'ns, and the descending Gods;
Then as I view the dazling Tracks of Angels,
Sigh to my Heart, and cry, See there, and there,
In full Perfect on thousand *Bellamira's*

*Mach.* My Lord, your Wound bleeds fast.

*Gand.* O *Machiavel*!
When I am shut for ever from the World,
Thou tenderest-hearted, gentlest, best of Friends,
Wilt visit me sometimes I know thou wilt.

*Mach.* Why do you droop thus? Lean upon my Arm
All shall be well. Yes, I will find a Way,
In spite of Fortune, yet to heal your Sorrows,
And pour the Balm of *Bellamira*'s Tears
Upon your Wound.

*Gand.* Could I but see her once
Before I die!

*Mach.* Once, twice, a hundred times;
Doubt not, you shall; but haste to your Apartment
[*Exit* Gandia.

Methinks if Mischief had but this to vaunt,
That, like a God, none knows her but her self,
It were enough to mount her o'er the World.
I love my self, and for my self, I love
Borgia my Prince. Who does not love himself?
Self-love's the universal Beam of Nature,
The Axel-tree that darts through all its Frame:
And he's a Child in Thought, who fears the Sting
Of Conscience; and will rather lose himself,
Than make his Fortune by another's Ruin!
Conscience, the Bug-bears Roar, the Nurses Howl,
Our Infant Lash, and Whip of Education.

*Enter* Adorna.

My Genius, my Love, my little Angel,
Hast thou the Letters?

*Ador.* First, my Lord,
If I have Breath to utter, let me tell you,
Never was Marriage solemniz'd like this.

*Mach.* Go on.

*Ador.* The Bride in Mourning Robes was led,
Or rather born like a pale Coarse along;
I saw her when she first approach'd the Temple,
How, rushing from the Arms of those that held her,
She threw her Body on the Marble Steps,
When strait the Bridegroom with a kindled Face
Drew near, and blushing, stretcht his bloody Arm,
Wrapt in a Scarf, and gave it to the Bride!
Then, bowing, wish'd the Priest perform his Duty.

*Mach.* What follow'd?

*Ador* Urg'd, or rather brib'd before,
The Priest, at old *Orsino*'s Intercession,
Soon join'd their Hands: All from the Temple haste,
*Orsino* and his Son in deep Discourse,
And *Bellamira* blind with weeping, led
This Way.

*Mach.* I am glad on't, for I wait to speak with her.
Prithee produce the Letters: Come, I know
Thou hast 'em: Nay, 'tis thy own Interest.

*Ador* See, *Bellamira* enters: Stay some time,
And I'll discover to your own Desire.

*Enter*

*Enter* Bellamira

*Mach* Madam, I would entreat a Word in private.

*Bell.* Can Misery, like mine, be worth Discourse?

*Mach.* The dead are only happy, and the dying:
The dead are still, and lasting Slumbers hold 'em,
He, who is near his Death, but turns about,
Shuffles a while to make his Pillow easie,
Then slips into his Shrowd, and rests for ever.

*Bella* My Mind presages, by the bloody Hand
That seiz'd me at the Altar.——

*Mach.* In their Nonage
A Sympathy unusual join'd their Loves;
They pair'd like Turtles, still together drank,
Together eat, nor quarrell'd for the Choice.
Like twining Streams both from one Fountain fell,
And as they ran, still mingled Smiles and Tears.
But oh, when Time had swell'd their Currents high,
This boundless World, this Ocean did divide 'em,
And now for ever they have lost each other.

*Bella.* For ever! Oh the Horror that invades me!
Thou seem'st to intimate some horrid Act:
I charge thee speak, how fares the Duke of *Gandia*?
Not answer me! Why dost thou shake thy Head,
And cross thy Arms, and turn thy Eyes away?
Has there been ought betwixt my Lord and him?

*Mach.* There has, they fought.

*Bella.* The Cause, the cursed Cause
Stands here, before thy Eyes she stands to blast thee.
I know 'tis thus, *Borgia* for me was wounded,
And, oh my Fears, by his relentless Hand,
Perhaps that poor despairing lost *Palante*
Is miserably slain. If it be so,
Spite of my Father, I'll renounce my Vows,
Forgo, forswear all Comforts in this Life,
And fly the World.

*Mach* Would I were out on't;
Nothing but Fraud and Cruelties reign here.
He is not slain, but, as his Surgeons bode,
I fear him much. Oh would you be so kind

To ſee the Wounds he ſuffers for your ſake,
And charm his Pains but with one parting View
Before your Lord return.——

*Bella* Alas! I dare not!

*Mach.* He graſpt me by the Wriſt, and weeping, vow'd
'Twould be a Heav'n, a lightning in his Grave,
Where elſe he muſt for ever lye unpity'd
Now, on my Soul, you muſt, you ought to ſee him,
Who, ballancing the Scales of doubtful Life,
Lyes in your way. A Glance, one grain of Favour
Turns him from Death. Come, come, you muſt have
Madam, I'll wait and intercept your Lord. [Mercy:

*Bella.* A Viſit! juſt upon our Marriage too——
But 'tis the laſt that he ſhall e'er receive,
Therefore I'll go, Nature, Compaſſion, Fate,
And Love, far more tyrannical than thoſe,
Forces me on. I feel him here; he throbs,
And beats a mournful March.

*Mach* Fear not, away:
I'll guard the Paſſage: look not back, but haſte.
[*Ex.* Bellamira.

If I remember Story well, old *Rome*
Was free from all this Weakneſs of the Mind;
For Women! Oh how ſlightly were they thought of,
When the great *Cato* gave his Friend his Wife,
To breed him Heirs, becauſe ſhe was a Teemer;
And after he was dead, again receiv'd her.
This was before the *Vandals* made us Slaves,
Who, mingling with our Wives, begot a Race
That nothing holds of the old Lion, Glory

*Enter* Borgia.

But huſh, more work, and now I am compos'd.

*Borg.* Welcome, my beſt of Friends, my *Machiavel!*
Let me unlade on thee my fraught of Joy,
For *Bellamira*'s mine, her Vows are mine,
Her Father gave her, and the holy Man
Has link'd our Hands. Fortune perhaps, ere long,
May join our Hearts. However dearly bought,
I ſay, ſhe's mine.

*Mach.* However dearly bought!

*Borg.*

*Borg* True *Machiavel*, moſt dearly, but alas,
He that would reach the Mine, muſt burſt the Quarry,
And labour to the Center —— Ha —— thou'rt cold,
Start from this Lethargy, and tell me why,
Why doſt thou ſhake my Joys with that ſtern Look?
Speak, for to me thy Face is as the Heav'ns,
And, when thou ſmil'ſt, I cannot fear a Storm
But now thy gather'd Brows prognoſticate
Ill Weather: Lightning ſparkles from thy Eyes:
Speak too, though Thunder follow.
*Mach* On what Conditions had the Prince his Life?
*Borg* It was agreed betwixt us ſolemnly,
And bound by Oath, that he who was ſubdu'd
Should never ſpeak to *Bellamira* more.
*Mach* I am ſatisfy'd.——
*Borg*. O *Machiavel*! is this friendly,
To hide the Cauſe of thy Diſorder from me?
Thou ſaid'ſt, I am ſatisfy'd, but at that moment
I ſaw two Furies leap from thy red Eyes,
That ſaid thou'rt not, thou art not ſatisfy'd.
This Coldneſs of thy Carriage! this dead Stillneſs,
Makes me more apprehend than all the Noiſe
That Mad-men raiſe. Speak then, but do not blaſt me,
Speak by degrees, let the Truth break away
In oblique Sounds; for if it come directly,
I fall at once, ſplit, ruin'd, daſh'd for ever,
So little am I Maſter of my Paſſion
*Mach*. Therefore I dare not tell you.
*Borg* Therefore 'tis horrid, ah!
Monſtrous! 'tis ſo, therefore thou dar'ſt not tell me:
But ſpeak, though trembling thus from Head to Foot,
I will be calm, preſs down the riſing Sighs,
And ſtifle all the Swellings in my Heart.
I will be Maſter far as Nature can.
*Mach* If that you knew ſuch Fire was in your Temper,
And thus would burn you up, why would you marry?
*Borg* Becauſe reſiſtleſs Love! reſiſtleſs Beauty,
Hurry'd me on But ſpeak, thou ſtav'ſt me off.
If thou haſt Senſe of Honour, tell me, *Machiavel*,
Speak, I conjure thee, as thou art my Friend.

*Mach*

*Mach.* The Fault's not great, and you may pardon it;
Yet 'twas a Fault, I think. Where did you leave
Your Bride?

*Borg.* Why dost thou ask? I know not where:
This Way they led her, and as I perswaded,
*Orsino*, though unwilling, judg'd it fit
She should retire again to her Apartment,
That her full Griefs might have a time to waste.

*Mach.* She is retir'd, my Lord.

*Borg.* Ha! whither? speak.
She is retir'd where she should not retire!
'Tis true, most plain, most undeniable,
I know it by the Fashion of thy Wit,
Thy Accent swears it, mouth thy Tale no more,
But say distinctly whither she's retir'd:
I charge thee, pray thee, and conjure thee, speak.
For what, with whom, and on what new Occasion?

*Mach.* You have a Brother.

*Borg.* O the perjur'd Traitor!
I have! what then?

*Mach.* She's with him now.

*Borg.* With whom?

*Mach.* Why with the Duke of *Gandia*; with your [Brother
*Palante*, Son or Nephew to the Pope.

*Borg.* What, *Bellamira* with him? Ponyards! Daggers!

*Mach.* This way, but now, I saw her come in haste;
Whether she guess'd the matter by your Wound,
I know not, but with faultring Speech she ask'd
How far'd *Palante*, if he were in being?
Whereon I nothing mus'd, but in plain Terms,
With Moderation, told her what I knew
But had you seen the Starts and Stops she made!

*Borg.* No doubt she did; ten thousand Curses, oh——
Go on, for yet I am a fangless Lion.

*Mach.* Had you but heard when first his Wound I men- [tion'd,
How she shriek'd out; how oft she forc'd me swear,
And swear, and swear again, it was not mortal!

*Borg.* Undone for ever! O Destruction seize her!

*Mach.* But when I told your Hurt, she seem'd scarce [griev'd,
And lessening Sorrow yielded to Attention,

I

I do not ſay ſhe flatly did rejoice,
But ſure I am, ſhe ſmil'd, and touch'd my Hand,
And begg'd me, if you came this way, to hold you
In Talk, while to the ſick ſhe made a Viſit.

*Borg* Thy Boſom be my Grave, bear me a while,
Or I ſhall burſt O *Bellamira*! Oh! [Fit

*Mach* Raiſe, raiſe your ſelf. Ha, Prince! is this the
We fear'd but now, that moſt tranſporting Fury?

*Borg* No more; 'tis gone: O Marriage! now I fin[d]
Thou coſtly Feaſt, on which with fear we feed, [thee,
As if each Golden Diſh we taſte were poiſon'd,
Where, by the fatal Tyranny of Cuſtom,
Our Honour, like a Sword juſt pointing o'er us,
Hangs by a Hair. Ha! but it comes, 'tis faln!
Like a fork'd Arrow ſtuck into my Skull.
No more. I am deaf as Adders, and as deadly:
Mercy! no more! thy Voice is quite uncharm'd;
All Pity thus be dry'd from my weak Eyes:
Here will I look my Mother's Softneſs off,
And gaze till Southern Fury ſteels my Soul,
'Till I am all my Father; 'till his Form,
All bloody o'er from Head to Foot with ſlaughter,
Skims o'er my poliſh'd Blade, in frowns to haſte me.

*Mach.* What mean you, Sir?

*Borg.* I know not what my ſelf!
Off from my Arms, away. I've oftentimes heard
At Princes Murders, Monſtrous Births forbode,
The Heavens themſelves rain Blood: Why, let it rain!
If my Heart holds her Purpoſe, with his Hand
I'll ſwell the Purple Deluge. Vengeance! Death and
Vengeance! [*Ex*

*Mach* No, my brave Warrior! 'tis not gone ſo far
Theſe Starts are but the haſty Harbingers
To the ſlow Murder that comes dragging on;
The Miſchief's yet but young, an Infant Fury;
'Tis the firſt Brawl of new-born Jealouſie.
But I have *Machiavellian* Magick here,
Shall nurſe this Brood of Hell to ſuch Perfection,
As ſhall ere long become the Devil's Manhood:
But hark! the Noiſe approaches, and the Time

Puts

Puts me in mind of *Bellamira*'s Letters—— [*Exit.*

*Enter* Borgia, Bellamira *and* Gandia.

*Borg.* Furies and Hell! yet ere thou dy'st, proud Villain,
Let me demand thee how thou dar'st abuse
My Mercy thus?

*Gand.* I give thee back the Title,
And have a Heart so well assur'd of Death,
That I disdain to answer.

*Borg.* Die then, Traitor!

*Bella.* Hold, *Borgia*, hold! Hear *Bellamira* speak.

*Borg.* Confusion! off, and play not thus with Thunder,
Lest it should blast thee too: Hence, off, I say:
Though thou deserv'st a Fate as sharp and sudden,
I will take leisure in thy Death. Be gone.

*Bella.* Behold, I grasp the Dagger, draw it through
And gash my Veins, and tear my Arteries;
I'll fix my Hand thus to the wounding Blade,
While Life will let me hold, and force thee hear me.

*Borg.* Say'st, ha! wilt thou? dar'st thou brave me thus?
Thus guilty too; once more forego my Ponyard.

*Bella.* No, draw it, Cruel, let thy bloody Deeds
Be swifter than thy Threats: I fear thee not;
But thus will wound my self, or quite disarm thee:
Now you shall hear me.

*Borg.* Is this possible?
Ha! *Borgia*! where! where is thy Fury now?
Where thy Revenge? O Woman in perfection!
Thou dazling Mixture of ten thousand *Circe's*,
In one bright heap cast by some hudling God,
How dar'st thou venture thus, how dar'st thou do this?
Yet heave thy Breasts, pant, breathe, and think on Mercy?

*Bella.* My Acts have shewn the Care indeed I take
To save my Life. No, Prince, not for my own
I would be heard, but for your innocent Brother's,
*Palante*

*Borg.* Ha! *Palante*! Yes, I know thee,
There hangs thy Joy, thy Pulse, thy Breath, and Motion,
Blood, Life, and Soul, thy Darling-Blessing's here,
And more than all the Joys of Heav'n hereafter.
O World of Horror! O Contagion, on

The

The Day when first I saw thee

*Bella.* Would you but hear——

*Borg.* Come off, I say! tear thy scarf'd Wound, tear't up,
With these distilling Drops, come glut thy Eyes,
Glut 'em with Blood, for *Borgia*'s Blood's thy Joy;
For say——when at the Altar I stood bleeding,
Speak Tygress, barbarous Wretch, thou she *Palante*,
Did'st thou once ask th' Occasion of my Wound?
No—— I remember thy uneasie Carriage,
How often thou look'st back with longing Eyes!
How oft in secret thou didst curse the Priest,
The tedious length of whose slow Ceremonies
Kept thee from flying to *Palante*'s Arms.

*Gand* Farewel, my Lord, think *Bellamira* guiltless,
And you shall never see *Palante* more.

*Borg* Stay, Sir; come back, I know your Wound's,
But the Reward I mean is worth your waiting. [Trouble
Here, take him, *Bellamira*, clasp him;
I give him thee, as our Physicians do
Prescribe last Remidies, to save thy Life!
I give him thee to save thy gasping Soul,
Which wou'd be damn'd without him, yet observe
There is a Deed that must, that shall be done,
Before you laugh and kiss. See here, my Bosom,
Strike, and strike deep, deep as *Palante* burns thee;
For in thy Heart, hot in thy inmost Veins,
I know the curs'd, the too lov'd Traitor lies.

*Gand* I do renounce the Name, and to the Giver
Retort it with an equal Indignation!

*Borg* Retort it! What?

*Gand.* The Name of Traitor.

*Borg* Ha!
Provoke me not, lest as I am unarm'd,
I crush thee with my Hands, and dash thee dead.

*Bella* Hold off, and hear me, noble *Borgia*, hear me!
Hear me, my Lord, my Husband, hear me kneeling,
Thou, whom the Heav'ns have destin'd to my Arms,
The constant Partner of my nicest Thoughts,
Doom'd to my Bed, whom I must learn to love,
And will, unless you turn my Heart to Stone.

Borg

*Borg.* Ha!
O! ſuch ſweet words ne'er fell from that fair Mouth
Before, nor can I truſt 'em now.
*Bella.* If you call back
The Vengeance which your impious Vows let ſlip,
I ſwear, thus ſinking on your Feet, I ſwear
Never from this ſad Hour, never to ſee,
Nor ſpeak, no, nor (if poſſible) to think
Of poor *Palante* more.
*Borg.* Go on, go on, I ſwear the Wind is turn'd,
And all thoſe furious and outragious Paſſions
Now bend another way
*Bella.* I will hereafter,
With ſtricteſt Duty, ſerve you as my Lord,
And give you ſigns of ſuch moſt faithful Love,
That it ſhall ſeem as if we languiſh'd long,
As if we had been us'd to mingle Sighs,
And from our Cradles interchang'd our Souls;
As if no Breach had ever been betwixt us,
As if no cruel Father forc'd the Marriage;
So reſigning as if always yours,
And you ſo mild, as if no other proof
But my Diſhonour e'er could make you angry.
*Borg.* O my Heart's Joy! Riſe, *Bellamira*, riſe!
There's nothing left, nothing of Rage to fright thee;
Thou haſt new-tun'd me, and the trembling Strings
Of my touch'd Heart dance to the Inſpiration,
As if no harſhneſs, nor no jars had been:
And theſe ſweet Sounds but met my entrance here,
My ghaſtly Fears and cloven Jealouſies,
With all the Monſters that made ſick my Brain,
Had fled (ſo ſoft and artful are thy Strains,)
Like ſullen Fiends before the Prophets Charms.
*Bella.* I came, 'tis true, my Lord, to ſee *Palante*,
But thought him on his Death-bed.
*Borg* O, no more!
I intreat thee mention that no more;
It's well; and we have mutually forgiven!
I love thee, *Bellamira*; therefore paſs
This Error by; yes, for thy ſelf I love thee!

 To

To glut my Fancy with thy endless Charms,
And snatch the Pleasures of all Woman-kind:
Thy fair Repentance, and thy graceful Vows,
Have turn'd the Eagerness of sworn Revenge
To furious Wishes for the promis'd Joy.

*Enter* Orsino

*Gand* O blasting Sight! O Death to all my Hopes!
Life, thou art vile, and I will wait no longer.

*Orsin* Ha! Traitor Prince! — Why, *Borgia*, does he live,
Who has himself broke all the ties of Blood?
Where is the lewd Adult'ress too, my Daughter?
For I will stab 'em in each others Arms.

*Borg.* Hold! *Orsino!* for Revenge is now
No more; thy Daughter is most Innocent,
And melts into my Arms. O happy Night!
Not to the weary Pilgrim half so welcome,
When after many a weary bleeding Step
With joyful Looks he spies his long'd-for Home.
See, see my Lord, the Effects of our Vexation!
Thus comes to the despairing Wretch, the glad
Reprieve 'Tis Mercy, Mercy at the Block:
Thus the toss'd Seaman, after boisterous Storms,
Lands on his Country's Breast, thus stands and gazes,
And runs it o'er with many a greedy Look;
Then shouts for Joy, as I should do, and makes
The eechoing Hills and all the Shoars resound.

*Orsin* Now Blessings on thy Heart; more Blessings on thee,
Than, on thy Disobedience, Curses Take him Girl,
And lay him to thy Heart, the warmest Gift
That Nature, or thy Father, can bestow!——

*Gand* Farewel, thrice happy Lover! never shall
This Wretch again disturb you. *Bellamira*,
O *Bellamira*——— [*Exit.*

*Bella* O farewel, for ever!

*Borg* Why dost thou weep? and pour into my Wounds
New Oil to make 'em blaze?

*Bella.* I've done, my Lord;
Let me but dry my Eyes, and I will wait you,
To Death, or to your Bed——

*Borg.* O ill compar'd!

Be

Be constant, *Bellamira*, to thy Vows,
So shall we shine, as in the in-most Heav'n,
The fixt and brightest Stars with silent Glory;
Where never Storm, nor Lightnings flash, nor stroak
Of Thunder comes, but if you fail in ought,
Then shall we fall like the cast Angels down,
Never to rise again: Therefore I warn thee——

*Bella* Fear not, my Lord.

*Borg* O! I must fear my Temper;
But I will purge it off with Resolution,
And with a Confidence thou wilt be mine.
For shouldst thou not · Hence *Gordon* Jealousie!
Cam'st thou uncall'd to set me on the Rack?
Be gone, I say, she's chaste, and I defie thee.
O plague me, Heav'n! plague me with all the Woes
That Man can suffer: Root up my Possessions,
Shipwrack my far-sought Ballast in the Haven;
Fire all my Cities, burn my Dukedoms down,
Let Midnight Wolves howl in my desart Chambers;
May the Earth yawn; shatter the frame of Nature;
Let the rack'd Orbs in Whirlwinds round me move,
But save me from the Rage of jealous Love. [*Exeunt*.

---

# ACT IV. SCENE I.

Soft Musick, with an *Epithalamium* to *Borgia* and *Bellamira*.

I.

*BLUSH not redder than the Morning,*
*Though the Virgins gave you warning,*
*Sigh not at the Chance befel ye,*
*Though they smile, and dare not tell ye.*

II.

*Maids, like* Turtles, *love the Cooing,*
*Bill and murmur in their Wooing.*

*Thus like you, they start and tremble,*
*And their troubled Joys dissemble.*

III.

*Grasp the Pleasure while 'tis coming,*
*Though your Beauties now are blooming;*
*Time at last your Joys will sever,*
*And they'll Part, they'll Part for ever.*

*Enter* Machiavel *and* Adorna.

*Mach.* Say'st thou, so loving?

*Adorn* O! he has got Ground
Beyond all Expectation: Had you seen
His graceful Manner, when the sighing Bride
Was last Night by your Arms given to his Bed;
When after she was laid, quite drown'd in Tears,
How, aw'd with trembling, he the Curtains drew,
And kneeling by her Bed-side, took her fair Hand,
With which she strove to hide her Blushes from him,
And sighing, swore upon t—if so she pleas'd,
If her cold Heart refus'd him utterly,
He would forgo his Joys, though Death ensu'd.
You muse, my Lord.

*Mach* This Day attend my Motion·
Soon as my Purpose hits, which you must watch,
I'll train the Bridegroom near *Palante*'s Lodgings,
Whence, as you were before by me instructed,
You with this Letter (which from all the Pacquets
I chose, and notably suits our Design)
Shall issue forth, and act as I inspir d—

*Adorn* I fear this Business,
Lest he should kill me. In this height of Fury,
Murder his Brother; or his innocent Lady.

*Mach.* I tell thee, though a Whirlwind drove him o
I'll make him calm. The Consequence of this
Is thine He drives *Palante* from the Palace,
Who else may linger after *Bellamira*,
And then thou know'st——

*Adorn* I will about it streight.
If I get clear of this, use me no more,

Fo

For I have ſworn to ceaſe——
*Mach.* Prithee, be gone——
Uſe me no more. For ſhe has ſworn to ceaſe, [*Ex* Ador.
To dip her Lady Finger in new Miſchief.
Yes——thou ſhalt ceaſe to live when I have us'd thee,
Poor uſeleſs thing.——But ſee the Bridegroom's here.
*Enter* Borgia.
My Lord, I give you Joy. Your Motion gives it,
Your wondrous Gallantry, and ſprightly Action.
But has ſhe wholly yielded to your Wiſhes,
Without the leaſt Reſerve?
*Borg.* Oh!
I cannot tell thee ought but this, I am happy
Above Expreſſion, bleſt beyond all Hope,
And ſure ſuch perfect Joy cannot laſt long,
Leſt we be Gods. O thou great Chymiſt Nature,
Who draw'ſt one Spirit ſo ſublimely perfect,
Thou mak'ſt a Dreg of all the World beſide.
*Mach.* Why, this at firſt I told you, but you fear'd,
And puſh'd the Bleſſing from you with both Hands.
I grant you that ſhe lov'd your Brother firſt,
I know he's young, and handſom, has a Wit
Moſt ſuitable to Woman's Inclination,
A ſubtle Genius, ſoft and voluble,
That winds with their Diſcourſe, and hits the Vein:
'Tis true, you are not of this ſubtle Mould;
But if you have enjoy'd her, 'tis all one,
My Life ſhe loves you: So the Act's reſolv'd,
Leave them to manage. O ye know 'em not.
Thoſe ſubtle Creatures, when Neceſſity
Forces Compliance, in a caſe like yours,
Will make the beſt on't.
*Borg.* How *Machiavel*, the beſt on't! Ha! how mean'ſt [thou?
*Mach.* Why thus; ſhe may, ev'n *Bellamira* may,
Spight of her Father's Will, her Vows in Marriage,
And all her After-Oaths, even in your Arms
Beſtow her ſelf upon the Duke of *Gandia*.
*Borg.* Ha!
*Mach.* I ſay not (pardon me!) ſhe does, or will;
But to make good my former Argument,

Affirm they may, they can, they will do thus.
As for Example, though your *Bellamira*,
Compell'd as all *Rome* knows, to this late Marriage,
Admits you to her Bed; you cannot think,
But her *Palante* had been much more welcome.

*Borg* Heav'n!

*Mach* 'Tis likely too her Fancy workt that Way
I urg'd before, she took you for *Palante*.
'Tis dark, she sees you not; you are his Brother,
Form'd in one Womb, of the same Flesh and Blood,
Therefore she yields as to foreknown Embraces:
And as you gently draw with trembling Arms
Her nicer Beauties to your heaving Breasts;
She shuts her Eyes with languishing Delight,
And whispers to her Heart, it is *Palante*

*Borg*. Cease *Machiavel*, hold; as thou lov'st my Life
I charge thee hold. O, 'tis most true I swear!
Thou know'st the very Depth of Woman-kind:
They are what thy Imagination paints 'em,
Charmers and Sorceresses. O, I'll tell thee,
When I the chastest, as I thought her then,
I am sure the sweetest of the Earth, embrac'd——
'Twas with Complainings, *Machiavel*; such Trembling,
I could have sworn her cold as Winter Streams.
But oh the Horrors thou hast conjur'd up!
Soon as soft Sleep had seal'd her melting Eyes,
I heard her sigh, (for 'till the Morn I wak'd)
*Palante* Oh——what we have done, *Palante*?

*Mach*. By Heav'n, that was too much.

*Borg* O much,——much more.
For stealing nearer me, her glowing Arm,
Cast o'er my Chek, thrice prest me to her Breast,
Ev'n that coy Arm, so nicely strange before,
Familiar grew, and circled in my Neck,
With all the Freedom of acquainted Love
And I too pity'd her, and thought that Nature
Work'd her imperfectly; but now I know,
I find, I see, it was her Heart's Design,
The black Contrivance of her blotted Fancy:
Blood, Blood and Death, thus has she set me down,

Throug

Through the whole Course of her polluted Nights,
To be her Bawd, her most industrious Groom,
The Drudge of her damn'd Lust——*Palante's* Stale——

*Mach.* Are you incens'd indeed? Or do you, Sir,
Put on this jealous Fit to make you Sport?
For if so small a Spark thus makes you glow,
A little more will blow you into Flame:
Therefore be serious in your Answer.

*Borg* Ha!
Thou know'st before my Marriage how I fear'd,
How when my Honour was engag'd by Vows,
Like Flax my jealous Temper caught the Flame,
And scarce could all her melting Sorrows quench me!

*Mach* I do remember well

*Borg* But now I have enjoy'd her, mark me, *Machiavel*,
If I was Flax before, I am Powder now,
And will fly up in general Conflagration
For I would chuse to scramble at a Door,
Make my loath'd Meals out of the common Basket
With Dungeon Villains, wallow in the Stews,
And get my Bread by poisoning my firm Limbs,
Ere pass an Hour with her I have espous'd,
If but in Thought consenting with another.

*Mach.* I am glad to find the Genius of your Climate
Inflames you thus; my Lord, give me your Hand:
Prepare your Soul, gather your Nobler Spirits,
And bid 'em stand to Arms, like Towns besieg'd,
That must receive no Quarter

*Borg.* Let me go·
So deep thou threaten'st, that I fear ev'n thee;
And from this Moment, like the fearful Plant,
Shrink back my Arms from every human Touch·
But speak, I charge thee, slip the strugling Thunder,
And foil my Soul.

*Mach.* This Morning, just before you enter'd here,
I saw in haste *Adorna* cross the Garden.
And as she ran, a Note dropt from her Bosom,
Which I took up, and in it read these Words;
*Mourn not, my dear* Palante, *for the time*

*Draws on, when spite of this inhuman* Borgia
*We will be happy.*

*Borg* Yes, she shall, she shall;
I'll join 'em Breast to Bosom, stab 'em through,
And clinch my Dagger on the other Side.

*Mach.* This, as I oft perus'd in great Amazement,
I saw her who had miss'd the Note, come back,
And briefly let her know that I had read it;
With Menaces, unless she told me all,
Immediately to carry you the Letters.
Why should I rack you longer? Your chaste Wife
Has, with the Help of this her Kinswoman,
Concluded, on the Date of your first Absence,
To admit your Brother

*Borg* 'Tis impossible!
'Tis mountainous to Faith, I'll not believe it:
For Hell it self ne'er teem'd with such a Falshood.

*Enter* Adorna

*Mach* Ha—— as I live, just from *Palante* now,
The private Way from his Apartment, see
Their Emissary comes

*Borg* Oh thou vile B..d!
Thou Midnight Hag: Thou most contagious Blast,
Which *Bellamira* with a Strumpet's Breath
Blows to *Palante*, and he back to her:
Whence com'st thou? Speak! What bear'st thou? Ha,
Or I will tear thee Limb from Limb. [produce it,

*Adorn* O Heav'ns! [my Life.
I am betray'd, undone, for ever ruin'd; and I shall lose

*Borg* Thou shalt be safe, I swear thou shalt, if thou confess the Truth.
But if thou hide ought from me, I will rack thee,
'Till with thy horrid Groans thou wake the Dead.

*Adorn* O my Lord!
I do confess that *Bellamira* sent me;
But sure no harm was in the Letter.

*Borg* None,
None at all, Hell knows her Innocence:
But speak——

*Adorn* I have, my Lord, confess'd already
All that I know, to my Lord *Machiavel.*

Borg.

*Borg.* Thou ly'ſt, damn'd Wretch! look here and dare not urge me,
Show me the Anſwer to the Morning Meſſage,
Or I will cut thee to Anatomy,
And ſearch through all thy Veins to find it out.
*Adorn.* O, ſave my Life! behold, my Lord, this Paper:
What it contains, I know not.
*Borg* 'Tis his Hand
*Mach* Be gone, and on thy Life no talk of this
[*Exit* Adorna.
Borg *reads* Palante *waits upon your Motion.* Death and Devils!
*And when you call, he comes, or the long Sleep*
*Shall huſh him ever.*
Daggers! Poiſon! Fire [*Tears the Letter.*
Woe, and ten thouſand Horrors on their Souls
*Mach.* What now, my Lord?
*Borg* Off——or I'll ſtab thee through!
Stab——I could mangle, tear up my own Breaſt,
Drag forth my Heart that holds her bleeding Image,
And daſh it in her Face.
*Mach* Talk no more on't; but do, Sir, do.
*Borg* Yes, *Machiavel,* I will——I will do Deeds
Grain'd as my Wrongs I will, I will be bloody
As *Pyrrhus,* daub'd in Murder at the Altar,
As *Tullia,* driving through her Father's Bowels;
As *Cæſar*'s Butchers in the Capitol;
As *Nero* bathing in his Mother's Womb;
With all ſucceeding Tyrants down to ours.
Lords of the Inquiſition, black Contrivers
Of Princes Deaths, and Heads of Maſſacres,
*Orſino, Vitellozzo,* Duke *Gravina,*
*Oliverotto* too, all, all at once,
Even the whole Race, a Hecatomb to Vengeance.
*Mach* Hear me one Word.
*Borg* Bid the Sea liſten, when the weeping Merchant,
To gorge its ravenous Jaws, hurles all his Wealth,
And ſtands himſelf upon the ſplitting Deck,
For the laſt Plunge No more! Let's ruſh together;
For Death rides poſt.
*Mach.* Though Death ſhould meet me,

More

More horrid than you name, I'd cross this Fury,
This blind, ungovern'd Rage. Sir, you shall hear me.

*Borg.* Barr'st thou my Vengeance?

*Mach.* No —— I'll further it.
You shall have Proof so plain, the World shall say,
The Pope himself, dear as he loves your Brother,
Shall say the Stroke was just. This Night I'll bring you
Into her Chamber, if with some Pretence
You seem t'absent your self. My Lord, I'll bring you
With a false Key into the Bridal Lodging;
Where you shall see, even with those Eyes behold,
And gaze upon their curst incestuous Loves.

*Borg.* Just reeking from my Arms! O thou Adulteress!
Whose Name to mention, sure would rot my Lungs,
And blister up my Tongue, Insatiate *Sylla*!
Bark'st thou for more? then let the Furies seize thee,
Whose burning Lust damns to the lowest Hell,
Smoaks to the Heav'ns, and sullies all the Stars.

*Mach.* Compose your Looks, smooth down that staring Hair,
And dry your Eyes, which spite of this Distraction
I see are full, brim full of gushing Tears.

*Borg.* Had she not fallen thus, O ten thousand Worlds
Could not have ballanc'd her, for Heav'n is in her;
And Joys which I must never dream of more;
I weep, 'tis true. But, *Machiavel*, I swear,
They're Tears of Vengeance, drops of liquid Fire:
So Marble weeps when Flames surround the Quarry,
And the pil'd Oaks spout forth such scalding Bubbles
Before the general blaze, for that she dies,
Though clinging to the Altar, Guardian Gods,
Though starting from their Shrines, shall not redeem her.

*Mach.* Pretend to Night, nor is it bare Pretence;
For, as I hear, the *Sinigallian* Victors
Come on to wait you here. Pretend to her,
To *Bellamira*, you can scarce return
In forty Hours.

*Borg.* I will do what I may.

*Mach.* Away then.

*Borg.* Ha! Methinks thou dost not share
In my Resentment, *Machiavel*, as thou ought'st:

If thou'rt my Friend, and art indeed concern'd,
Relieve my weary'd Fury, beat my Vengeance,
Call up a friendly Rage, and curſe 'em, *Machiavel*,
Curſe theſe Triumphers o'er thy *Borgia*'s Ruin

*Mach.* Diſeaſes wait 'em: Wherefore ſhould I curſe
If that my Breath were ſulph'rous as the Light'ning ['em?
That murders with a Blaſt, or like the Vapours,
The choaking Stench, which thoſe that die of Plagues
Send with their parting Groans, then I would curſe 'em
With Accents that ſhould poiſon from my Tongue,
Deliver'd ſtrongly through my gnaſhing Teeth,
More harſh, more horrible, and more outragious,
Than Envy in her Cave, or Madmen in their Dens

*Borg.* Excellent *Machiavel!* more, more, to lull me.

*Mach.* My Tongue ſhould ſtammer in my earneſt Words;
My Eyes ſhould ſparkle like the beaten Flint.

*Borg.* This hoary Hair ſhould ſtart, and ſtand an end,
And all thy ſhaking Joints ſhould ſeem to curſe 'em.

*Mach* Nay, ſince you urge me, Sir, my Heart will
Unleſs I curſe 'em! Poiſon be their Drink. [break,

*Borg* Gall, Gall, and Wormwood, Hemlock! Hemlock! quench 'em

*Mach.* Their ſweeteſt Shade, a Dell of duskiſh Adders.

*Borg* Their faireſt Proſpect, Fields of *Baſilisks*
Their ſofteſt Touch, as ſmart as Vipers Teeth

*Mach.* Their Muſick horrid as the Hiſs of Dragons,
All the foul Terrors of dark-ſeated Hell.

*Borg.* No more; thou art one Piece with me my ſelf:
And now I take a Pride in my Revenge.

*Mach* You bid me ban, and will you bid me ceaſe?
Now, by your Wrongs that turn my Heart to Steel,
Well could I curſe away a Winter's Night,
Though ſtanding naked on a Mountain's Top,
And think it but a Minute ſpent in Sport.

*Borg.* Thou beſt of Friends! come to my Arms my Bro-
But the time calls, and Vengeance bids us part, [ther,
Henceforth, be thou the Miſtreſs of my Heart. [*Exit.*

*Mach* Now it grows ripe; the *Orſins*, and *Vitelli*,
Are bury'd by my Wit, without a Noiſe
O 'tis the ſafer Courſe, for Threats are dang'rous

But

But there's no Danger in the Execution,
For he that's dead, ne'er thinks upon Revenge.
What, hoa——*Alonzo!*——

*Enter* Alonzo.

*Alonz.* Here, my Lord.

*Mach.* Are the Gloves brought I sent to the Perfumer?

*Alonz.* They are.

*Mach.* Where is *Adorna*?

*Alonz.* She waits without.

*Mach.* As you see her enter,
Bring me the Gloves: 'Twere easie strangling her,
But this is quainter.——O my bright *Adorna*!

*Enter* Adorna.

With confidence I swear the Duke is thine.

*Adorn.* May I believe it?

*Mach.* Be judge, thy self, whether I have been id[le].
These were a Present from the King of *Spain*,
To the *Pope*'s Niece, of whom the fond young Duke
Begg'd 'em for thee.

*Adorn.* Is't possible?

*Mach.* Stay, Madam——we must change
One Present for another. Lend me the Key
To *Bellamira*'s Chamber.

*Adorn.* For what?

*Mach.* Nay, if we barter words.

*Adorn.* Here, here, my Lord.
Now give me the dear Present.
See, see, my Lord, they are emboss'd with Jewels,
And cast so rich an Odour, they o'ercome me——
Help me----my Lord---O help me----lend your Arm
The Earth turns round with me! O Mercy, Heav'n——

[*Di*[es.]

*Mach.* Remove the Body——
Then haste and find the Duke of *Gandia* out,
Ere he removes, as he intends to Night,
Having Commission from the *Pope* to lead
Th' *Italian* Armies, earnestly entreat him,
To honour me by making one last Visit,
Which equally imports him as his Life.

*Ent*[er]

*Enter* Borgia *and* Bellamira

*Borg.* Upon the instant, Fairest, I must leave you,
The Lord of *Firmo*, with the Duke your Uncle,
Have taken *Sinigallia* by surprize:
What else, but meeting thy Victorious Kinsmen,
Should draw me from thy Arms? yet thus divided
But for a Day or two, methinks I part,
As Souls are sever'd from their warmer Mansions,
To wander in the bleak and desart Air.
O *Bellamira*!

*Bell.* Why do you sigh, my Lord?
If 'tis your Pleasure, let 'em wait you here;
Or if my Presence can dispel these Clouds
That make you sad, I will attend you thither;
For while Life lasts I will be all Obedience.

*Borg.* Could'st thou hold there, how might we laugh [at Fate!
So kindled both by Love, and by Ambition,
How would I sweep, like Tempests, with a waste
Over all *Italy*, and Crown thee Empress
Here in the Heart of *Rome* — my bright *Augusta*,
But 'tis impossible.

*Bell.* Then you conclude, my Lord, I am not true.

*Borg.* Why, art thou? Is there such a thing in Nature
As a true Wife? No, *Bellamira*, no———
Thou would'st be monstrous then, ev'n to derision:
For the whole Flock of common Wives would whoot [thee,
And drive thee, like a Bird, without one Feather
Of thy own kind.

*Bell.* Once more upon my Knees,
In view of all the Hierarchy of Heav'n,
I here attest my spotless Innocence.

*Borg.* Still *Machiavel*, still let us keep to Death;
His Principle, that we are Dust when dead,
For were there any Hell, or any Devil
But hot enough to make an Exhalation,
Would he not fetch her now? would he not damn her?
I believe thee guiltless: Therefore rise;
And since thou art so confidently clear,
Dear *Bellamira*, if I prove thee false,
What e'er I threat, nay, though I put in act

Those

Those Menaces, thou wilt not call me Tyrant.

*Bell.* I swear by Heav'n I will submit my Life
To the severest stroke of your Revenge

*Borg* If then I prove thee false, O *Bellamira*!
Not that Celestial Copy, ev'n thy Face,
Shall scape, but I will race the Draught, as if
It ne'er had been the Pattern of the Gods.

*Bell.* Act what you please, but speak no more, my Lord,
For every Word's a blot, and strikes me dead

*Borg* If thou art false, and if I prove thee so,
That Skin of thine, that matchless West of Heav'n,
Which some more curious Angel cast about thee,
Will I tear off, though cleaving to the Shrine.

*Bell* Speak to him, *Machiavel*! O fatal Marriage!

*Borg.* If thou dost play me false, think not of Mercy,
Thy Father shall be burnt before thy Eyes.

*Bell* O horrid Thought!

*Borg* Thy Uncles, Brothers, Sisters,
All that have any relish of thy Blood,
I'll rack to Death, and throw their Limbs before thee!
Therefore look to't; beware, if thou art false,
I'll take thee unprepar'd, and sink thy Soul:
Therefore, I say again, beware! I've warn'd thee;
Body and Soul, ev'n everlasting Ruin;
For so may Heav'n have Mercy upon mine
At my last gasp, as I'll have none on thine— [*Exit.*

*Bell* O 'tis too plain! I am lost, undone for ever
What, but one Night, ev'n the first Nuptial Night,
So sought, so courted, and so hardly won;
And the next Day, nay, the succeeding Morn
To be us'd thus—Let me go, let me go,
For I'll proclaim him through the Streets of *Rome*
The Traitor, Monster— O, I could shake the World
With thundering forth my Wrongs; Hollow his Name
To the resounding Hills! *Borgia*! Traitor *Borgia*!
Methinks that Word, that Spell, that horrid Sound,
That groan of Air could cleave the Neighbouring Rocks
And scare the babling Ecchoes from their Dens

*Mach* Perhaps some busie Slave has whisper'd him
I know not what, that chafes his Melancholly
Against your Honour.

*Bell* That's impossible!
d I deny'd to admit him to my Bed,
me seeming cause, some reason for Distrust
ght then be given, but the bright Heav'ns know
ad resolv'd to take him for my Lord,
d love him too, or force my Inclination,
subtly had he wrought by deep dissembling
on my plain and undiscerning Weakness.
t now he's gorg'd, the Monster shews himself,
pears all Beast, and I must die, he cries,
Cruelty! and all my wretched Race
*Mach.* Madam, you know how near a Friendship grows
twixt the Duke of *Gandia*, and my self.
ter this Night you'll never see him more:
t, ere he goes, as he to Night is order'd,
will unfold, if you permit him leave,
e only means to save your Father's Life;
y, and the Lives of all your Family.
*Bell.* O *Machiavel*! now, where is thy Advice?
d I not reason for my dreadful Fears?
Father dies, and by whose Hand but *Borgia*'s?
hat shall I do? where shall I go? and whither shall I
n thousand horrours! O, instruct me, *Machiavel*, [run?
r I grow desperate!
*Mach.* Admit the Duke of *Gandia*;
is Night, for one last Conference Your Husband
nnot return, unless he ride the Wind,
forty hours——
*Bell* Here I am lost again:
ould he return, and find *Palante* with me,
hom I have sworn never to see, discourse,
ever to hear of, scarce to think of more,
at Mountains then should hide me from his Fury?
t if I see him not, my poor old Father,
ith all his Children, Brothers, and Relations,
p, Root and Branches, all must be cut down.
ar, Heav'n, hear! I must kneel to thee for Succour;
aid my Virtue, and support my Weakness
thinks I am inspir'd, some Guardian Spirit
hispers me, Save, O save thy Fathers Life!

Bring

Bring him then, *Machiavel*, bring the Duke of *Gandi*
Yet ſtay! methinks I ſee the Tyrant there!
My bloody Husband, with his Ponyard drawn,
Juſt at the Door: Stop, ſtop the Duke of *Gandia*,
He ſhall not come: Why, then thy Father dies;
O horrid ſtate! weep Eyes, and bleed, O Heart!
Let Nature burſt with theſe unheard of Suff'rings!
Forbid him, *Machiavel*, or let him come,
All have their Fate, and I'll expect my Doom.—

[*Ex ſeveral*

## ACT V. SCENE I.

*Enter* Machiavel, *and* Alonzo.

*Alon* MY Lord, I have been diligent.
*Mach*. And always wert my ſubtle Emiſſar,
My Glance of Death, and Lanthorn to my Miſchiefs.
*Alonz* I met the Duke of *Gandia* at the Head
Of his new Forces, and acquainted him
As you directed; and he'll ſtraight attend you.
But as I whiſper'd him, Duke *Valentine*
With a vaſt Train come up to take his leave,
Being call'd (as Fame reports) to *Sinigallia*.
But had you ſeen the Embraces, heard the Vows
Which *Borgia* ſwore ſhould be inviolable,
And ratify'd 'em with a parting Kiſs.
*Mach* 'Tis my own *Borgia*, a very Limb of me,
And when he dies, thou'lt ſee me halt, *Alonzo*.

*Enter* Gandia.

My Lord, moſt welcome! *Alonzo*—hence—O Prince

[*Ex*. Alonzo

Was ever Slave ſo careful for his Lord,
That watch'd his Nod, as I have been for you?
*Gand* I muſt with ſhame to Death acknowledge it.
But didſt thou know, or couldſt thou gueſs how near
The loſs of *Bellamira* touches me,
Thou would'ſt forgive me.

*Mach*

*Mach* I have excus'd you, Sir:
nd for a witneſs of my faſter Friendſhip,
This Night have ſent the Duke to *Smigallia*,
That you might take your laſt farewel of Love,
And *Bellamira*.

*Gand*. And has the cruel Fair conſented to it?

*Mach*. She has conſented, rather by Conſtraint,
Than her own Will; I was forc'd to tell her,
How you had ſignify'd to me, her Father
Was in great Hazard; but if ſhe vouchſaf'd
A Viſit, you would ſatisfie her better.

*Enter* Alonzo.

*Gand*. Ha! what's this? A ſudden fall of Spirits——

*Alonz* My Lord, he's in's Litter muffled up,
In a dark Avenue behind the Palace;
And bid me fly to tell you, *Tarquin*'s Poppies
Are bound up all together in one Sheaf. [The Time

*Mach* Haſte thee, and make my Anſwer thus——
Calls for their Heads. This Key, my Lord, admits you----

*Gand*. 'Tis now no Time for Thanks, but if I live——

[*Exit*.

*Mach* Why, this is true *Italian*! turning thus
A Key with *Machiavellian* ſlight of Hand,
Two Families of the beſt *Southern* Blood,
With the firſt Prince in *Rome*, are quite extinct:
What foggy *Northern* Brain would dream of this?

Borgia *muffled in a Cloak*.

*Borg* My *Machiavel*!

*Mach* My Prince, my God-like *Borgia*!

*Borg* Tell me, my Boſom-ſin, am I awake?
...ve? And may I credit this thy Summons?

*Mach* No ſooner were you gone, but your Chaſte Wife,
Whom I imagin'd dead with what you utter'd:
...y, this Wife, this heavenly Wife of yours,
...aring her Head, and wiping her dry Eyes,
...opping her Chin, to make her Smile more ſcornful,
...'d out, Lord *Machiavel*, you ſee, you ſee,
What things theſe Husbands are; and left the Room.

*Borg*. Racks, Racks, and Fire! Caldrons of molten Lead!
...w ſhall I torture her?

*Mach* Streight, by her walking Pacquet,
She signify'd her Pleasure to the Duke,
Who soon approach'd, and with a matchless Boldness
Desir'd my Friendship in this private Business:
I smil'd, and promis'd that I would not see,
Though I beheld *Adorna* let him in,
Whom since I poison'd, lest she should betray
The Secret of your coming.

*Borg* By Death and Vengeance
I could turn *Cannibal*, and with my Teeth
Tear her alive. But let us talk no more.

*Enter D.* Michael.

What hoa, Don *Michael!* when I stamp my Foot
Against the Ground, bring forth the Prisoners,
And execute as I shall order. [*Ex.* Mich.

*Mach* Pass the back Way, my Lord; this Door
If that be shut too, force it open, while [lock
I set a Guard on this: Millions to one,
But when she hears your Voice, she'll hide the Duke
And then deny him boldly to your Face.
'Tis like those subtle Creatures.

*Borg* Damn 'em, Serpents!
What needs this Aggravation? Revenge! away— [E

*Mach.* Now like a Grey-hound barking in the l
Death struggles for a loose; I must be gone,
And lurk in Shadows till the Murder's done.
Hark, 'tis doing, the Doors are thunder'd down!
O! for an Earth-quake now to swallow all,
All that oppose my Tyrant, to the Center—— [

SCENE *draws.* Borgia, Bellamira, *Duke of* Ga
dia *disarm'd* D. Michael, *&c.*

*Borg* Slave, run you down, and bar the Palace G
Let not a Soldier stir on pain of Death,
Till I appoint. What's he you have disarm'd?
Haste, drag him forth, and put the Tapers near h
Lightning and Thunder! Ha! the Duke of *Gandia*
Rage burn me up? It is not possible:
Woman, O Woman!

*Bell.* O Heav'ns! O all ye Powers!
Is there not one, one Door for Mercy left?

*Borg.* Pull off his Robes, and bind him to a Chair;
Ply him with Fire and Wounds—Yes, *Bellamira*,
There is a Flood-gate——but it is of Blood;
A Gate for Mercy wide, as thou hast shown
For Honour, Chastity, and Bridal Virtue.
See here the Sluce I draw, through Doors of Wounds;
Thy Vows, this sulphurous stench thy Kisses.

*Bell* Hold, hold, Tormentors!

*Borg* Seize the Fury's Arms,
nd execute my Orders

*Gand* O unmerciful!
O *Borgia:* When, when shall my Torments end?

*Bell.* Ha! is it doing! Wretches, Villains, Dogs,
Miscreants, Sons of Hell, and Broods of Darkness!

*Gand.* Humanity can bear no more. My Heart, strike [there.

*Bell.* 'Tis done; O the dark Deed is done!
O let me gather all the Rage of Woman,
nd tell this Tyrant to his Teeth, he is a Villain.

*Gand* Mercy, gentle *Borgia*, Mercy!

*Bell* He gentle, then theDevils themselves have Mercy.
O Monster, rocky Villain, Tyger, Hell-hound,
eze him you Fiends, and Furies damn him, damn him,
ay Hell have infinite stories, and this Devil
e damn'd beneath the bottomless Foundation.

*Borg* By Heav'n she weeps. Here, dip her Handker-
ip't in his Blood, and bid her dry her Eyes. [chief,

*Bell* O thou eternal Mover of the Heav'ns,
Where are thy Bolts?

*Gand* I go, O *Bellamira*!
hink'st thou, alas, that we shall know each other
n the bright World; I fear we shall not——Oh!
*orgia* farewel: Thy Bride is Innocent:
et *Bellamira* live, and I forgive thee.—— [*Dies.*

*Bell* He's gone, to Heav'n he's gone, as sure as thou
halt sink to Hell, thou Tyrant, double damn'd.
ay, thou wouldst have me rage, and I will rage,
nd weep, and rage, and show thee to the World,
hou Priest, Archbishop, Cardinal, and Duke,
hou that hast run through all Religious Orders,
nd with a form of Virtue cloak'd thy Horrors!

Thou proper Son of that old curſed Serpent,
Who daubs the holy Chair with Blood and Murders,
But ſure the Everlaſting has a Chain
To bind your Charms, and link you both together:
Hell's Vicar, and his firſt begotten Devil,
Hotter than *Lucifer* in all his Flames.

*Enter* Alonzo.

*Borg* What, hoa, *Alonzo*! ſtrangle the Priſoners;
*Orſino*, *Vitellozzo* Haſte, I ſay,
Without reply.——

*Bell.* O ſpare him! ſpare my Father!
And I'll unſay, forſwear all that I have ſaid:
O, I have play'd the Woman now indeed,
A lying, fooliſh, vext, outragious Woman!
To ſet your Wrath againſt the Innocent.
There was a ſeeming Cauſe for the Duke's Death
And mine, But, oh! what has *Orſino* done?
*Orſino* loves you. Oh, that good old Man!
Your Father——For ſo a thouſand times
I've heard you call him, ſeen you kiſs, embrace him
Therefore he muſt not, cannot die!

*Borg* *Alonzo*!

*Alonz* My Lord!

*Borg.* Slave, I'll ſtrangle thee [*Strikes* h
With my own Hands! if thou delay'ſt my Vengeance
Say, Villain, what, not dead?

*Alonz* My Lord, they are:
And if I live, you ſhall repent this Blow—— [*A*

*Borg.* Go, draw the Curtain, glut her Eyes with Dea
And ſtrangle her My Veins are all on Fire,
And I could wade up to the Eyes in Blood.
Draw, draw the Curtain.

[Orſin Vitellez D Gravina, Oliverotto, *appear diſguiſ*

*Bell* *Gorgon*, *Meduſa*, Horror,
Yet I will ſhoot through Daggers, ruſh through Fla
To claſp him in my Arms O wretched *Paul*,
O noble *Orſin*, what, quite cold? pale, dead?
And you, dear Images, will you not give
One gaſp of Breath, one Groan, one laſt Farewel?
Horror! Confuſion! and eternal Shame

ht on thee for this Deed I tell thee, *Borgia*,
e thee on thy Death-Bed, all on Fire,
if some Hellish Poison had inflam'd thee;
e thee thrown ten Fathom in a Well,
still come up, like *Etna*'s belching Flames.
*org* I hope thou wilt go mad, and prophesie!
*ell* Yes Tyrant, thus, thus to thy Face I brave thee,
tell thee in despite of Threats, ere long
u and thy holy Father shall be seiz'd,
carry'd to the everlasting Goal,
m whence not all your *Spanish* Cardinals,
r Bailiffs in red Liveries, shall redeem you——
*org* Die in thy Prophesie; *Alonzo*, end her ——
*ell.* Thus, on my Knees then —— And for Terror to
r my last Prayer, and mark my dying Words. [thee,
in Thought, in Word, in private Act
e yielded up this Body to the Arms
ought that's Mortal, but inhuman *Borgia*!
hou impartial and most awful Judge!
t, shut thy Gates of Bliss against my Soul,
if my tortur'd Virtue merits Glory,
on my Frailties, see with what Joy
ave this Life, and bring me to Perfection.

[*She is strangled.*

*org* What, at her Death! she that believ'd a Heav'n,
fear'd a Hell, yet to depart a Liar:
how know I that she believ'd a Heav'n?
why with Hopes that in the pangs of Death
ould reprieve her, might she not deny
Whoredom to the last? But that's unnatural!
at wouldst thou then? I will no more of this,
louds my Brain Hence, *Alonzo* bear,
r the Duke of *Gandia*'s Body to the *Tyber*
ome close Chair, tie at his Neck a Weight,
plunge him to the Bottom.
*lonz* My Lord 'tis done.

[*Ex. Executioners with the Body*

*org* I swear I have been cruel to my self,
that I lov'd her, is as true, as she
ast the Sense on't. She is cold already.———

*Enter* Machiavel. [Fo

*Mach.* Ha! this is stately Mischief! what, my fo
Of *Florence*! but they are Dumb. Ha! gazing there,
I like not that——

*Borg* Her Lips are lovely still;
The Buds, tho' gather'd, keep their Damask Colour;
Yes, and their Odour too! haste *Machiavel*,
Rush to my Aid. I grow in Love with Death.
She shall not dye! Run Slaves! fetch hither Spirits,
I will recover her again!

*Mach.* Again to Plague?
To meet again another Duke of *Gandia*?

*Borg* Death on that Thought: no, let her dye and ro
The damn'd Adultress! perish the Thoughts of her.
Ha, tell me, come: I will no more of her.
How shall the Bodies be dispos'd? I sent
My Brother to the *Tiber*.

*Mach* That's a trouble,
I'll find an easier way for these, and her
That sleeps within my Closet. Go, Don *Michael*,
Bury 'em all together in quick Lime;
In some few Hours the Flesh will be consum'd:
Then burn the Bones, and all is Dust and Ashes.

[*Draw here the Curtains on* 'e

*Borg.* I swear this Body shall not be consum'd,
I'll have't embalm'd to last a thousand Years.
O *Machiavel*! I swear, I know not why,
But with a World of Horror on my Soul,
With Tremblings here, Convulsions of the Heart;
As if I heard some God thus whisper to me,
Thou ou_ht'st to grieve for *Bellamira*'s Death

*Mach* My Lord, a very fond and foolish Fancy.

*Borg.* I say, my Lord, your Policy is out:
Furies and Hell! how should you judge of Love,
That never lov'd? Thou hast no taste of Love,
No sense, no relish——Why did I trust thee then?
Had any Softness dwelt in that lean Bosom,
My *Bellamira* now had been alive:
Though I had cause to kill her, thou hadst none
To set me on, but Honour, jealous Honour!

Oh the last Night! I tell thee, Politician!
When I run o'er the vast Delight I curse thee,
And curse my self; nay wish I had been found
Dead in her Arms, but take her, bear her hence!
And if thou lov'st me, drive her from my Memory
[*They remove her*
Tell me my Brother's Murder is discover'd;
That the four Ghosts are up again in Arms:
Say any thing to make me mad, and lose
This Melancholly, which will else destroy me
*Mach.* I hear the *Pope* has sent to *Sinigallia*
To call you back.
*Borg* By Heav'n, I had forgot,
And thou most opportunely hast remembred:
You know twelve Cardinals were then created,
That solemn Morn that I receiv'd the *Rose*;
And I will tell thee, half those Fools ere Morrow,
That bought so high, shall veil their Caps for ever.
*Mach* He mends apace; 'tis but another shrug,
And then this Love, this Ague Fit is lost.
*Borg* I swear——I'll to the Wars, and ne'er return
To *Rome*, till I have brav'd this haughty *French Man*
That menac'd so of late.
*Mach* Why this is *Borgia*.
Come, come, you must not droop; look up, my Lord,
Methinks I see you Crown'd *Rome*'s Emperor
No doubt, Sir, but among your glorious Plunder,
You'll find some Woman——
*Borg*. Ha! no more, I charge thee.
I swear I was at ease, and had forgot her·
Why didst thou wake me then, to turn me wild,
And rouze the slumb'ring Orders of my Soul?
To my charm'd Ears no more of Woman tell,
Name not a Woman, and I shall be well
Like a poor Lunatick that makes his Moan,
And for a time beguiles the Lookers on,
He reasons well, his Eyes their wildness lose,
And vows the Keepers his wrong'd Sense abuse:
But if you hit the Cause that hurt his Brain,
Then his Teeth gnash, he foams, he shakes his Chain,
His Eye-balls rowl, and he is mad again. [*Exeunt*

*Enter one Executioner with a Dark Lanthorn, follow'd by another at a distance; they part often, look up and down, and Hem to the rest*

1 *Exec* The Coast is clear, and all the Guards are gone

2 *Exec* Hark, hark; what Noise was that?

1 *Exec* The Clock struck three:

2 *Exec* See, the Moon shines, haste, and call our
Hem to 'em, that's the Sign. [Fellows

1 *Exec* They come, they come.

*Enter Four Executioners more, Two carry the Body of the Duke of* Gandia *in a Chair, the others follow, and scout behind.*

1 *Exec* So —— set him down, and let 'em bear the..
For I am weary—— [part

4 *Exec.* And so am I. I sweat, but 'tis with Fear

1 *Exec.* Make no more Words on't; take him from the Chair

2 *Exec* A ghastly Sight The Weight about his Neck
Has bent him almost double I'll not touch him ——

3 *Exec.* Cowardly Villain — Come, my Princely Ma-
The Fishes want their Break-fast [ster,

4 *Exec* Joyn all together,
And hurl him o'er this Wall into the *Tiber* [Guard..

2 *Exec.* Fly, fl, ---I hear a noise. The Guards, the

3 *Exec* He lies, he lies, the Coynage of his Fears,
Once more, I say, joyn all your Hands together.
Remember the Reward, two thousand Crowns
A Man But for that Milk-sop, I suspect him;
Therefore let's watch our time, decoy him on;
And when this Business is a little o'er,
Strangle him in some Corner, least he prate
Of what's done Now, now's the time, away——

[*They joyn all together, take him by the Legs and Arms, and hurl him over the Wall into the* Tiber *A noise is heard, as of a Body falling into the Water---They look about once more, then start, take up the Chair, and run out---Scene shuts.*

## SCENE II.

*Enter* Borgia *and* Machiavel.

*Mach* Though *Orsino*, the *Vitelli*, and *Colonni*
Are hush'd; the *Spaniard*, and the *French*, no doubt

ould buy your Friendſhip at the deareſt rate.
y more, I yield you Lord of *Tuſcany*,
d Maſter of ſuch Forces as might march
ainſt the haughtieſt Power of Chriſtendom:
t Prince, forgive me, if I am too free,
o you remember whence this Glory comes,
d how this Golden Fortune is deriv'd?
e Pope--from that rich Scource theſe Currents rowl;
d when another Pope ſucceeds, who knows
t he may ſtrip you bare of all thoſe Honours
hich this has given, and turn you to the World?
*Borg.* No, *Machiavel*, I am prepar'd for Fate,
hough *Alexander* ſhould expire to Night.
rſt, who is left of all the Families
have defac'd, if a new Pope were made,
o ſay I wrong'd 'em, none that I remember.
is not my way to lop, for then the Tree
ay ſprout again, but root him, and he lies
ever to bluſter. But I will tell thee,
ite to unhinge that hold, no Pope ſhall e'er
e fixt in *Rome*, while *Borgia* is alive,
ut by this Hand. The Gentry are all mine
or ever, gain'd by Preſents and Preferments:
he *Spaniſh* Cardinals are mine devoted,
ith all that are conſpicuous in the College.
hat then can Fortune do? I laugh at her,
purn all thoſe Shrines and Altars, which weak Wretches,
ero's and Fools, devoutly raiſe to gain her.
*Mach.* Yet hear me, *Borgia*, hear the oddeſt Story
hat ever Melancholly told the World.
his Morning, being early in the *Vatican*,
ar in the Library, at the upper end,
ethought I ſaw two ſtately Human Forms,
ying at diſtance, wrapt in Linnen Shrouds,
pproaching nearer with a ſtedfaſt Gaze,
s now I look upon the Prince I honour,
ſaw the Figure of the Pope your Father
tretch'd on the Floor, pale, ghaſtly, cold and dead,
nd by his Side, with horrour upon horrour,
nd double tremblings, ſaw my Lord, your ſelf,

My

My very *Cæsar*, like a new-laid Ghost,
Swoln black, and bloated, while your inclos'd Eyes,
All blod-shot, fixt on mine their dreadful Beams. [Phleg-
*Borg.* Fumes, Fumes, my *Machiavel*, the effects of
Gross Humours, Fumes, which from thy thicker Blood
Stream up like Vapours from a foggy Pool.
*Mach* I am apt to think it but a leap of Fancy,
A jading of the Mind, which, quite tired out
With Thought's eternal toil, strikes from the Road·
Yet, as you prize your Life, let me conjure you,
Beware *Ascanio*, his long red Coat
Hides a most mortal and inveterate Foe.
*Borg.* I know him *Machiavel*, and sooth him on,
As he would me But *Borgia* does assure thee,
That he, that scarlet poisonous Luxury,
With his adherent Brothers, shall this Night,
Even in the midst of Kisses, Oaths, Embraces,
Burst in the *Vatican*, and shed their Venom
*Mach* Your Father is a Master of his Breast,
The occasion gives new Life, fresh Vigour to him,
Even at the very verge of bottomless Death,
He stands and smiles as careless and undaunted,
As wanton Swimmers on a Rivers brink
Laugh at the rapid Stream.
*Borg* Therefore my Friend,
Let us despise this Torrent of the World,
Fortune, I mean, and dam her up with Fences,
Banks, Bulworks, all the Fortresses, which Virtue,
Resolv'd and mann'd like ours, can raise against her;
That if she does o'er-flow, she may at least
Bring but half Ruin to our great designs:
That being at last asham'd of her own Weakness,
Like a low-bated Flood, she may retire
To her own Bounds, and we with Pride o're-look her.

*Enter Don* Michael *and the Butler.*

*D. Mich.* My Lord, your Servant waits as you ap-
*Borg* Are my Provisions come? [pointed.
*Butl.* They are, my Lord
*Borg.* Do you remember what I gave in charge?
*Butl.* That none should touch the gilded flask of Wine.

Borg.

*Borg* I charge thee none, but ſuch as I ſhall order.
Don *Michael*, is my Father yet arriv'd?

*D Mich.* He is, my Lord, and gone.

*Borg* Say'ſt thou?

*D Mich.* When firſt he enter'd, quite o'ercome with
Thirſting, and faint with the hot Seaſon's Rage,[Heat,
He call'd for Wine, and though diſſwaded from it,
Drank largely, mingled with the Cardinals,
And walk'd, and laugh'd, play'd with *Columbus* Boys,
Heard their rude Muſick, and beheld 'em dance;
When on a ſudden ſtarting up, he ask'd
For you, my Lord; bow'd, as his Cuſtóm is,
With deep humility to all, deſir'd 'em
To ſit, and ſo went out——but with a promiſe
Of a moſt quick Return——

SCENE *draws, and diſcovers a Chair of State under a Canopy, a large Table, with a rich Banquet——and many Candles on't.*

*Enter* Aſcanio, Adrian, Enna, Ange, *two Cardinals more.*

*Aſcan.* My Lord, the Vatican Society,
Who were oblig'd to ſacrifice this Night,
As every looſer Genius ſhould inſpire,
To Air, and Wine, and warmer Converſation,
Grow dull for want of you. His Holineſs
Himſelf's retir'd——Therefore let us intreat you——

*Borg.* O my good Lord *Aſcanio*, I am born
To be at your command———my Lords, I wait you.
Sirrah, remember him———I charge thee fill
Of the gilt Flaſk to him——

*Butl* My Lord ———I ſhall.
This Wine is ſure the richeſt of the World,
Becauſe he charges me ſo ſtrictly of it
That Cardinal's a Friend, and he muſt taſte it.

*Aſcan* Lord *Machiavel*, you have been charitable, I thank your Love;
Nay, with my Life, I thank you——

*Mach* My Lord--I wiſh you would explain your ſelf.

*Aſcan.* It needs not Sir, for this the meaneſt know,
The Rabble, baſe Mechanicks talk of Murders

I saw a sweating Weaver in his Shirt,
Ran puffing with his Shuttle in his Hand,
To ask a neighbour Butcher of the News,
Who with his Knife in's Mouth abruptly tells
*Orsino*'s Death, yes, and his Daughter's too
Then comes a Taylor with his Hair tuck'd back,
Behind his Ears, on tiptoes, in his Slippers,
And cries in haste, the Duke of *Gandia*'s murder'd:
Then spits upon his Iron, casts up his Eyes,
Threads through the Company, as 'twere a Needle,
And vanishes. no more, my Lord, I thank you.
Nay, by my Life, but for the Company,
I'd kiss the bottom of your Robe, your Lordship's ever
Your Highness Servant My Lord, let's drink a Health to
His Holiness--But in my Heart, I say the Devil take him

*Borg* Lord *Machiavel*, you are my Guest to Night
Were the Society made up of Gods,
As sure it is of Saints, Spirits above
The common Elevation, yet this Man
I say, my Lords, this Human Prodigy,
Would not be set to wait, but fix'd among 'em,
To dazle with the brightest Being here.
Wine there! —— My Lord *Ascanio Sforza*,
Health to all here, and to the general Joy —— [*Drinks*

*Ascan* Fine work, my Lords, fine work, I say, look to't,
The Duke of *Gandia*'s murder'd.

*Adrian* 'Tis the common Rumour

*Em.* The Pope this Morning in the Consistory,
When first he heard the News, leap'd from his Throne,
Crossing his Breast, and looking up to Heav'n,
He vow'd hereafter most severe amendment,
As from this time to fast for Forty Hours,
And all his Life wear next his humble Flesh
A Shirt of Hair

*Ascan* A Shirt of Hair, bating *Lucretian* Nights:
She'll not endure't, look you, her Skin's too tender:
A Shirt of Hair, a very prickling Penance.
Now, by my Holy Dame, meer Letchery:
Don't I know him? Slave, more Wine, I say;
Fill up my Glass, Come, come, my Lords, 'tis time

To

To look about us, and reform the Church—[*Drinks*
Prune it I say, or else like *Babylon*,
Like *Babel*'s Whore, 'twill run up all to Seed.
Hark you, Lord *Ange*.

*Ang* My Lord.

*Ascan* My Lord of *Enna* too, we four are
As one Soul. This Pope's a very leud
And wicked Head,—he's never well, but
When he's plotting Murders. Why, look you, Sirs,
If a Man cannot speak his Mind of
State Affairs,— but he must streight be
Dogg'd by Hell-hounds, Blood-suckers, Decoyers,
Rascals, that watch to throttle him in some
By-corner, then quoit him like a Cat into
The River, 'tis very fine, Now by my Holy-dame,
It may be our turn next—by the Mass it may,
I say, my Lord, it may— [*The* Indian *Boys dance.*
Ha, my Lords, how do you
Like the motion? Very pretty, very fine.
O brave *Columbus*! More Wine there, a bigger
Glass: I'll drink *Columbus*'s Health—Now, by my
Holy dame, I am frolicksome, and will be active.
Ha, my Lords, ha, I learnt at *Paris*, when I was
A Stripling; yet these are pretty Children, very fine Boys--

*Enter D.* Michael.

*D Mich.* My Lord, I grieve to bring you Mortal
Which were I silent, yet in some few Minutes [News,
Must wound your Ears; your Father's dead.

*Borg* Hence, Raven,
Thou Boder of the blackest deed of Death!
My Lords, this Villain say's the Pope's dead;
Went he not hence but now, sound, firm, and healthful,
And promis'd to return?

*D Mich* My Lord, he did:
But 'tis most certain, ere he went from hence,
As all our best Physicians give on Oath,
He was by some pernicious Traitor poison'd

*Borg* O *Machiavel*, where is our Forecast now?
My Heart misgives me, and my Bosom's hot.
Who ministred? who gave my Father Wine?

*D. Mich.*

*D. Mich* Your Servant: For when first your Fath
His own Provisions were not come. [enter
*Borg.* O Confusion!
Answer me Villain! ha! fill'd you his Wine?
*Butl* My Lord, I did. [trembl
*Borg.* What, from the gilded Flask? Why dost tho
Horror consume thee, gnaw thee, burn thy Entrails,
Wilt thou not speak?
*Butl* My Lord, by your strict Charge,
That none should taste thoseFlasks but whom you order
I judg'd the Wine most Excellent, and gave
Part of it to your Father——
*Borg* O damn'd Dolt!
Curst, senseless Dog! Now, *Machiavel*, where are w
Ha! by the Furies that invade my Breast,
And crumble all my Bowels into Dust,
I am caught my self! Speak, tell me, horrid Villain
Or I will have thee dragg'd in thousand Pieces;
Torn by mad Horses like the flesh of Dogs: [Traito
Thou gav'st me Wine too from the gilded Flasks! h
Come, double damn thy self, and swear thou didst not
*Butl* My Lord—I must confess I gave the same
To you, that was directed for your Friend,
My Lord *Ascanio.* [pou
*Borg.* Take thy Reward then, which the Devil th
Into my Breast, thus gives thee back again!
O *Machiavel*, O do not look upon me:
I am below thy Scorn, thus vilely caught,
O basely, basely sold by my own Wile [De
*Asca* Oh, oh, oh—I have my Share on't too, t
Thank you—Fire, Fire, Fire! oh my Guts—Brimsto
And Fire——haste there———fly for Antidotes.
*Borg* None, none on Earth,
I tell thee, Priest, can save thy rotten Carkass,
No Cardinal, lie down, lie down, and roar,
Think on thy Scarlet Sins, and fear Damnation.
*Asca.* Legions of Furies here, Hell is broke loose,
And all the Devils are quarter'd in my Bowels.
Run Slave! and for a last Revenge, produce
His mangled Bastard——that's some Pleasure yet.

Borg

*Borg.* O *Machiavel*, thy Hand, I am all flames;
Yet thou shalt hear no noise. sit down, my Friend,
Upon the Earth——for there's my Mansion now,
Dust, and no more———and yet methinks 'twas hard
That this Elaborate Scheme of mighty Man,
This Parchment, where the Lines of *Roman* Greatness
By thee so well were drawn, should by the Hand
Of scribbling Chance be blotted thus for ever

*Ascan* I burn, I burn, I toste, I roste, and my Guts fry,
They blaze, they snap, they bounce like Squibs
And Crackers· I am all Fire———

*Mach* Is't possible that you can bear the Pangs
Of violent Poison, thus unmov'd?

*Borg.* 'Tis little
To one resolv'd: No, let the Coward Statesman,
Women, and Priests, whine at the Thoughts of Death;
For me, whose Mind was ever fierce and active,
Death is unwelcome, only for this Reason,
Because 'tis an eternal Laziness———

*Enter* Alonzo, *leading in* Seraphino, *with his Eyes out, and Face cut.*

*Mach.* I must confess my Mind, by what I saw
This Morning, and by what has happen'd since,
Is deeply shock'd, even from her own Foundation.

*Asca.* Bear the blind Bastard to his Father, go,
And bid him laugh——oh!

*Mach.* Horror! new horror!
My Lord, your Son, by that most bloody Cardinal,
Mangled and blind

*Borg.* Why dost thou wonder at it?
'Tis all the work of Chance, and trick of Fortune:
Yet this methinks is horrible indeed
Come hither Boy———

*Serap* Alas, I hear your Voice,
And cannot find the Way,
But am like one benighted in a Wood.

*Borg.* A Wood indeed,
But oh the Brambles there have us'd thee vilely.

*Serap* O Father, you are arm'd, and have a Sword;
Will you not, for your *Seraphino*'s sake,

Cut

Cut down those Thorns that prick'd out both my Ey[es]
I know you will; for you were always kind
And tender of me: Oft-times have you held me,
Fast in your Arms, and smil'd, and plaid with me;
Though you're a Prince, a very busie Prince,
And call'd me little Eyes, little indeed,
For now they're out, and all my Face is cut:
Nay, they have starv'd me too.

*Borg.* Death and Horror!

*Serap.* Why do you press me thus between your Ar[ms]
As if you lov'd me still? I am sure you cannot.
Pray let me hide my Face within your Bosom,
For if you look upon me I shall fright you.
O! I've a Pain here just about my Heart!
When you, my Lord, a long time after me
Shall die, will you not lay my little Bones
By yours? Alas! my Pain encreases——Oh—— [*Dies.*

*Borg.* Revenge thee, Boy! I ask but that from Fa[te]
And see 't is given me Through a thousand Wounds,
Thus, horrid Priest! purge out thy lustful Blood,
[*Stabs Asca.*

And vomit thy black Soul——

*Asca.* Oh! Devil! Devil! Devil—— [*Dies.*

*Borg.* No, *Machiavel,* 'tis now fit time to rave,
For I am now enrag'd to that Degree,
That I will live even in despight of Fortune,
Stars! Fates! and all the Juggles of a Heav'n.
Hence, bear me, Slaves, and plunge me into *Tyber,*
Deep as I sunk the Duke of *Gandia* down!
Till I have quench'd this Hell within my Bowels,
Then flay me an Ox hide and swaddle me,
Like *Hercules* in the *Nemean* Skin
'Till all my poison'd Flesh like Bark peels off,
And my bare Trunk stands every brushing Wind!

*Enna.* Where are our Guards? My Lords, I judge it
That *Machiavel* and *Borgia* should be seiz'd. [tion

*Borg.* Seize me! what sawcy Priest durst start that M[otion?]
Am I not Tyrant here? The Lord of *Rome*?
Does not *France* dread my Frown? and *Spain* adore me?
Who then dares talk of seizing me? What, he?

Ti[...]

This wag-tail Priest, with the black picked Beard,
That scowers the Country round for freckled Wenches?
Or was it you, my Lord of *Enna*? Hah!
Death, where's my Majesty? Or vail your Caps,
Or I will trample you beneath my Feet;
You, *Ange*! that could prostitute your Sister
To gain a Hat? Lie there Lord of St. *Peter*:
You Cardinal *ad Vincula*, you pack of Hell-hounds,
That trace me by the Blood. On, on I say,
On to the brink of Hell: Thence plunge together,
Where, on his Throne, behold the Master Devil
With a great pair of glowing Horns red hot
To gore you for your Lives Incontinence,
You Ravishers, you Virgin Pioneers,
You Cuckold-makers of the forked World

*Ange.* Where are our Guards?

*Borg.* Hark, I hear 'em coming:
Or is it Dooms-Day? Ha——by Hell it is:
And see, the Heav'ns, and Earth, and Air are all
On fire the very Seas, like molten Glass,
Rowl their bright Waves, and from the smoaky Deep
Cast up the glaring Dead: The Trumpet sounds,
And the swift Angels skim about the Globe
To summon all Mankind. *Rome*, *Rome* is call'd!
Work, work for Hell Hoa, Satan! *Belzebub*!
*Bal* and *Baal*——Whence this Thunderclap?
They've blown us up with Wild-fire in the Air;
And look how the ball'd *Fryers* in russet Gowns
Croak like old Vultures, how the flutt'ring *Jesuits*,
In black and white, chatter about the Heav'ns!
Capuchins, *Monks*, with the whole Tribe of Knaves!
Then let me burst my Spleen! Look how the Tassels,
Caps, Hats and Cardinals Coats, and Cowls and Hoods
Are tost about——the sport, the sport of Winds——
Indulgences, Dispences, Pardons, Bulls, see yonder!
Priest, they fly——they're whirl'd aloft. They fly,
They fly o'er the backside o'th' World,
Into a Limbo large, and broad, since call'd the Paradise
Of Fools

 *Enna.*

*Enna* 'Tis just we give him way! this fit of Rage
Has wasted him to Death, see he breaths short.
The Taper's spent, and this is his last Blaze

*Borg* Ha! Breath I short? Prelate thou ly'st: my Pulse
Beats with a constant Fire and sprightly Motion;
The Strings of my tough Heart as strong as ever:
No—I will live; in spight of Fate I'll live
To be the Scourge of *Rome*: I'll live to act
New Mischiefs, and create new wicked *Popes*,
To ponyard *Heritick* Princes, that refuse
To lay their Necks beneath the holy Slipper.
Murder successively two Kings of *France*;
*Britain* attempt, though her most watchful Angel
Saves the lov'd Monarch of that happy Isle,
And turns upon our selves the plotted Wound,
That sinks me to the Earth: yet still we'll on,
And hatch new Deeds of Darkness: O Hell, and Furies,
Why should we not, since the great Head himself
Will back my Plots, joyn me in Blood and Honor,
And after give me Bond for my Salvation.
I swear I will——I'll have it——nay, Sir, you shall—
Or I will thunder to your Holiness
But hark he whispers, what a little Gold———
With all my heart thus Devils buy Souls for trash—
I'll fee your itching Palm for Absolution,
Gold for my Pardon, hey——'tis seal'd and given!
And for a Ducat thus I purchase Heav'n——    [Di

*Mach* The mighty Soul there forc'd her furious Passage
And plunges now in deep Eternity ———
I see my Lords, you have resolv'd to guard me,
And I submit to strict Examination:
By you to be acquitted or condemn'd
Yet this I must avow before you all,
Though you should cast me to the Inquisition,
Skill'd as I am in all Affairs of Earth,
Known both to Popes and Kings, and often honour'd
With Cabinet Councils of Imperial Heads;
I here resolve on this, as my last Judgment,
No Power is safe, nor no Religion good,
Whose Principles of Growth are laid in Blood

EP

# EPILOGUE.

*WELL, then be you his Judges; what Pretence*
*Made them roar out, this Play would give*
*Offence?*
*Had he the Pope's Effigies meant to burn,*
*And kept for Sport his Ashes in an Urn;*
*To try if Reliques would perform, at home,*
*But half those Miracles they do at* Rome;
*More could not have been said, nor more been done,*
*To damn this Play about the Court and Town:*
*Not if he had shown their Philters, Charms and*
*Rage,*
*Nay conjur'd up Pope* Jone *to please the Age,*
*And had her Breeches search'd upon the Stage.*
*First then, he brings a Scandal on the Gown,*
*And makes a Priest both Leacher and Buffoon:*
*Why, was no Fool yet ever made a Flamen;*
*But Dulness quite entail'd upon the Lay-men?*
*Or was it ever heard in* Rome *before,*
*That any Priest was question'd for his Whore?*
*Yet more, the horrid Chair the Midnight show—*
*He says 'twas done two hundred Years ago:*
*He only points their ways of murdering then;*
*If you must damn, spare the Historian's Pen,*
*And damn those Rogues that act 'em o'er again.*
*But* Dominicks, Franciscans, Hermits, Fryars,
*Shall breed no more a Race of Zealous Lyars;*
*Villains, who for Religion's Propagation,*
*Come here disguis'd in ev'ry mean Vocation,*
*And sit in Stalls to spy upon the Nation.*
*Old Emissaries shall their Trade forbear,*
*Spread no more* Savoy *Reliques, Bones and Hair,*
*Shall sell no more like Baubles in a Fair.*

 *Monks*

## EPILOGUE.

*Monks under Ground shall cease to Earth like Moles,*
*And Father* Lewis *leave his lurking Holes;*
*Get no more Thirty Pounds for a blind Story,*
*Of freeing a* Welch *Soul from Purgatory.*
*Jesuits in* Rome *shall quite forswear their Function,*
*And not for Gold give Whores the* Extreme Unction·
*High* English *Whores, that have all Vices past,*
*Shall cease to turn true Catholicks at last,*
*When Poets write, tho' by exactest Rules,*
*And are not judg'd by Knaves, and damn'd by Fools.*

# *Lucius Junius Brutus;*

## Father of his Country.

A

# TRAGEDY.

—*cæloque invectus aperto*
*Flectit equos, curruque volans dat lora Secunda* Virg. l 4.

Printed in the YEAR 1712.

To the Right Honourable

# CHARLES,

## Earl *of* Dorset *and* Middlesex, *One of the Gentlemen of His Majesties Bed-Chamber*, &c.

*MY LORD*,

ITH an Assurance I hope becoming the Justice of my Cause I lay this Tragedy at your Lordship's Feet, not as a common Persecution, but as an Offering suitable to your Virtue, and worthy of the Greatness of your Name. There are some Subjects that require but half the Strength of a Great Poet, but when *Greece* or Old *Rome* come in play, the Nature, Wit and Vigour of foremost *Shakespear*, the Judgment and Force of *Johnson*, with all his borrowed Mastery from the Ancients, will scarce suffice for so terrible a Grapple. The Poet must elevate his Fancy with the mightiest Imagination, must run back so many Hundred Years, take a just Prospect of the Spirit of those Times without the least Thought of Ours; for if his Eye should swerve so low, his Muse will grow giddy with the Vastness of the Distance, fall at once, and for ever lose the Majesty of the First Design. He that will pretend to be a Critick of such a Work must not have a Grain of *Cecilius*, he must be *Longin* throughout, or nothing, where even the nicest, best Remarks must pass but for Allay to the Imperial Fury of this Old *Roman* Gold. There must be no Dross through the whole Mass, the Furnace must be justly heated, and the Bullion stamp'd with an unerring Hand. In such a Writing there must be Greatness of Thought without Bombast, Remoteness without Monstrousness, Virtue arm'd with Severity, not in Iron Bodice, Solid Wit without Modern Affectation; Smoothness without Gloss, Speaking out without cracking the Voice, or straining the Lungs. In short, my Lord, he that will Write as he ought on so Noble an Occasion, must Write like You. But I fear there are few that know how to Copy after so Great an Original as your Lordship, because there is scarce One Genius Extant of your own Size that can follow you *passibus æquis*; that has the Felicity and Mastery of the Old Poets, or can half Match the Thoughtfulness of your Soul. How far short I am cast of such Inimitable Excellence, I must with Shame, my Lord, confess I am but too too sensible Nature, 'tis believ'd (if I am not flattered, and do not flatter my self) has not been niggardly to me in the Portion of a Genius, tho' I have been so far from improving it, that I am half afraid I have lost of the Principal. It behoves e then for the Future to look about me, to ſee hether I am a Lag in the Race, to look up to ur Lordſhip, and ſtrain upon the Track of ſo r a Glory. I muſt acknowledge, however I ve behav'd my ſelf in drawing, nothing ever eſented it ſelf to my Fancy with that Solid Plea-re as *Brutus* did in Sacrificing his Sons. Before ead *Machivel*'s Notes upon the Place, I con-ded it the greateſt Action that was ever ſeen roughout all Ages on the greateſt Occaſion. For y own Endeavour, I thought I never painted y Man ſo to the Life before.

*Vis & Tarquinios reges animamque ſuperbam*
*Ultoris Bruti, faſceſque videre receptos?*
*Infelix utcunque ferent ea facta Minores?*

No doubt that Divine Poet imagined it might be o great for any People but his own, perhaps I have und it ſo, but *Johnſon*'s *Catiline* met no better te, as his Motto from *Horace* tells us.

———*His non plebecula gaudet, &c.*

ay, *Shakeſpear*'s *Brutus* with much ado beat mſelf into the Heads of a blockiſh Age, ſo knot- were the Oaks he had to deal with. For my vn Opinion, in ſpight of all the Obſtacles my odeſty could raiſe, I could not help inſerting a aunt in the Title Page, *Cœloque, &c.*

*And having gain'd the Liſt that he deſign'd,*
*Bold as the Billows driving with the Wind,*
*He loos'd the Muſe that wing'd his free-born Mind.*

On

On this I arm'd, and reſolv'd not to be ſtirr with the little Exceptions of a ſparkiſh Generati on, that have an Antipathy to Thought: But al how frail are our beſt Reſolves in our own Co cerns? I ſhow'd no Paſſion outward; but wheth through an Over-conceit of the Work, or becau perhaps there was indeed ſome Merit, the Fi burnt inward, and I was troubled for my dum Play, like a Father for his dead Child. 'Tis e nough that I have eas'd my Heart by this Dedica tion to your Lordſhip. I comfort my ſelf tha whatever our partial Youth alledge, your Lor ſhip will find ſomething in it worth your Obſer vation; which with my future Diligence, Reſo lution to Study, Devotion to Virtue, and you Lordſhip's Service, may render me not altogeth unworthy the Protection of your Lordſhip.

*My Lord,*

Your Lordſhip's moſt humble

and devoted Servant,

*Nat: Lee.*

PRO

# PROLOGUE,

## Written by Mr. *Duke*.

*Ong has the Tribe of Poets on the Stage*
*Groan'd under persecuting Criticks Rage;*
*with the sound of Railing and of Rhime,*
*Bees united by the tinkling Chime,*
*little stinging Insects swarm the more,*
*Buz is greater than it was before*
*oh! you leading Voters of the Pit,*
*infect others with your too much Wit,*
*well-affected Members do seduce,*
*with your Malice poyson half the House,*
*your Ill-manag'd Arbitrary Sway*
*be no more indur'd, but ends this Day.*
*rs of abler Conduct we will chuse,*
*more indulgent to a trembling Muse;*
*men for Ends of Government more fit,*
*men shall Rule the Boxes and the Pit,*
*Laws to Love, and Influence to Wit.*
*me one Man of Sense in all your Roll,*
*m some one Woman has not made a Fool.*
*Business, that intolerable Load,*
*r which Man does Groan, and yet is Proud,*
*h better they can Manage wou'd they please,*
*not their want of Wit, but love of Ease*
*spite of Art, more Wit in them appears,*
*we boast ours, and they dissemble theirs.*
*once was ours, and shot up for a while,*
*hallow in a hot and barren Soil,*
*when transplanted to a richer Ground,*
*in their Eden its Perfection found*
*'tis but just they shou'd our Wit invade,*
*lst we set up their painting, patching Trade;*
*or our Courage, to our Shame 'tis known,*
*hey can raise it, they can pull it down.*
*heir own Weapons they our Bullies awe,*
*h let them make an Antisalick Law,*
*cribe to all Mankind, as well as Plays,*
*wear the Breeches, as they wear the Bays.*

Dra-

# Dramatis Personæ.

## MEN.

| | | |
|---|---|---|
| Lucius Junius Brutus, | | Mr. *Betterton* |
| Titus, | | Mr. *Smith.* |
| Tiberius, | | Mr. *William* |
| Collatinus, | | Mr. *Wiltshir* |
| Valerius, | | Mr. *Gillow.* |
| Horatius, | | Mr. *Norris.* |
| Aquilius. | | |
| Vitellius. | | |
| Junius. | | |
| Fecilian Priests, | Mr. *Percival.* | Mr *Freeman* |
| Vindicius, | | Mr. *Nokes.* |
| Fabritius, | | Mr. *Jeron.* |
| Citizens, *&c.* | | |

## WOMEN

| | |
|---|---|
| Sempronia, | Lady *Sling* |
| Lucretia, | Mrs *Better* |
| Teraminta, | Mrs *Barret* |

## SCENE *ROME.*

*Luci*

# ucius Junius Brutus;

# Father of his Country.

## CT I. SCENE I.

Enter *Titus* and *Teraminta*.

*TITUS.*

*Teraminta*, why this Face of Tears?
Since first I saw thee, till this happy Day,
Thus hast thou past thy Melancholly Hours,
Ev'n in the Court retir'd, stretch'd on a Bed
In some dark Room, with all the Curtains drawn,
r in some Garden o'er a Flowry Bank
eting thy Sorrows in the murm'ring Stream;
n some pathless Wilderness amusing,
king the mossie Bark of some old Tree,
poring, like a *Sybil*, on the Leaves:
at, now the Priest should join us! O, the Gods!
at can you proffer me in vast Exchange
this ensuing Night? Not all the Days
Crowning Kings, of Conquering Generals,
all the Expectation of hereafter,
th what bright Fame can give in th'other World,
u'd purchase thee this Night one Minute from me.

Ter.

*Ter.* O, *Titus!* if since first I saw the Light,
Since I began to think on my Misfortunes,
And take a Prospect of my certain Woes,
If my sad Soul has entertain'd a Hope
Of Pleasure here, or harbour'd any Joy,
But what the Presence of my *Titus* gave me;
Add, add, you cruel Gods, to what I bear,
And break my Heart before him. [

*Tit.* Break first th' eternal Chain, for when tho
The World to me is *Chaos* Yes, *Teraminta*,
So close the everlasting Sisters wove us,
When e'er we part, the Strings of both must crack
Once more I do intreat thee give the Grave
Thy Sadness; let me press thee in my Arms,
My fairest Bride, my only Lightness here,
Tune of my Heart, and Charmer of my Eyes;
Nay, thou shalt learn the Extasie from me,
I'll make thee smile with my extravagant Passion,
Drive thy pale Fears away; and e'er the Morn
I swear, O *Teraminta*, O my Love,
Cold as thou art, I'll warm thee into Blushes

*Ter* O *Titus!* may I, ought I to believe you?
Remember, Sir, I am the Blood of *Tarquin*,
The basest too

*Tit.* Thou art the Blood of Heav'n,
The kindest Influence of the teeming Stars
No Seed of *Tarquin*, no, 'tis forg'd t' abuse thee.
A God thy Father was, a Goddess was his Wife,
The Wood-Nymphs found thee on a Bed of Roses,
Lapt in the Sweets and Beauties of the Spring,
*Diana* foster'd thee with Nectar Dews,
Thus tender, blooming, chaste, she gave thee me,
To build a Temple sacred to her Name,
Which I will do, and wed thee there again. [

*Ter.* Swear then, my *Titus*, swear you'll ne'er upbr
Swear that your Love shall last like mine for ever,
No turn of State or Empire, no Misfortune,
Shall e'er estrange you from me. Swear, I say,
That, if you should prove false, I may at least
Have something still to answer to my Fate,

Swe

wear, ſwear, my Lord, that you will never hate me,
ut ,to your Death ſtill cheriſh in your Boſom
he poor, the fond, the wretched *Teraminta*
*Tit* 'Till Death! nay, after Death, if poſſible.
iſſolve me ſtill with Queſtions of this Nature,
Vhile I return my Anſwer all in Oaths.
ore than thou canſt demand I ſwear to do.
his Night, this Night ſhall tell thee how I love thee·
Vhen Words are at a Loſs, and the mute Soul
ours out her ſelf in Sighs and gaſping Joys,
he graſps, the Pangs of Bliſs, and murmuring Pleaſures,
hou ſhalt confeſs all Language then is vile,
nd yet believe me moſt without my Vowing

*Enter* Brutus *with a* Flamen.

ut ſee, my Father with a *Flamen* here!
he Court comes on, let's ſlip the buſie Croud,
nd ſteal into th' Eternal Knot of Love. [*Exeunt.*

*Brut* Did *Sextus*, ſay'ſt thou, lye at *Collatia*,
*Collatine*'s Houſe, laſt Night?
*Fla* My Lord, he did.
here he, with *Collatine*, and many others,
d been ſome Nights before.
*Brut* Ha! if before,
hy did he come again?
*Fla* Becauſe, as Rumour ſpreads,
fell moſt paſſionately in Love with her.
*Brut* What then?
*Fla* Why, is't not ſtrange?
*Brut* Is ſhe not handſome?
*Fla* O, very handſome.
*Brut* Then 'tis not ſtrange at all.
it, for a King's Son to love another Man's Wife!
y Sir, I've known the King has done the ſame.
h, I my ſelf, who am not us'd to caper,
e ſometimes had th'unlawful Itch upon me
y, prithee Prieſt, come thou and help the Number.
my old Boy; the Company is not ſcandalous.
s go to Hell together, confeſs the Truth,
'ſt thou ne'er ſteal from the Gods an Hour, or ſo,
mumble a new Prayer———

With

With a young fleshly Whore in a Baudy Corner? h[a
*Fla* My Lord, your Servant. Is this the Fool? Th[
Let him be what he will, he spoke the Truth:[Madman
If other Fools be thus, they're dangerous Fellows.[Ex[
*Brut solus.* Occasion seems in view; something there
In *Tarquin*'s last Abode at *Collatine*'s:
Late entertain'd, and early gone this Morning?
The Matron ruffled, wet, and dropping Tears,
As if she had lost her Wealth in some Black Storm!
As in the Body, on some great Surprize,
The Heart still calls from the discolour'd Face,
From every part the Life and Spirits down:
So *Lucrece* comes to *Rome*, and summons all her Blood
*Lucrece* is fair, but chaste, as the fann'd Snow
Twice bolted o'er by the bleak Nothern Blasts.
So lies this Starry, Cold and Frozen Beauty,
Still watch'd and guarded by her waking Virtue,
A Pattern, tho' I fear inimitable,
For all succeeding Wives O *Brutus*! *Brutus*!
When will the tedious Gods permit thy Soul
To walk abroad in her own Majesty,
And throw this Vizor of thy Madness from thee?
O, what but infinite Spirit, propt by Fate,
For Empire's Weight to turn on, could endure,
As thou hast done, the Labours of an Age,
All Follies, Scoffs, Reproaches, Pities, Scorns,
Indignities almost to Blows sustain'd,
For twenty pressing Years, and by a *Roman*?
To act Deformity in thousand Shapes,
To please the greater Monster of the two,
That cries, bring forth the Beast, and let him tumble
With all Variety of Aping Madness,
To bray, and bear more than the Asses Burden,
Sometimes to whoot and scream like Midnight Owls
Then screw my Limbs like a distorted Satyr,
The World's Grimace, th'eternal Laughing-stock
Of Town and Court, the Block, the Jest of *Rome*,
Yet all the while not to my dearest Friend,
To my own Children, nor my Bosome Wife,
Disclose the weighty Secret of my Soul.

*Rome*, O Mother, be thou th'impartial Judge
this be Virtue, which yet wants a Name.
hich never any Age could parallel,
d worthy of the foremost of thy Sons.

*Enter* Horatius, *and* Mutius.

*Mut. Horatius* heard'st thou where *Sextus* was last Night?
*Hor* Yes, at *Collatia*. 'Tis the Buz of *Rome*,
is more than guess'd that there has been foul Play,
se, why should *Lucrece* come in this sad manner
old *Lucretius* House, and summon thither
r Father, Husband, each distinct Relation?

*Enter* Fabritius, *with Courtiers*

*Mut* Scatter it through the City, raise the People,
d find *Valerius* out. Away, *Horatius*. [*Exeunt severally*.

*Fab*. Prithee let's talk no more on't. Look, here's Lord
*utus*. Come, come, we'll divert our selves; for 'tis
t just, that we who sit at the Helm should now and
n unruffle our State Affairs with the Impertinence of a
ol. Prithee, *Brutus*, what's a Clock?

*Brut Clotho*, *Lachesis*, *Atropos*, the Fates are Three. Let
em but strike, and I'll lead you a Dance, my Masters.

*Fab* But hark you, *Brutus*, dost thou hear the News
*Lucrece*?

*Brut* Yes, yes; and I heard of the Wager that was
d among you, among you whoring Lords at the Siege
*Ardea*; ha, Boy! about your handsome Wives.

*Fab* Well, and how, and how?

*Brut* How you bounc'd from the Board, to k Horse,
d rode like Madmen, to find the gentle *Lucrece* at *Col-*
*tia* But how found her? Why, working with her
aids at Midnight Was not this Monstrous, and quite out
the Fashion? Fine Stuff indeed, for a Lady of Honour,
hen her Husband was out of the way, to sit weaving,
d pinking, and pricking of *Arras*? Now, by this Light,
y Lord, your Wife made better use of her Pincusheon.

*Fab* My Wife, my Lord? By *Mars*, my Wife!

*Brut* Why should she not, when all the Royal Nur-
do the same? What? What, my Lord, did you not
d 'em at it, when you came from *Collatia* to *Rome*?
*rtius*, your Wife; and yours, *Flaminius*? with *Tullia*'s

 Boys;

Boys, turning the Cristals up, dashing the Window and the Fates defying? Now, by the Gods, I think 'twas Civil in you, discreetly done, Sirs not to interrupt 'em. But for your Wife, *Fabritius*, I'll be sworn for her, she would not keep 'em Company.

*Fab* No marry would she not; she hates Debauche. How have I heard her Rail at *Terentia*, and tell her next her Heart upon the Qualms, that drinking Wi so late, and tippling Spirits, would be the Death of her.

*Brut.* Hark you, Gentlemen, if you would but be secret now, I could unfould such a business; my Life on a very Plot upon the Court.

*Fab* Out with it; we swear Secresie.

*Brut.* Why thus then To morow *Tullia* goes to the Camp; and I being Master of the Houshold, have Command to sweep the Court of all its Furniture, and send it packing to the Wars. Pandars, Sycophants, smart Rogues, fine Knaves, and surly Rascals, Flatterers, easie, supple, cringing, passing, smiling Villains, all to the Wars

*Fab* By *Mars*, I do not like this Plot.

*Brut* Why, is it not a Plot? A Plot upon your selves, your Persons, Families, and your Relations, even your Wives, Mothers, Sisters, all your Kindred? Whores too are included, Setters too, and Whore-procurers, Bag and Baggage; all, all to the Wars. hence, all Rubbish, Lumber out, and not a Bawd left behind, to put you in Hope of hatching Wh hereafter.

*Fab.* Hark, *Lartius*, he'll run from Fooling to dir Madness, and beat our Brains out. The Devil take the hindmost. Your Servant, sweet *Brutus*; Noble, Honourable *Brutus* [*Exeunt*

*Enter* Titus.

*Tit.* 'Tis done, 'tis done, Auspicious Heav'n has jo And I this Night shall hold her in my Arms. Oh, Sir!

*Brut* Oh, Sir! that Exclamation was too high. Such Raptures ill become the troubled Times, No more of 'em And by the way, my *Titus*, Renounce your *Teraminta*,

*Tit.* Ha, my Lord!
*Brut* How now, my Boy?
*Tit* Your Counsel comes too late, Sir.
*Tit* Your Reply, Sir,
mes too ill-manner'd, pert and sawcy, Sir.
*Tit.* Sir I am Marry'd.
*Brut.* What, without my Knowledge?
*Tit.* My Lord, I ask your Pardon, but that *Hymen*--
*Brut.* Thou ly'st that Honorable God would scorn it,
me bawdy Flamen shuffled you together,
*apus* lock'd you, while the *Bachanals*
ng your detested *Epithalamium.*
hich of thy Blood were the curs'd Witnesses?
ho would be there at such polluted Rites
*Goats, Baboons,* some chatt'ring old *Silenus;*
*Satyrs,* grinning at your slimy Joys?
*Tit* Oh, all the Gods! my Lord, your Son is Marry'd
*Tarquin's*——
*Brut* Bastard.
*Tit* No, his Daughter.
*Brut* No matter:
any of his Blood, if it be his,
re is such natural Contagion in it,
h a Congenial Devil in his Spirit,
me, Lineage, Stock, that but to own a Part
his Relation, is to profess thy self
rn Slave of Hell, and Bondman to the Furies.
u art not Marry'd
*Tit* O, is this possible?
s Change that I behold? No Part of him
e same, nor Eyes, nor Mien, nor Voice, nor Gesture!
*rut.* Oh, that the Gods would give my Arm the Vigor
shake this soft, effeminate, lazy Soul
h from thy Bosom. No, degenerate Boy,
*us* is not the same; the Gods have wak'd him
m dead Stupidity, to be a Scourge,
ving Torment to thy Disobedience.
k on my Face, view my Eyes flame, and tell me
ght thou seest but Glory and Revenge,
lood-shot Anger, and a burst of Fury,

When I but think of *Tarquin*. Damn the Monster,
Fetch him, you Judges of th' eternal Deep,
Arraign him, chain him, plunge him in double Fires:
If after this thou seest a Tenderness,
A Woman's Tear come o'er my Resolution,
Think, *Titus*, think, my Son, 'tis Nature's Fault,
Not *Roman Brutus*, but a Father now.

*Tit*. Oh, let me fall low as the Earth permits me,
And thank the Gods for this most happy Change,
That you are now, altho' to my Confusion,
That awful, Godlike, and Commanding *Brutus*,
Which I so oft have wish'd you; which sometimes
I thought imperfectly you were, or might be,
When I have taken unawares your Soul
At a broad Glance, and forc'd her to retire.
Ah, my dear Lord, you need not add new Threats,
New Marks of Anger to compleat my Ruin,
Your *Titus* has enough to break his Heart,
When he remembers that you durst not trust him:
Yes, yes, my Lord, I have a thousand Frailties;
The Mould you cast me in, the Breath, the Blood,
And Spirit which you gave me, are unlike
The Godlike Author, yet you gave 'em, Sir:
And sure, if you had pleas'd to honour me,
T'immortalize my Name to after Ages,
By imparting your high Cares, I should have found
At least so much Hereditary Virtue
As not to have divulg'd them.

*Brut*. Rise, my Son;
Be satisfy'd thou art the first that know'st me.
A thousand Accidents and fated Causes
Rush against every Bulwark I can raise,
And half unhinge my Soul. For now's the time,
To shake the Building of the Tyrant down.
As from Night's Womb the glorious Day breaks forth
And seems to kindle from the setting Stars;
So from the Blackness of young *Tarquin*'s Crime
And Furnace of his Lust, the Virtuous Soul
Of *Junius Brutus* catches bright Occasion.
I see the Pillars of his Kingdom totter:

he Rape of *Lucrece* is the Midnight Lanthorn
hat lights my Genius down to the Foundation.
eave me to Work, my *Titus*; O, my Son,
or from this Spark a Lightning shall arise,
hat must ere Night purge all the *Roman* Air:
nd then the Thunder of his Ruin follows.
o more; but haste thee to *Lucretius*
ear the Multitude, and must among them.
way, my Son.

*Tit* Bound, and obedient ever. [*Exit.*

*Enter* Vinditius *with* Plebeians.

1 *Cit* *Jupiter*, defend us! I think the Firmament is on a light Fire Now, Neighbour, as you were ing, as to the Cause of Lightning and Thunder, and the Nature of Prodigies.

*Vin* What! a Taylor, and talk of Lightning and hunder? Why, thou walking Shred, thou moving ttom, thou upright Needle, thou shaving edging irt, thou Flip-flap of a Man, thou vaulting Flea, u Nit, thou Nothing, dost thou talk of Prodigies en I am by? *O tempora! O mores!* But, Neighbours, was saying, what think you of *Valerius*?

*All* *Valerius*, *Valerius*!

*Vin.* I know you are piping hot for Sedition; you all e for Rebellion. But what's the near? For look you, , we the People in the Body Politick are but the ts of Government; therefore we may rumble and mble, and croke our Hearts out, if we have never a ad: Why, how shall we be nourish'd? Therefore y, let us get us a Head, a Head, my Masters.

*Brut* Protect me, *Jove*, and guard me from the Fantom!
this so horrid Apparition be?
is it but the making of my Fancy?

*Vin* Ha, *Brutus*! What, where is this Apparition?

*Cit.* This is the Tribune of the *Celeres*;
otable Head-piece, and the King's Jester.

*Brut* By *Jove*, a Prodigy!

*Vind.* Nay, like enough; the Gods are very angry,
ow they are, they told me so themselves,
look you, Neighbours, I for my own Part [a half.
e seen to Day Fourscore and Nineteen Prodigies and

*Brut* But this is a whole one O most horrible!
Look, *Vindityus*, yonder, o'er that part
O'th' Capitol, just, just there, Man, yonder, look
*Vin* Ha, my Lord!
*Brut.* I always took thee for a quick-sighted Fellow
What, art thou blind? Why, yonder, all o' Fire,
It vomits Lightning; 'tis a monstrous Dragon.
*Vin* O, I see it. O *Jupiter* and *Juno*! By the Gods I see
O Neighbours, look, look, look, on his filthy Nostrils
'T has Eyes like flaming Saucers; and a Belly
Like a burning Caldron With such a swinging Tail
And O, a thing, a thing that's all o' Fire!
*Brut* Ha! now it fronts us with a Head that's mark'd
With *Tarquin*'s Name: And see, 'tis Thunder-struck
Look yonder how it whizzes through the Air!
The Gods have struck it down; 'tis gone, 'tis vanish'd
O! Neighbours, what, what should this Portent mean
*Vin* Mean! why, it's plain; did we not see the M
Upon the Beast? *Tarquin*'s the Dragon, Neighbours,
*Tarquin*'s the Dragon, and the Gods shall swinge him
*All* A Dragon, a *Tarquin*
1 *Cit.* For my Part I saw nothing
*Vin.* How, Rogue? Why, this is Prodigy on Prodig
Down with him, knock him down, what, not see t
Dragon?
1 *Cit* Mercy: I did, I did; a huge monstrous Drag
*Brut* So; not a word of this, my Masters, not for yo
Lives.
Meet me anon at the *Forum*, but not a Word.
*Vindityus*, tell 'em the Tribune of the *Celeres*
Intends this Night to give them an Oration.
[*Ex* Vindit. *and Rab*
*Enter* Lucrece, Valerius, Lucretius, Mutius, Herminius, Horatius, Titus, Tiberius, Collatinus.
*Brut* Ha! in the open Air? So near, you Gods!
So ripe your Judgments? Nay, then let 'em break,
And burst the Hearts of those that have deserv'd them
*Lucr* O *Collatine*! Art thou come?
Alas, my Husband! O my Love! my Lord!

*Coll* O *Lucrece*! See, I have obey'd thy Summons:
have thee in my Arms, but speak, my Fair,
ay, is all well?

*Lucr*. Away, and do not touch me:
and near, but touch me not. My Father too!
*ucretius*, art thou here?

*Luc*. Thou seest I am
aste, and relate thy lamentable Story.

*Lucr* If there be Gods, O, will not they revenge me?
raw near, my Lord; for sure you have a Share
n these strange Woes. Ah, Sir, what have you done?
Why did you bring that Monster of Mankind
he other Night, to curse *Collatia*'s Walls?
Why did you blast me with that horrid Visage,
nd blot my Honour with the Blood of *Tarquin*?

*Coll*. O all the Gods!

*Lucr* Alas, they are far off;
r sure they would have help'd the wretched *Lucrece*.
ear then and tell it to the wondring World,
ast Night the Lustful Bloody *Sextus* came
ate, and benighted, to *Collatia*,
ntending, as he said, for *Rome* next Morning;
ut in the dead of Night, just when soft Sleep
ad seal'd my Eyes, and quite becalm'd my Soul,
ethought a horrid Voice thus thunder'd in my Ear,
*ucrece*, thou'rt mine, arise and meet my Arms;
hen strait I wak'd, and found young *Tarquin* by me,
is Robe unbutton'd, red and sparkling Eyes,
he flushing Blood that mounted in his Face,
he trembling Eagerness that quite devour'd him,
ith only one grim Slave that held a Taper,
 that dead Stillness of the murd'ring Night,
fficiently declar'd his horrid Purpose.

*Coll*. O, *Lucrece*, O!

*Lucr* How is it possible to speak the Passion,
he Fright, the Throes, and Labour of my Soul?
, *Collatine*! half dead I turn'd away
 hide my Shame, my Anger, and my Blushes,
hile he at first with a dissembled Mildness
tempted on my Honour;——

But hastily repuls'd, and with Disdain,
He drew his Sword, and locking his Left Hand
Fast in my Hair, he held it to my Breast:
Protesting by the Gods, the Fiends and Furies,
If I refus'd him he would give me Death,
And swear he found me with that Swarthy Slave,
Whom he would leave there murder'd by my Side.

*Brut.* Villain! Damn'd Villain!

*Lucr* Ah *Collatine*! Oh Father! *Junius Brutus!*
All that are kin to this dishonour'd Blood,
How will you view me now? Ah, how forgive me?
Yet think not, *Collatine*, with my last Tears,
With these last Sighs, these dying Groans, I beg you,
I do conjure my Love, my Lord, my Husband,
O think me not consenting once in Thought,
Tho' he in Act possess'd his furious Pleasure:
For, oh the Name! the Name of an Adultress!——
But here I faint? Oh help me
Imagine me, my Lord, but what I was,
And what I shortly shall be; cold and dead.

*Coll.* Oh you avenging Gods! *Lucrece*; my Love,
I swear I do not think thy Soul consenting,
And therefore I forgive thee.

*Lucr.* Ah, my Lord!
Were I to live, how should I answer this?
All that I ask you now is to revenge me;
Revenge me, Father, Husband, oh revenge me;
Revenge me, *Brutus*, you his Sons revenge me;
*Herminius*, *Mutius*, thou *Horatius* too;
And thou *Valerius*; all; revenge me all:
Revenge the Honour of the Ravish'd *Lucrece*.

*All* We will Revenge thee.

*Lucr* I thank you all, I thank you, noble *Romans*
And that my Life, tho' well I know you wish it,
May not hereafter ever give Example
To any that, like me, shall be dishonour'd,
To live beneath so loath'd an Infamy;
Thus I for ever loose it, thus set free
My Soul my Life and Honour all together:
Revenge me; Oh Revenge, Revenge, Revenge. [Di[es]
L[illegible]

*Luc.* Struck to the Heart, already motionless.
*Coll* O give me way t' embalm her with my Tears;
For who has that Propriety of Sorrow?
Who dares to claim an equal Share with me?
*Brut.* That, Sir, dare I, and every *Roman* here.
What now? At your Laments? Your puling Sighs?
And Womans Drops? Shall these quit Scores for Blood?
For *Chastity*, for *Rome*, and violated Honour?
Now, by the Gods, my Soul disdains your Tears:
There's not a common Harlot in the Shambles
But for a Drachm shall outweep you all
Advance the Body nearer See, my Lords,
Behold, you dazled *Romans*, from the Wound
Of this dead Beauty, thus I draw the Dagger,
All stain'd and reeking with her Sacred Blood,
Thus to my Lips I put the hollow'd Blade,
To yours *Lucretius*, *Collatinus* yours;
To yours *Herminius*, *Mutius*, and *Horatius*,
And yours *Valerius*: Kiss the Ponnyard round:
Now join your Hands with mine, and swear, swear all,
By this chaste Blood, chaste ere the Royal Villain
Mixt his foul Spirits with the spotless Mass,
Swear, and let all the Gods be Witnesses,
That you with me will drive proud *Tarquin* out,
His Wife, th' Imperial Fury, and her Sons,
With all the Race, drive 'em with Sword and Fire
To the World's Limits, Profligate accurst.
Swear from this time never to suffer them,
Nor any other King, to reign in *Rome*.
*All* We swear.
*Brut.* Well have you sworn; and oh, methinks I see
The hovering Spirit of the ravish'd Matron
Look down, she bows her Airy Head to bless you,
And Crown th' Auspicious Sacrament with Smiles.
Thus with her Body high expos'd to View,
March to the *Forum* with this Pomp of Death.
*Lucrece*! Oh!
When to the Clouds thy Pile of Fame is rais'd
While *Rome* is free thy Memory shall be prais'd:

Senate

Senate and People, Wives and Virgins all,
Shall once a Year before thy Statue fall;
Cursing the *Tarquins*, they thy Fate shall mourn:
But, when the Thoughts of Liberty return,
Shall bless the happy Hour when thou wert born
[*Exe*

---

## ACT II. SCENE I.

### SCENE *The* Forum.

*Tiberius, Fabritius, Lartius, Flaminius.*

*Tib* FAbritius, Lartius, and Flaminius,
As you are *Romans*, and oblig'd by *Tarqu*
I dare confide in you, I say again,
Tho' I could not refuse the Oath he gave us,
I disapprove my Father's Undertaking.
I'm Loyal to the last, and so will stand.
I am in haste, and must to *Tullia*

*Fab.* Leave me, my Lord, to deal with the Multi

*Tib* Remember this in short A King is one
To whom you may complain when you are wrong'd
The Throne lyes open in your Way for Justice:
You may be angry, and may be forgiven,
There's room for Favour, and for Benefit,
Where Friends and Enemies may come together,
Have present Hearing, present Composition,
Without recourse to the litigious Laws;
Laws that are cruel, deaf, inexorable,
That cast the Vile and Noble all together;
Where, if you should exceed the Bounds of Order,
There is no Pardon O! 'tis dangerous,
To have all Actions judg'd by rigorous Law.
What, to depend on Innocence alone,
Among so many Accidents and Errors
That wait on Human Life? Consider it;
Stand fast, be Loyal, I must to the Queen: [*E*

*Fab* A pretty Speech, by *Mercury*! Look *Lartius*, when the Words lye like a low *Wre* round, close and short, squat, pat and pithy.

*Lar.* But what should we do here, *Fabritius*? The ultitude will tear us in Pieces

*Fab.* 'Tis true, *Lartius*, the Multitude is a mad thing? strange blunder-headed Monster, and very unruly: t Eloquence is such a thing, a fine, moving, florid, thetical Speech! But see, the *Hidra* comes Let me ne, fear not, I say fear not.

*Enter* Vinditius, *with* Plebeians

*Vin* Come, Neighbours, rank your selves, plant ur selves, set your selves in Order, the Gods are very gry, I'll say that for 'em · Pough, pough, I begin to eat already, and they'll find us Work enough to y, I'll tell you that. And to say Truth, I never lik'd rquin, before I saw the Mark in his Forehead · For k you, Sirs, I am a true Commonwealthsman, and not naturally love Kings, tho' they be good; for y should any One Man have more Power than the ople? Is he bigger, or wiser than the People? Has more Guts, or more Brains than the People? What n he do for the People, that the People can't do for emselves? Can he make Corn grow in a Famine? n he give us Rain in Drought? Or make our Pots il, tho' the Devil piss in the Fire?

1 *Cit* For my part, I hate all Courtiers; and I think ave Reason for't.

*Vin.* Thou Reason! Well, Taylor, and what's thy eason?

1 *Cit* Why, Sir, there was a Crew of 'em t'other ght got drunk, broke my Windows, and handled Wife.

*Vin* How, Neighbours? Nay, now the Fellow has eason, look you. His Wife handled! Why, this is a atter of Moment.

1 *Cit* Nay, I know there were some of the Prin-s, for I heard *Sextus* his Name.

*Vin* Ay, ay, the King's Sons, my Life for't; some of e King's Sons. Well, these roaring Lords never do y Good among us Citizens: They are ever breaking e Peace, running in our Debts, and swinging our ives.

*Fab*

*Fab.* How long at length, thou many-headed Monster,
You Bulls, and Bears, you roaring Beasts and Bandogs,
Porters and Coblers, Tinkers, Taylors, all!
You Rascally Sons of Whores in a Civil Government,
How long, I say, dare you abuse our Patience?
Does not the Thought of Rods and Axes fright you?
Does not our Presence, ha, these Eyes, these Faces
Strike you with trembling? Ha!

*Vin.* Why, what have we here? a very Spit-fire, the Crack-fart of the Court. Hold, let me see him nearer. Yes, Neighbours, this is one of 'em, one of your Roaring Squires that poke us in the Night, beat the Watch, and deflower our Wives. I know him, Neighbours, for all his Bouncing and his Swearing, this is a Court-Pimp, a Bawd, One of *Tarquin*'s Bawds.

*Fab.* Peace thou obstreperous Rascal; I am a Man of Honour. One of the Equestrian Order, my Name *Fabritius*.

*Vin.* *Fabritius!* Your Servant, *Fabritius*. Down with him, Neighbours; an upstart Rogue; this is he that was the Queen's Coachman, and drove the Chariot over her Father's Body, Down with him, down with 'em all; Bawds, Pimps, Pandars.

*Fab.* O Mercy, Mercy, Mercy!

*Vin.* Hold, Neighbours, hold. As we are Great, let us be Just. You, Sirrah; you of the Equestrian Order, Knight? Now, by *Jove*, he has the Look of a Pimp, I find we can't save him, Rise, Sir Knight, and tell me before the Majesty of the People, what have you to say, that you should not have your Neck broke down the *Tarpeian* Rock, your Body burnt, and your Ashes thrown in the *Tiber*?

*Fab.* Oh! oh! oh!

*Vin.* A Courtier! a Sheep-biter. Leave off your blubbering, and confess.

*Fab.* Oh! I will confess, I will confess.

*Vin.* Answer me then. Was not you once the Queen's Coachman?

*Fab.* I was, I was.

Vin.

*Vin.* Did you not drive her Chariot over the Body f her Father, the dead King *Tullus*?

*Fab.* I did, I did; tho' it went against my Conscience.

*Vin* So much the worse Have you not since a-used the good People, by seducing the Citizens Wives Court for the King's Sons? Have you not by your awds Tricks been the occasion of their making Assault the Bodies of many a virtuous dispos'd Gentlewoman?

*Fab* I have, I have

*Vin.* Have you not wickedly held the Door, while e Daughters of the wise Citizens have had their Vesls broken up?

*Fab* Oh, I confess many a time and often.

*Vin.* For all which Services to your Princes, and so ghly deserving of the Commonwealth, you have reiv'd the Honour of Knighthood?

*Fab* Mercy, Mercy, I confess it all

*Vin* Hitherto I have helpt you to spell, now pray it together for your self, and confess the whole Matr in Three Words

*Fab* I was at first the Son of a Carman, came to the onour of being *Tullia*'s Coachman, have been a Pimp, d remain a Knight at the Mercy o'the People.

*Vin* Well, I am mov'd, my Bowels are stir'd; take n away, and let 'em only be hang'd Away with 'em, ay with 'em.

*Fab* Oh Mercy! Help, help

*Vin* Hang 'em, Rogues, Pimps, hang 'em I say hy, look you, Neighbours, this is Law, Right, and stice· This is the Peoples Law, and I think that's tter than the Arbitrary Power of Kings. Why, here as Trial, Condemnation, and Execution, without ore ado. Hark, hark, what have we here? Look, ok, the Tribune of the *Celeres*! Bring forth the Pul-t, the Pulpit.

*Trumpits ſound a Dead March.*

*Enter* Brutus, Valerius, Herminius, Mutius, Horatiu[s] Lucretius, Collatinus, Tiberius, Titus, *with the B[ody]* *of* Lucrece.

*Val.* I charge you Fathers, Nobles, *Romans*, Frien[ds]
Magiſtrates, all you People, hear *Valerius*.
This Day, O *Romans*, is a Day of Wonders,
The Villanies of *Tarquin* are compleat:
To lay whoſe Vices open to your View,
To give you Reaſons for his Baniſhment,
With the Expulſion of his wicked Race,
The Gods have choſen *Lucius Junius Brutus*,
The ſtupid, ſenſeleſs, and illiterate *Brutus*,
Their Orator in this prodigious Cauſe:
Let him aſcend, and Silence be proclaim'd.

*Vin.* A *Brutus*, a *Brutus*, a *Brutus!* Silence there;
Silence, I ſay, Silence on Pain of Death

*Brut* Patricians, People, Friends, and *Romans* all,
Had not th'inſpiring Gods by Wonder brought me
From clouded Senſe, to this full Day of Reaſon,
Whence, with a Prophet's Proſpect, I behold
The State of *Rome*, and Danger of the World,
Yet in a Cauſe like this, methinks the weak,
Enervate, ſtupid *Brutus* might ſuffice·
O the Eternal Gods! Bring but the Statues
Of *Romulus* and *Numa*, plant 'em here
On either Hand of this cold *Roman* Wife,
Only to ſtand and point that Publick Wound;
O *Romans*, Oh, what Uſe would be of Tongues!
What Orator need ſpeak while they were by?
Would not the Majeſty of thoſe dumb Forms
Inſpire your Souls, and arm you for the Cauſe?
Would you not curſe the Author of the Murder,
And drive him from the Earth with Sword and Fire?
But where, methinks I hear the People ſhout,
I hear the Cry of *Rome*, where is the Monſter?
Bring *Tarquin* forth, bring the Deſtroyer out,
By whoſe curs'd Off-ſpring, Luſtful Bloody *Sextus*,
This perfect Mould of *Roman* Chaſtity,

T

is Star of ſpotleſs and immortal Fame,
is Pattern for all Wives, the *Roman Lucrece*,
as foully brought to a diſaſt'rous End.
*Vin* O, Neighbours, oh! I bury'd ſeven Wives with-
y, I never wept before in all my Life. [out crying,
*Brut* O the Immortal Gods, and thou great Stayer
falling *Rome*, if to his own Relations,
r *Collatinus* is a *Tarquin* too,)
Wrongs ſo great to them, to his own Blood,
hat then to us, the Nobles and the Commons?
ot to remember you of his paſt Crimes,
e black Ambition of his furious Queen,
ho drove her Chariot through the *Cyprian* Street,
ſuch a damn'd Deſign as might have turn'd
e Steeds of Day, and ſhock'd the ſtaring Gods,
ſt as they are, with an uneaſie Moment
d yet to this, oh! add the horrid Slaughter
all the Princes of the *Roman* Senate,
ding Fundamental Right and Juſtice,
aking the ancient Cuſtoms, Statutes, Laws,
th poſitive Pow'r, and arbitrary Luſt,
those Affairs which were before diſpatch'd
ublick by the Fathers, now are forc'd
his own Palace, there to be determin'd
e and his Portentous Council pleaſe.
then for you
*Vin* Ay, for the People, come,
then, my Mirmydons, to pot with him
*ut* I ſay, if thus the Nobles have been wrong'd,
at Tongue can ſpeak the Grievance of the People?
*n* Alas, poor People!
*ut* You that were once a Free-born People, fam'd
is Forefather's Days for Wars abroad,
Conquerors of the World, Oh *Rome*! Oh Glory!
t are you now? What has the Tyrant made you?
Slaves, the Beaſts, the Aſſes of the Earth,
Soldiers of the Gods mechanick Labourers,
vers of Water, Taskers, Timber-fellers,
'd you like Bulls, his very Jades for Luggage,
e you with Scourges down to dig in Quarries,

To

To cleanse his Sinks, the Scavengers o'th' Court;
While his lewd Sons, tho' not on Work so hard,
Employ'd your Daughters and your Wives at Home.

*Vin.* Yes, marry did they.

*Brut* O all the Gods! What are you *Romans*? Ha!
If this be true, why have you been so backward?
Oh sluggish Souls! Oh Fall of former Glory!
That would not rouze unless a Woman wak'd you!
Behold she comes, and calls you to revenge her,
Her Spirit hovers in the Air, and cries
To Arms, to Arms; drive, drive the *Tarquins* out.
Behold this Dagger, taken from her Wound,
She bids you fix this Trophy on your Standard,
This Poniard which she stabb'd into her Heart,
And bear her Body in your Battel's Front:
Or will you stay till *Tarquin* does return,
To see your Wives and Children dragg'd about,
Your Houses burnt, the Temples all profan'd,
The City fill'd with Rapes, Adulteries,
The *Tiber* choak'd with Bodies, all the Shores
And neighb'ring Rocks besmear'd with *Roman* Blood!

*Vin* Away, away, let's burn his Palace first

*Brut.* Hold, hold, my Friends, as I have been th' Inspi[rer]
Of this most just Revenge, so I intreat you,
Oh worthy *Romans*, take me with you still:
Drive *Tullia* out, and all of *Tarquin*'s Race,
Expel 'em without Damage to their Persons,
Tho' not without Reproach *Vinditius*, you
I trust in this. So prosper us the Gods,
Prosper our Cause, prosper the Common-wealth,
Guard and defend the Liberty of *Rome*.

*Vin* Liberty, Liberty, Liberty.

*All* Liberty, &c. [*Exeu[nt]*

*Val.* O *Brutus*, as a God we all survey thee;
Let then the Gratitude we should express
Be lost in Admiration Well, we know
Virtue like thine, so fierce, so like the Gods,
That more than thou presents we could not bear,
Looks with Disdain on Ceremonious Honours,
Therefore accept in short the Thanks of *Rome*:

Fi[...]

ſt with our Bodies thus we worſhip thee,
ou Guardian *Genius* of the Commonwealth,
ou Father and Redeemer of thy Country,
ext we, as Friends, with equal Arms embrace thee,
at *Brutus* may remember, tho' his Virtue
ar to the Gods, he is a *Roman* ſtill.
*Brut.* And when I am not ſo, or once in Thought
nſpire the Bondage of my Countrymen,
ke me, you Gods, tear me, O *Romans*, piece-meal;
d let your *Brutus* be more loath'd than *Tarquin*.
t now to thoſe Affairs that want a View.
agine then the Fame of what is done
s reach'd to *Ardea*, whence the trembling King,
Guilt and Nature quick and apprehenſive,
ith a bent Brow comes poſt for his Revenge,
make Examples of the Mutiniers·
t him come on. *Lucretius*, to your Care
e Charge and Cuſtody of *Rome* is given,
hile we, with all the Force that can be rais'd,
aving the *Tarquins* on the common Road,
ſolve to join the Army at the Camp
hat thinks *Valerius* of the Conſequence?
*Val.* As of a lucky Hit. There is a Number
Malecontents that wiſh for ſuch a Time:
ink that only Speed is neceſſary
Crown the whole Event.
*Brut* Go then your ſelf,
th theſe Aſſiſtants, and make inſtant Head
ell as you can, Numbers will not be wanting
*Mars* his Field; I have but ſome few Orders
leave with *Titus* that muſt be diſpers'd,
d *Brutus* ſhall attend you.
*Val.* The Gods direct you.
[*Exeunt with the Body of* Lucrece.
*Manent* Brutus, *and* Titus.
*Brut.* *Titus*, my Son?
*Tit* My ever honour'd Lord.
*Brut* I think, my *Titus*,
y by the Gods, I dare proteſt it to thee,
ve thee more than any of my Children

 Tit.

*Tit.* How, Sir, oh how, my Lord, have I deserv'd it?
*Brut* Therefore I love thee more, because, my Son,
Thou hast deserv'd it; for to speak sincerely,
There's such a Sweetness still in all thy Manners,
An Air so open, and a Brow so clear,
A Temper so remov'd from Villany,
With such a manly Plainness in thy Dealing,
That not to love thee, O my Son, my *Titus*,
Were to be envious of so great a Virtue.
*Tit.* O all the Gods, where will this Kindness end?
Why do you thus, O my too gracious Lord,
Dissolve at once the Being that you gave me;
Unless you mean to screw me to Performance
Beyond the reach of Man?
Ah why, my Lord, do you oblige me more
Than my Humanity can e'er return?
*Brut* Yes, *Titus*, thou conceiv'st thy Father right;
I find our *Genii* know each other well,
And Minds, my Son, of our uncommon Make,
When once the Mark's in View, never shoot wide,
But in a Line come level to the White,
And hit the very Heart of our Design,
Then to the shocking Purpose Once again
I say, I swear, I love thee, O my Son;
I like thy Frame, the Fingers of the Gods
I see have left their Mastery upon thee,
They have been tapering up thy *Roman* Form,
And the Majestick Prints at large appear
Yet something they have left for me to finish,
Which thus I press thee to, thus in my Arms
I fashion thee, I mould thee to my Heart
What? Dost thou kneel? Nay, stand up now a *Roman*
Shake from thy Lids that Dew that hangs upon 'em,
*And* answer to th' Austerity of my Virtue
*Tit.* If I must die, you Gods, I am prepar'd.
Let then my Fate suffice; but do not rack me
With something more.
*Brut. Titus*, as I remember,
You told me you were Marry'd.
*Tit.* My Lord, I did.
*Brut.* To *Teramnta*, *Tarquin*'s natural Daughter.

Th

*Tit* Most true, my Lord, to that Poor Virtuous [Maid,
our *Titus*, Sir, your most unhappy Son,
join'd for ever.

*Brut* No, *Titus*, not for ever
ot but I know the Virgin Beautiful,
or I did oft converse her when I seem'd
ot to converse at all · Yet more, my Son,
think her chastely Good, most sweetly Fram'd;
ithout the smallest Tincture of her Father,
et, *Titus*,——Ha! What, Man? What, all in Tears?
rt thou so soft, that only saying yet
as dash'd thee thus? Nay, then I'll plunge thee down;
own to the bottom of this foolish Stream,
hose Brink thus makes thee tremble No, my Son,
thou art mine thou art not *Teremmta*'s.
r if thou art, I swear thou must not be;
hou shalt not be hereafter.

*Tit.* O the Gods!
orgive me, Blood and Duty, all Respects
ue to a Father's Name, not *Teramınta*'s!

*Brut* No, by the Gods I swear, not *Teramınta*'s,
o, *Titus*, by th' Eternal Fates, that hang
hope Auspicious o'er the Head of *Rome*,
ll grapple with thee on this Spot of Earth
bout this Theme till one of us fall Dead:
ll struggle with thee for this Point of Honour,
nd tug with *Teramınta* for thy Heart,
s I have done for *Rome*, Yes, ere we part,
ix'd as you are by Wedlock join'd and fast,
ll set you far asunder. Nay, on this,
his spotted Blade, bath'd in the Blood of *Lucrece*,
l make thee swear on this thy Wedding Night
hou wilt not touch thy Wife

*Tit* Conscience, Heart and Bowels,
m I a Man? Have I my Flesh about me?

*Brut.* I know thou hast too much of Flesh about thee,
is that, my Son, that and thy Blood I fear,
ore than thy Spirit, which is truly *Roman* ·
t let the heated Channels of thy Veins
il o'er, I still am obstinate in this:

Thou ſhalt renounce thy Father or thy Love.
Either reſolve to part with *Teraminta*,
To ſend her forth, with *Tullia*, to her Father,
Or ſhake Hands with me, part, and be accurs'd;
Make me believe thy Mother play'd me falſe,
And, in my Abſence, ſtamp'd thee with a *Tarquin*

*Tit* Hold, Sir, I do conjure you by the Gods
Wrong not my Mother, tho' you doom me dead,
Curſe me not till you hear what I reſolve;
Give me a little time to rouze my Spirits,
To muſter all the Tyrant-man about me,
All that is fierce, auſtere, and greatly cruel,
To *Titus* and his *Teraminta*'s Ruin

*Brut* Remember me, look on thy Father's Suff'ring
What he has born for Twenty rolling Years,
If thou haſt Nature, Worth, or Honour in thee,
The Contemplation of my cruel Labours
Will ſtir thee up to this new Act of Glory:
Thou want'ſt the Image of thy Father's Wrongs,
O take it then, reflected with the Warmth
Of all the Tenderneſs that I can give thee:
Perhaps it ſtood in a wrong Light before,
I'll try all Ways to place it to Advantage.
Learn by my rigorous *Roman* Reſolution
To ſtiffen thy unharraſs'd Infant Virtue:
I do allow thee Fond, Young, Soft, and Gentle,
Train'd by the Charms of one that is moſt Lovely,
Yet, *Titus*, this muſt all be loſt, when Honour,
When *Rome*, the World, and the Gods come to claim it
Think then thou heard'ſt 'em cry, obey thy Father,
If thou art falſe, or perjur'd, there he ſtands
Accountable to us, but ſwear t'obey,
Implicitly believe him, that, if ought
Be ſworn amiſs, thou may'ſt have nought to anſwer.

*Tit.* What is it, Sir, that you would have me ſwear
That I may ſcape your Curſe, and gain your Bleſſing

*Brut.* That thou this Night wilt part with *Teraminta*
For once again I ſwear if here ſhe ſtays,
What for the Hatred of the Multitude,
And my Reſolves to drive out *Tarquin*'s Race,

He

r Perſon is not ſafe

*Tit* Here, take me, Sir,

ke me before I cool I ſwear this Night

at I will part with (oh!) my *Teraminta.*

*Brut.* Swear too, and by the Soul of Raviſh'd *Lucrece*,

o' on thy Bridal Night, thou wilt not touch her.

*Tit* I ſwear, ev'n by the Soul of her you nam'd,

e Raviſh'd *Lucrece*, oh th' Immortal Gods!

ill not touch her.

*rut.* So, I truſt thy Virtue:

d by the Gods I thank thee for the Conqueſt.

ce more, with al the Bleſſings I can give thee,

ke thee to my Arms; thus on my Breaſt,

hard and rugged Pillow of thy Honour,

ean thee from thy Love: Farewel; be faſt

what thou'ſt ſworn, and I am thine for ever. [*Exit.*

*it. ſolus.* To what thou'ſt ſworn! Oh Heav'n and

Earth what's that?

at have I ſworn? To part with *Teraminta*?

part with ſomething dearer to my Heart

n my Life's Drops? What! Not this Night enjoy her?

ounce my Vows, the Rights, the Dues of Marriage,

ich now I gave her, and the Prieſt was Witneſs,

'd with a Flood that ſtream'd from both our Eyes,

ſeal'd with Sighs, and Smiles, and deathleſs Kiſſes,

after this to ſwear thou wilt not touch her!

all the Gods, I did forſwear my ſelf

earing that, and will forſwear again:

touch her! O thou perjur'd Braggard, where,

re are thy Vaunts, thy Proteſtations now?

*Enter* Teraminta.

omes to ſtrike thy ſtaggering Duty down:

all'n, 'tis gone. Oh *Teraminta*, come,

to my Arms thou only Joy of *Titus*,

to my Cares thou Maſs of hoarded Sweets,

ed Hour of all Life's happy Moments;

shall I ſay to thee?

Say any thing;

hile you ſpeak methinks a ſudden Calm,

ght of all the Horror that ſurrounds me,

Falls upon every frighted Faculty,
And puts my Soul in Tune. O *Titus*, oh!
Methinks my Spirit shivers in her House,
Shruging, as if she long'd to be at rest;
With this Foresight, to die thus in your Arms
Were to prevent a World of following Ills.

*Tit* What Ills, my Love? What Power has Fortu[ne]
But we can brave? 'Tis true, my *Teraminta*, [no]
The Body of the World is out of Frame,
The vast distorted Limbs are on the Rack,
And all the Cable Sinews stretch'd to bursting,
The Blood ferments, and the Majestick Spirits,
Like *Hercules* in the invenom'd Shirt,
Lye in a Fever on the horrid Pile:
My Father, like an *Æsculapius*
Sent by the Gods, comes boldly to the Cure;
But how, my Love? By violent Remedies,
And says that *Rome*, e'er yet she can be well,
Must purge and cast, purge all th' infected Humours
Through the whole Mass, and vastly, vastly bleed.

*Ter* Ah, *Titus*! I my self but now beheld
Th' Expulsion of the Queen, driv'n from her Pala[ce]
By the inrag'd and madding Multitude,
And hardly scap'd my self to find you here.

*Tit* Why yet, my *Teraminta*, we may smile.
Come then to Bed, ere yet the Night descends
With her Black Wings to brood o'er all the Worl[d]
Why, what care we? Let us enjoy those Pleasures
The Gods have giv'n; lock'd in each other's Arm[s]
We'll lye for ever thus, and laugh at Fate.

*Ter* No, no, my Lord, there's more than you h[...]
There's something at your Heart that I must find, [...]
I claim it with the Privilege of a Wife
Keep close your Joys, but for your Griefs, my *Titus*
I must not, will not lose my Share in them.
Ah, the good Gods, what is it stirs you thus?
Speak, speak, my Lord, or *Teraminta* dies.
Oh Heav'ns, he weeps! Nay, then upon my Knees
I thus conjure you speak, or give me Death.

*Tit.* Rise, *Teraminta*. Oh, if I should speak

What I have rashly sworn against my Love,
fear that I should give thee Death indeed
*Ter.* Against your Love! No, that's impossible,
know your God-like Truth Nay, should you swear,
wear to me now that you forswore your Love,
would not credit it No, no, my Lord,
ee, I know, I read it in your Eyes,
ou love the wretched *Teraminta* still
he very Manner of your hiding it,
he Tears you shed, your Backwardness to speak
What you affirm you swore against your Love,
ell me, my Lord, you love me more than ever.
*Tit* By all the Gods I do: Oh *Teraminta*,
y Heart's Discerner, whither wilt thou drive me?
l tell thee then. My Father wrought me up,
now not how, to swear I know not what,
hat I would send thee hence with *Tullia*,
wear not to touch thee, though my Wife, yet, oh,
d'st thou been by thy self, and but beheld him,
ou would'st have thought, such was his Majesty,
hat the Gods Lightned from his awful Eyes,
d Thunder'd from his Tongue.
*Ter* No more, my Lord:
o conjure you by all those Powers
hich we invok'd together at the Altar,
d beg you by the Love I know you bear me,
let this Passion trouble you no farther,
, my dear Lord, my honour'd God-like Husband,
m your Wife, and one that seeks your Honour:
Heav'n I would have sworn you thus my self
hat, on the Shock of Empire, on the Turn
State, and Universal Change of Things,
lye at Home and languish for a Woman!
, *Titus*, he that makes himself thus Vile,
t him not dare pretend to ought that's Princely;
t be, as all the Warlike World shall judge him,
e Droll o' th' People, and the Scorn of Kings.

*Enter* Horatius.

*Hor.* My Lord, your Father gives you thus in Charge
member what you swore: The Guard is ready;

And I am ordered to Conduct your Bride,
While you attend your Father.

*Tit.* Oh *Teraminta*!
Then we must part,

*Ter.* We must, we must, my Lord,
Therefore be swift, and snatch your self away,
Or I shall die with lingring.

*Tit* Oh, a Kiss.
Balmy as Cordials that recover Souls,
Chaste as Maids Sighs, and keen as longing Mothers,
Preserve thy self; look well to that, my Love,
Think on our Covenant: When either dies
The other is no more.

*Ter.* I do remember,
But have no Language left.

*Tit.* Yet we shall meet,
In spight of Sighs we shall, at least in Heav'n.
Oh *Teraminta*, once more to my Heart,
Once to my Lips, and ever to my Soul.
Thus the soft Mother, tho' her Babe is dead,
Will have the Darling on her Bosom laid,
Will talk, and rave, and with the Nurses strive,
And fond it still, as if it were alive,
Knows it must go, yet struggles with the Croud,
And shrieks to see 'em wrap it in the Shroud. [*Exeunt.*

## ACT III. SCENE I.

*Collatinus, Tiberius, Vitellius, Aquilius.*

*Coll.* TH' Expulsion of the *Tarquins* now must stand;
Their Camp to be surpriz'd, while *Tarquin* here
Was scolded from our Walls! I blush to think
That such a Master in the Art of War
Should so forget himself.

*Vit.* Triumphant *Brutus*,
Like *Jove* when follow'd by a Train of Gods,
To mingle with the Fates, and Doom the World,
Ascends the Brazen Steps o'th' Capitol,

With

th all the humming Senate at his Heels,
n in that Capitol which the King built
th the Expence of all the Royal Treasure,
rateful *Brutus* there in Pomp appears,
d sits the Purple Judge of *Tarquin*'s Downfall.
*Aquil* But why, my Lord, why are not you there too?
re you not chosen Consul by whole *Rome*?
y are you not saluted too like him?
here are your Lictors? Where your Rods and Axes?
are you but the Ape, the Mimic God
this new Thunderer, who appropriates
ose Bolts of Power which ought to be divided?
*Tib* Now by the Gods I hate his upstart Pride,
Rebel Thoughts of the Imperial Race,
abject Soul that stoops to Court the Vulgar,
Scorn of Princes, and his Lust to th' People.
*Collatine*, have you not Eyes to find him?
hy are you rais'd, but to set off his Honours?
Taper by the Sun, whose sickly Beams
swallow'd in the Blaze of his full Glory:
like a *Meteor*, wades th' Abyss of Light,
hile your faint Lustre adds but to the Beard
at awes the World. When late through *Rome* he pass'd,
t on his Courser, mark'd you how he bow'd
this, on that Side, to the gazing Heads
at pav'd the Streets, and all imboss'd the Windows,
at gap'd with eagerness to speak, but could not,
fast their Spirits flow'd to Admiration,
d that to Joy, which thus at last broke forth:
*tus*, God *Brutus*, Father of thy Country!
l *Genius*, hail! Deliverer of lost *Rome*!
eld of the Common-wealth, and Sword of Justice!
l, Scourge of Tyrants, Lash for Lawless Kings!
hail, they cry'd, while the long Peal of Praises,
mented with a thousand Eccho'ing Cries,
n like the Volly of the Gods along.
*Coll.* No more on't, I grow sick with the Remem-[brance.
*Tib* But when you follow'd, how did their bellying [Bodies,
at ventur'd from the Casements more than half
look at *Brutus*, nay, that stuck like Snails

Upon

Upon the Walls, and from the Houses tops
Hung down like clust'ring Bees upon each other,
How did they all draw back at Sight of you,
To laze, and loll, and yawn, and rest from Rapture
Are you a Man? Have you the Blood of Kings
And suffer this?

*Coll* Ha! is he not his Father?

*Tib.* I grant he is
Consider this, and rouze your self at Home:
Commend my Fire, and rail at your own Slackness,
Yet more, remember but your last Disgrace,
When you propos'd, with Reverence to the Gods,
A King of Sacrifices should be chosen,
And from the Consuls, did he not oppose you?
Fearing, as well he might, your sure Election,
Saying, it smelt too much of Royalty;
And that it might rub up the Memory
Of those that lov'd the Tyrant? Nay, yet more,
That if the People chose you for the Place,
The Name of King would light upon a *Tarquin*
Of one that's doubly Royal, being descended
From two great Princes that were Kings of *Rome*?

*Coll.* But after all this, whither would'st thou drive

*Tib.* I would to Justice, for the Restauration
Of our most Lawful Prince Yes, *Collatine*,
I look upon my Father as a Traitor,
I find that neither you, nor Brave *Aquilius*,
Nor young *Vitellius*, dare confide in me·
But that you may, and firmly, to the Hazard
Of all the World holds precious, once again,
I say, I look on *Brutus* as a Traitor;
No more my Father, by th' Immortal Gods.
And to redeem the time, to fix the King
On his Imperial Throne, some Means propos'd
That savour of a govern'd Policy,
Where there is Strength and Life to hope a Fortune,
Not to throw all upon one desperate Chance;
I'll on as far as he that laughs at dying.

*Coll.* Come to my Arms: O thou, so truly Brave,
Thou may'st redeem the Errors of thy Race!

*Aquili-*

*uilius*, and *Vitellius*, O embrace him,
d ask his Pardon, that so long we fear'd
trust so rich a Virtue. But behold,

*Enter* Brutus *and* Valerius.

*utus* appears Young Man, be satisfy'd,
ound thy Politick Father to the bottom,
otting the Assumption of *Valerius*.
e means to cast me from the Consulship.
t now I heard how he cajol'd the People
ith h's known Industry, and my Remissness,
at still in all our Votes, Proscriptions, Edicts,
ainst the King, he found I acted faintly,
ll closing every Sentence, he's a *Tarquin*
*Brut* No, my *Valerius*, 'till thou art my Mate,
int Master in this great Authority,
owever calm the Face of things appear,
*me* is not safe· By the Majestick Gods
wear, while *Collatine* sits at the Helm
Universal Wrack is to be fear'd·
ave Intelligence of his Transactions,
e mingles with the young hot Blood of *Rome*,
aws himself inward, grudges my Applause,
omotes Cabals with highest Quality,
ch headlong Youth as spurning Laws and Manners,
ar'd in the late Debaucheries of *Sextus*,
nd therefore wish the Tyrant here again:
the inverted Seasons shock wise Men,
nd the most fix'd Philosophy must start
t sultry Winters, and at frosty Summers;
at this most unnatural Stilness here,
his more than Midnight Silence through all *Rome*,
his deadness of Discourse, and dreadful Calm
pon so great a Change, I more admire,
han if a hundred Politick Heads were met,
nd nodded Mutiny to one another;
ore Fear than if a thousand lying Libels
ere spread abroad, nay dropt among the Senate.
*Val.* I have my self employ'd a busie Slave,
is Name *Vinditius*, given him Wealth and Freedom,
o watch the Motions of *Vitellius*,

And

And those of the *Aquilian* Family:
*Vitellius* has already entertain'd him;
And something thence Important may be gather'd,
For these of all the Youth of Quality
Are most inclin'd to *Tarquin* and his Race,
By Blood and Humour.

*Brut* O *Valerius*!
That Boy, observ'st thou? O, I fear, my Friend,
He is a Weed, but rooted in my Heart,
And grafted to my Stock, if he prove rank,
By *Mars* no more but thus, away with him:
I'll tear him from me, though the Blood should follow
*Tiberius*.

*Tib*. My Lord!

*Brut*. Sirrah, no more of that *Vitellius*;
I warn'd you too of young *Aquilius*:
Are my Words Wind, that thus you let 'em pass?
Hast thou forgot thy Father?

*Tib* No, my Lord.

*Brut*. Thou ly'st. But tho' thou 'scape a Father's Rod,
The Consul's Ax may reach thee: Think on that.
I know thy Vanity, and blind Ambition;
Thou dost associate with my Enemies:
When I refus'd the Consul *Collatine*
To be the King of Sacrifices, strait,
As if thou hadst been sworn his Bosom Fool,
He nam'd thee for the Office. And since that,
Since I refus'd thy Madness that Preferment,
Because I would have none of *Brutus* Blood
Pretend to be a King, thou hang'st thy Head,
Contriv'st to give thy Father new Displeasure,
As if Imperial Toil were not enough
To break my Heart without thy Disobedience.
But by the Majesty of *Rome* I swear,
If after double Warning thou despise me,
By all the Gods, I'll cast thee from my Blood,
Doom thee to Forks and Whips as a *Barbarian*,
And leave thee to the Lashes of the Lictor.
*Tarquinius Collatinus*, you are summon'd
To meet the Senate on the instant Time.

Co

*Coll.* Lead on: My Duty is to follow *Brutus*,
[*Ex.* Brut Val.

*Tib* Now, by those Gods with which he menac'd me,
here put off all Nature, since he turns me
hus desperate to the World, I do renounce him:
d when we meet again he is my Foe.
l Blood, all Reverence, Fondness be forgot:
ke a grown Savage on the Common Wild,
at runs at all, and cares not who begot him,
meet my Lion Sire, and roar Defiance,
if he ne'er had nurs'd me in his Den.

*nter* Vinditius, *with the People, and two* Fecialian *Priests, Crown'd with Lawrel · Two Spears in their Hands; one Bloody and half burnt.*

*Vin* Make Way there, hey, News from the Tyrant, e come Envoys, Heralds, Ambassadors, whether in Gods Name or in the Devils I know not; but here y come, your *Fecialian* Priests: Well, good People, ke not these Priests; why, what the Devil have they lo with State Affairs? What side soever they are for y'll have Heaven for their Part I'll warrant you. ey'll lug the Gods in whether they will or no.

*Pri* Hear, *Jupiter*; and thou, O *Juno*, hear;
, O *Quirinus*, hear us all you Gods,
estial, Terrestrial, and Infernal. [People.

*Pri* Be thou, O *Rome*, our Judge. Hear all you

*Vin* Fine canting Rogues! I told you how they'd be king the Gods in at first dash: Why, the Gods are r Tools and Tackle, they work with Heaven and , and let me tell you, as Things go your Priests a hopeful Trade on't.

*Pri.* I come Ambassador to thee, O *Rome*,
ed and Just, the Legate of the King.

*Pri* If we demand, or purpose to require,
one from *Rome* that's contrary to Justice,
we be ever banish'd from our Country,
never hope to taste this vital Air

*b* *Vinditius*, lead the Multitude away:
*lius*, with *Vitellius* and my self,
straight conduct 'em to the Capitol.

*Vin.*

*Vin.* I go, my Lord; but have a care of 'em· Rogues I warrant 'em. Mark that first Priest; you see how he leers? A lying Elder; the true Cast of Holy Jugler. Come, my Masters, I would think of a Priest, but that he has a Commission to dissemble: A Patent Hypocrite, that takes Pay to forge Lies, Law, and lives by the Sins of the People

[*Exeunt with Peo*

*Aquil* My Life upon't, you may speak out, and free*Tiberius* is the Heart of our Design [commen

1 *Pri.* The Gods be prais'd. Thus then, the King
Your generous Resolves, longs to be with you,
And those you have engag'd, divides his Heart
Amongst you; which more clearly will be seen
When you have read these Packets· As we go
I'll spread the Bosom of the King before you.

[*Exeu*

## SCENE II. *The Senate.*

*Brut* Patricians, that long stood, and scap'd the T
The Venerable Moulds of your Forefathers,
That represent the Wisdom of the Dead;
And you the Conscript chosen for the People,
Engines of Power, severest Counsellors,
Courts that examine Treasons to the Head:
All Hail. The Consul begs th' Auspicious Gods,
And binds *Quirinus* by his Tutelar Vow,
That Plenty, Peace, and lasting Liberty
May be your Portion, and the Lot of *Rome.*
Laws, Rules, and Bounds, prescrib'd for raging Kings
Like Banks and Bulwarks for the Mother Seas,
Tho' 'tis impossible they should prevent
A thousand daily Wracks and Nightly Ruins,
Yet help to break those rowling Inundations,
Which else would overflow and drown the World.
*Tarquin*, to feed whose Fathomless Ambition
And Ocean Luxury, the noblest Veins
Of all true *Romans* were like Rivers empty'd,

ut from *Rome*, and now he flows full on;
, Fathers, ought we much to fear his Ebb,
d strictly watch the Dams that we have rais'd.
hy should I go about? The *Roman* People
, with once Voice, accuse my Fellow Consul
*oll.* The People may; I hope the Nobles will not:
e People! *Brutus* does indulge the People
*Brut.* Consul, in what is right I will indulge 'em:
d much I think 'tis better so to do,
an see 'em run in Tumults through the Streets,
ming Cabals, plotting against the Senate,
itting their Shops, and flying from the Town,
if the Gods had sent the Plague among 'em.
now too well, you and your Royal Tribe
rn the good People, scorn the late Election,
ause we chose these Fathers for the People,
fill the Place of those whom *Tarquin* murder'd:
d tho' you laugh at this, you and your Train,
e Irreligious Harebrain'd Youth of *Rome*,
e Ignorant, the Slothful, and the Base;
wise Men know, 'tis very rarely seen,
at a free People should desire the Hurt
Common Liberty. No, *Collatine*,
those Desires arise from their Oppression,
from Suspicion they are falling to it;
put the Case that those their Fears were false,
ys may be found to rectifie their Errors;
grant the People ignorant of themselves,
they are capable of being told,
will conceive a Truth from Worthy Men.
n you they will not, nor from your Adherents,
r's Infamous and Execrable Youth,
s to Religion and the Commonwealth,
Virtue, Learning, and all sober Arts
t bring Renown and Profit to Mankind;
h as had rather bleed beneath a Tyrant
become dreadful to the Populace,
spread their Lusts and Dissoluteness round,
' at the daily Hazard of their Lives,
n live at Peace in a free Government,

Where

Where every Man is Master of his own,
Sole Lord at home, and Monarch of his House;
Where Rancour and Ambition are extinguish'd;
Where Universal Peace extends her Wings,
As if the Golden Age return'd; where all
The People do agree, and live secure,
The Nobles and the Princes lov'd and reverenc'd
The World in Triumph, and the Gods ador'd

*Coll.* The Consul, Conscript Fathers, says the Peop[le]
For divers Reasons, grudge the Dignity,
Which I possess'd by general Approbation;
I hear their Murmurs, and would know of *Brutus*
What they would have me do, what's their Desire.

*Brut* Take hence the Royal Name, resign thy Offic[e]
Go as a Friend, and of thy own accord,
Lest thou be forc'd to what may seem thy Will:
The City renders thee what is thy own
With vast Increase, so thou resolve to go;
For till the Name, the Race and Family
Of *Tarquin* be remov'd, *Rome* is not free.

*Coll* *Brutus*, I yeild my Office to *Valerius*,
Hoping, when *Rome* has try'd my Faith by Exile,
She will recall me: So the Gods preserve you [Ex[it]

*Brut.* Welcome *Publicola*, true Son of *Rome*;
On such a Pilot in the roughest Storm
She may securely sleep, and rest her Cares.

*Enter* Tiberius, Aquinius, Vitellius, *and the Priests.*

1 *Pri.* Hear *Jupiter*, *Quirinus*, all you Gods,
Thou Father, Judge, commission'd for the Message,
*Pater Patratus* for the Ambassie,
And Sacred Oaths which I must swear for Truth,
Dost thou Commission me to seal the Peace,
If Peace they chuse, or hurl this Bloody Spear
Half burnt in Fire, if they inforce a War?

2 *Pri* Speak to the Senate, and the *Alban* People,
The Words of *Tarquin* This is your Commission

1 *Pri* The King, to shew he has more Moderati[on]
Than those that drove him from his lawful Empire,
Demands but Restitution of his own,
His Royal Houshold-stuff, Imperial Treasure,

Gold, his Jewels, and his proper State
be transported where he now resides:
wear that this is all the King requires,
hold his Signet, set upon the Wax
is Seal'd and Written in these Sacred Tables.
this I swear; and as my Oath is Just,
ccra and Punctual, without all Deceit,
ay *Jupiter* and all the Gods reward me
if I act, or otherwise imagine,
ink, or design, than what I here have sworn,
you the *Alban* People being safe,
e in your Country, Temples, Sepulchers,
e in your Laws, and proper Houshold Gods,
me alone be struck, fall, perish, die,
now this Stone falls from my Hand to Earth.
*Bru.* The Things you ask being very controversial
quire some Time. Should we deny the Tyrant
hat was his own 'twould seem a strange Injustice,
o' he had never Reign'd in *Rome*; yet, Fathers,
we consent to yield to his Demand,
e give him then full Power to make a War.
s known to you, the *Fecialian* Priests,
Act of Senate after Sun-set stands,
erefore your Offers being of great Moment,
e shall defer your Bus'ness till the Morn;
ith whose first Dawn we summon all the Fathers
give th' Affair Dispatch. So *Jove* protect,
ard, and defend the Commonwealth of *Rome* [*Exeunt.*
*Manent* Tiberius, Aquilius, Vitellius, *Priests.*
*Tib* Now to the Garden, where I'll bring my Brother:
r not, my Lord, we have the Means to work him,
annot fail
*Pri.* And you, *Vitellius*, haste
ith good *Aquilius*, spread the News through *Rome*
all of Royal Spirit; most to those
ung Noblemen that us'd to range with *Sextus*,
swade a Restitution of the King,
ve 'em the Hint to let him in by Night,
d joyn their Forces with th' Imperial Troops,
'tis a Shove, a Push of Fate, must bear it,

For you, the Hearts and Souls of Enterprize,
I need not urge a Reason after this:
What Good can come of such a Government,
Where tho' Two Consuls, wise and able Persons
As are throughout the World, sit at the Helm,
A very Trifle cannot be resolv'd,
A Trick, a Start, a Shadow of a Business,
That would receive Dispatch in half a Minute,
Were the Authority but rightly plac'd
In *Rome*'s most lawful King? But now no more;
The *Fecialian* Garden is the Place,
Where more of our sworn Function will be ready
To help the Royal Plot Disperse, and Prosper

## SCENE III. *The* Fecialian *Garden.*

*Titus Solus.*

*Tit.* She's gone, and I shall never see her more:
Gone to the Camp, to the harsh Trade of War,
Driven from thy Bed, just warm within thy Breast,
Torn from her Harbour by thy Father's Hand,
Perhaps to starve upon the barren Plain.
Thy Virgin Wife, the very Blush of Maids,
The softest Bosom, sweet, and not enjoy'd.
O the Immortal Gods! And as she went,
Howe'er she seem'd to bear our Parting well,
Methoughts she mixt her Melting with Disdain,
A Cast of Anger through her shining Tears:
So to abuse her Hopes, and blast her Wishes,
By making her my Bride, but not a Woman!

*Enter* Tiberius, Aquilius, Vitellius, *and Priests*, Teraminta.

*Tib* See where he stands, drown'd in his Melancholy
1 *Pri.* Madam, you know the Pleasure of the Queen
And what the Royal *Tullia* did command
I've sworn to execute,
*Ter.* I am instructed.
Since then my Life's at stake, you need not doubt
But I will act with all the Force I can.
Let me intreat you leave me here alone

S

e Minutes, and I'll call you to the Conquest.
[*Ex* Tib Aquil Vitel *Pri.*
*Tit* Chuse then the gloomy'st Place through all the
ow thy abandon'd Body on the Ground, [Grove,
th thy bare Breast lye wedded to the Dew;
en, as thou drink'st the Tears that trickle from thee,
stretch'd resolve to lye till Death shall seize thee
y sorrowful Head hung o'er some tumbling Stream,
ock thy Griefs with melancholy Sounds,
th broken Murmurs, and redoubled Groans,
help the gurgling of the Waters Fall.
*Ter* Oh, *Titus*, oh, what Scene of Death is this! [*Aside.*
*Tit* Or if thy Passion will not be kept in,
n that Glass of Nature thou shalt view
y swoln drown'd Eyes with the inverted Banks,
Tops of Willows, and their Blossoms turn'd,
h all the under Sky ten Fathom down,
sh that the Shadow of the swimming Globe
re so indeed, that thou might'st leap at Fate,
hurl thy Fortune headlong at the Stars:
y do not bear it, turn thy watry Face
yond' misguided Orb, and ask the Gods
what bold Sin they doom the wretched *Titus*
ch a Loss as that of *Teraminta*?
*raminta*! I will groan thy Name
he tir'd Eccho faint with Repetition,
ll the breathless Grove and quiet Myrtles
with my Sighs, as if a Tempest bow'd 'em.
ng but *Teraminta*. O *Teraminta*!
Nothing but *Titus*, *Titus* and *Teraminta*!
let me rob the Fountains and the Groves,
gird me to thee with the fastest Knot
ms and Spirits that would clasp thee through;
s thou art, and wet with Night's faln Dews,
arer so, thus richly dress'd with Sorrows,
f the Gods had hung thee round with Kingdoms.
*Titus*! O!
I find thee, *Teraminta*,
from a fearful Dream, and hold thee fast:
al, and I give thee back thy Joys,

Thy boundless Love with Pleasures running o'er;
Nay, as thou art, thus with thy Trappings, come,
Leap to my Heart, and ride upon the Pants,
Triumphing thus, and now defie our Stars.
But, oh, why do we lose this precious Moment!
The Bliss may yet be barr'd if we delay,
As 'twas before. Come to thy Husband's Bed,
I will not think this true till there I hold thee,
Lock'd in my Arms Leave this contagious Air;
There will be time for Talk how thou cam'st hither
When we have been beforehand with the Gods
Till then———

*Ter.* O, *Titus*, you must hear me first.
I bring a Message from the furious Queen;
I promised, nay, she swore me not to touch you,
Till I had charm'd you to the Part of *Tarquin*

*Tit* Ha, *Teraminta*! Not to touch thy Husband
Unless he prove a Villain?

*Ter.* *Titus*, no·
I'm sworn to tell you that you are a Traitor,
If you refuse to fight the Royal Cause.

*Tit* Hold, *Teraminta*

*Ter* No, my Lord; 'tis plain,
And I am sworn to lay my Reasons home
Rouze then, awake, recal your sleeping Virtue;
Side with the King, and arm against your Father,
Take part with those that loyally have sworn
To let him in by Night: *Vitellius*,
*Aquilius*, and your Brother wait without;
Therefore I charge you haste, subscribe your Name
And send your vow'd Obedience to the King
'Tis *Teraminta* that intreats you thus,
Charms, and conjures you; tell the Royal Heralds
You'll head their Enterprize; and then, my Lord,
My Love, my noble Husband, I'll obey you,
And follow to your Bed.

*Tit.* Never I swear
O, *Teraminta*, thou hast broke my Heart:
By all the Gods from thee this was too much.
Farewel, and take this with thee. For thy Sake

...ill not fight against the King, nor for him.
...fly my Father, Brother, Friends for ever,
...sake the haunts of Men, converse no more
With ought that's Human, dwell with endless Darkness:
...since the Sight of thee is now unwelcome,
What has the World besides that I can bear?

*Ter.* Come back, my Lord. By those Immortal Pow'rs
...now invok'd, I'll fix you in this Virtue.
...r *Teraminta* did but try how strong
...r Honour stood, and now she finds it lasting,
...ll die to root you in this solid Glory.
..., *Titus*, tho' the Queen has sworn to end me,
...o' both the *Fecialians* have Commission
...stab me in your Presence, if not wrought
...serve the King, yet by the Gods I charge you
...p to the Point your Constancy has gain'd.
...quin, altho' my Father, is a Tyrant,
...Bloody, Black Usurper, so I beg you
... in my Death to view him.

*Tit.* Oh you Gods!

*Ter.* Yet guilty as he is, if you behold him
...eafter with his Wounds upon the Earth,
..., for my sake, for poor *Teraminta*,
...o rather dy'd than you should lose your Honour,
...not you strike him, do not dip your Sword
...arquin's Blood, because he was my Father.

*Tit.* No, *Teraminta*, no, by all the Gods
...ll defend him, e'en against my Father.
... see, my Love, behold the Flight I take:
...at all the Charms of thy expected Bed
...ld not once move my Soul to think of acting,
... Fears and menac'd Death, by which thou striv'st
...ix me to the Principles of Glory,
... wrought me off. Yes, yes, you cruel Gods,
...the eternal Bolts that bind this Frame
... from their Order: Since you push me thus,
... to the Margin of this wide Despair,
...ld I plunge at once in this Dishonour,
...ere there is neither Shore, nor hope of Heav'n,
...loating Mark through all the dismal Vast;

'Tis Rockless too, no Cliff to clamber up,
To gaze about and pause upon the Ruin.

*Ter.* Is then your purpos'd Honour come to this?
What now, my Lord?

*Tit.* Thy Death, thy Death, my Love:
I'll think on that, and laugh at all the Gods.
Glory, Blood, Nature, Ties of Reverence,
The Dues of Birth, Respect of Parents, all,
All are as this, the Air I drive before me.
What hoa! *Vitellius*, and *Aquilius*, come,
And you the *Fecialian* Hera'ds, haste,
I'm ready for the Leap, I'll take it with you,
Tho' deep as to the Fiends

*Ter.* Thus hear me, *Titus*.

*Tit.* Off from my Knees, away. [Ra[illegible]
What on this Theme, thy Death? Nay, stabb'd be[illegible]

*Enter Priests, with* Tiberius, Aquilius, Vitellius.

Speak not, I will not know thee on this Subject,
But push thee from my Heart, with all Persuasions
That now are lost upon me O *Tiberius*,
*Aquilius*, and *Vitellius*, welcome, welcome,
I'll join you in the Conjuration, come
I am as free as he that dares be foremost.

*Ter.* My Lord, my Husband.

*Tit.* Take this Woman from me.
Nay, look you, Sirs, I am not yet so gone,
So headlong neither in his damn'd Design,
To quench this horrid Thirst with *Brutus'* Blood:
No, by th' Eternal Gods I barr you that;
My Father shall not bleed.

*Tib.* You could not think
Your Brother sure so monstrous in his Kind,
As not to make our Father's Life his Care.

*Tit.* Thus then, my Lords, I list my self among you,
And with my Stile in short subscribe my self
The Servant to the King; my Words are these.
*Titus* to the King.
Sir, you need only know my Brother's Mind
To judge of me, who am resolv'd to serve you.

1 *Pri.* 'Tis full enough.

Ti[illegible]

*Vit* Then leave me to the Hire
[*Ex* Tib. Aquil. Vit *and Priests.*
this hard Labour, to the dear-bought Prize;
Whose Life I purchas'd with my Loss of Honour:
me to my Breasts thou Tempest-beaten Flower,
m full of Rain, and stick upon my Heart.
short-liv'd Rose! Yet I some Hours will wear thee:
, by the Gods I'll smell thee 'till I languish,
le thy Sweets, and run thee o'er and o'er,
l like the Night upon thy folding Beauties,
d clasp thee dead Then, like the Morning Sun,
th a new Heat kiss th e to Life again,
d make the Pleasure equal to the Pain. [*Exeunt.*

---

## ACT IV. SCENE I.

Tiberius, Vitellius.

HArk, are we not pursu'd?
*Vit.* No, 'tis the Tread
our own Friends that follow in the Dark.
*ib* What's now the time?
*it* Just dead of Night.
d 'tis the blackest that e'er mask'd a Murder
*ib.* It likes me better; for I love the Scoul,
e grimmest Lowre of Fate on such a Deed,
ould have all the Charnel-houses yawn,
e dusty Urns, and monumental Bones,
nov'd, to make our Massacre a Tomb.
*b* Who was that that hollow'd Fire?
*it* A Slave
at snores i' th' Hall, he bellows in his Sleep,
l cries, The Capitol's o' Fire.
*ib* I would it were,
*Tarquin* at the Gates: 'Twould be a Blaze,
eacon fit to light a King of Blood,
at vows at once the Slaughter of the World:
wn with their Temples, set 'em on a Flame;
at should they do with Houses for the Gods,
Fools, the lazy Magistrates of *Rome*,

Wise Citizens, the politick Heads o'th' People,
That preach Rebellion to the Multitude?
Why, let 'em off, and rowl into their Graves:
I long to be at Work See, good *Aquilius*,
*Trebonius* too, *Servilius* and *Minutius*,
*Pomponius* ha! Nay, now you may unmask,
Brow-beat the Fates, and say they are your Slaves.

*Aqu.* What are those Bodies for?

*Tib.* A Sacrifice.
These were two very busie Commonwealths men,
That, ere the King was banish'd by the Senate,
First set the Plot on Foot in publick Meetings.
That would be holding forth, 'Twas possible
That Kings themselves might err, and were but Men,
The People were not Beasts for Sacrifice;
Then jogg'd his Brother, this cramm'd Statesman here,
The bolder Rogue, whom ev'n with open Mouth
I heard once belch Sedition from a Stall
Go, bear him to the Priests, he is a Victim
That comes as wish'd for them, the Cooks of Heav'n,
And they will carve this Brawn of fat Rebellion,
As if he were a Dish the Gods might feed on

Vin. (*From a Window*) Oh, the Gods! Oh the Gods!
What will they do with him? O these Priests, Rogues,
Cut-throats! a Dish for the Gods, but the Devil's Cooks
to dress him.

*Tib.* Thus then The *Fecialians* have set down
A Platform, copy'd from the King's Design:
The *Pandane*, or the *Romulide*, the *Roman*,
*Carmental* and *Janiculan* Ports of *Rome*,
The *Circ*, the *Capital*, and *Sublician* Bridge,
Must all be seiz'd by us that are within,
'Twill not be hard in the Surprize of Night
By us, the Consuls Children and their Nephews,
To kill the drowsie Guards, and keep the Holds,
At least so long till *Tarquin* force his Entrance
With all the Royalists that come to join us:
Therefore to make his broader Squadrons Way,
*Tarquinian* is design'd to be the Entry
Of his most pompous and resolv'd Revenge.

Aqui.

*Aquil.* The first decreed in this great Execution
here set down your Father and *Valerius.*

*Tib.* That's as the King shall please; but for *Valerius,*
take my self the Honour of his Head,
d wear it on my Spear. The Senate all
ithout Exception shall be sacrific'd:
d those that are the mutinous Heads o' th' People,
hom I have mark'd to be the Soldiers Spoil,
Plunder must be given, and who so fit
those notorious Limbs, your Commonwealths-men?
eir Daughters to be ravish'd, and their Sons
arter'd like Brutes upon the common Shambles

*Vit.* Now for the Letters, which the *Fecialians*
quire us all to Sign, and send to *Tarquin,*
ho will not else be apt to trust his Heralds
thout Credentials under every Hand,
e Bus'ness being indeed of vast Import,
which the Hazard of his Life and Empire,
well as all our Fortunes, does depend.

*Tib.* It were a Break to the whole Enterprize
make a Scruple in our great Affair:
ill Sign first: And for my Brother *Titus,*
hom his new Wife detains, I have his Hand
Seal to show, as fast and firm as any.

*Vin.* O Villany! Villany! What would they do with if they should catch me peeping? Knock out my ns at least; another Dish for the Priests, who uld make fine Sauce of 'em for the Hanch of a Fat izen!

[Hearts

*Tib.* All Hands have here subscrib'd: and that your
ve resolute to what your Hands have giv'n,
old the Messengers of Heav'n to bind you,
rms of Religion, Sacred Conjurations,
th Sounds of Execration, Words of Horror,
t to disclose or make least Signs or Show
what you have both heard, and seen, and sworn,
bear your selves as if it ne'er had been:
ear by the Gods Celestial and Infernal,
*Pluto,* Mother Earth, and by the Furies,
t to reveal, tho' Racks were set before you,
llable of what is past and done.

Hark

Hark how the offer'd Brutes begin to roar!
O that the Hearts of all the Traitor Senate,
And Heads of all that foul *Hydra* Multitude,
Were frying with their Fat upon this Pile,
That we might make an Off'ring worth an Empire,
And Sacrifice Rebellion to the King.

*The* SCENE *draws, showing the Sacrifice, one Burning and another Crucify'd, the Priests coming forward with Goblets in their Hands, fill'd with Human Blood*

1 *Pri.* Kneel all you Heroes of this black Design,
Each take his Goblet fill'd with Blood and Wine,
Swear by the Thunderer, swear by *Jove*,
Swear by the Hundred Gods above,
Swear by *Dis*, by *Proserpine*,
Swear by the *Berecynthian* Queen,
2 *Pri* To keep it close till *Tarquin* comes,
With Trumpet Sound and Beat of Drums,
But then to thunder forth the Deed,
That *Rome* may blush, and Traitors bleed.
Swear all

*All* We swear.

1 *Pri.* Now drink the Blood,
To make the Conjuration good.

*Tib.* Methinks I feel the Slaves exalted Blood
Warm at my Heart O that it were the Spirits
Of *Rome*'s best Life, drawn from her grizled Fathers!
That were a Draught indeed to quench Ambition,
And give new Fierceness to the King's Revenge.

*Vin* Oh the Gods! What, burn a Man alive! O Cannibals, Hellhounds! Eat one Man, and drink another! Well, I'll to *Valerius*, *Brutus* will not believe me, because his Sons and Nephews are in the Business. What, drink a Man's Blood! Roast him and eat him alive! A whole Man roasted! Would not an Ox serve the Turn? Priests to do this! O you Immortal Gods! For my part if this be your Worship I renounce you No, if a Man can't go to Heav'n, unless your Priests eat him, and drink him, and roast him alive, I'll be for the Broad Way, and the Devil shall have me at a Venture [*Ex*

*Exe*

*Enter* Titus.

*Tit* What ho, *Tiberius*! Give me back my Hand.
hat have you done? Horrors and Midnight Murders!
he Gods, the Gods awake you to Repentance,
they have me Would'st thou believe me, Brother?
nce I deliver'd thee that Fatal Scroul,
at Writing to the King, my Heart rebell'd
ainst it self; my Thoughts were up in Arms,
in a Roar, like Seamen in a Storm,
y Reason and my Faculties were wrack'd,
e Mast, the Rudder and the Tackling gone,
y Body, like the Hull of some lost Vessel,
aten and tumbled with my Rowling Fears,
erefore I charge thee give me back my Writing.
*Tib.* What means my Brother?
*Tit* O *Tiberius*, O!
rk as it seems, I tell thee that the Gods
ok through a Day of Lightning on our City;
e Heav'n's on Fire; and from the flaming Vault
tentous Blood pours like a Torrent down.
ere are a Hundred Gods in *Rome* to Night,
every larger Spirit is abroad,
numents empty'd, every Urn is shaken
fright the State, and put the World in Arms.
now I saw Three *Romans* stand amaz'd
ore a Flaming Sword, then dropt down dead,
self untouch'd; while through the blazing Air
leeting Head, like a full-riding Moon,
c'd by, and cry'd, *Titus*, I am *Egeria*,
ent, repent, or certain Death attends thee;
son and Tyranny shall not prevail:
gdom shall be no more; *Egeria* says it:
that vast turn Imperial Fate design'd
, O *Titus*, on th' eternal Loom,
ripe, 'tis perfect, and is doom'd to stand.
*Tit* Fumes, Fumes, the Fantoms of an ill Digestion,
Gods are as good quiet Gods as may be,
're fast asleep, and mean not to disturb us,
ss your Frenzy wake 'em

*Tit*

*Tit.* Peace, Fury, Peace,
May the Gods doom me to the Pains of Hell
If I enjoy'd the Beauties that I sav'd:
The Horror of my Treason shock'd my Joys,
Enervated my Purpose, while I lay
Colder than Marble by her Virgin Side;
As if I had drunk the Blood of Elephants,
Drousie Mandragora, or the Juice of Hemlock.

1 *Pri* I like him not, I think we had best dispatch hi[m]

*Tit* Nothing but Images of Horror round me;
*Rome* all in Blood, the Ravish'd Vestals raving,
The Sacred Fire put out; robb'd Mothers Shrieks
Deaf'ning the Gods with Clamours from their Babes,
That sprawl'd aloft upon the Soldiers Spears,
The Beard of Age pluck'd off by barbarous Hands,
While from his piteous Wounds and horrid Gashe[s]
The labouring Life flow'd faster than the Blood.

*Enter* Valerius, Vinditius, *with Guards, who seize all b[ut] the Priests, who slip away* · Vinditius *follows them.*

*Val* Horror upon me! What will this Night bri[ng]
Yes, you immortal Gods, strike, strike the Consul, [for]
Since these are here, the Crime will look less horrid
In me, than in his Sons. *Titus, Tiberius!*
O from this time let me be Blind and Dumb,
But haste there; *Mutius*, fly; call hither *Brutus*,
Bid him for ever leave the Down of Rest,
And sleep no more If *Rome* were all on Fire,
And *Tarquin* in the Streets bestriding Slaughter,
He would less wonder than at *Titus* here.

*Tit* Stop there, O stop that Messenger of Fate
Here, bind, *Valerius*, bind this Villain's Hands,
Tear off my Robes, put me upon the Forks,
And lash me like a Slave, till I shall howl
My Soul away; or hang me on a Cross,
Rack me a Year within some Horrid Dungeon;
So deep, so near the Hells that I must suffer,
That I may groan my Torments to the Damn'd.
I do submit, this Traitor, this curs'd Villain,
To all the Stings of most Ingenious Horror,

thou dispatch me ere my Father comes.
t hark, I hear the Tread of fatal *Brutus*;
y all the Gods, and by the lowest Furies,
cannot bear his Face. Away with me,
l like a Whirlwind I will tear my Way,
care not whither. [*Exit with* Tiberius.

*Val* Take 'em hence together.

*Enter* Vinditius *with the Priests.*

*Vin* Here, here, my Lord, I have unkennell'd Two:
hose there are Rascals made of Flesh and Blood,
hose are but Men, but these are the Gods Rogues.

*Val* Go, good *Vinditius*, haste, and stop the People,
et 'em together to the Capitol·
here all the Senate, with the Consuls early,
ill see strict Justice done upon the Traitors.
or thee the Senate shall decree Rewards
reat as thy Service.

*Vin.* I humbly thank your Lordship.
hy, what, they'll make me a Senator at least,
nd then a Consul, O th' Immortal Gods!
My Lord, I go—To have the Rods and Axes carry'd
efore me, and a long Purple Gown trailing behind my
onourable Heels: Well, I am made for ever. [*Exit.*

*Enter* Brutus, *attended.*

*Bru.* O, my *Valerius*, are these Horrors true?
ast thou, O Gods, this Night embowell'd me?
ansack'd thy *Brutus*, Veins, thy Fellow Consul,
nd found Two Villains lurking in my Blood?

*Val* The blackest Treason that e'er Darkness brooded,
nd who, to hatch these Horrors for the World,
ho to seduce the Noble Youth of *Rome*,
o draw 'em to so damn'd a Conjuration,
o bind 'em too by new invented Oaths,
eligious Forms, and Devilish Sacrifices,
Sacrament of Blood, for which *Rome* suffer'd
Two the worthiest of her Martyr'd Sons;
ho to do this, but Messengers from Heav'n?
hese Holy Men that swore so solemnly
efore the Senate, call'd the Gods to curse 'em,
they intended ought against the State,

Or

Or harbour'd Treaſon more than what they utter'd?
*Bru* Now all the Fiends and Furies thank 'em for't
You Sons of *Murder*, *that get drunk with Blood*,
Then ſtab at Princes, poiſon Commonwealths,
Deſtroy whole Hecatombs of Innocent Souls,
Pile 'em like Bulls and Sheep upon your Altars,
As you would ſmoke the Gods from out their Dwellings;
You Shame of Earth, and Scandal of the Heav'ns,
You deeper Fiends than any of the Furies,
That ſcorn to whiſper Envy, Hate, Sedition;
But with a Blaſt of Priviledge proclaim it,
Prieſts that are Inſtruments deſign'd to damn us,
Fit Speaking-Trumpets for the Mouth of Hell
Hence with 'em, Guards; ſecure 'em in the Priſon
Of *Ancus Martius* Read the Packets o'er,
I'll bear it as I'm able, read 'em out.
*Val.* The Sum of the Conſpiracy to the King.
It ſhall begin with both the Conſuls Deaths,
And then the Senate; every Man muſt bleed,
But thoſe that have engag'd to ſerve the King.
Be ready therefore, Sir, to ſend your Troops
By Twelve to morrow Night, and come your ſelf
In Perſon, if you'll reaſcend the Throne.
All that have ſworn to ſerve your Majeſty
Subſcribe themſelves by Name your faithful Subjects.
*Tiberius*, *Aquilius*, *Vitellius*,
*Trebonius*, *Servilius*, *Minutius*,
*Pomponius*, and your *Fecialian* Prieſts
*Bru* Ha! my *Valerius*, is not *Titus* there?
*Val.* He's here, my Lord; a Paper by it ſelf.
*Titus* to the King.
Sir, you need only know my Brother's Mind
To judge of me, who am reſolv'd to ſerve you.
What do you think, my Lord?
*Bru* Think, my *Valerius*!
By my Heart, I know not:
I'm at a Loſs of Thought; and muſt acknowledge
The Councils of the Gods are fathomleſs;
Nay, 'tis the hardeſt Task perhaps of Life
To be aſſur'd of what is Vice or Virtue

Whether

hether when we raise up Temples to the Gods
e do not then Blaspheme 'em O, behold me,
hold the Game that laughing Fortune plays,
te, or the Will of Heav'n, call't what you please,
at marrs the best Designs that Prudence lays,
at brings Events about perhaps to mock
Humane Reach, and sport with Expectation.
nsider this, and wonder not at *Brutus*,
is *Philosophy* seems at a stand;
thou behold'st him shed unmanly Tears
see his Blood, his Children, his own Bowels
nspire the Death of him that gave 'em Being
*Val* What Heart, but yours, could bear it without [breaking?
*Bru.* No, my *Valerius*, I were a Beast indeed
ot to be mov'd with such prodigious Suffering,
after all I justifie the Gods,
d will conclude there's Reason supernatural
at guides us through the World with vast Discretion,
ho we have not Souls to comprehend it:
hich makes by wondrous Methods the same Causes
oduce Effects, tho' of a different Nature;
ce then, for Man's Instruction, and the Glory
the Immortal Gods, it is decreed
ere must be Patterns drawn of fiercest Virtue,
*us* submits to the Eternal Doom.
*al.* May I believe there can be such Perfection,
h a Resolve in Man?
*ru* First, as I am their Father,
rdon both of 'em this black Design;
as I am *Rome*'s Consul, I abhor 'em,
cast 'em from my Soul with Detestation:
nearer to my Blood, the deeper grain'd
Colour of their Fault, and they shall bleed.
my *Valerius*, both my Sons shall die:

*Enter* Teraminta.

, I will stand unbowell'd by the Altar,
something dearer to me than my Entrails
play'd before the Gods and *Roman* People:
Sacrifice of Justice and Revenge.
*er.* What Sacrifice, what Victims, Sir, are these
Which

Which you intend? O, you Eternal Powers,
How shall I vent my Sorrows! Oh, my Lord,
Yet ere you seal the Death you have design'd,
The Death of all that's lovely in the World,
Hear what the Witness of his Soul can say,
The only Evidence that can, or dare
Appear for your unhappy guiltless Son;
The Gods command you, Virtue, Truth, and Justice
Which you with so much Rigor have ador'd,
Beg you would hear the wretched *Teraminta*

*Brut.* Cease thy Laments: Tho' of the Blood of *Tarq*
Yet more, the Wife of my forgotten Son;
Thou shalt be heard.

*Ter.* Have you forgot him then?
Have you forgot your self? The Image of you,
The very Picture of your Excellence,
The Portraiture of all your Manly Virtues,
Your Visage stampt upon him; just those Eyes,
The moving Greatness of 'em, all the Mercy,
The shedding Goodness; not so quite severe,
Yet still most like. And can you then forget him?

*Brut.* Will you proceed?

*Ter.* My Lord, I will. Know then,
After your Son, your Son that loves you more
Than I love him, after our common *Titus*,
The Wealth o'th' World, unless you rob 'em of it,
Had long endur'd th' Assaults of the Rebellious,
And still kept fix'd to what you had enjoin'd him;
I, as Fate order'd it, was sent from *Tullia*,
With my Death menac'd, ev'n before his Eyes,
Doom'd to be stabb'd before him by the Priests,
Unless he yielded not t' oppose the King.
Consider, Sir; oh make it your own Case;
Just wedded, just on the expected Joys,
Warm for my Bed, and rushing to my Arms,
So loving too, alas, as we did love.
Granted in Haste, in Heat, in Flame of Passion
He knew not what himself, and so subscrib'd.
But now, Sir, now, my Lord, behold a Wonder,
Behold a Miracle to move your Soul!

ho' in my Arms, just in the Grasps of Pleasure.
is noble Heart, struck with the Thoughts of *Brutus*,
f what he promis'd you, till then forgot,
apt in his Breast, and dash'd him from Enjoyment;
shriek'd, Y' Immortal Gods, what have I done!
o, *Teraminta*, let us rather perish,
vide for ever with whole Seas betwixt us,
ther than Sin against so good a Father
ho' he before had barr'd your Life and Fortune,
t would not trust the Traitors with the Safety
him he call'd the Image of the Gods
*Val* O Saint like Virtue of a *Roman* Wife!
Eloquence Divine! Now all the Arts
Womens Tongues, the Rhetoric of the Gods
pire thy soft and tender Soul to move him.
*Ter.* On this he rous'd Swore by the Powers Divine
would fetch back the Paper that he gave,
leave his Life amongst 'em: Kept his Word,
came to challenge it, but, oh! too late;
, in the midst of all his Piety,
strong Perswasions to a swift Repentance,
Vows to lay their horrid Treasons open,
Execration of the barbarous Priests,
w he abhorr'd that Bloody Sacrament
much as you, and curs'd the Conjuration;
*dutus* came, that had before alarm'd
wise *Valerius*, who with all the Guards
nd *Titus* here, believ'd him like the rest,
seiz'd him too, as guilty of the Treason.
*al* But, by the Gods, my Soul does now acquit him.
t le thy Tongue, blest the auspicious Gods
t sent thee, O true Pattern of Perfection!
plead his bleeding Cause There needs no more,
his Father's mov'd: Behold a Joy,
atry Comfort rising in his Eyes,
t says, 'Tis more than half a Heav'n to hear thee.
*ut* Haste, O *Valerius*, haste, and send for *Titus*.
*r* For *Titus*! Oh, that is a Word too distant;
for your Son, for your Beloved Son,
Darling of the World, the Joy of Heav'n,

 The

The Hope of Earth, your Eyes not dearer to you,
Your Soul's best Wish, and Comfort of your Age.

*Enter* Titus, *with* Valerius.

*Tit* Ah, Sir! Oh whither shall I run to hide me?
Where shall I lower fall? How shall I lye
More groveling in your View, and howl for Mercy?
Yet 'tis some Comfort to my wild Despair,
Some Joy in Death, that I may kiss your Feet,
And swear upon 'em by these streaming Tears,
Black as I am with all my Guilt upon me,
I never harbour'd ought against your Person:
Ev'n in the Height of my full-fraught Distraction,
Your Life, my Lord, was Sacred; ever dear,
And ever precious to unhappy *Titus*.

*Brut* Rise, *Titus*. Rise, my Son.

*Tit* Alas, I dare not;
I have not Strength to see the Majesty
Which I have brav'd If thus far I aspire,
If on your Knees I hang and vent my Groans,
It is too much, too much for thousand Lives.

*Brut* I pity thee, my Son, and I forgive thee:
And, that thou may'st believe my Mercy true,
I take thee in my Arms

*Tit* O all the Gods!

*Brut.* Now rise, I charge thee, on my Blessing, ri[se]

*Ter* Ah! See, Sir, see, against his Will behold
He does obey, tho' he would chuse to kneel
An Age before you, see how he stands and trembles!
Now, by my Hopes of Mercy he's so lost,
His Heart's so full, brim full of Tenderness,
The Sense of what you've done has struck him speechless
Nor can he thank you now but with his Tears.

*Brut* My dear *Valerius*, let me now intreat thee
Withdraw a while with gentle *Teraminta*,
And leave us to our selves

*Ter* Ah, Sir, I fear you now;
Nor can I leave you with the humble *Titus*,
Unless you promise me you will not chide,
Nor fall again to Anger. Do not, Sir,
Do not upbraid his soft and melting Temper

W[ith]

With what is paſt. Behold he ſighs again!
Now by the Gods that hitherto have bleſt us,
My Heart forebodes a Storm, I know not why.
But ſay, my Lord, give me your God-like Word
You'll not be cruel, and I'll not truſt my Heart,
Howe'er it leaps, and fills me with new Horror.

*Brut.* I promiſe thee.

*Ter.* Why, then I thank you, Sir,
Ev'n from my Soul I thank you for this Goodneſs:
The Great, Good, Gracious Gods reward and bleſs you.
Ah *Titus*, ah, my Soul's Eternal Treaſure,
I fear I leave thee with a hard Uſurer;
But I perforce muſt truſt thee. Oh Farewel.
[*Ex. with* Val.

*Brut.* Well, *Titus*, ſpeak, how is it with thee now?
I would attend a while this mighty Motion,
Wait till the Tempeſt were quite overblown,
That I might take thee in the Calm of Nature,
With all thy gentler Virtues brooding on thee,
So huſh'd a Stillneſs, as if all the Gods
Look'd down, and liſten'd to what we were ſaying;
Speak then, and tell me, O my beſt belov'd,
My Son, my *Titus*, is all well again?

*Tit.* So well, that ſaying how muſt make it nothing;
So well, that I could wiſh to die this Moment,
For ſo my Heart with pow'rful Throbs perſwades me:
That were indeed to make you Reparation,
That were, my Lord, to thank you home, to die,
And that for *Titus* too would be moſt happy.

*Brut.* How's that, my Son? Would Death for thee be [happy?

*Tit.* Moſt certain, Sir, for in my Grave I 'ſcape
All thoſe Affronts which I in Life muſt look for,
All thoſe Reproaches which the Eyes, and Fingers,
And Tongues of *Rome* will daily caſt upon me;
From whom, to a Soul ſo ſenſible as mine,
Each ſingle Scorn would be far worſe than dying:
Beſides, I 'ſcape the Stings of my own Conſcience,
Which will for ever rack me with Remembrance,
Haunt me by Day, and torture me by Night,

Casting my blotted Honour in the Way
Where-e'er my melancholy Thoughts shall guide me,
*Brut* But is not Death a very dreadful Thing?
*Tit* Not to a Mind resolv'd. No, Sir, to me
It seems as natural as to be Born.
Groans, and Convulsions, and discolour'd Faces,
Friends weeping round us, Blacks, and Obsequies,
Make it a dreadful Thing, the Pomp of Death
Is far more terrible than Death it self
Yes, Sir, I call the Powers of Heav'n to witness
*Titus* dares die, if so you have decreed,
Nay, he shall die with Joy, to honour *Brutus*,
To make your Justice famous through the World,
And fix the Liberty of *Rome* for ever:
Not but I must confess my Weakness too;
Yet it is great thus to resolve against it,
To have the Frailty of a Mortal Man,
But the Security of th' Immortal Gods.
*Brut* O *Titus*! Oh thou absolute Young Man!
Thou flatt'ring Mirror of thy Father's Image,
Where I behold my self at such Advantage!
Thou perfect Glory of the *Human* Race!
Let me endear thee once more to my Bosom,
Groan an Eternal Farewel to thy Soul,
Instead of Tears weep Blood, if possible,
Blood, the Heart-Blood of *Brutus*, on his Child,
For thou must die, my *Titus*, die, my Son,
I swear the Gods have doom'd thee to the Grave.
The violated *Genius* of thy Country
Rears his sad Head, and passes Sentence on thee
This Morning Sun, that lights my Sorrows on
To the Tribunal of this Horrid Vengeance,
Shall never see thee more.
*Tit* Alas, my Lord!
Why are you mov'd thus? Why am I worth your Sorrow?
Why should the God-like *Brutus* shake to doom me?
Why all these Trappings for a Traitor's Hearse?
The Gods will have it so
*Brut* They will, my *Titus*
Nor Heav'n, nor Earth, can have it otherwise,

ay, *Titus*, mark; the d eper that I ſearch,
y harraſs'd Soul returns the more confirm'd:
ethinks I ſee the very Hand of *Jove*
oving the dreadful Wheels of this Affair,
hat whirl thee, like a Machine, to thy Fate.
ſeems as if the Gods had pre-ordain'd it,
o fix the reeling Spirits of the People,
nd ſettle the looſe Liberty of *Rome*
'Tis fix'd, O therefore let not Fancy fond thee.
o fix'd thy Death, that 'tis not in the Power
f Gods or Men to ſave thee from the Ax
*Tit* The Ax! O Heav'n! Then muſt I fall ſo baſely?
hat, ſhall I periſh by the Common Hangman?
*Brut* If thou deny me this thou giv'ſt me nothing.
es, *Titus*, ſince the Gods have ſo decreed
hat I muſt loſe thee, I will take th' Advantage
f thy Important Fate, cement *Rome*'s Flaws,
nd heal her wounded Freedom with thy Blood.
will aſcend my ſelf the ſad Tribunal,
nd ſit upon my Sons, on thee, my *Titus*;
hold thee ſuffer all the Shame of Death,
he Lictor's Laſhes, bleed before People;
hen with thy Hopes and all thy Youth upon thee,
e thy Head taken by the Common Ax,
ithout a Groan, without one pitying Tear,
that the Gods can hold me to my Purpoſe,
o make my Juſtice quite tranſcend Example.
*Tit* Scourg'd like a Bondman! Ha! a beaten Slave!
t I deſerve it all, yet here I fail
he Image of this Suff'ring quite unmans me,
or can I longer ſtop the guſhing Tears.
Sir! O *Brutus*! Muſt I call you Father,
et have no Token of your Tenderneſs?
o Sign of Mercy? What, not bate me that!
an you reſolve, O all th' Extremity
f cruel Rigour! to behold me too?
o ſit unmov'd, and ſee me whipt to Death?
here are your Bowels now? Is this a Father?
h, Sir, why ſhould you make my Heart ſuſpect

That all your late Compassion was dissembled?
How can I think that you did ever love me?
*Brut* Think that I love thee by my present Passion,
By these unmanly Tears, these Earthquakes here,
These Sighs that twitch the very Strings of Life
Think that no other Cause on Earth could move me
To tremble thus, to sob, or shed a Tear,
Nor shake my solid Virtue from her Point,
But *Titus'* Death O do not call it shameful
That thus shall fix the Glory of the World.
I own thy Suff'rings ought t'unman me thus,
To make me throw my Body on the Ground,
To bellow like a Beast, to gnaw the Earth,
To tear my Hair, to curse the Cruel Fates
That force a Father thus to drag his Bowels.
*Tit* O rise, thou violated Majesty,
Rise from the Earth, or I shall beg those Fates
Which you would curse to bolt me to the Centre
I now submit to all your threaten'd Vengeance.
Come forth you Executioners of Justice,
Nay, all you Lictors, Slaves, and common Hangmen
Come, strip me bare, unrobe me in his Sight,
And lash me till I bleed, whip me like Furies;
And when you've scourg'd me till I foam and fall,
For want of Spirits groveling in the Dust,
Then take my Head, and give it his Revenge
By all the Gods I greedily resign it
*Brut.* No more, Farewel, eternally Farewel.
If there be Gods they will reserve a Room,
A Throne for thee in Heav'n. One last Embrace
What is it makes thy Eyes thus swim again?
*Tit* I had forgot. Be good to *Teraminta*
When I am Ashes.
*Brut* Leave her to my Care.
See her thou must not, for thou canst not bear it
O for one more, this Pull, this Tug of Heart-strings!
Farewel for ever
*Tit* O *Brutus*! O my Father!
*Brut.* Canst thou not say Farewel?

*Tit* Farewel, for ever.
*Brut* For ever then, but Oh my Tears run o'er,
oans choak my Words, and I can speak no more [*Exeunt.*

## ACT V. SCENE I.

*Valerius, Horatius, Herminius, Mutius.*

*r* HIS Sons condemn'd?
*Val* Doom'd to the Rods and Axes.
*Hor* What, both of 'em?
*Val* Both, Sir, both, both his Sons
*Hor* What, *Titus* too?
*Val* Yes, Sir his Darling *Titus*,
, tho' he knows him Innocent as I am,
s all one, Sir his Sentence stands like Fate.
*Hor* Yet I'll intreat him
*Mut* So will I.
*Herm* And I.
*Val* Intreat him! Yes, you may, my Lords, and move
I have done: Why, he's no more a Man, [him,
is not cast in the same common Mould,
s Spirit moves not with our Springs and Wards,
looks and talks as if that *Jove* had sent him
be the Judge of all the under World,
lls me, this Palace of the Universe,
ith that vast Moat, the Ocean running round us,
' Eternal Stars so fiercely rowling o'er us,
ith all that Circulation of Heav'ns Orbs,
re so establish'd from before all Ages
be the Dowry of Majestick *Rome*
en looks as if he had a Patent for it
take Account of all this great Expence,
d see the Layings out of the round World
*Herm* What shall be done then? For it grieves my Soul
think of *Titus'* Loss
*Val* There is no Help,
t thus to shake your Head, and cross your Arms,
d wonder what the Gods and he intend

*Herm* There's ſcarce one Man of this Conſpiracy
But is ſome Way related, if not nearly,
To *Junius Brutus* Some of the *Aquilians*
Are Nephews to him; and *Vitellius*' Siſter,
The Grave *Sempronia*, is the Conſul's Wife.

*Val* Therefore I have engag'd that groaning Matron
To plead the Cauſe of her unhappy Sons.

*Enter* Titus *with* Lictors.

But ſee, O Gods, behold the Gallant *Titus*,
The Mirror of all Sons, the White of Virtue,
Fill'd up with Blots, and writ all o'er with Blood,
Bowing with Shame his Body to the Ground,
Whipt out of Breath by theſe Inhuman Slaves!
O *Titus*! Is this poſſible? this Shame?

*Tit.* O my *Valerius*, call it not my Shame;
By all the Gods it is to *Titus*, Honour;
My conſtant Suff'rings are my only Glory.
What have I left beſides? But ask, *Valerius*,
Ask theſe good Men that have perform'd their Duty,
If all the while they whipt me like a Slave,
If when the Blood from every Part ran down,
I gave one Groan, or ſhed a Woman's Tear:
I think, I ſwear, I think, O my *Valerius*,
That I have born it well, and like a *Roman*.
But O, far better ſhall I bear my Death,
Which, as it brings leſs Pain, has leſs Diſhonour.

*Enter* Teraminta *Wounded*

*Ter* Where is he? Where, where is this God-like Son
Of an Inhuman, Barbarous, Bloody Father?
O bear me to him

*Tit* Ha! My *Teraminta*!
Is't poſſible? The very Top of Beauty,
This perfect Face drawn by the Gods at Council,
Which they were long a making, as they had Reaſon,
For they ſhall never hit the like again,
Defil'd and mangled thus! What Barbarous Wretch
Has thus Blaſphem'd this bright Original?

*Ter* For me it matters not, nor my Abuſes,
But, oh, for thee, why have they us'd thee thus?
Whipt, *Titus*, whipt! And could the Gods look on?

Th

he Glory of the World thus basely us'd?
sh'd, whipt, and beaten by these upright Dogs?
hose Souls, with all the Virtue of the Senate,
ill be but Foils to any Fault of thine,
ho hast a Beauty e'en in thy offending
nd did thy Father doom thee thus? Oh *Titus*,
rgive thy dying Part, if she believes
Wretch so barbarous never could produce thee.
me God, some God, my *Titus*, watch'd his Absence,
pt to thy Mother's Bed, and gave thee to the World.
*Tit* Oh this last Wound, this Stab to all my Courage!
d'st thou been well I could have born more Lashes:
d is it thus my Father does protect thee?
*Ter.* Ah *Titus*! What, thy Murd'rer my Protector!
, let me fall again among the People,
t me be whooted like a common Strumpet,
s'd as I was, and dragg d about the Streets,
e Bastard of a *Tarquin*, foil'd in Dirt,
e Cry of all those Bloodhounds that did hunt me
us to the Goal of Death, this happy End
all my Miseries, here to pant my last,
wash thy Gashes with my Farewel Tears,
murmur, sob, and lean my aking Head
on thy Breast, thus, like a Cradle Babe,
suck thy Wounds, and bubble out my Soul.
*Enter* Sempronia, Aquilia, Vitellia, *Mourners*,&c
*Semp.* Come Ladies, haste, and let us to the Senate;
he Gods give us leave we'll be to Day
t of the Council Oh, my Son, my *Titus*!
here the Bloody Justice of a Father,
low the Vengeance rains from his own Bowels!
e n t mad? If he refuse to hear us
'll bind his Hands as one bereft of Reason
te then. Oh *Titus*, I would stay to moan thee,
that I fear h s Orders are gone out
something worse, for Death, to take the Heads
al the Kindred of these Wretched Women
*er* Come then, I think I have some Spirits left
join thee, O most pious, best of Mothers,
melt this rocky Heart. Give me your Hand,

Thus

Thus let us march before this wretched Host,
And offer to that God of Blood our Vows:
If there be ought that's Human left about him,
Perhaps my Wounds and horrible Abuses,
Helpt with the Tears and Groan of this sad Troop,
May batter down the best of his Resolves

*Tit.* Hark, *Teraminta.*

*Ter* No, my Lord, away. [Exit

*Tit* Oh, my *Valerius!* Was there ever Day
Through all the Legends of recorded Time
So sad as this? But see, my Father comes!

*Enter* Brutus, Tiberius, Lictors.

*Tiberius* too has undergone the Lash
Give him the Patience, Gods, of martyr'd *Titus*,
And he will bless those Hands that have chastis'd him.

*Tib* Enjoy the bloody Conquest of thy Pride,
Thou more Tyrannical than any *Tarquin*,
Thou fiercer Sire of these unhappy Sons,
Than Impious *Saturn*, or the gorg'd *Thyestes*
This Cormorant sees, and owns us for his Children,
Yet preys upon his Intrails, tears his Bowels
With Thirst of Blood, and Hunger fetch'd from Hell,
Which famish'd *Tantalus* would start to think on,
But end, *Barbarian*, end the horrid Vengeance
Which thou so impiously hast begun,
Perfect thy Justice, as thou, Tyrant, call'st it,
Sit like a Fury on thy Black Tribunal,
Grasp with thy monstrous Hands these gory Heads
And let thy Flatt'ring Orators adore thee,
For Triumphs which shall make thee smile at Hor[...]

*Brut* Lead to the Senate

*Tib* Go then to the Senate,
There make thy Boast how thou hast doom'd thy Chil[dren]
To Forks and Whips, for which the Gods reward [...]
Away; my Spirit scorns more Conference with thee
The Ax will be as Laughter, but the Whips
That drew these Stains, for this I beg the Gods
With my last Breath, for every Drop that falls
From these vile Wounds, to thunder Curses on thee [...]

*Brut* *Valerius*, haste; the Senate does attend us [E...]

*it Valerius*, ere you go let me conjure thee,
all the Earth holds great or honourable,
thou art truly *Roman*, stampt a Man,
nt to thy dying *Titus* one Request
*al* I'll grant thee any thing, but do not talk
dying yet, for much I dare confide
hat sad Company that's gone before.
ow they'll move him to preserve his *Titus*,
tho' you mark'd him not, as hence he parted
uld perceive with Joy a silent Shower
down his Silver Beard, therefore have Hope.
*it* Hope, say'st thou! O the Gods! What hope of
live, to live! And after this Dishonour! [Life?
my *Valerius*, do not make me rave,
if thou hast a Soul that's sensible,
me conjure thee, when we reach the Senate,
thrust me through the Heart.
*al* Not for the World.
*it* Do't, or I swear thou hast no Friendship for me.
, thou wilt save me from the hated Ax,
Hangman's Hand, for by the Gods I tell thee
u may'st as well stop the Eternal Sun,
drive him back, as turn my Father's Purpose:
, and what most my Soul intreats thee for,
ll perhaps in Death procure his Pity;
to dye thus, beneath his killing Frown,
mning me before my Ex cution
*al* 'Tis granted, by the Gods I swear to end thee;
when I weigh with my more serious Thought
Father's Conduct in this dreadful Justice,
d it is impossible to save thee
e then, I'll lead thee, O thou glorious *Victim*,
s to the Altar of untimely Death,
s in thy Trim, with all thy Bloom of Youth,
le Virtues on thee, whose Eternal Spring
l Blossom on thy Monumental Marble
h never-fading Glory.
. Let me clasp thee,
out my Thanks thus with my Farewel Spirits:
now away, the Taper's almost out,

To

To lose the Light of this dear World for ever!
Never, *Valerius*, to be kindled more:
Or if it be, my Friend, it shall continue,
Burn through all Winds against the Puff of Fortune,
To dazle still, and shine like the fix'd Stars,
With Beams of Glory that shall last for ever [*Exe*.

## Scena Ultima. *The Senate.*

*Brut.* Health to the Senate! To the Fathers hail!
*Jupiter*, *Horsius* and *Diespiter*,
*Hospital* and *Feretrian*, *Jove* the Stayer,
With all the Hundred Gods and Goddesses,
Guard and defend the Liberty of *Rome*
It has been found a famous Truth in Story,
Left by the Ancient Sages to their Sons,
That on the Change of Empires, or of Kingdoms,
Some sudden Execution, fierce and great,
Such as may draw the World to Admiration,
Is necessary to be put in Act
Against the Enemies of the present State.
Had *Hector*, when the *Greeks* and *Trojans* met
Upon the Truce, and mingled with each other,
Brought to the Banquet of those D my Gods
The Fatal Head of that Illustrious Whore,
*Troy* might have stood till now, but that was wanting
*Jove* having from Eternity set down
*Rome* to be Head of all the under-World
Rais'd with this Thought, and big with Prophesie
Of what vast Good may grow by such Examples,
*Brutus* stands forth to do a dreadful Justice.
I come, O Conscript Fathers, to a Deed
Wholly protentous, new, and wonderful,
Such as, perhaps, has never yet been found
In all Memorials of former Ages,
Nor ever will again My Sons are Traitors,
Their Tongues and Hands are Witnesses confest,
Therefore I have already past their Sentence,
And wait with you to see their Execution.
*Hor* Consul, the Senate does not ask their De-
They are content with what's already done,

all intreat you to remit the Ax
*rut.* I thank you, Fathers, but refuse the Offer.
the assaulted Majesty of *Rome*
ear there is no Way to quit the Grace,
right the Commonwealth, and thank the Gods,
by the Sacrificing of my Bowels
e then, you sad Revengers of the Publick,
se Traitors hence, strike off their Heads, and then
*Sons* No more: Their Doom is past. Away.
, shall we stop the Mouth of loud Sedition,
s show the difference betwixt the Sway
Partial Tyrants, and of a Free-born People,
ere no Man shall offend because he's Great,
re none need doubt his Wife's or Daughter's Honour,
ere all enjoy their own without Suspicion,
ere there's no Innovation of Religion,
Change of Laws, nor Breach of Privilege,
desperate Factions gaping for Rebellion,
Hopes of Pardon for Assassinates,
rash Advancements of the Base or Stranger,
Luxury, for Wit, or Glorious Vice;
on the contrary, a Ballanc'd Trade,
ts encourag'd, Manufactors cherish'd,
bonds, Walkers, Drones, and swarming Braves,
Froth of States, scumm'd from the Commonwealth,
e's banish'd, all Excess repress'd,
Riots check'd by Sumptuary Laws.
Conscript Fathers! 'Tis on these Foundations
*Rome* shall build her Empire to the Stars,
her Command is with her Armies forth,
ame the World, and give the Nations Law;
uls, Proconsuls, who to the Capitol
ride upon the Necks of Conquer'd Kings,
when they dye, mount from the gorgeous Pile
ames of Spice, and mingle with the Gods.
*r* Excellent *Brutus*! All the Senate thanks thee,
says that thou thy self art half a God.

Sempronii, Teraminta, *with the rest of the Mourners*, Titus, Valerius, Junius.

*n.* Gone, gone, to Death! Already Sentenc'd! Doom'd

What, my *Tiberius* too! Ah, Barbarous *Brutus*!
Send, haste, revoke the order of their Fate
By all the Pledges of our Marriage Bed,
If thou, Inhuman Judge, hast left me one
To put thee yet in Mind thou art a Father,
Speak to him, Oh you Mothers of sad *Rome*,
Sisters and Daughters, ere the Execution
Of all your Blood, haste, haste, and run about him,
Groan, sob, howl out the Terrors of your Souls,
Nay, fly upon him like robb'd Savages,
And tear him from your Young.

*Brut.* Away, and leave me.

*Sem.* Or if you think it better for your Purpose,
Because he has the Pow'r of Life and Death,
Intreat him thus Throw all your Heartless Breasts
Low at his Feet, and like a God adore him,
Nay, make a Rampier round him with your Bodies,
And block him up I see he would be going,
Yet that's a Sign that our Complaints have mov'd him
Continu'd Falls of Ever-streaming Tears,
Such, and so many, and the chastest too
Of all the Pious Matrons throughout *Rome*,
Perhaps may melt this *Adamantine* Temper.
Not yet! Nay, hang your Bodies then upon him,
Some on his Arms, and some upon his Knees,
And lay this Innocent about his Neck,
This little smiling Image of his Father
See how he bends, and stretches to his Bosom!
Oh all you pitying Pow'rs, the Darling weeps,
His pretty Eyes, ruddy and wet with Tears,
Like two burst Cherries rowling in a Storm,
Plead for our Griefs more than a Thousand Tongues

*Jun.* Yes, yes, my Father will be good to us,
And spare my Brothers, Oh, I know he will:
Why, do you think he ever was in Earnest?
What, to cut off their Heads? I warrant you
He will not, no, he only meant to fright 'em,
As he will me, when I have done a Fault
Why, Mother, he has whipt 'em for't already,
And do you think he has the Heart to kill 'em?

, no, he would not cut their Little Fingers
all the World: Or if he should, I'm sure
e Gods would pay him for't.

*Brut* What hoa! Without there!
ves, Villains, Ha! are not my Orders heard?

*Ter* Oh *Brutus*, see, they are too well perform'd!
here the Bodies of the *Roman* Youth
headless by your Doom, and there *Tiberius*

*er* See, Si, behold, is not this horrid Slaughter,
is cutting off one Limb from your own Body,
not enough? Oh, will it not suffice
stop the Mouth of the most Bloody Law?
it were highest Sin to make a Doubt,
ask you now to save the Innocent *Titus*,
common Wish and general Petition
ll the *Roman* Senate, Matrons, Wives,
dows, and Babes; nay, e'en the madding People
out at last that Treason is reveng'd,
ask no more: Oh, therefore spare him, Sir!

*ut.* I must not hear you: Hark, *Valerius*

*er* By all these Wounds upon my Virgin Breast,
ich I have suffer'd by your Cruelty,
o' you promis'd *Titus* to defend me

*mp* Yet hold thy bloody Hand, Tyrannick *Brutus*,
I'll forgive thee for that headless Horror:
t me my *Titus*, oh in Death I ask thee
u hast already broke *Sempronia*'s Heart,
I will pardon that so *Titus* live
Cruel Judge! Thou pitiless Avenger!
t art thou whisp'ring? Speak the Horror out,
n thy glaring Eyes I read a Murder.

*ut* I charge thee by thy Oath, *Valerius*,
hou art here deputed by the Gods,
not a Subject for a Woman's Folly,
e him away, and drag him to the Ax.

*al* It shall be thus then, not the Hangman's Hand

[*Runs him through, the Women shriek.*

*t.* Oh bravely struck! thou hast hit me to the Earth
obly that I shall rebound to Heav'n,
re I will thank thee for this Gallant Wound.

[Semp *Sounds*

*Brut.*

*Brut.* Take hence this Woman; haste and bear [him]
Why, my *Valerius*, did'st thou rob my Justice? [hos
*Tit* I wrought him to it, Sir, that thus in Death
I might have leave to pay my last Obedience,
And beg your Blessing for the other World
*Ter.* Oh do not take it, *Titus*; whate'er comes
From such a monstrous Nature must be blasting
Ah, thou Inhuman Tyrant! But alas
I loiter here, when *Titus* stays for me:
Look here my Love, thou shalt not be before me.
[*Stabs her s*
Thus, to thy Arms then. Oh, make haste, my *Titus*,
I'm got already in the Grove of Death;
The Heav'n is all benighted, not one Star
To light us through the dark and pathless Maze.
I have lost thy Spirit, Oh, I grope about
But cannot find thee. Now I sink in Shadows [Di
*Tit* I come, thou matchless Virtue Oh my Heart!
Farewel my Love, we'll meet in Heav'n again
My Lord, I hope you Justice is aton'd;
I hope the Glorious Libert of *Rome*,
Thus water'd by the Blood of both your Sons,
Will get Imperial Growth, and flourish long
*Brut* Thou hast so nobly born thy self in dying,
That not to bless thee were to curse my self,
Therefore I give thee thus my last Embrace,
Print this last Kiss upon thy trembling Lips.
And ere thou goest I beg thee to report me
To the great Shades of *Romulus* and *Numa*,
Just with that Majesty and rugged Virtue
Which they inspir'd, and which the World has seen
So, for I see thou'rt gone, farewel for ever.
Eternal *Jove*, the King of Gods and Men,
Reward and Crown thee in the other World
*Tit* What Happiness has Life to equal this?
By all the Gods I would not live again,
For what can *Jove*, or all the Gods give more,
To fall thus Crown'd with Virtue's fullest Charms,
And die thus blest in such a Father's Arms? [D
*Val* He's gone, the gallant Spirit's fled for ever
How fares this Noble Vessel, that is robb'd

f all its Wealth, ſpoil'd of its topmoſt Glory,
nd now lyes floating in this World of Ruin?
*Brut.* Peace, Conſul, Peace, let us not ſoil the Pomp
f this Majeſtick Fate with Womans Brawls.
ncel Fathers, Friends, kneel all you *Roman* People,
uſh'd as dead Calms, while I conceive a Pray'r
hat ſhall be worthy *Rome*, and worthy *Jove*
*Val.* Inſpire him, Gods, and thou, oh *Rome*, attend.
*Brut.* Let Heav'n and Earth for ever keep their Bound,
e Stars unſhaken go their conſtant Round,
harmleſs Labour be our Steel employ'd,
d endleſs Peace through all the World enjoy'd.
t every Bark the Waves in Safety plough,
angry Tempeſt curl the Ocean's Brow;
darted Flames from Heav'n make Mortals fear,
Thunder fright the weeping Paſſenger,
not poor Swains for Storms at Harveſt mourn,
ſmile to ſee their Hoards of bladed Corn:
dreadful Comets threaten from the Skies,
Venom fall, nor poys'nous Vapours riſe:
u *Jove*, who doſt the Fates of Empires doom,
rd and defend the Liberty of *Rome*.

---

# EPILOGUE.

Spoken by Mrs *Barrey*.

*O Cringing Sirs, the Poet's Champion I*
*Have ſworn to ſtand, and ev'ry Judge defie,*
*hy each Bullying Critick ſhou'd I name*
*dge, whoſe only Buſineſs is to damn?*
*you your Arbitrary Fiſt advance*
*it, and duſt it like a Boor of* France,
*without ſhow of Reaſon or Pretence*
*mn a Man to die for ſpeaking Senſe,*
*er we term'd you once the Wiſe, the Strong,*
*we have born your Impotence too long,*

# EPILOGUE.

*You that above your Sizes presume to soar,*
*And are but Copies dawb'd in Miniature;*
*You that have nothing right in Heart nor Tongue,*
*But only to be resolute in Wrong*
*Who Sense affect with such an aukward Air,*
*As if a* Frenchman *should become severe,*
*Or an* Italian *make his Wife a Jest,*
*Like* Spaniards *pleasant, or like* Dutchmen *drest,*
*That rank the Noblest Poets with the Vile,*
*And look your selves in a* Plebeian *Stile,*
*But with an Oath———————*
*False as your Wit and Judgment now I swear,*
*By the known Maidenheads of each Theatre,*
*Nay, by my own, the Poets shall not stand,*
*Like* Shrovetide *Cocks, the Palt of every Hand.*
*Let not the Purblind Critick's Sentence pass,*
*That shoots the Poet through an Optick Glass,*
*No Peals of ill-plac'd Praise from Galleries come,*
*Nor Punk below to Clap or Hiss presume,*
*Let her not Cackle at the Fops that Flout her,*
*Nor Cluck the Squires that use to Pipp about her,*
*No full-blown Blockhead, bloated, like an Ox,*
*Traverse the Pit with Damme, what a Pox,*
*Know then for ev'ry Misdemeanor here*
*I'll be more Stabbing, Sharp, and more Severe,*
*Than the Fell-she that on her Keeper comes,*
*Who in his Drink last Night laid waste her Rooms,*
*Thunder'd her China, damn'd her Quality,*
*Her Glasses broke, and tore her Point Venice;*
*That dragg'd her by the Hair, and broke her Head,*
*A Chamber Lion, but a Lamb in Bed,*
*Like her I'll teize you for your Midnight storming,*
*For your all talking, and your no performing*
*You that with monstrous Judgment force the Stage,*
*To the fribling, fumbling Keepers of the Age.*

# CONSTANTINE

THE

# GREAT;

A

# TRAGEDY.

Printed in the YEAR 1712.

# PROLOGUE.

## *Spoken by Mr.* Goodman.

*WHAT think ye meant wise Providence, when first*
Poets *were made? I'd tell you, if I durst,*
*That 'twas in Contradiction to Heav'ns Word,*
*That when its Spirit o'er the Waters stir'd,*
*When it saw All, and said That All was good,*
*The Creature* Poet *was not understood.*
*For, were it worth the Pains of six long Days,*
*To mould Retailers of dull Third-Day Plays,*
*That starve out Threescore Years in hopes of Bays?*
*'Tis plain they ne'er were of the first Creation,*
*But came by meer Equiv'cal Generation.*
*Like Rats in Ships, without Coition bred;*
*As hated too as they are, and unfed.*
*Nature their Species sure must needs disown,*
*Scarce knowing* Poets, *less by* Poets *known.*
*Yet this poor Thing, so scorn'd, and set at nought,*
*We all pretend to, and would fain be thought.*
*Disabl'd wasting* Whore-Masters *are not*
*Prouder to own the Brats they never got,*
*Than Fumbling, Itching Rhimers of the Town,*
*T' adopt some base-born Song that's not their own.*
*Spite of his State,* My Lord *sometimes descends,*
*To please the Importunity of Friends.*
*The dullest he thought most for Business fit,*
*Will venture his bought Place, to aim at Wit,*
*And though he sinks with his Imploys of State,*
*Till Common Sense forsake him, he'll Translate.*
*The* Poet *and the* Whore *alike complains,*
*Of trading Quality, that spoils their Gains;*
*The Lords will Write, and Ladies will have Swains.*
*Therefore, all you who have Male Issue born,*
*Under the Starving Sign of* Capricorn;
*Prevent the Malice of their Stars in time,*
*And warn them early from the Sin of Rhime:*
*Tell 'em how* Spencer *starv'd, how* Cowley *mourn'd,*
*How* Butler's *Faith and Service was return'd;*

*And if ſuch Warning they refuſe to take,*
*This laſt Experiment, O Parents! make:*
*With Hands behind them ſee th' Offender ty'd,*
*The Pariſh Whip, and Beadle by his ſide*
*Then lead him to ſome Stall that does expoſe*
*The Authors he loves moſt, there rub his Noſe;*
*Till like a Spaniel laſh'd, to know Command,*
*He by the due Correction underſtand,*
*To keep his Brains clean, and not foul the Land.*
*Till he againſt his Nature learn to ſtrive,*
*And get the Knack of Dullneſs how to thrive.*

---

# Dramatis Perſonæ.

## MEN.

| | |
|---|---|
| Conſtantine, | Mr. *Smith.* |
| Dalmatius, | Mr *Griffin.* |
| Criſpus, | Mr. *Betterton.* |
| Annibal, | Mr. *Goodman.* |
| Lycinius, | Mr. *Wiltſhire.* |
| Arius, | Mr. *Gillo.* |
| Labienus, | Mr *Perin* |
| Eubolus, | Mr *Saunders* |
| Sylveſter, | Mr. *Bowman* |

## WOMEN.

| | |
|---|---|
| Fauſta, | Mrs. *Barrey.* |
| Serena, | Mrs. *Cook.* |

*Angels, Prieſts, Guards, and Attendants.*

# Constantine *the Great*.

## ACT I. SCENE I.

*Constantine sleeping in a Pavilion,* Silvester *standing at distance, two Angels descend with Banners in their Hands.*

This Motto, *In hoc signo vince,* writ in Gold.

1 *Ang* Sing.

AWake · O *Constantine*! awake;
Or in thy Sleep the Prospect take·
Here in this hallow'd streaming Gold,
The Prospect of thy Life behold.
This Emblem of a bleeding Love,
Shall both thy Cross and Triumph prove.
For, alas! 'tis decreed by the Heav'nly Doom,
To purge thy past Crimes, there's a Torment to come.

2 *Ang* Yet, after the Storm, believe in me,
No more disturb'd thy Thoughts shall be,
But all Serene as a breathless Sea.

*Chor* And still thy Handmaid Victory,
Where-e'er thou go'st, shall wait on thee;
And all shall end in Harmony.

3 *Ang speaks.* Awake, and ponder the Celestial Song;
Thy vow'd Conversion is delay'd too long.
Awake, remember the Celestial Doom,
That threaten'd Torments, and a Cross to come.
Yet after all the Menaces of Fate,

Be waſh'd: And Calms ſhall on thoſe Tempeſts wait:
For true Repentance never comes too late. [*Angels aſcend.*
Conſtantine *awakes.*

*Conſt.* Stay! I adjure you, by the Holy Name
That bows your Airy Heads, I charge you ſtay
They're gone, thoſe Beauteous Legates of the Skies,
And left me puzling here to die in doubt
Unleſs *Silveſter* guide me with a Clew,
Through the dark Mazes of this folding Dream

*Silv.* To purge your paſt Crimes, there's a Torment,
Ay, there the Torment too repeated thrice. [con

*Conſt.* But ſay, what Torment?

*Silv.* A dangerous Torment, govern'd by ill Stars
Which were I Emperor ſhould be ſoon prevented.

*Conſt.* By Heav'n it ſhall by me

*Silv.* You muſt not ſwear,
Leſt you ſhou'd be forſworn.

*Conſt.* If Heav'n require
My Life as an Atonement for my Sins,
Lead to the Altar, Saint, and I will bleed.

*Silv.* I dare believe you would: But this is more.

*Conſt.* More than my Life? Why, then 'tis Reputation
But I have learnt in Chriſtian Schools to lay
My Honour down, and own my ſelf a Worm.
To waſh the Pilgrims Feet, to bid the Saints
Tread on this Earth, this traſh, this heap of Sin.

*Silv.* But there's a Boſom Foe to conquer yet,
And there's my fear.

*Conſt.* Your fear, my Saint, after what I have ſaid

*Silv.* My fear, my Emperor, though you had ſworn

*Conſt.* Had I a Race of Sons like *Criſpus* dear,
Hope of my Vows, my Soldier and my Love,
Early Renown'd, and Pious from the Womb;
Yet were my Bowels Foes to that Religion,
Whoſe Infant growth I water'd with my Blood,
I ſwear by Heav'n, they ſhould be mine no more

*Silv.* Your Son's the Angels care, and when he dies
The foremoſt of the Quire ſhall meet him with a Crown
But have you not a Wife?

*Conſt.* You know I had

dear one, and by much my better Part.

*Silv.* But hav you not another?

*Const.* When she dy'd,

] Beauty fled with her.

*Silv.* This Beauty lives:

n you deny a Truth?

*Const.* *Silvester*, why,

hy dost thou press me thus, to my Confusion?

*Silv.* Because this Beauty, Sir, may bring Confusion.

*Const.* Large as an Angel's Knowledge be your own,

d at one View receive whole Nature in,

t if you tax my Choice with least Dishonour,

must declare you wrong her.

*Silv.* Then you are at least contracted to *Maximinus* [Daughter:

Heathen born?

*Const.* But bred a *Cherubin*,

has all the Beauties of her Sex below,

d equal Virtues with the blest above.

*Silv.* Dares *Constantine*, the Christian so Renown'd,

this to me?

*Const.* Dares any Saint deny't?

*Silv.* That *Fausta* is not Guilty!

*Const.* Ha! of what?

*Silv.* Of all the Ills that shall attend your Life,

all——

*Const.* Hold, hold——lest I fall out with Heav'n.

*Silv.* Of all the Blots, that shall in After-Times

in your white Character, and blast your Fame;

hile weeping Readers shall lament your Story.

erefore away with her.

*Const.* First, let me die.

*urious* Heav'n, and oh! thou niggard Saint,

I not offer you my Darling Son,

th all my Race, as Victims to your Shrines,

hey were guilty in a Point of Faith,

wash their Heresies with Royal Blood?

l do you grudge me one, but one poor Pleasure,

all the Pains of my Unwearied Wars?

'n take my Life, take Empire, Glory, all,

e all I offer'd this Ungrateful Priest,

Who

Who in requital will allow me nothing
*Silv* Forgive me, Heav'n! my too officious Care,
For interposing in thy dark Decrees
In Christian Patience he is yet but young
Chastise him now. And make the Tryal strong.
*Const* What have I said, that I am past Forgiveness
Your Silence argues me undone for ever
Yet think me not so lost in desperate Love,
But while offending I can kneel for Pardon.
*Silv* What I have offer'd to your Choice,
Was not Commission'd me to say from Heav'n,
Therefore the Pardon must be mutual
All I have urg'd was but a thoughtful boding.
No more of that; be happy in your Love.
*Const* Oh! you have charm'd me into Life again,
And fear not but she shall become a Christian,
I must confess, that yet she is a Heathen,
As such I lov'd her, in her Father's Court,
Where first we plighted Vows in *Arius* Hands
But the dark Contract was so close contriv'd,
I wonder how you reach'd the Truth so soon.
But Heav'n reveal'd it, or you cou'd not know it;
Since I may swear, she is not yet enjoy'd
*Silv* By you!
*Const* By me? Your Answer's short and home
Who shou'd possess her else?
*Silv* Young and a Heathen?
Left in the Sensual *Maximinian*'s Court?
*Const* No, Sir; she's guarded, and secure at Rome
*Crispus*, not yet acquainted with our Contract,
Is sent in show, for I had other purpose,
To make his Judgment of my *Fausta*'s Person,
Whether to be preserv'd, or like her Father,
To hinder Insurrections, be destroy'd
But hark! What March is this? Perhaps 'tis he!
And these his Trumpets, with the Legions Rais'd
[*Trumpets* within.

*Enter* Arius, *and* Eubolus.

*Both.* Long live the Emperor.
*Const.* Is *Crispus* come,

th those Auxiliar Legions we requir'd,
Mony sent to pay the last Arrears?
*rt.* Nothing obey'd: When first your Orders came,
ich by your Brother were in the *Forum* read,
ver saw so sudden a Revolt
once they cry'd, Our Liberty's betray'd,
Courts of Justice robb'd; Old Rights infring'd;
Gods must down, our Shrines and Temples burn:
all for a Phantastick Old Wives Tale;
ross they cry'd, one of *Silvester*'s Lies,
ich never yet was seen by waking Eyes,
either feign'd, or dreamt of in the Skies.
*nst.* Is this their Answer to my strict Commands?
*n Crispus* by this return'd to join your Brother;
en straight some Devil whisper'd in their Ears,
r Son already had begun the Change,
Statue of *Apollo* was pull'd down,
make his Father's Place Whereon they cry'd
Image should be burnt, and with a Breath
Cockle, and the Corn, bow'd all that way.
*b* But were reversed by a more powerful Gale,
Brother and your Son appear'd like Gods,
stopt the Madmen in their full Career.
*t* At close of Day, in dark Cabals they met,
in the Morning gave their final Answer,
*us,* who that Night was brought a Captive,
race the Triumph of your first Appearance,
first propos'd to share th' Imperial Power
they demand a general Persecution
l the Christians, and *Silvester*'s Head.
*st* Tell 'em their City shall be Ashes first
l for this, with hazard of my Life,
redeem'd 'em from their Tyrants Racks,
all their Streets were but one hideous Grave;
Wives and Daughters ravisht in their View?
Age was drain'd of its last ebbing Drop,
Babes were snatch'd their earliest Breath to give,
y'd ere knowing what it was to live

*Trumpets* ——*Enter* Dalmatius.

Treason——*Arms,* or do the Slaves repent?

My

My Brother here Still to my Arms, and Heart,
Thou Nerve of all my Wars: How fares my Friend,
And my beloved?

*Dalm* *Crispus*, our Care, is well.
And the late Tempest, which must reach your Ear,
By skilful Pilots rockt into a Calm.
Believe me Sir, your Presence gains the Cause,
Therefore upon the Instant march to *Rome*,
Vanquish'd *Licinius* waits to grace your Triumph.
Bless me! Is't possible? *Arius* with you, Sir?
*Arius* the Traitor?

*Const* Have you found him so?

*Dalm* The subtlest Snake, the softest Civil Vill[ain]
That ever warm'd himself in Prince's Bosom,
Diseases, Blasts, Plagues, Death and Hell are in h[is]
What e'er his Outside seems: This shameless Trait[or]
Was the foul Spring of all these poison'd Water[s],
That late had like to overflow the Empire,
Yet while his Emissaries fired the People,
This *Judas* on my side appear'd an Angel:
For after the first Mutiny was quell'd,
Though he had sworn to justifie your Cause,
He warn'd the Slaves, I have his Hand to show,
Next Day to make those Impudent Demands

*Ari* Plots on my Innocence; as I am a Christi[an]
If e'er I set my Hand to such a Treason,
May these rot off, which thus I hold to Heav'n
As I am of Priestly Order——

*Dalm* A Devil ordain'd——
Sir, if I do not prove him——

*Const* I believe you,
I know him Heretick, a seditious Traitor,
But yet have Reasons to defer his Ruin,
Therefore no more at present. *Arius* hence,
And let me hear no further of these Mischiefs
I have pardon'd you, be gone you *Eubulus*, and [. . .]
I come Embattel'd now for my Revenge, [Re[. . .]
My Standard, and my Banners, bear the Cross
Tell 'em *Lycinius*, whom once before
I took to Grace, and marry'd to my Sister,
Their new Petition'd *Cæsar*, soon shall bleed.

*lv* Forgive your Enemies.

*onst.* But not my Friends.

*nius* was my Friend, and has betray'd me,
erefore I'll execute him in their View.
ay and warn him, for the Doom that's given.

[*Ex.* Arius, Eubulus.

not by halfs that we will worship Heav'n.
, my *Dalmatius*, I have made a Vow,
e *Romans*, or their Emperor shall bow.
ey're Subjects, and 'tis fit Nay, bow they shall,
*Cæsar* in th' Attempt their Victim fall,
to the Man, whom Heav'n ordain'd for Sway,
in his great Vicegerent learn their Maker to obey

[*Exeunt*

## SCENE II. *Rome. Constantine's* Palace.

*Enter* Lycinius, Labienus.

*abi.* The Mischief's ripe, and ready for our wish:
nfusion to the House of *Constantine*,
Fortune points their Fate. For mark the Method:
Father sends the Son to see the Prisoner,
Son, not knowing of his Father's Contract,
ears a God to *Fausta*'s charming Eyes,
marry'd her.

*ycin* How came you by the Secret? [the Son,

*abi* *Arius* told me, he who betroth'd the Father weds
stands for ever bound to serve *Lycinius*

*ycin.* He's voted Heretick among the Christians.

*abi* No matter what they vote him, Sir; He's yours,
Foe to all Religion, but his Friends.

*ycin* By *Mars*, he falls the righter to my Purpose
as my self bred up in Blood and Wars,
aught, and Scoft at by these Civil Cowards,
erefore I hate Religion, Arts and Learning,
if I ever Mount the *Cæsar*'s Throne,
raise another General Persecution,
e *Nero*, Bait these Christian Dogs to Death,
build the Temples of the Old Gods again.

*Labi.*

*Labi.* And be a God your self: In the mean time,
Let your Wife's Tears prevail upon your Temper,
Supple your haughty Spirit, bow your Body,
Low as the Earth, before the Emperor's Feet.

*Lycin* I had rather die If he thinks fit to save me,
'Tis well, if not, why let him take my Head

*Labi* Yet for the sake of those whom you must govern
Rebate this Martial Fire, and hear your Wife:
Hear what Return our long'd-for *Arius* brings.

*Enter* Crispus, *with* Annibal

But soft! the Bridegroom *Crispus* and his Friend
*Constantia* with Impatience waits your coming,
*Constantia*, who has Power to save your Head,
Though *Cæsar* with an Oath had doom'd you Dead,

[*Ex.* Lycinius, Labienus

*Crisp* How *Annibal*! What! out of Temper now?
When Crowns are offer'd, and the *Cæsar*'s Purple?
What, though not born in the immediate Way?
Yet thou art Collaterally Great as I
And if I ever Heir this spacious Empire,
By Heav'n, thou shalt not share, but guide, engross
My Heart's best Love, and all the World beside

*Annib.* Your Heart? Ay there you eccho'd my Desire
Enrich me there, and trowle your empy Globe
To those crown'd Slaves, that know no other Greatness
But tell me, O my *Crispus*! all Mens Joy,
Tell me, and truly from thy generous Soul,
Hast thou a Friend whom more thou lov'st than me?

*Crisp* Not more belov'd, more fonded than my Friend,
But more——————

*Annib* Nay add not to that broken Truth,
There's more in that, no more, than thou had'st Sr.

*Crisp* Wilt thou not hear me out?

*Annib.* There needs no more;
Thou art no Friend, that lov'st another more·
Nay half so much But now I find that all
The former Flatteries of thy glozing Friendship
Were Courtiers Promises, and Womens Vows.
But let me know his Name.

*Crisp.* Thy Father, *Annibal*, my Godlike Friend,
*lmatius*, who before thou could'st write Man,
ugg'd *Crispus* to his Heart: Like Lambs in Peace
gether we lay down, together rose,
Wa like Lions, coupled on a side;
e yet thy Infant Arms a Sword could wield,
d drove like Herds the Nations from the Field.

*Annib.* Why then we're Friends again, more fast than
t since we have happen'd into this Disorder, [ever.
make a Tryal of renew'd Affection,
put thee to the Test.

*Crisp.* Name the Danger, [thee.
ough Kin to Death, my Arm, young Man, shall right

*Annib.* 'Tis Death indeed Most certain Death to me,
nless thy softning Charms have Pow'r to save me

*Crisp.* Speak his close Grief, that wrings thee with the
am not Eloquent in such a Cause, [Anguish:
t out my Tongue.

*Annib.* My Life is in the Hands
one that hates me, or, what wounds me more,
one, my *Crispus*, that can never love me. [that?

*Crisp.* Not love thee? O ye Powers! What Heart is

*Annib.* Hast thou not seen the beauteous Prisoners?

*Crisp.* Ha!
hat, *Fausta* mean'st thou?

*Annib.* *Fausta* and *Serena.* [thee?

*Crisp.* Say which of 'em? which Beauty has Inflam'd

*Annib.* Which shou'd, but the most soft and artless
e Languishing—— [Melter?

*Crisp.* The killing Beauteous——Come——

*Annib.* Ha! *Crispus* thou art concern'd!

*Crisp.* I am to help thee——
Name?

*Annib.* Why take it then, the Fair *Serena.*

*Crisp.* O she's the softest, sweetest, killing Fair.
Heav'n — I am glad——I'm ravisht that 'tis she!
his Embrace I promise thee Success,
now her Temper well——No more, but leave me.
as upon the Instant when I met thee,
ing to their Apartment,——Nay look up——
trust thy Friend.

*Annib.*

*Annib.* Plead then for my Life,
I beg thee as a God to plead my Cause;
Thou canst not know o'th' sudden how 'tis with me,
How great, how mortal, and how deep the Wound.
May all the Saints, and Powers that pity Love,
Inspire thy Breast, as if twere possible
That *Annibal*'s Soul cou'd actuate thy Body.
So sigh, weep, languish, and for Mercy sue,
As were I *Crispus*, I my self wou'd do. [*Ex.* Ann.
*Crisp.* The Youth is haughty, martial, hot and b...
Right for the Field, unhappy parts for Love.
Therefore perhaps the Virgin likes him not
But thou hast luckier Stars. No sooner seen [Transp.
But lik'd——Lov'd, Marry'd——Ha!——but where...
Without thy Father's Knowledge thou wert marry'd.
'Tis the first Fault of my unhappy Youth,
Yet tis a Fault——but 'tis the Fault of Love.
Had he not lov'd, *Crispus* had not been here,
Away, you Damps, and darkning Images,
Be gone I say——Behold she comes to meet me;

*Enter* Fausta

Last as I am, in this great Race of Love——
O *Fausta*, *Fausta*!
*Faust* O my *Constantine*!
*Crisp* Ha!
*Faust.* A Mistake, my Fear out-went my Love
*Crisp* My *Constantine*! Thy Fear——By Heav'n't
What Cause hast thou to fear? [Comm...
*Faust* Bondage and Death.
Are not those Reasons for a Virgin's Fear?
*Crisp* Yes for another, *Fausta*, not for thine.
For oh! when he has seen and heard, like me,
Th' Abstracted Charms of all this beauteous World,
Expect not Death, but Offers of a Throne
*Faust* 'Tis possible Yet by thy self I swear,
By dear lov'd thee, my *Crispus* in a Cottage
Shall be prefer'd to all the Thrones on Earth
*Crisp* And thou, forgive me Heav'n! I had almost...
To Heav'n it self No *Fausta*, that's the Jar,
Religion makes this Discord in my Soul
I find it now Hence come my Starts and Fears,

L

en in the height of my expected Joys,
t Time, the Saints and Miracles must win thee.

*Faust* No Time, no Miracle, no Saint but thou:
h, thou art all the Wonders of the Earth,
Saint, my Heart's Religion, and my Heav'n;
ith thee I am imbarkt to live or perish,
t only here but in the World hereafter.

*Crisp* O Extacy! Oh Pattern for thy Sex.
shalt thou Master me by this Subjection.
e me thy Hand. Thy Lip——the Sweets are richer,
e Taste enobled. Oh! my ravisht Love [open'd;
ws with the pointed Charms. The Heav'ns are
I behold thee Crown'd a Saint already
I will hold thee fast, lest that the Angels snatch thee
we have mingled Souls——

*Faust* Oh not to Night!

*Crisp* Ha! not to Night? Not on this lov'd Confession?
when thou hast set my Spirits all on fire?
now enjoy thee? Thou mak'st my Fears return,
more extravagant than they were before,
ere we join an Apoplex shou'd seize me,
Palace fall, and thousand other Chances,
t awe th' Imagination of my Love.
come——

*Faust* I will, and with these longing Arms
thee 'til Morn: And from that Morn 'till Evening:
n Evening to Mid-day: From Day to Night:
n Night to Death——I'll clasp thee thus for ever.

*Crisp* Let's haste then, while the beckning Minute

*Faust* But I must swear thee first. [smiles.

*Crisp* Take Oath on Oath.
ear to obey thee without asking why.

*Faust.* Swear thou wilt never leave thy wedded *Fausta*,
t ever dreadful Chance, or strange Misfortune,
'd start to undo me, almost to a Crime. [Heav'n,

*Crisp* No Crime, but want of Love Nor that, by
make me hate thee, though it bring me Death.
hou soft Death! if ever I forsake thee,
y last hour may I despair of Mercy;
may those Saints, that knew the Wrong I did thee,

When at Heav'ns Gate I beg for Entrance, answer,
Remember what thou didst to *Fausta* swear:
Be gone, for ever leave this happy Sphere,
For perjur'd Lovers have no Mansion here.
[*Exeu*

## ACT II. SCENE I.

### SCENE *Rome*.

*Enter* Arius, Labienus, *and* Eubolus.

*Ari.* WE have done our Work by halfs, follo
by the Scent,
Trac'd to our Holes! Oh I could play the Mad ma
Men of our Make so poorly hide a Murder,
That Dogs can rake it up Spies, Spies by Hell!
The Course of former Councils was too slow,
I am proclaim'd a Traitor, Heretick,
And Poniards must proclaim my Accuser nothing.
*Labi.* Were it not better to comply?
*Ari.* Impossible!
The Genius of the proud Imperial Brothers
And mine, by Nature mortally oppos'd,
Hate strongly at first sight, which Hate improv'd,
By the late flaw I found in their Religion
They hear too how I tainted Infant *Julian*.
Yet being made the Emperor's Confident
In the late Contract, all might have been retriev'd,
And I at Helm, had not his hated Brother
Thus interpos'd to my eternal Ruin——
Poison and Poniard——
*Eub* Is it come to that?
*Ari.* It is; without dispatch, we are all undone.
Oh for a Slave to mould, some Malecontent,
His Blood adust, and blackned with the Blows
Of adverse Fortune; yet of Soul elate,
And to be flush'd for Fame, or Hire,
To any kind of daring!

*Labi.* Why?

*Ar.* I would work the Melancholy Brave
o stab *Dalmatius.*

*Eub.* Why not *Constantine*?

*Ar* Because ten *Constantines* live at least in him;
he one's not half so open to Destruction,
t'other close, and on the Guard to save him,
has unravell'd our close Web of Thought,
d from the bottom of our dark Design
rawn Treason forth, perhaps to hang us all

*Lab.* 'Tis justly thought, this Lett must be remov'd;
d who so fit to hew it into pieces
that ambitious, brawny Fool, *Lycinius*?

*Ar.* Thou hast hit the Man my busie Brain had lost.
e Emperor dooms him dead; By whose Advice?
l me, I hear the dull *Lycinius* cry,
at ere I fall the Victim of the War,
ay at once destroy his Life and Name.

*Enter* Lycinius. *Guards.*

see he comes! I bring you News.

*Lycin* Ha! of my Death! I read it in thy Face.

*Ar* The Emperor, as at first I told your Story,
clin'd to Mercy: But fierce *Dalmatius*
peal'd the hint of your half granted Pardon,
forc'd him to your Death.

*ycin* By *Mars* I'll fight him.

*r* 'Tis not in your Power,
're Pris'ner of War

*ycin* Yet I may Curse
Tongue is not their Prisoner; therefore I'll curse,
erly curse *Dalmatius*, curse 'em all.

*r* Curse for the loss of Empire, and of Life!
rly curse! Why Whores will there out-do you.
sh to think the great *Lycinius*
uld e'er be brought in such Comparison!
uld it not seem more worthy your past Honour
trike than say? Strike, if I may advise,
ere you suffer.——

*cin.* Kill *Dalmatius*,
*ntine*, *Crispus*, *Annibal*, nay all,——

Quite root up all th' Imperial Stock at once:

*Ari.* This Dagger then be yours; the Legacy
Of an old Prophetess, who dying, told me,
He that had Courage to employ it well,
And where it ought, should make himself the Greatest.
[*Trumpet at distance*

*Lycin.* It shall be well employ'd, and where it ought.
But hark! the Emperor comes!

*Ari* Rather *Dalmatius*,
Perhaps commission'd for your Execution!

*Lycin.* Why then I'll forth and meet him. By the Fates
If I must fall, he shall not live to laugh:
And in remembrance of this solemn Oath,
I kiss the ominous Gift thou hast bequeath'd me;
I'll treasure it next my Heart, where it shall rest,
Till sheath'd by Vengeance in *Dalmatius*' Breast
[*Ex*

*Ari.* Or live or die, thou art contriv'd for Mischief
Next I must mend the Heresies I've broach'd,
And reconcile my self, by some bold Offer,
With *Constantine*; which while I undertake,
Be it your Care to spread th' old poisonous Doctrine:
Sow it in all Habits, Persons, Forms, and Places,
Grow with the Times, and cultivate Sedition.

*Enter* Serena.

My fair Devotess,—— but hence, as I have order'd,
And meet me at the Trial of *Lycinius*.
[*Ex* Labi *and* Eu

*Seren* The Morning's come, and fain I would have rest
Who all the Night have wak'd upon my Pillow,
And made it wet with Tears · My solitary Groans,
That pierc'd Heav'ns Vaults (tho' Heav'n was deaf,
Deaf to redress) have made my Breast so sore [*wh*
That I can sigh no longer.
*Crispus* and *Fausta*! Oh you happy Lovers!
Not so with you the gladsome Minutes past:
For, ere 'twas Day, I left my tedious Bed,
And listen'd to your Joys.

*Ari.* Her Sorrows lull me,
And I grow good, I know not how, o' th' sudden.

*Seren* Such soft Expressions flow'd from the charming
did but aggravate my Passion more; [*Crispus,*
t hide it, O *Serena!* though thou diest,
ll it to none, but to the midnight Groves,
e Flocks and Streams, and those unhappy Stars
hose merciless Fires thus fated thy undoing.
*Ari.* What! not to *Arius!* to thy Confessor;
him who has a Privilege from Heav'n?
*Seren.* Oh *Arius!* would I had the Power to hide it;
t you have heard it all;
d will, perhaps, proclaim a Virgin's Frailty.
, Sir, I shall not long survive my Shame:
d since 'tis known, confess it to the World;
nfess, that Passion has dethron'd my Reason;
at unbelov'd, I love the best of Men,
d sigh unheard, and without Witness mourn,
d dote to Death without the least Return
*Ari.* 'Tis said, young *Annibal* is vow'd your Servant.
*Seren* O *Arius!* mark the Malice of our Fates!
at Prince loves me, as *Crispus* is belov'd,
d failing in his Suit, employ'd his Friend
plead his Cause! Oh had it been his own!——
t all my Pray'rs, alas! are now in vain,
d wanting *Crispus,* I must wed my Grave.
erefore I beg you, Sir, procure his Picture
entertain my melancholy Thoughts,
ce him himself I ne'er must see again.
*Ari* That, and all Helps which *Arius* can command.
*Seren* I thank you Sir, by the blest Saints I do,
hank you for this Favour, from my Heart.
t hark! they come! *Crispus* and *Fausta* come!
Heart! why dost thou leap against my Bosom
e a Cag'd Bird, and beat thy self to Death
r an impossible Freedom?
*Ari.* Stay to salute 'em.
*Seren.* No *Arius,* no, I cannot, dare not stand 'em.
t see, they come, wreath'd in each others Arms,
d mingling Kisses. Has not then the Night
n long enough, but you must love by Day?

Do *Fausta*, do, be stifled with the Joy.
Follow him from thy Chamber to the Grove,
To Garden haunts, and clasp him in the Bowers,
Thence to your golden Beds again; while I
Sink to my Grave, and there forgotten lye. [Ex.
*Art.* *Crispus* to Court *Serena* for his Friend!
His Picture! she shall have it—— Mischief! Hell!
And if it be thy Will thy Slave obeys.
*Crispus* and *Annibal*, that late were Friends,
Shall strait be Foes. But hush, the Lovers come.—
This Closet hides me to discover more.

*Enter* Crispus *and* Fausta.

This Closet be my School, to learn their Language.
*Faust* Your Father's Trumpets call you. Let 'em c[all]
You shall not go. Oh are there any Sounds
To charm, more powerful than your *Fausta*'s Cries?
*Crisp* No, not the Tongues of Angels! O best Jo[y]
Of my abounding Soul! What shall I call thee?
By Heav'n, thou art all Heav'n, all Paradise;
Talk not then of going from thee For I'll stay till A[ge]
Has Snow'd a hundred Winters on my Head,
Yet give and take Enjoyments then, as now.
*Faust.* And oh, for thee, thou dearest of the Wo[rld]
My Soul's best Life, and my Heart's grasp'd Desire,
Oh what Return! The Mother on her Throws,
After the Rack when hanging o'er her Babe,
With bleeding Joys, wild Looks, and earning Smiles,
Loves not her Darling more than I love *Crispus*.
Thou shalt not leave me, *Crispus*.
*Crisp* Yes, to meet again;
Our Loves approv'd by him that gave me Being,
And then——
*Faust* What then? He dooms me to that place,
Where in his Shrowd the poor *Maximian* lies,
Where I shall lye as I had never been,
Nor think of *Crispus* more.——
*Crisp.* Canst thou fear Death,
While I have Life?
*Faust.* Oh do not trust thy Father!
Trust not the Passions of a Conqueror;

or in his fatal Look, when last he left me,
omething I saw, that bid me fly his Presence;
y to the Verge of Earth, and leap the Bounds,
ather than ever meet his Eyes again

*Crisp* Thy Father's Fate makes thee mistrust thy own.

*Faust* No *Crispus*, not Mistrust, but certain Danger;
hich, like a moulding Promontory, hangs
ursting above our Heads; and threatens Death,
nless we House betimes, and scape the Fall.

*Crisp* What Danger? Death? What Fall?

*Faust.* Thy Father.

*Crisp* Ha!

*Faust* Thy Father, *Crispus*——

*Crisp* Knows not we are marry'd,
it shall, and will I hope forgive my Passion.

*Faust.* I dreamt last Night, thy Father was in Love;
love with me, my *Crispus*, catch'd us clasp'd,
nd with his Dagger stabb'd us in the fold.

*Crisp* Is't possible?

*Faust.* Most true

*Crisp* And catch'd thee with me?

*Faust* Catch'd us in Bed.

*Crisp.* There?

*Faust* Here. Why dost thou wonder?
was but a Dream.

*Crisp* Yet there is wonder in't,
cause, by Heav'n, I dreamt the very same.
it not strange?

*Faust* If it should happen true!

*Crisp.* That would be strange indeed.

*Faust.* Therefore let's fear the worst, and arm against [it,
or oh, why should I hide a Secret from thee?
hen I beheld him last, he languished,
nd wrung my Hand at parting.

*Crisp* But what said he?

*Faust* I will not tell you *Crispus*, till you answer
hat you would do with me, my dearest Joy,
it were true indeed, your Father lov'd me.

*Crisp.* What, at your parting? ha!

*Faust* Why if 'twere true,
Would you forsake me?

*Crisp* Be my own Murderer!
I know not what, but speak your parting. Oh!

*Faust*. Why are you so enrag'd? I dare not tell you [...]

*Crisp* If ought thou hid'st, by Heav'n thou dost not lo[...]

*Faust* By Heav'n! I hope no other Heav'n, but th[...]
What if he talk'd a little? Age will talk,
And think of it no more.

*Crisp* What was your Talk?
I'll know each Syllable

*Faust*. Why so you shall;
But then be Calm. What if he talk'd of Love?
And what? Oh be not angry and I'll tell you,
What if, to save my Life, I promis'd him?——

*Crisp* Ha! promis'd, *Fausta*?
Promise the Father, and engage the Son?
But speak, I stand upon a Precipice;
For if 'tis true, that e'er so little past
Of Love before——

*Faust*. What then?

*Crisp*. And thou hast promis'd?

*Faust* Suppose I have sworn.

*Crisp* Suppose then thy Dishonour:
Suppose me never to behold thee more;
Suppose my Death, both Soul and Body's Ruin.

*Faust*. Suppose no more, but what my Soul hath swo[...]
To love his Son, none but the lovely *Crispus*,
O therefore clear thy Brow, and take me to thee,
Be still my Love, forgive this little Fault,
And Jealousie shall ne'er offend thee more.

*Crisp* O Charmer! Beauty! what! where was the[...]
Why hast thou kept me on the Rack so long?
Tho' taken down, I feel the Strains upon me,
And shall, I fear, too long But hark they call, [*Trump*[...]
And I must go.

*Faust*. But will you then return?

*Crisp*. Quick as thy Wishes, or my own Desires,
But make no more such Tryal. Hark again [*Trumpets ag*[...]

*Faust*. I cannot part with you, tho' for a Mome[...]

*Crisp* I'll but enquire whether my Father's come.
*Faust* Swear to come back then, swear, before you see
give me one Look more. [him,
*Crisp.* What needs an Oath?
re I speak with him——
*Faust.* You'll speak with me,
r I have much to say of mighty moment;
ear therefore to return
*Crisp* Swear on thy Lips,
us with my Heart I seal my Vows for ever. [*Ex.*
*Faust* Heart and the holiest Vows deep writ in Blood;
ood and Dishonour Take then, take my Cause,
ou that hast made me sin, O mighty Love!
d let thy Mother plead it with her Tears:
sees his Father and my Crime at once,
d then resolves never to see me more.

*Enter* Arius.

*Ari* What then?
*Faust.* What then! O *Arius*, dost thou know me?
d ask what then, when he ne'er sees me more?
l tell thee then, I'll never see the Day
aces, Night and Death, Despair and Dungeons hold
hen those dear Eyes shall never light me more [me,
*Ari* Since you enjoy'd him, let the Tides of Love
swallow'd in the Ocean of Ambition.
*Faust* Ambition, Pomp, and Greatness of the World,
l empty sounds to Love! But thine's a downward Sense,
ou hast no Taste of these sublimer Joys
t haste! look out, Why comes he not again?
swore he would, but he has seen his Father!
ho stops him, with my first unhappy Contract.
*Ari* I see him yonder
*Faust* Blessings on thy Tongue;
t I'll run forth to meet him, and no longer
nceal the innocent Deceit of Love.
*Ari* Hold Madam, stay, *Dalmatius* comes; retire.
*Faust* *Dalmatius*! Let me see my self.
*Ari.* They come
*Faust* *Dalmatius*! Gods, 'tis he, he tells him all;
' Emperor told it him. Nay it must out,

I

I am lost, undone; But gentle *Arius*, wait,
And watch, and bring me word, how *Crispus* bears it;
Oh that I were a Spirit to stand unseen!
To mark his Passions how they rise and fall,
With every Glance of those dear, dreadful Eyes:
But see they come, and yet I cannot stir,
I grow distracted with my Hope and Fear,
Compell'd to go; yet long to tarry here. [*Ex.* Fau[sta.]

*Enter* Dalmatius *and* Crispus *to* Arius.

*Dalm.* I have much against you, *Crispus*, and you kn[ow it,]
Therefore with all the freedom of a Friend,
Tell me what is the Cause you have not been
So free as formerly.

*Crisp* You know I am.

*Dalm* I'll press you, Sir, no more; only remember
There stands a Villain, whom I have seen you whisp[er]
[*Ex.* Ar[ius.]

*Crisp.* I'll tell you all.

*Dalm* You dare not Come, there is a Guilt at bott[om]
You blush to own, a Crime of such a nature
As will admit no Pardon. Thou hast sinn'd
Against the great Divinity of Friendship;
Which my Soul takes to death.

*Crisp.* Can it be
Ever too late to gain a Pardon here?

*Dalm* I cannot tell, Yet I can tell thee this,
There was a time, not many days are past,
Since I preferr'd thy Friendship to the World,
When I cou'd say, Why yonder goes the Man,
Whom my Soul worships more than *Constantine*,
And loves beyond my Son By Heav'n thy Fault
Is ominous, and grinds my Temper through

*Crisp.* That Son you nam'd unhappily's in Love.

*Dalm.* Then he's a Fool With whom?

*Crisp* *Maximian*'s Daughter;
The younger Beauty.

*Dalm* Ha! And you Love the Elder:
My Life on't some such masterly design
This makes you shun the Camp, to lurk beneath
The Eves of Palaces, and droop in Corners.

t, Sir, your Pardon. I almost forgot
urge your swiftest Speed, to wait your Father.

*Crisp* I will but take my leave.

*Dalm* I fear there is
o much already taken, but no more——
ou have ought to say, I'll visit for you.——

*Crisp* Be all as you would have it! Oh your Hand,
y, I will force my Entrance to your Heart,
opening all my own, and so farewell. [*Ex* Crispus.

*Dalm* I blame my Friend for walking in the Dark,
hide my self, who when I seem most strange
fondest of his Love. So Sir, what now?

*Enter* Annibal.

*Annib* The fair *Constantia*, with condemn'd *Lycinius*,
elt in the saddest Glass of dying Sorrow,
s coming to entreat you for his Pardon;
soon as she had heard, from weeping *Arius*,
r Husband's doom, she in our Arms expir'd.

*Dalm* I mourn her Fate, But for *Lycinius*,
g'd at first, and still resolve, his Death
ecessary to the Emperor's Life.
r should a few weak drops, by Women shed,
a Decree so Absolute and Royal

*Annib* He comes attended with a mournful Crowd
lue for Life.

*Dalm* I'll have him executed in their View;
*Annibal*, and shew thy Youth a Pattern
the old *Romans*, for thy Imitation;
o hast but poorly copy'd from thy Father.

*Annib* Why Sir, What Villain has traduc'd my Virtue?

*Dalm* No Villain, but thy Prince has own'd thy
says thou lov'st a Captive Foe of *Rome* [Weakness;

*Annib* The Virgin's beautiful, and greatly born.

*Dalm* Perhaps the Virgin may as greatly die,
yield her Beauties to the Fatal Stroke.

*Annib.* To the Fatal Stroke! Oh all ye Powers!
Sir, the fair *Serena* shall not die
ile I wear this.

*Dalm.* Ha Rebel! Traitor! How!
at the Emperor's Doom?

*Annib.*

*Annib.* No nor at yours,
That gave me, Sir, my Being; take it again,
Unleſs you give me leave to lay it there,
Where I have plac'd my Love.

*Dalm.* The Emperor
Decrees thee *Cappadocia* Wilt thou forfeit
The noble Heritage of ſuch Ambition,
For Infamous Love?

*Annib.* Wrong not a Paſſion,
That equals your own Virtue For could *Cæſar*
Give with a Daughter of his own the World,
I would prefer my Love in this condition,
To all the proffers of his Blood and Empire.

*Dalm.* Hence from my ſight; and till thou brea[k]
See me no more. [this Paſſ[ion]

*Annib* Then I muſt never ſee you
For when I ceaſe to Love, where I have vow'd,
I am no more; therefore upon my Knees,
I beg you to recall this dreadful Sentence.
Repeal my Baniſhment, and give me leave
To win the Heart of this unhappy Maid,
Or bid me die before you.

*Dalm* Riſe my Boy,
Thou lov'ſt indeed, who canſt refuſe a Kingdom

*Enter* Arius, Lycinius, Labienus, Eubolus, *wit[h] the Populace.*

But ſee *Lycinius* with his Followers here;
Take to the habit of thy former Wars,
And ſoften not my Juſtice by thy Sorrows.

*Annib* I have heard *Lycinius* lately threatned yo[u]
Therefore your Guardian's Eye be watchful o'er yo[u]

*Dalm.* Fear not, I'm arm'd againſt 'em Know, *Lyci[nius]*
The Emperor has decreed to ſhew his Subjects
What weary'd Mercy dares reſolve to do.
*Cleanthes*, you the Captain of the Guard,
Lead to the *Forum*, and in the Peoples view
Strike off his Head.

*Lycin* I bear the Sentence as becomes my Honour
And all the favour which I beg in Death,
Is to reveal a Secret to your Ear,

Wi[th]

hich may import the Emperor's Life, and yours.

*Dalm* What would you, Sir?

*Lycin.* My Lord, are you in earneſt?
is there room for Hope?

*Dalm.* Sir, be not flatter'd·
pe is the fawning Traitor of the Mind,
hich while it cozens with a colour'd Friendſhip,
bs us of our laſt Virtue, Reſolution.

*Lycin.* Speak then the force of Reſolution—Thus.

*Annib.* No Villain—Thus.

[Annibal *diſarms and offers to Stab him.*

*Dalm.* Hold, *Annibal*! hold thy Hand.
Executioner in the beſt of Cauſes,
vile Trade for honourable Men,
erefore let Slaves diſpatch him.

*Annib.* Rack him firſt,
know who counſel'd him to this damn'd Deed.

*Dalm* No To *Sylveſter* let him own his Fault,
d die a Chriſtian; I am ſatisfy'd.

*Lycin* Ha ha!—A Chriſtian! What, and fall a Sheep?
nfeſs! No, as he urg'd, bring forth the Rack;
re draw my Limbs, ſpin all my Nerves like Hairs,
d work my tortur'd Fleſh as thin as Flame,
u ſhall not know a tittle more than this;
as ſet on to ſtab *Dalmatius*,
d would the Emperor, were he in my reach.
ho were the Gods that prompted thus my Arm,
u Chriſtian Curs ſhall never know from me,
erefore go learn the Myſtery in Hell
us much I may acquaint you, they are living,
arm in your Boſoms, and I hope will ſting you;
ng you to Death Plagues, Famine, Sword, and Fire;
e from the Gods on your proud City fall,
d with that dying Curſe I leave you all [ *Ex Guarded.*

*Dalm* His Fate was juſt Now *Romans* to the Triumph;
forth and meet your Emperor, whoſe Mercy
tends her peaceful Wings to all that ſeek him;
d is the darling Attribute of his Soul.
hark! He comes! the Saviour of your Empire;
ng forth his Statues; Crown his Images;

Meet

Meet him with Garlands, Songs, and Shouts of Trium[ph]
But ſee his Entrance is already made,
And there he comes, with *Criſpus* in his Arms

*Enter* Conſtantine, Criſpus, *&c to the Triumph.*

*Conſt.* *Dalmatius*, I muſt thank thee for the Fate
Of that too ſtubborn Troubler of our Reign·
*Sylveſter* to his Hermitage retires,
And ſays the Saints are ſad at my delay·
Tell him, ere long, and urge him to return,
The Emperor and the Court ſhall be baptiz'd. [mo[...]

*Dalm* Take to your former Freedom, Mirth and [...]
For 'tis obſerv'd you are not as you were.

*Conſt* Oh Brother' Friend! In all my Hazards try'[d]
This Son ſhall ſhare the Heart and Empire too
Of my lov'd *Criſpus*, whom for ſome few Minute[s]
I would diſcourſe alone.

*Dalm* Your Wiſhes on you;
Peace to your Thoughts, and Heav'n ſtill guide y[our]
Councils. [*Exit*

*Manent* Conſtantine, Criſpus.

*Conſt* Haſt thou perform'd thy Embaſſie, my *Cri[ſpus]*
And ſeen the Daughter of *Maximian?*

*Criſp.* I have ſeen her Sir; and ſeen her beauteous Siſ[ter]

*Conſt* How lik'ſt thou? Ha' Are they not charm[ing]
Both Beautiful? [both

*Criſp* They are But why Sir both?

*Conſt.* Becauſe the latter only catch'd thy Praiſe,
When *Fauſta*, in the Pride of Blooming Nature,
As much tranſcends her, as the Summer's Roſe
The little Beauties of a backward Spring.

*Criſp* 'Tis true, ſhe is the Elder.

*Conſt.* And the Fairer,
In all Compariſons to be preferr'd,
Not only to her Siſter, but the World.

*Criſp* Is't poſſible?

*Conſt* That thou ſhould'ſt be ſo dull
To ask the Queſtion, having ſeen the Wonder'

*Criſp* But Sir, when I was ſent you talk'd of De[...]

*Conſt* Death to my ſelf, and thee, and all Mank[ind]
Rather then wound a Part of my lov'd *Fauſta* [th[...]

*Criſp.* Oh Heav'n? What ſaid you? Do you love [...]

*onst.* Love her, my Son? In Age I love her more,
an in my Youth I lov'd the Chace of Glory.
*risp* And does she know you love her?
*onst* Know? Approves,
proving join'd, and seal'd the Contract sure.
*risp.* Death and Despair! Approv'd, Joyn'd, Seal'd,
w Seal'd? and how Contracted? [Contracted!
*onst* Why, our Lips
ve sign'd and seal'd an Everlasting Love.
*risp* What, kiss'd her? Ha! But I'm too credulous:
you have said is but to try my Temper,
w much your Son can bear.
*onst* I must confess
Fears were just, hadst thou another Father;
as I am, I swear whatever Issue
ve by *Fausta*, thou shalt heir my Power.
*risp.* Talk not of Power, but tell me of your Love;
ract me not with these ambiguous Answers,
tell me, swear to save my loss of Reason,
s you love, you are by *Fausta* lov'd.
*onst* That I love *Fausta*, is as true by Heav'n,
love thee, But whether I am lov'd
h just return, is hard indeed to swear:
, as I said before, our Hands have joyn'd,
Lips have seal'd, and binding Oaths have past.
*risp* What Oaths?
*onst.* Betrothing Oaths.
*risp* Oh, all ye Saints!
you contracted too?
*onst* Ah *Crispus*, we're contracted;
ep not my Son, I swear by this Embrace,
u shalt not less be lov'd than heretofore. [her?
*risp* Betroth'd! Oh Heav'n! And have you, Sir, enjoy'd
*onst* No *Crispus*, That's a Heav'n I have to come.
*risp.* A Hell! All Hell! And if not yet enjoy'd,
me conjure you by my Mother's Ashes,
ch her not for the World
*onst* What means my Son?
e decreed to marry her this Night,
taste the Sweets of long expected Joys
*risp.* By Heav'n I swear those Sweets have Poison in 'em,

Bane to your Soul, your Empire, Life and Glory.
*Conſt* Take heed, my *Criſpus*, that thou do not wro
I know the hazard of Succeſſion frights thee. [
*Criſp.* No By your Sacred Life, nothing but Hon
Provoks me in the point She's falſe, forſworn,
And to my certain Knowledge loves another
Oh! therefore touch her not, and, to convince you
That Empire could not work me thus, this Night
I'll turn a Hermit, and renounce the World.
*Conſt* If ſhe be falſe I know his Temper well,
And Nature cannot make ſuch Faults o'th' ſudden.
If ſhe be falſe! By Heav'n, thou haſt mov'd me *Criſ*
But ſpeak the Traitor's Name, who thus has wrong'd
*Criſp* Pardon me, Sir, his Name, he could not w
Becauſe he knew not. [
*Conſt* What?
*Criſp* Your Love.
*Conſt.* His Name,
There's more in this; his Name, again I charge th
Not only name him, but produce his Perſon;
Or I ſhall think all Forgery thou haſt ſworn
*Criſp.* O let me beg you, wed her not to Night,
And when I ſee you next I'll tell you more,
Perhaps betray the Innocent to Death.
*Conſt.* Let that be prov'd, I ſwear he ſhall not d
Thou art it ſeems his Friend, as well as mine,
But look you calm the Tempeſt you have rais'd,
Or I will make thee Stranger to my Soul: [
*Criſp ſolus* I am content; if that ſome pitying Po
Would make me too a Stranger to my ſelf
But hold my Heart a while, till I have found her.
Yet there's a lucid Joy in theſe Diſtractions,
To know he has not Bedded her, then had follow'd
Her Death and mine, and conſequent Damnation'
Yet leſt ſhe ſhould conſent, I'll haſte, and warn her
When warn'd I'll watch, and if ſhe after yield,
Through Love or Fear, to his Inceſtuous Charms,
I'll Ruſh through all, and ſtab her in his Arms [

A C

1

## ACT III. SCENE I.

*Enter* Annibal *and* Serena.

*Annib.* IS this your Answer then, you cannot love me;
This the Reward for Offers of my Blood,
nd braving a stern Father to preserve you?
his the Effect of *Crispus'* Eloquence!
o make his Friend a most untimely Grave?
r, bear it as you please, or laugh or grieve,
will not be a Trouble to you long.

*Seren* What shall I say? Alas! I might delude you,
ke other faithless Beauties of the Age;
t the Gods fram'd me of so plain a Temper,
annot hide my Thoughts, though to my undoing.
t something more there is, if you could bear it,
turn your desp'rate Love for ever from me.

*Annib* Produce it then; for, what can Nature shew me
an Death more dreadful, wilder than Despair,
hich now are my Familiars?

*Seren.* Take it, Sir,
e only Secret of my wounded Soul.
ve, I languish, and despair like you.

*Annib.* What, do you love another?

*Seren* Love him to death, nor does he know I love him;
if he did, he would not make Return.

*Annib* Can this be possible! but where, where is he?
t I may rush with all my Rage upon him,
l bear him with me, to the other World. [him----

*Seren* Not for a thousand Worlds you must not hate

*Annib* Plagues! Curses on his Head, Rage and Despair.
his then the Return of all my Vows,
make my setting yet more deep in Blood?
give me quick his Quality and Name. [geance!

*Seren* His Name! what, after such Resolves of Ven-
r Fate and mine should not compel it now.

*Annib* What, not to save my Life!

*Seren.* No; for what Life can stand in Competition,
When his is threaten'd? Better you, and I,
And all the rest of human Kind, should perish,
Than he, the Master-piece of Nature, suffer.
And should you know him, spite of your Resolves,
Sir, you would kneel and worship too like me
*Annib.* Show me the God then, if I must adore.
*Seren.* No, since you have sworn, I should do ill to tru[st]
Yet, for his Preservation, I must tell you, [yea]
Whene'er he dies *Serena* too shall bleed.
From the same Hand the same Dispatch I crave,
And if at last one Monument we have,
What Joys can Life compare with such a Grave!
[Ex[it]

*Enter* Arius *with* Crispus's *Picture.*

*Annib* Death, Hell, and Furies, if my Sword ha[ve]
Which never fail'd me yet, I'll find him out, [Charm]
This Rival God———
And drive him from the World.
*Ari* Ha! goes it there?
Then to my Task!
*Annib.* *Arius* in Contemplation!
'Twere worth my while to spy · *Crispus'* Picture!
Forgive me, *Arius*, if I rob your Hand
Of what's so deep ingraven in my Heart.
For whom this pretty Present? [great Secre[t]
*Ari.* Your Pardon——The Mystery is one of Love
*Annib* *Crispus* in Love, and hide it from his Frien[ds]
From *Annibal*, that open'd all to him!
'Twas much unkind *Arius*, I am concern'd·
And you must tell me where his Heart's engag'd,
Ere I return the Picture.
*Arius.* Sir, I am in haste,
And dare not tell her Name; therefore I beg you:
She waits my coming.—— Good my Lord,——she lov[es]
To that degree, each Moment's stay is Death.
Therefore let me conjure you.
*Annib.* Thou dost but raise my Admiration more:
Therefore, your Business, or farewel.——

A

*Ari.* Stay, Stay!
y Lord, you are his Friend! yet 'tis a Breach
Trust, but since there is no other help,
d the fair Mistress of his Heart may pine
death upon the Loss, restore the Picture,
d take the Secret, Sir; her Name's *Serena* [tects thee,
*Annib.* Traitor, thou ly'st; and, but thy Robe pro-
uld'st feel, even now, th' Effects of my Revenge.
*Ari.* To clear th' Aspersion, bear it Sir, your self,
d to *Serena's* Face I'll justifie
e Secret of her Love, tho' *Crispus* kill me.
*nnib* By Heav'n, thou dost recall a dreadful Image.
fore I met him, ere I made my Visit
her thou hast nam'd, and ask'd him of my Love!
seem'd in haste! his Answers were abrupt;
Count'nance sad; and thus in short return'd,
t not a Bubble Beauty, like a Boy;
like a Man, and let your Rest be Fame.
so it shall If what thou say'st be true,
evel him with Earth
*ri* What said you, Sir?
*nnib* Yet I will have more Proof, she shall, her self,
itness to the Fall of this high Virtue.
n Friendship to the Winds, like meeting Tides,
l fight the Tempest out, nor give it o'er,
one lies dasht and broken on the Shore [*Exit.*
*ri.* Thus far the Devil is the best mounted yet,
Heresie at last shall win the Race

*Enter* Labienus *and* Eubolus.

*Labienus* here,
my *Eubolus*, we shall shortly govern.
*ub* I met the Emperor of late, alone,
o ask'd for you
*ri.* I'll instantly attend him
re is his Son?
*b* I left him with *Dalmatius*
*ri.* Unloading his sick Heart upon his Friend.

*Enter* Dalmatius *and* Crispus.

ee, the Master Enemy's at Hand,
to your Posts, and dive in Mists away.
[*Ex.* Ari. Lab. Eub.

*Crisp* Now my *Dalmatius*, now thou hast my Hea[rt]
And make good use on't, if I ne'er see thee more
By Heav'n, my Friend, I have not hid a Point
Of that sad Story that must make my Ruin.

*Dalm.* Would thou hadst told me half of it before
I might have sav'd thee many a Sigh and Tear:
Pray Heav'n no worse come on't, but 'tis no Time
T' upbraid thee now What wou'dst thou have me d[o]

*Crisp* Persuade my Father from enjoying her,
For if that be to Night, as once he vow'd,
Thou shalt behold thy *Crispus* dead to morrow.

*Dalm* And what of *Fausta*?

*Crisp* I know not what
That subtle false one, that has thus deceiv'd me,
And with her Charms ensnar'd my Innocent Soul.
But I will hence

*Dalm* For what?

*Crisp.* To execute
The Vows I made.

*Dalm* Go then and kill her.

*Crisp.* Ha!

*Dalm.* Kill the Adultress, this incestuous Charm[er]
And have her born in Triumph to thy Father
Then tell thy Tragick Story like a Man;
And greatly thus Atone for both your Crimes.

*Crisp* Farewel: I'll find another Way to end he[r]

*Dalm* Tongue-kill her, go; or swear, and be forsw[orn]
Thou ne'er wilt see her more Heav'n! That a Ma[n]
Born to the Empire of the World, should dote
On such slight stuff as Woman!

*Crisp* See my Father,
Look thou to him, as I'll be Guard on her.
Incest! Dishonour! to all future Ages——
Think,— —think on that——and push him from his [...]

[*Ex.* Cr[isp.]

*Enter* Constantine, *and* Sylvester.

*Const.* What say the People to the Rumor spre[ad]
Of my new Contract?

*Silv.* All the Christians mourn,
And sicken in their Souls, as if Heav'n warn'd

e Earth, of some unheard Calamity.
e Heathens on the other side rejoice,
d cry, a Persecution is at Hand

*Const.* No matter, to the Point, know'st thou the Man
hom *Fausta* loves?

*[illegible]* I told you, Sir, before,
ould be dumb for ever on this Theme [him:

*Const* Yet this implies thou know'st, but wilt not show
know him, all, all but he that shou'd;
*Crispus* has confess'd,
hides the Name, —— But I'll find out one,
meriting Respect, whom Racks shall force

*Dalm* If you intend your Empire's Safety, Sir,
*Fausta* from your Bosom, turn her out,
with her—— far let her be Exil'd,
h all her Race; for Death is in her Beauty.

*Const* My Brother offer this!
h in her Beauty?

*Dalm* Violent, sudden Death,
h to your Health, and Ruin to your Glory.

*Const* Perhaps he is the Man Her Lover! Yes
thus conceals his Flame with covert Rage,
lse what Cause could thus provoke his Passion?
is the Publick Interest here concern'd?
r Murmurings, or their Joys, which with a nod
Power can hush By Heav'n there's more at bottom,
I will find it out, their Looks betray 'em
, Princes, all engag'd, and for some Great One.

*Enter* Arius

old——here comes my Man! Brother, I've thought.
will consider further what you urg'd,
nst my Wife.

*Dalm.* We leave you to Heav'ns Care,
wish you to beware that waiting Fiend.

[*Ex.* Dalm Sil

*st* So, now your Business, *Arius*!

Sir

*st* Your Business?
Coast is clear; be your Confession so,
peak what all the Court have sworn to hide

*Ari* Sir, *Labienus* gave me your Commands,
That I shou'd wait
*Const* Dost thou dally with me?
Thou know'st the least of thy enormous Crimes
Deserve a lengthen'd Death · Think on thy Treason,
Atheism, Blasphemies against the Highest,
Think on the purpos'd Murther of my Brother,
Wrought by thy Charms, thou damn'd one; after[illegible]
Let thy affrighted Soul despise my Wrath,
And if she dares be dumb to my Demands.
*Ari* What must I answer?
*Const* Give me Truth for Truth
Once more then, and this Warning be thy last,
Show me the Robber of my Heart's Repose,
Friend to my *Crispus*, but his Father's Foe;
The Conqu'ring Rival of my ravisht Love.
*Ari.* What, has your Son reveal'd?
*Const* He says she's false, but tells me not to wh[illegible]
Swears she's forsworn; and when I see him next,
I shall know more,
*Ari* What if you never see him?
*Const* Why dost thou start a Question so unlikely?
*Ari* I cannot think he will betray his Friend,
He who betrays his Friend, betrays himself,
And rather than do that, I judge he'll leave
Your Sight, the Empire, and his Love for ever.
*Const* Love, *Arius*! ha! his Love! what Love?
*Ari* Why Love to you: [wh[illegible]
What other Love shou'd *Crispus* entertain?
He has no Mistress sure!
*Const* Thou seem'st to hint
As if he had Mark thy foregoing Words:
He who betrays his Friend, betrays himself·
By Heav'n! thou hast set my anxious Soul a' work
For when thou said'st, he has no Mistress, sure—
Thy Meaning was, to make me think he had,
And that this Mistress could be none but *Fausta*.
*Ari* I hope, dread Sir, you will not wrest my Wo[illegible]
And innocent Thoughts, to any evil Purpose.

Cri[illegible]

*Const.* What, at your Tricks again? Be quick my Traitor,
d spread at once thy double Heart before me,
t thou not judge my Son his Father's Rival?
*Ari.* If you would know my Heart, indeed I do.
*Const.* Why, what a Devil wert thou then to deny't?
pitifully play the Hypocrite!
d scrue that lying Face into a show
Innocence,
hen Nature stampt thee for a Villain!
*Ari.* Forgive me, Sir, if I avow 'twas Fear,
t Villany, that made me hide my Thought.
*Const.* All Fear, but Fear of Heav'n, betrays a Guilt,
d Guilt is Villany. But let thy Fear
duce what past betwixt the wicked Pair;
w me th' Adultress and Adulterer,
here, how, and when, this Incest was committed,
ho was the Instrument and cursed Bawd,
d damn'd Contriver of their horrid Joys.
*Ari.* Oh Heav'n!
*Const.* O Hell! for there shalt thou be hurl'd,
d rost in Sulphur, if thou not tell me all,
ou, who perhaps thy self wert the Contriver,
e Bawd I nam'd, and Instrument of their Lust
*Ari.* Hold Sir! and I'll confess: I've seen your Son,
ner than I have wish'd, attend your *Fausta*,
d seen him late from her Apartment come;
heard him praise her long, and when the Praise
s finish'd, sigh, that he durst praise no longer.
least I thought so, but my Thought's no Proof
*Const.* No, *Arius*, not enough for *Crispus*' Death,
there's enough to turn my Spirit from him,
make me loath his Form, when next we meet,
m Head to Foot to measure him with my Eye,
h as an Object of my Scorn and Hate.
*Ari.* That Love has past betwixt 'em is past Doubt,
for enjoying———
*Const.* Know'st thou ought of that?
*Ari.* Not I, by Heav'n!
*Const.* Why didst thou start it then?

*Ari.* Sir to be satisfy'd, what you wou'd do,
Upon the Demonstration.
*Const.* Both shou'd bleed,
Both dye, as sure as we are living, *Arius*,
For him, 'twere Sacrilege to think to save him,
If thus he has transgrest, not then my Vows,
Not all the Conquests of his blooming Years,
With my whole Empires Knees and lifted Hands,
Not the remembrance of his Mother's Tears,
When on her Death-Bed she bequeathed his Safety
To my best Care and Love, shall once redeem him.
*Ari.* What shall be done to him that finds the Tr[uth]
*Const* Reward and Honour. He shall be my Fri[end]
*Ari.* I ask no more; henceforth I'm yours,
To search, tho' at the Peril of my Life,
The bottom of this Business.
*Const* Say and do———
But send my Wardrope now to *Fausta*'s side,
Bear her the Diadem, with stile of Empress;
And say this Night I bed her.
*Ari.* That will prove her———
If she refuse, you know Sir what to judge.
Nor would it be amiss to break discourse
About your Son, and sift her subtle Soul.
*Const.* I apprehend thee But as I commanded—
Away—Oh *Constantine*! Yet e'er this search, [Ex[it]
Whate'er comes, remember he's thy Son,
Son of thy Love, and once was next thy Soul
But as the best are worst, when once corrupted,
If he has sinn'd at all, he has sinn'd to Death,
The Thought distracts me; Heav'n remove this Tr[ea]
Or I shall run to my old Gods again
But hush a while I'll bear my Passion cold,
I'll curb it while the Reins of Reason hold,
But if they break, then Nature, where's thy Call?
Be deaf to Reason, Nature, Judgment, All—
The Precipice is Fate, and if we roul,
The Fault is theirs that fool'd us with a Soul [E[xit]

SCE[NE]

## SCENE II.

*Enter* Criſpus *with a Dagger, and* Fauſta.

*auſt.* Hold, hold thy Hand———
*iſp.* Think not I meant to kill thee——
thou Seducer, were thy Stains more deep,
*nk not* Deſpair and Rage cou'd ſo unman me
hurt a Woman. Yet thou ſhalt hear me, *Fauſta:*
if the Story of thy Crimes can kill thee,
ay thy Wounds wide open to the Air;
lay the Perjuries of thy bleeding Heart,
to thy Inceſt, add at laſt a Murder.
*uſt.* Stab with thy Dagger then, but let thy Tongue
roy no more
*iſp* O all ye Powers, who that had known laſt Night,
Joys which I have known, could once have thought it!
that had heard her Vows, when on my Breaſt,
ried with Oaths, and out of Breath with Kiſſes,
panting ſwore! and wiſh'd Deſtruction ſeize her,
e were not content, ſo one Night more
raviſh'd Soul like that might entertain,
ive her Miſeries and paſt Life again.
*uſt.* By all thoſe Powers you name, and by your own,
h ſo ſtill
*iſp* Yet at that very Minute
n thus ſhe ſwore, to know ſhe was forſworn,
cious her Faith was plighted to another!
who that other pick'd from all Mankind,
make her more abhor'd, but my own Father?
*uſt.* What, Load on Load?
*iſp* Her violated Hands
e plighted faſt with his; and Kiſſes paſt.——
*uſt* Hold, hold, and let my Tears atone, my Lord,
ink upon the Earth.
*iſp* The Center, *Fauſta,*
Center cannot hide thee from the Horrors
y own Conſcience, which are my Avengers:
whereſoe'er thou fly'ſt, ſhall follow thee

With

With inward Hells, for the base Wrong thou hast d
*Faust.* O *Crispus*! never, never, wilt thou end?
*Crisp* By Heav'n! I know thy damnable design:
Thou hast this Night contriv'd to ruin Nature,
To make the Angels sick with such a Crime,
As equals hers that first betray'd the World
*Faust* I'll stop thee with my Kisses!
*Crisp* Off, Crocodile!
*Faust.* Why use thy Ponyard then.
*Crisp* Nor that, nor this.
I had design'd, 'tis true, to stab my self;
But second Thoughts instruct me thus to haunt thee
Like an eternal Fiend to follow thee.
To hollow still Damnation in thy Ear,
And hinder thee from Incest with my Father.
Oh horrid Thought!
*Faust* Oh horrid Thought indeed!
*Crisp* Why does it not possess thee!
Thou fair insinuating Snake! would'st thou then gil
Swear on my Ponyard, swear, and damn thy self, [Pe
Thou hast not plotted, as this Night, to twist
Thy incestuous Arms about my Father's Neck!
*Faust* Yes, I will swear. But let me lean my H
Against thy Breast, while I recover Breath.
For I am faint with Groans.
*Crisp* Oh Heart! Oh Love!
She grasps so hard, and locks so with her Charms,
I cannot put her from me! *Fausta*! is't possible!
Is it then possible! thou canst be good?
So good at least, as being thus gone in Sin,
To go no further?
*Faust* Let me swear;
For I will face the Gods in such a Cause;
And standing on the Guard of Innocence,
Swear, all I've done was but th' Effect of Love
*Crisp* Again thou'rt fallen, for thou art guilty, Fa
Of Impious Treason, and incestuous Love.
*Faust* I am not, *Crispus*
*Crisp* Ha! not guilty, *Fausta*?
Then farewel all!

*ust* Hold, hold, not guilty to my *Crispus*
not to Rage again, and I'll confess
as compell'd to be contracted to him.
wedded, nor possest
*isp.* Why didst thou hide thy Contract?
*ust.* Because 'twas forc'd by Fear, nor did I dare
eal it to thee, ere I had thee sure. So much I lov'd
thee, *Crispus*
*isp.* But what hadst thou decreed to do to Night,
fatal Night, if that the Emperor
sworn to enjoy thee?
*ust* Stop him with my Tears,
f they fail'd, to dam his Passion thus,
sheath this hidden Ponyard in my Heart
*isp* Is't possible thou should'st so greatly dare?
*ust.* Yes, *Crispus.* Thou shalt see, by what's to come.
therefore take me to thy Breast, and swear——
*isp* Swear first thy self, he never shall possess thee.
*ust* What needs an Oath after possessing thee?
*isp* Yet, for the Satisfaction of my Soul,
Cement of our everlasting Loves,
ar thou wilt never
*ust* Never *Crispus*, never.
Heav'n and Earth, by all that's great and holy,
ar thy Father never shall embrace me.
*isp.* What, never! Oh yet closer! Never, *Fausta*?
*ust* By all this Dearness, never *Crispus*, never

*Enter* Arius

*r.* What Faults are gone and past, it matters not:
you had best beware of what's to come ——
Sir away.--See there the Beds prepar'd--[*Scene draws.*
Diadem, and Name of Empress given ——
Father's at my Heels! hark! you are warn'd.

*Soft Musick.*

r him come, and wish you Sir away. [*Ex.* Arius.
*isp* Oh *Fausta*!
*ust* Take no thought.
*isp* If he should charm thee,
are thee to Compliance——
*ust.* That Distrust

Again!

Again! by Heav'n I'll dye before he enters.

*Crisp* Hold thee, my Heart! my Life, my Love,
I'll stay---and hazard all---but hark! he comes. [S
I would advise——Live, if thou canst with Honou
If not--he's here, fall, and I'll follow thee [*Ex.* Cris

*Re-enter* Arius *with* Constantine.

*Const* Ha *Arius*! see'st thou there!

*Ari* *Crispus*, I think.

*Const.* Did'st thou not see him?

*Ari.* Yes

*Const.* Why dost thou then suppose it but thy Thou

*Ari* Because I do not like his being here.

*Const* Nor I, by Heav'n! Withdraw, and wait my C
[Ar *re*

What now, my *Fausta*! Ha! in Tears my Fair!
What, on thy Wedding Night? Why dost thou fly
Am I a Ravisher? Howe'er reputed
Bloody in Fi lds, in Chambers I am gentle
As thy own Thoughts.
Therefore let our Vows be seal'd, and then to Bed

*Faust* What said you, Sir?

*Const* Why, to Bed my Love,
And hide thy Virgin Fears. Thou wilt be bolder th

*Faust* Alas! I dare not

*Const* Why?

*Faust* I've sworn, my Lord.——

*Const.* What, and to whom?

*Faust* To Heav'n I've sworn,
Howe'er contracted, that I will not wed you

*Const.* When?

*Faust.* Not to Night.

*Const* When then?

*Faust* Press me no further,
For I can only answer with my Tears.

*Const* Speak, for I'll know th' Extremity to Nig
Why then to morrow, but by Heav'n no longer,
For now I've sworn too

*Faust.* But I vow'd first
And swear again to keep that Vow till Death
To morrow and to morrow, add to those
To Millions more You never shall embrace me

*Conſt* Is't poſſible! after thy Faith was given!
*Fauſt.* Not given, but by a Conqueror compell'd.
*Conſt.* And haſt thou rightly ſcan'd the Conqueror's [Rage?
*Fauſta!* Haſt thou plac'd thy Father's Fate
ore thy Eyes? And thought upon thy own?
*Fauſt* Juſt to your purpoſe I'm prepar'd for Death,
her than entertain you in my Bed.
refore if you ſet down t'enjoy me, Sir,
doom me dead, upon the Earth I beg you
ſpeak your Will, and *Fauſta* ſhall revenge you.
, Ponyard ſtrait ſhall act your vow'd Revenge,
take her from the World——
*Conſt.* Riſe, *Fauſta* riſe——
Heav'n I find 'tis vain to ſtrive againſt thee!
e then what more thou valu'ſt than the World,
what, in ſpite of me, the Fates ordain thee ——
*Criſpus* for thy Love——
*Fauſt* Ah, Sir, what mean you? [ſhows?
*Conſt* Why would'ſt thou ſtrive to hide what Nature
*naturus*, *Arius*, and *Sylveſter*, know it.
over-wrought me, for my Empire's Safety,
this great Act, to yield thee to my Son [you
*Fauſt* Did *Arius* too? No ſure, they rather wrought
yield me to my Grave——
*Conſt* No; to my Throne.
ady 'tis decreed, my *Cæſar* weds thee.
but I own I came to work thee from him.
ſince not Death it ſelf can daunt thy Love,
id it Heav'n, that I ſhould break ſuch Union.
e *Arius*! call my Son. I'll give him now,
while my Reaſon lets me ſee my Dotage.
ill ſuch Autumn ſuits thy Beauty's Spring!
haſte and bring him, while the Heat is on me;
I will have you wedded in my Preſence.
if thy Heart conſent to make a turn,
range as kind; this Night he ſhall enjoy thee
*Fauſt* Oh Heav'n, inſtruct my Frailty what to anſwer!
this be real Sir! Is't poſſible?
*Conſt* My Council know it, and confirm the Order
*Fauſt.* That I ſhall wed your Son?

Conſt.

*Const.* Why thus repeated?

*Faust.* And you approve it?

*Const.* Canst thou doubt me still?

*Faust.* No I will own Sir, since you approve it,
Own it to Death, I love him more than Life.

*Const.* O *Fausta*!

*Faust.* Ha! What now? He turns away.
He blushes! Gods——I'm lost, betray'd, undone!
Undone for ever. *Crispus* is betray'd:
The innocent *Crispus*.——

*Const.* Guilty, guilty *Crispus*——
And guilty *Fausta*! Guilty both to Death;
But most my Son who wrought thee to this Ruin.

*Faust.* O say not so 'Twas *Fausta* wrought your Son-
And over-lov'd him, to his own Destruction.
Therefore as you are powerful be just,
And let the stroak of Vengeance light on me
But Sir, for him——

*Const.* For him! each Syllable
Thou plead'st in his behalf but Wings his Death.

*Faust.* By the just Heav'ns! and by the Saint that bo[re you]
B[y] [yo]ur Religion Sir, I do conjure you,
Sp[are] [h]is, spare his Innocence——

*Const.* If thou consent,
That I this Night shall wed thee.

*Faust.* Wed me, *Constantine*!

*Const.* *Fausta*, why not?
Art thou enjoy'd already, married? Speak, confess—
That I may pardon thee——

*Faust.* What you know, you know;
You have betray'd me once, but shall no more
More! There's no more, but that I love your Son,
And whether he loves me, the Gods can tell.
I know the natural Goodness of your Temper,
How e'er transported, will not let you kill him.
Therefore I leave you——

*Const.* Stay and tell me when,
When I may hope Love's Consummation sure?

*Faust.* When you behold me wedded to your Son,
As you engag'd, and past your Royal Word;

hen after many rowling Years I bring you
ace of ſmiling Boys to bleſs your Age,
play about your Throne, and be your *Cæſars*:
en may your Happineſs compleated be,
en may your Eyes the Conſummation ſee,
never hope for other Joys from me. [*Ex* Fauſta.

*onſt.* What *Arius!* help and free me from this plunge
Love and Nature. She loves, ſhe loves to Death;
d tho' ſhe hides it, is belov'd again

*Ari* What's your Reſolve? To give her to your Son?

*onſt.* No *Arius*, firſt I'll give her to the Grave——
ign my Empire: All——

*Ari* Then *Criſpus* dies———

*onſt.* If he has not enjoy'd her, he ſhall live;
that I lov'd him once is full as true
hat, tho' now he has ſinn'd, I cannot hate him.
if enjoy'd! how ſhall I find it out?
eize and rack him.

*Ari* How Sir, rack your Son!

*nſt.* By Heav'n 'twas well remember'd by a Villain:
refore I ſwear thou ſhalt be rack'd thy ſelf.

*r* Who I, my Lord?

*nſt* Ay Villain, Traitor, thou!
ack the Racker, till I find it out;
my miſgiving Heart ſays thou know'ſt more:
refore, when next I ſee thee, bring me proof
s not enjoy'd, her Vows and Virtue clear;
, or thy Death ſhall teach ſucceeding Kings
more by falſe Reports to be abus'd,
trait confront th' Accuſer with the Accus'd,
rove the Treaſons urg'd againſt the Throne,
now the Sycophants that ſet 'em on.
all the Sovereign Pow'r unclouded ſway.
n ſuch Court Devils ſhun the glorious Ray,
drive like Fogs, before the riſing Day. [*Exeunt*

ACT

## ACT IV. SCENE I.

*Enter* Annibal *and* Serena.

*Annib.* THEN you confess you did bespeak the Pictu[re]
Gods! and you own you love him! love t[he]
Traitor?

*Seren.* Call him not Traitor, *Annibal*, he who spoke
The kindest things of you.

*Annib.* Wondrous kind!
Accurst Dissembler! That could speak for me,
But acted for himself.

*Seren.* Just contrary.
For when by Signs, which Passion could not hide,
I let him know my Love, he turn'd away,
Shaking his Head as loath to understand me,
Anger and Pity combating in his Face,
And with his Blushes taught *Serena* Shame.

*Annib.* Shameless himself, and Traitor to my Friend[ship]
For all I have heard, your Love has forg'd to save h[im]

*Seren.* Heav'n knows 'tis true! Nothing was left uns[aid]
To his own Disgrace and your Immortal Honour.
In the most melting Terms and sweetest Words
That Heart could think, or Friendship could invent.
Therefore forgo, my Lord, this fruitless Passion,
And speak for *Crispus* as he spoke for you.

*Annib.* I will, and speak so loud the Gods shall hear
There! take his Picture, feed your hungry Passion,
Till with my Sword I carve another Feast,
To glut your Fatal Eyes——

*Seren.* Hold, whither go you?
And what fierce Purpose has your Heart in hand?

*Annib.* I'll tell thee, and if possible [illegible] a W[arm]
In that cold Breast, kindle a dying Spark
In that inhospitable Land of Love,
And never see thee more——I go to die,
To blot my Youth and Glory from the World;
Tho' Conquests waits my Sword, I swear to die,
And make thee sport with my untimely Fall.

*Seren.* To die! By whom? for what?
*Annib* For Love of thee.
[...] if I suffer by the Hand of *Crispus*,
[...]d Perjury should prosper in my Ruin,
[...]en you may revel in each others Arms,
[...]d laugh indeed at my ridiculous Fortune.
[...], if revenging Ghosts have power to rise,
[...]pect me at the Riot of your Joys;
[...]th hollow Eyes, to stare you in the Face:
[...]midnight, look to have your Curtains drawn;
[...]pect me in your Bed, a Coarse of Clay,
[...]clasp your trembling Limbs with cold Embraces,
[...]d print my gelid Kisses on your Lips,
[...]o revenge my Death upon your Scorn,
[...]d groan about you till the dawning Morn [*Exit.*
*[...]ren* Stay——and I'll tell thee, 'tis impossible----
*[...]ur* already is in love with *Fausta* ——
[...]s gone to the Execution of his Purpose——
[...]d *Crispus* must be slain Why then my Hour
[...]Fate is come. What's that to *Crispus*' Murder?
[...]s gone to fight, perhaps not give him leave,
[...]take the Innocent at unawares,
[...]e after him, and by thy own Destruction,
[...]vent both Ruins Follow the Fate that wafts thee,
[...] let no Interrupter cross thy Passage [*Exit.*

*Enter* Constantine, Silvester *and* Dalmatius.

*[...]nst* Were you both Fathers, and in love like me,
[...] more doubt what you would put in Act,
[...]n now I doubt my self, who am resov'd ——
*[...]alm* On what?
*[...]nst* On Death.
*[...]v* Of whom?
*[...]nst* Of any Man
[...] knows, yet hides this secret Treason from me:
*[...]alm* Has *Crispus* own'd he loves her?
*[...]nst* Yes, in effect,
[...]when I first reveal'd this Contract to him,
[...]opt me from enjoying her with Oaths.
[...]new her false, forsworn To whom? To him;
[...]im himself. For this last Night I prov'd,

Drawing the Secret from her by a Wile,
Which she before as craftily conceal'd
*Dalm.* But have you marry'd and enjoy'd her, Sir?
*Const.* O no, the Ceremonies and the Dues,
Without a Blush were frontlesly deny'd·
In all the heat of boyling Love deny'd:
Not only from possessing her that Night,
But, matchless Impudence! deny'd for ever.
Now judge if 'tis not fit I should let go
The struggling Thunder, and destroy 'em both.
*Dalm.* Not both——for yet you have not heard yo
Hear him but plead—— [S
*Const.* Then let him plead in Time. [*Ex* D
The Bolts are brandish'd, and 'twill be too late
To lift his blasted Hands, when I have hurl'd.
*Silv* How far, Sir, would your utmost Search exten
*Const* To know if actually they have embrac'd
Each other, as in Will th' have done already.
*Silv* Be not too hasty in your Answer, Sir,
If I should ask, What then, what then must follow
*Const* Death certain, on the Instant; imminent De
Death, and I swear not all the Gods shall save him.
*Silv* Ruin of Piety! Not all the Gods!
That your Religion?
*Const.* Oh forgive me, Saint,
I am eaten up with Passion· So o'er-wrought
With racking Love, I knew not what I said.
But if he has enjoy'd her, By that Power
Whom thou remember'st well, I now adore,
His Death must wash th' incestuous Guilt away
*Silv* Not Incest, Sir.
*Const* Not if he has enjoy'd her?
*Silv.* No; for to prove the Guilt compleated Inc
You must have married and enjoy'd her first [De
*Const.* True, but what makes his Crime deter
More than imputed Treason, Incest, all;
All Faults by Art and Nature join'd in one.
If he has touch'd her, she must ne'er be mine,
And that's a Cause so pointing to his Fate,
That Death's their due that offer to excuse him.

*Silv.* He comes —— I'm silenc'd. Nature, now or never.

*Enter* Crispus *and* Dalmatius.

*Crisp.* O Emperor! for I dare not call you Father,
hold me at your Feet prepar'd for Death.
*Const.* O *Crispus*! for I must not call thee Son,
ftice surveys thee as a Criminal,
rise and speak, plead like a Man for Life.
me on, and look thy Father in the Face,
all thee Traitor, and I'll prove thee one,
ho impiously, for all my former Love,
st dar'd to violate my sacred Bed.
w answer, Criminal. What canst thou say
at Sentence should not pass upon thy Treason?
*Crisp.* Most awful Emperor, my Judge and Father!
her, alas! I would have offer'd first;
since you are not pleas'd it should be so,
do as Criminals use, and you command.
plead my Innocence at your Judgment-Bar;
ther, Sir, I saw or lov'd the Princess,
were the only Cause, 'twas you that sent me:
ar from once but hinting thus your Contract,
told me, Sir, her Fate was yet in doubt:
ich made me wonder when I saw the Virgin,
nnocent, so beautiful, so young:
ich Charms did more my Admiration move,
nder begot my Pity; that my Love.
*nst.* But if I told you that her Fate was doubtful,
you too, she was a Foe to *Rome*;
fore, to think of loving her was Treason.
*isp.* If Love be Treason, Sir, I own I am guilty;
ty indeed, because it was a Fault,
y Case to wed without your knowledge:
yet I hop'd, in time you might forgive me;
so my Conscience tells me still you would,
you not been engag'd your self before.
*st.* Rebellion, not thy Pardon, was thy Thought:
herwise, how canst thou answer, Traitor,
ot confessing all when first I met thee?
*sp.* Pardon me, Sir, for that I had done too,
ou not told me first you were betroth'd;

But conscious then how closely I was link'd,
I durst not tempt your Wrath
*Const* How closely, Traitor! hast thou then enjoy'd h[er]
*Crisp* Can you forgive me?
*Const.* No, By this shaking Flesh,
Tho' there my Mother kneel'd too by thy side
If thou hast touch'd her, Death and Curses on the[e]
*Crisp.* Oh by those Knees and Hands which I must b[...]
Racks, Racks, and Death, but not your Curses, S[ir]
*Const.* If thou would'st have my Blessing, swear t[...]
Thou hast not enjoy'd her [la...]
*Crisp* Swear then to forgive me.
*Const* Forgive thee, Villain! if thou hast possest h[er]
Speak, or be curst.
*Crisp* I will but give me time. [...]
*Const* Let go What time? Thou hast confes[s'd]
By that Demand; I swear thou hast enjoy'd her
*Crisp* Swear not, and I'll confess this Moment.
*Const.* What!
*Crisp* O Heav'n,
What if your Son has plighted holy Vows?
*Const.* Why then I make that Vow and Marriage [...]
Therefore, if thou hast not embrac'd her yet,
I charge thee, on my Blessing, never hope it,
Nor never think of loving her again
*Crisp* Impossibilities! Were you a God,
And doom'd me thus, I could not, Sir, obey you
For I have sworn to love her while I have Life
And if I love her I must hope Enjoyment
*Const* Death then and Curses on thy Disobed[ience]
Off Villain! Traitor! grovel there on Earth
What, are you Plotters too? Nay, then 'tis time
To haste his Ruin Ruin is thy Doom,
And wing'd with all my Curses it shall come
[*Ex. with* Dalm. *and* Silve[ster]
*Crisp* *Dalmatius* and *Silvester*! Call him back,
And I'll renounce my Love. Heav'n, 'tis too much
But hark! I hear a Voice cry, *Crispus* come,
Come to the thoughtless Grave where all is still.
It shall be so: Up then, and fall a Man.

ne forth, thou Miniſter of others Fates,
 be thy Maſter's now! Where art thou, *Fauſta*?
ere is my Love to cloſe my dying Eyes?

*Enter* Annibal

*Annib* Ha, Traitor! art thou then prepar'd for Death?
*uſp* Yes *Annibal*, I will receive it calmly,
m any Hand but thine What have I done
t he ſhould call me Traitor?
*Annib* Guard thy ſelf,
lſe by Heav'n thou dy'ſt
*uſp* Hold. Is't poſſible! ſo quickly?
the deſire of Empire loſe a Friend!
Father I offended, but not thee;
cute then the Ruin which he dooms,
rateful Man I will not make Defence,
ſpread my Arms t'embrace the Death he ſends me.
*nnib* What thou deſerv'ſt from him I neither know
 care, reſolv'd upon my own Revenge;
 but I think the Man who did his Friend
orrible a Wrong as thou haſt done,
 for any Miſchief. Therefore guard thee.
*uſp* Never to fight with thee, not tho' my Father
uld grant my Love. Therefore I ſheath my Sword.
*nnib* Traitor, Coward.
*uſp* Oh *Annibal*, I know I am no Traitor.
 thou, whoſe Life I have ſo oft preſerv'd,
w'ſt but too well I am no Coward.
*nnib* Draw
 then, or periſh By the Gods I'll kill thee,
hat thou wilt, and take this to provoke thee.

[*Strikes him with his Sword.*

*uſp* Well *Annibal*. 'Tis well Thou haſt done well.
thus much Villany am I content to bear;
onger, oh ungrateful, for thy ſake,
 injur'ſt me, yet will not tell the Cauſe.
or thy noble Father I will ſpare thee,
 thee thus far, ſo thou reſolve to leave me.
*nnib* Not yet? Why then another.
*uſp* But the next
ine. Humanity can bear no further. [Annib. *falls.*

*Annib* I have my Death: and now my Heart relent
*Crisp.* Cut off my Hand.
*Annib* *Crispus*, thou hast wrong'd me.
*Crisp* Speak how, and where?
*Enter* Serena.
*Annib* See, she comes to tell thee.
*Serena*, oh *Serena*! [D
*Crisp* Gone for ever!
*Seren* Oh, never to return! and I, alas,
Who could not love again, the wretched Cause!
*Crisp* The cursed Cause.
*Seren* Call me not cursed, *Crispus*,
Who think no Blessing equal to thy Love.
*Crisp* Wert thou a Man, by Heav'n such Love I bear th
I think that I should seek thee through the World,
To give thee Death———
*Seren.* Take then the Death you threaten,
Prepare to suffer by a Virgin's Hand.
*Crisp* Kill me, and I'll forgive thee *Annibal's* De
But take this Sword, yet reeking with his Blood,
And thrust it through my Heart
*Seren.* Yet hold, *Serena*·
What will become of him when thou art slain?
Kill himself last, and that I would prevent.
*Crisp.* Why dost thou stay?
*Enter* Sylvester. [hea
*Sylv* *Crispus*, I come to tell thee, thy Father will
*Seren* Take these Swords, *Sylvester*, bear 'em hen
Without Reply,——or *Crispus* kills himself.——A
*Sylv.* *Crispus* Death!
I thank thee Heav'n that sent me to preserve him. [E
*Crisp.* Why hast thou thus delay'd my Ruin?
*Seren.* To make thy Torments lasting,
Live, that my Ghost and *Annibal's* may haunt thee
Yet when I come, believe, for all my Threatnings,
My Soul shall seek thee in a gentle form·
Court thee to Cells, and to the Garden Shade,
And tell thee there, what Love with us is made,
What Fires the Fiends for willful Murder make,
And what my Spirit suffers for thy sake.
But hark! I'm call'd——behold the Dead awake.

ey waft me, *Crispus*, to the sleepy Shore,
d I shall never, never see thee more. [*Ex.* Seren.
*Crisp* She's gone, and takes the means of Death too
from me
what's the next? What have the Fates to add
my past Sufferings? Lightning blast me,
untains fall on me, gape to the Center Earth,
hide me from my Friend

*Enter* Dalmatius.

*Dalm* Why, my dearest *Crispus*! but alas——
vain I urg'd thy Father, deaf to all
r Prayers, remorsless, rocky and unmov'd;
t think not but I press'd with all my Love
*Crisp* Therefore in great requital for thy Love
ok there, and let thy Blood congeal to Stone;
hold thy *Annibal* butcher'd by this Hand.
*Dalm* Cold, cold my Boy! *Crispus*, have I--have I?
t I waste Time by such unmanly wailing.
ke to thy Sword.
*Crisp* Thou seest I've none: but strike——
*Dalm.* What could provoke thee to this horrid Deed?
*Crisp* His Jealousie, and Anger of the Heav'ns.
lous I robb'd him of *Serena*'s Love,
call'd me Traitor, Coward, struck me twice
ore I drew, than ran upon my Sword.
*Dalm* Whatever happen'd---I'm a wretched Father,
d thou hast robb'd me of an only Child,
erefore hereafter we no more are one.
here-e'er I go I'll ask before I enter
*Crispus* be not there? that I may shun thee.
erefore if thou hast any Gratitude
r those kind Offices which I have done thee,
these sad Eyes, as I will run from thine,
moan my Son, and howl my Life away [*Exit*
*risp sol* And whither thou? thou heap of walking woe!
ou that hast pull'd thy Father's Curse upon thee,
ll'd thy best Friend, and ruin'd all that lov'd thee--
here will at last thy cruel Fortune drive thee?
nce tear thy Robes, and Naked fly the World,
mantled to the Weather, wander on
some dark Wild, where Sun-beam never shone. [*Exit.*

## SCENE II.

*Enter* Constantine, Arius, Fausta, Sylvester.

*Faust.* Consider, Sir, his Youth——
*Const.* I have consider'd all——
But find thy Love so rooted in my Heart,
I must forgo my Life, or lose my Claim.
Yet mark how deep thy Tears have wrought my Temp[er]
If thou wilt swear to null thy Marriage with him,
By wedding me in Publick, and this Night,
By making me thy Lord———
*Faust* No Sir, 'tis impossible; yet if you'll swear
To save your Son, if I should prove him guiltless,
I'll tell you Wonders, Sir, which otherwise
Not Racks shall e'er compell.
*Const.* Forbid it, Heav'n! I should destroy the guiltle[ss]
Tho' Strangers to my Blood, much less my Son:
Therefore I swear by Heav'n and all the Saints,
Prove *Crispus* innocent he shall not die.
*Faust.* Be witness, oh *Arius* and *Sylvester*!
What he has sworn Let *Crispus* strait be call'd,
And quitted of his Crime: Run, *Arius*, haste,
That I may see the Royal Friendship made. [*Ex.* Ari[us]
*Const* By an entire Surrender of thy self
To me.
*Faust.* To *Crispus*.
*Const* By all thy former Oaths, I swear to me.
*Faust* I told you 'twas impossible, before,
And now confirm it.
*Const.* How?
*Faust* I am married.
*Const* Curses and Vengeance. Married! say by who[m]
*Faust* To *Crispus*.
*Const* When, thou false one? When? and where?
*Faust.* Here in your Palace, on that happy Night
Before you made your dreadful Triumph.
*Const* Dreadful indeed. for now the Wretch shall d[ie]
Tho' Angels pleaded——

Sy[l.]

*Sylv* Emperor, you have ſworn.

*Conſt.* I know it Sir, to ſpare the innocent Blood;
it I will prove him now———

*Fauſt.* White as the Saints,
y all the Powers of Heav'n and Earth I ſwear,
was I that puſh'd the Marriage, Conſcious before
hat I had ſworn to you; nay caſt the Veil
f Modeſty aſide to make him ſure,
nd after Marriage, you may gueſs the reſt.

*Conſt* Oh Curſes! Vengeance! Curſes yet unthought!
ch Curſes as thou wilt let fly at me,
hen thou ſhalt ſee his Head beneath the Ax,
ven Womans Curſes on thee

*Sylv* How Sir, the Ax!

*Enter* Arius *with* Criſpus.

*Conſt* Doſt thou not find the Traitor?
t ſee, he comes . Oh thou Diſſembler, anſwer,
oſt thou not tell me, when thy Life was ſtak'd,
his Marriage was not yet conſummate, ſpeak.

*Criſp* 'Tis true, dread Sir.

*Conſt.* Mark all he has confeſs'd'
is own Mouth has condemn'd him——he ſhall die.

*Criſp.* I own'd Sir, I was marry'd—but confeſs'd
o further

*Conſt* How, Traitor!
id I not force the Queſtion often?

*Criſp* True,
hich I as often wav'd with low Submiſſions—

*Conſt* Yet thoſe thy low Submiſſions all were Lies.
r well thou know'ſt thy ſubtle working wrought me
o a Satisfaction that thou hadſt not poſſeſt her.

*Criſp* That was alas my Crime.

*Conſt* That Crime was Treaſon
rpos'd Abuſe. A Plot upon thy Father.
ay the whole Cozenage ſhows thee rank in Sin,
Ha!——How know I yet ſhe is enjoy'd?
ave but thy word and her's, and both are Traitors.
t ſee my Brother comes to join my Juſtice.

*Enter* Dalmatius.

*Dalm.* What, *Criſpus* here?

*Const.* Stay, my *Dalmatius*, stay.

*Dalm.* Your Pardon Sir,
There's one among you whom I cannot suffer,
And *Crispus* knows the Cause. [*Exit* Dal-

*Crisp.* Come back, and hear it then,
Hear thou unhappy Father, hear me own
The Murder which this cursed Hand committed,
That Hand that slew the wretched *Annibal*

*Const* *Annibal* slain! O Traitor! And by thee!
Is Murder added to thy Treason too?

*Crisp.* It shall not stand me, Sir, in stead to say,
Mistaken *Annibal* forc'd me to his Ruin.
For see I lay my Body at your Feet,
And plead for Death, as others beg for Life

*Const.* *Cleanthes*, take him——*Crispus*, thou shalt dy
Therefore be this our fatal last Farewel——
One struggle more. His Mother's in his Eyes.

*Faust.* And where's his Father; but in all his Form
His every Grace, his Smiles——all but his Frowns
So exact in Body, qualities of Mind,
That if you kill your Son, you kill your self.
Oh therefore listen to the Call of Nature,
And once more view him with an Eye of Mercy.

*Const.* I have look'd my last, and now am Judge agai
*Cleanthes*, take 'em both They're both your Prisone
*Crispus* and *Fausta*. *Arius*——look you to 'em!
Keep 'em apart, and wait me in my Closet——
What yet again? 'Tis the last Tugg of Nature.—
And yet another——Why that Sigh uncall'd?—
And these wet Eyes? Oh——if I longer stay!
My vows of Justice will dissolve away—— [*E*

*Manent* Crispus, Fausta, Arius, *Guard*

*Faust.* Ruin on Ruin, let Destruction come,
With all the Wings of the most violent Death,
Yet arm'd with Innocence, I'll face the Gorgon,
And brave his bloodiest Terrors: But thy Death,
My *Crispus'* Death, my Spirit cannot bear——
Therefore I have resolv'd, and think not *Crispus*,
Think not thy Tears shall move me from my Purpo

*Crisp.* Speak, *Fausta*, speak, how come these Earthquakes here?

A

nd those o'erflowings? Why do thy Sighs redouble?
*Faust.* Because my dearest Life, my all, my *Crispus*,
oul of my Soul, that's Martyr'd for thy love——
m resolv'd, rather than see thy Death,
o wed thy Father.——
*Crisp.* Ha! do I hear thee truly?
ut speak again, for I'll not trust my Senses.
*Faust.* To wed him, *Crispus.*
*Crisp.* Sorrow sure distracts thee——
*Faust.* No——'tis the effect of Reason——
h t makes me desperate in this last Resolve——
*Crisp.* No more of this. Haste, cast the Poison up,
'is Hell that tempts thee to Eternal Ruin
herefore if thou desir'st my Spirit shou'd part
Peace, and leave my Love and Blessing with thee;
epent this last Result of thy Despair,
est I conclude thee false.——
*Faust.* How false, my *Crispus*?
*Crisp.* False to thy Vows, unconstant to thy Love;
nd that thy Soul, unable for a Ruin,
hose rather to sustain an infamous Life,
han dye with Honour.
*Faust.* Oh I cannot bear it!
*Crisp.* Not when I beg thee with my latest Breath---
*Faust.* Thy Death, my Dear! And I the hated Cause?
*Crisp.* Therefore I love thee: And would dye again
r such another Proof of thy Affection.
*Faust.* As wrought thy Death?——
*Crisp.* Thy Purpose was to save me,
nd dye thy self. Therefore let's fall together——
e not cast down, my Fair, but raise thy Eyes,
hose Watry setting Suns shine forth, my *Fausta*,
nd make our Love look beautiful in Ruin.——

*Enter* Soldier.

*Ar.* The Emperor sends again to have you parted.
*Faust.* Oh *Crispus*! Whither now?
*Crisp.* To our long Home,
here purer Spirits drink immortal Air,
nd thin-clad Souls in flying Chariots move,
nd give, and take, an Everlasting Love.

Faust.

*Faust* Such Love, grant Heav'n, our meeting Sou[l]
Which no inhuman Father may divide: [beti[d]
Where at first sight, our Minds enlarg'd may spread
Thro' all the Space, and know the mighty Dead
Such is my Hope. But, *Crispus*, what my Fear?
If I should seek, but never find you there——

*Crisp.* One last Embrace! Oh *Fausta*! do not stain
Our Bliss, with Fears we ne'er shall meet again
Through all the Heav'n, in all their Mansions blest,
To ev'ry Saint my Prayers shall be addrest,
Nor shall the happy taste a Moment's Rest,
Till some kind Angel guides my wandring Eyes,
And shews me where thy charming Spirit flies.
Then crown'd with Joys, we never knew before,
We'll waste the stock of Love's Immortal Store,
And cruel Fate shall never part us more. [*Exeunt*

---

## ACT V. SCENE I.

*Enter* Dalmatius *and* Serena.

*Seren.* NOw Sir, you have it all, the whole sad Sto[ry]
Of your unhappy Son, his Love and mine:
*Serena*'s Guilt, and *Crispus*' Innocence;
Therefore if you ask Blood, and would revenge him,
Here waits his Murdress for the stroke of Death
But hate not *Crispus*, hate not the Innocent,
Much less proceed to the Murder of your Friend,
Your faultless, guiltless, too deserving Friend,
The gentlest, best, of all th' Imperial Race.

*Dalm* No more, there needs no more My Son is dead
Eternal Peace attend him. A few sad Drops,
And now no more *Serena*, I believe thee.
My Heart avows th' Innocence of my Friend;
Which I had own'd before, had not the Wounds
Of *Annibal* lain green upon my Soul;
But that I now forgive him be thou witness,
Be witness Heav'n, and this last Resolution,
I now put on to save my *Crispus*' Life,

O[h]

or lose my own

*Seren* O let me kneel to such exalted Virtue.
ut Sir, be quick to save him, or this Goodness
Will come too late.

*Dalm.* Where is the Emperor?

*Seren* Lock'd in his Closet, deaf to the Peoples Cries:
ly Sir, I saw him pass in Fury by,
With *Arius* in discourse.

*Dalm* I fear that Traitor.

*Seren.* Your Fears, my Lord, are mine. I never lik'd him,
he Picture which he gave your Son, has shown him:
e has all the Marks we Virgins reckon Ominous,
pale, down Look, red Hair, and leering Eyes,
ischief is in him. He's with th' Emperor now,
erhaps solliciting the Fate we fear
met 'em, Sir, and interrupted *Cæsar*,
Who first receiv'd me kindly, but at the Name
f *Crispus* frown'd, and shook me from his Arm.

*Dalm* Fear not, as thou hast counsel'd, I will join
*lester* on the instant.

*Seren* Force the Door,
he refuse to let you in, do all
hat Pity, Love, and Friendship can inspire,
o all that I would do, were I *Dalmatius* [*Ex. severally*

## SCENE II. *A Bedchamber.*

*A Bowl and a Dagger on the Table.*

*Enter* Constantine *and* Arius.

*Const* *Arius!*

*Ari* Sir.

*Const* I am resolv'd to be at Rest,
hou art my Friend, Physician, I am sick;
ck even to death Reach me that Goblet hither:
he Dagger too.

*Ari* Sir

*Const* What an easie matter
were for any Man, in any Case,
ho' rack'd with th' Gout, Stone, any kind of Torture,

With one of these to Sleep?

*Ari* For ever, Sir?

*Const* Right, *Arius.*

*Ari* Then there is Poison in the Bowl?

*Const.* There is most deadly.

*Ari* May I, Sir, presume
To ask for what?

*Const* *Arius*, thou art my Friend,
I think too, thou would'st venture Life. Why yes!
'Tis Poison, and I'll tell thee too for what:
To see how long a Dog will be a dying.
Or say, what if we try'd it on a Man;
Some Enemy that Laws will not take hold of?

*Ari.* Sir, I understand you

*Const* Look then you do · How dost thou understand m[e]

*Ari* Why thus, you past your Oath, your Son shou[ld]
If *Fausta* prov'd him Innocent. [Li...

*Const.* 'Tis true
And spite of my Revenge, my Heart must clear h[im]

*Ari.* Right Sir, I find it, you are grip'd in Conscien[ce]
Now if a Friend should help you, so; or Fate,
Not always answering most Mens Expectations,
Should call your Son to Heav'n.

*Const.* To Heav'n, *Arius*!

*Ari.* To Heav'n, or Hell, it matters not for that,
So he be out o'th' way, and you not know't.

*Const.* And I not know't?

*Ari* No Sir, not I. What then?
How then! you never see him more.
And so farewell ——I'll take this Poison with me.

*Const.* Stay, stay! Come back.
How strange a Guilt is mine, who dare not speak,
But indirectly, what my Soul desires
Directly done. Why should I hide my Thoughts
From thee?

*Ari.* Why Sir indeed?

*Const.* When no Eye sees.

*Ari.* None.

*Const.* None but the Eye of Heav'n.
But Walls they say have Ears; therefore we'll whisp[er]

Th[...]

is horrid, barbarous, and unnatural Murder!
e him his Choice. Tell him I cannot live,
ess he dies. Tell him I strove to save him,
d Nature pleaded wonders in his Cause.
*Arr.* I'll stab him first, and tell him after.——
*ust* No, Poison's the gentler Fate. Thou art too
loud——
Conscience! how it heaves within my Bosom——
*Arr* Conscience! The Soul's rising of the Lights.
Drink Blood ——
*ust* Blood, say'st thou! What, the Blood of *Crispus*?
Hark!
o's there? Run to the Door! Say I am not well,
not be seen to night
*rr* Your Fancy, Sir.
*ust* I thought I heard my Mother's Voice
she's long dead 'Twas, as thou say'st, my Fancy.
Fear, my Guilt that haunts me. But be gone.
must fall there is no hiding it·
it no longer Murder, but a Justice,
ey him as a Thief that robb'd thy Soul
ll its wealth· *Arrus*——how am I now?
*r* All Emperor And, Sir, I'll haste to obey you.
*st* Thou shalt: But go not *Arrus*, till I send thee——
Emperor, and Judge. But where's the Father?
k me there Nature, save him if thou canst;
ember him as once thy bosom-love.
*r* I like not this Remembrance.
*ust.* Remember the whole Progress of his Life;
dient all, ev'n in his Infant Years
n every Morning to my Bed-side he came,
as I blest him, thank'd me with his Tears.

Serena *knocking without.*

*en* My Lord, the Emperor.
*ust.* *Arrus*, hark. Who's there?
'tis my Wife. Run to the door. My Wife!
risen from the dead to save my Son.
*en* I will have Audience.
Madam, you must not enter.
*st.* *Arrus*, let her in.

*Enter*

*Enter* Serena.

*Seren* *Cæsar*, save thy Son;
Save him in time, the People are in Arms.
*Dalmatius*, with the Guards, is gone to quell 'em

*Const* How! mutiny? And in my Son's behalf?
Is this the course to save him? *Arius*, hence—
And execute my Orders

*Seren* May I think it?
A Bowl of Poison, Sir! Is that your Order?

*Const.* There is no Mystery now to be conceal'd—
'Tis as you said And *Crispus* dies this Minute.
*Arius* away

*Seren.* He sha'nt, till you hear me.
Think Sir, oh think!

*Const.* I've thought too much already:
But with this last Revolt my Heart is steel'd,
Though as you enter'd I was fooling Time
With Thoughts of Mercy.

*Seren* And has this cursed Wretch prevented you!

*Const.* *Dalmatius* and *Sylvester* will be here
To hinder Justice: Break her hold Away.

*Seren* Fall then *Serena* first, and stay that Fury [*Stabs her s*

*Const* *Arius*, come back What hast thou done, *Sere*

*Seren.* I've paid the Debt of Nature ere my Time.

*Const* 'Twas a too honest part What was the Ca

*Seren* The Love of *Crispus*: Love of him you ha
But let this Victim to Despair suffice.

*Enter* Dalmatius *and* Sylvester.

Your Brother here! *Dalmatius* pardon me.
Your Son is now reveng'd. Restrain the Emperor—
And look to *Arius*. Oh! [*She d*

*Dalm.* The Joys of Heav'n,
And an eternal Requiem waft thy Soul.

*Const* Brother, how are the People?

*Dalm* All hush'd again
Why will you harbour, Sir, that Snake about you,
That puts you on these fatal Resolutions?
For, else could it be possible a Prince
So good, so full of every Kingly Grace,

Sho

uld once conceive a Thought to put his Son,
guiltless Son, to an untimely Death,
thout the Instigation of a Devil?

*Syv.* Consider, *Cæsar*, you that have had the Glory
Miracles from Heav'n to be converted
know your Passion manacles your Reason,
here are Hands to help you.

*Const.* Is that then the Result of all your Reason?
hope for sober Actions from a Mad-man?

*Dalm* Not till the Frenzy leaves him. But we know
u are not so far gone, to lose all Temper.
ur Hopes, and Fears, your broken Resolutions,
Symptoms all of a most noble Nature,
here Judgment seems half sunk, but not quite drown'd.

*Const.* Why this I can alledge as well as you;
ow the Lawrels which I've worn so long
st wither If my Son should find a Grave,
present Fame, and Glory too hereafter,
ll upon the hazard But what then?
e the Storm before me threatning Wrack,
e the Shelves, but who can point the Shore?

*Syl.* Cast over-board the Casket of your Love,
ow 'tis precious, but 'twill sink you, Sir.
orce her, Sir; and give her to your Son.

*Const.* Forgo my *Fausta*! 'tis impossible.

*Dalm* Nothing's impossible to a Mind resolv'd.
pass beyond *Sylvester*'s mild Remonstrance,
d ease your Love by Death, by *Fausta*'s Death,
hen she is past recall, you'll love no more;
y no more

*Const* If that could be resolv'd——
e Conquest were a great one. [will strike you.

*Dalm.* The more you think, the more the Thought
but the difference of Counsellors;
hat Colours good and bad can give to Reason.
d *Arius* stay'd, by this time you had doom'd
ur Son to Death, who now have gain'd the Conquest.

*Const.* Would half were gain'd: yet, since the Start
try to win in this Olympick Race. [was noble,
o' hilly all the way, and at the Gole
e Summit touches Heav'n.

*Dalm.* Urge the necessity; she or *Crispus* dies.
Th' innocent *Crispus*, or the guilty *Fausta*,
That after all her Vows, could thus deceive you,
Deceive you both. Who, if your Son were dead,
No doubt, as quick would practise with another
*Const.* By Heav'n, why not? She that could swe
Forsworn, may swear and be forsworn again [and
Oh! I remember now with what a Look,
An Angel-look, she vow'd
*Dalm.* Yet with that Look,
This Angel, like a Devil, drew in your Son.
Methinks the very grossness of the Cheat
Should make you loath her.
*Const.* Ha!
*Dalm.* Detest and scorn her.
*Const.* Scorn on her Scorn, and Death Disdain
By Majesty, by Empire, she shall bleed. [ce
*Sylv.* Banish her, *Cæsar.*——
*Dalm.* No, Sir; Death, or nothing.
Banish her to day, and she'll be here to morrow
Down with her, down; dwell on her perjur'd Vo
When the same Breath that swore her yours for ever
Dom'd her anothers.
*Const.* *Arius*, bring her forth.
She dies! I'll sweat and bleed, but I will conquer—
Call, call my Son——Henceforth but name a Wo
'Tis Treason to my Ear. Why, what a Plague
Might she have here engender'd! Forc'd a Fathe
To put his guiltless Son to horrid Death.
*Dalm.* Royally urg'd. By Heav'n 'twas ever thus
Where Women had to do. Therefore behold her
As a Gangreen to the State
*Const.* And cut her off
*Dalm.* The Bane of Empire——
*Const.* And the Rott of Power!
Yet there I'll stay and fix my Imagination,
On all their Mischiefs, Murders, Massacres,
And Seas of Blood they have spilt in former Ages
Woman, no more. And when my Heart is going,
Sound but that Name, the pow'rful Spell shall bind

ond Circean and Ægyptian Charms:
will raise the lowest Devils up in swarms,
hinge the Globe, and put the World in Arms
oman that dooms us all to one sure Grave,
d rather damns than Providence can save [Exe.

Enter Constantine and Fausta

Const Fausta, thou art false, forsworn,
Fausta I say so too.
Const Therefore shalt dye
Faust I have no other Wish
Const. What, not to live,
should pardon thee?
Faust. That were Life indeed;
gain your Pardon, and to live for Crispus
Const. No, Wretch! remember as you swore to me,
ow return, it is impossible
thou shalt dye for Crispus
Faust And not with him, Sir?
Const No; I've decreed
n thou shalt dye to save him
Faust. But have you, Sir, decreed to love him too
Fausta's Death?
Const I have.
Faust Oh! then the Gods
ve heard my Pray'rs, which, next to living for him,
s, still to dye to save him.
t grant me, Sir, in Death
e last Farewel.
Const No, thou hast look'd thy last
Faust. Yet you may let 'em bear me by his Window;
t be possible to snatch a Glance,
d not delay my Execution, Sir
Const She weeps; and there is Magick in her Tears.
hall weep too. Bring forth the Poison. Haste——
e shall not stay the making of a Bath.
hat, Artus!
Art Sir.
Const. Give her the Poison. Haste and see her dye.
Faust. Stay, Sir, come back. I have no load upon me——
t what you all may know: give me the Bowl;

I'll drink it for my Love. Alas my Lord,
Methinks one last Farewel had not been much,
But since you judge it, Sir, unfit——I'll dye,
Without complaining. Therefore tell my Love—
That my last Pray'r was for his Life and yours

*Const* Hold, *Fausta*: *Arius*, take the Poison from
And bring the Bath My Son shall see her dye
Call *Crispus* hither. Since her Fate's decreed,
'Twere just he shou'd be harden'd with the view,
She weeps again, and with the trick unmans me,
Spite of my Vows, she works my Lyon Heart,
And melts me into Love. How fares my *Fausta*?

*Faust* Sir

*Const*. Thy Hand, before we part for ever, *Fausta*
I am lost——I'm vanquish'd. With a Touch o'ercom

*Dalm* Wake Sir Where are you?

*Const* Ha!

*Dalm* *Sylvester*'s here:
And *Crispus* waits

*Const* Why then she dies again.
Haste, bring him in, bring him to my Relief
The earning of a Father comes upon me,
And my Soul longs to meet him. *Fausta*, turn;
Turn thy bright Eyes on Death: And carry Fires
To scorch new Worlds; but warm the old no more
For here's the rising Sun, to eclipse thy Beams

*Enter* Crispus *with* Sylvester

O *Crispus*! Who that has beheld our distance,
That infinite space that Passion cast betwixt us,
Would e'er have thought we thus should meet again

*Crisp* What can be added, Heav'n, to such a Kind

*Const*. What, *Crispus*! What indeed, to make it last
See'st thou that fair one?

*Crisp*. Sir, you give me Hopes; tho' dash'd with Fe
But hold, perhaps I have to Death offended,
For sinning but in wish: A dawning Joy
Shines in her Eyes, and revels in her Smiles,
Which seem to tell me, we shall both be happy.

*Const* Would'st thou be happy in thy Father's Lo

*Crisp* Judge me, you Powers, if that be not my Thoug

utmoſt reach of my extended Soul,
ich knows no other wiſh, but *Fauſta*'s Love———
*uſt.* And that's the Love, which you, by my Example,
t learn to hate.
*iſp.* To hate, Sir? What?
*uſt.* Hate thy Love
what's all one, to bear the effect of Hate,
Execution here before thy Eyes.
*iſp* My *Fauſta*'s Death?

ENE *draws* Arius, Labienus, Eubolus, *with a Bath.*

*uſt.* Behold the Poiſon'd Bath. [Veins:
*iſp* For me---I am ready Sir. Haſte, launch my
that are deſtin'd here for my Deſtruction,
obe me——haſte———
*uſt.* None touch him, on your Lives.
y may as ſafely launch their Emperor,
ound his Son. But *Fauſta* muſt prepare,
e is no other way to reconcile us.
*iſp.* Then hold me, Sir, at everlaſting diſtance,
me again for ever from your ſight.
ſh me, Curſe me, as you did before———
make not *Fauſta*'s Death the curſed Cauſe,
ſave his Villain's Life, this hangman Traitor,
Coward that can live and hear her threaten'd!
*uſt* My Love, my Lord, blame not thy noble Father,
Curſe thy ſelf, for this was all my ſeeking.——
*iſp* Thy ſeeking. Ha! And ſeek'ſt thou my Embraces——.——
the baſe Diſhonour thou haſt done me?
e from my Arms———
*uſt* I will not, I will hold thee
my laſt gaſp, and graſp thee after Death
puſh me yet again. Nay, ſtrike me *Criſpus*,
ll not leave thy Boſom.
*iſp* See he's going——
, bleſt Mother's Soul, let me come at him——
*uſt* *Arius*, ſee it done.
Prayers are vain, ſome of you break his hold.
*iſp* *Dalmatius* and *Sylveſter* will not ſure,
for the reſt, let me but ſee who dares.

*Const.* Their Emperor commands 'em---help to for[ce]
I charge thee *Crispus*, leave me, [hi...]
And dare not by this Willfulness provoke me.

*Crisp.* I have no Willfulness, but these stubborn Tea[rs]
Hear my last Sighs, for Groans quite choak my Wor[ds]
My *Fausta*'s Life, or break my Heart before you.

*Faust.* Sir, do not hear him, snatch your self away
And leave us here——I'll hush him, ere I die,
And send him weeping to you for his Pardon.

*Const.* He sees 'tis vain; and has let go his hold
Withdraw——yet Brother, we'll observe unseen—
I do not like this sudden Sullenness———
*Fausta* farewel. *Arius* dispatch No more. [Ex[eunt]

Crispus, Arius, Fausta, *Executioners*

*Faust.* Now *Crispus*, now my Dear, wilt thou forg[ive]
This glorious Conquest of triumphing Love?

*Crisp.* No By my Soul, and by my hopes of Hea[ven]
Not at thy parting Groan, will I forgive thee,
But rather curse the Hour when first I saw thee,
Curse our first Kisses, Marriage and Embraces,
Unless thou join me —Ha——come forwarder
With *Arius*, join me, to provide some Means,
That I may bear thee Company in Death
If this thou dost deny me, by the Saints,
By all our Loves——I swear thou never Lov'st me—

*Ari.* By Heav'n my Lord I pity you; and if—

*Faust.* If, *Arius*! What? thou wilt not joyn his M[eans]

*Crisp.* Hark *Arius* By our Friendship---I conjure th[ee]
For I have sworn I will not eat nor drink,
Tho' I survive this Hour———

*Ari.* I have the Means.

*Crisp.* A Dagger Blessings on thee---give't me, I sa[y]

*Faust.* [Ar]ius, thou art a Villain!

[illegible] [I']l tell my Father, that I forc'd it from thee

[illegible] [K]eep keep it from him, or I'll tell the Emp[eror]

[illegible] [y]ou that first betray'd him to my Love,

[illegible] us.

[illegible] Madam! let me beg you———

[illegible] Love, I am [illegible] thee

[illegible] call the Emperor.

hat damn'd Villain, Traitor, Devil, *Arius*.
i there without. *Crispus* is murder'd. Help——
*n*. Nay then 'tis time to fly——

Constantine *meets him with the rest*

*nst*. Yes Fiend, to Hell,
ere thou shalt make thy damn'd Account.——In with him——
the unblooded Villain in the Bath,
ich he prepar'd for others Throw him in.
*In*. Hold Sir, the Bath's not poison'd.
*nst* How!
*in*. Compassion for your Empress,
de me contrive this only way to save her
*nst*. Thou hast done well. Yet in with him, to try.
*in*. Hold Sir! And I'll confess, it is, it is,
poison'd——Pardon
*nst* Down with him, keep him down
he be dead. Then give him to his Slaves ——

[*The Bath sinks with him*

*rispus*——Why? why dost thou eye me thus
h snatch'd Regards? Why dost thou eye thy Father?
looking on thy Dagger, now on *Fausta*——
'twere possible to deny her still?
*risp* Deny her? Why, Sir? mean you then to give her?
*nst* Or let me stand a Curse to After-Ages.
the Hand of Heav'n, not mine, that gives her:
Treasons of the perjur'd *Arius*
urn my Soul, and quite reduce my Reason,
t I will give her thee without a Pang.
e her, my Son, and with her all the Blessings,
all the Love, my loaded Bosom bears;
Dews of Heav'n, and these thy Father's Tears.
*risp*. Oh Joys!
*ust* Oh Heav'n!
*risp* *Fausta*!
*ust* *Crispus*! *Cæsar*!
*risp* Father!
let us prostrate——as a God, approach him——
u glorious Image of the Deity!
n shall we answer?

*Const. Crispus! Fausta* —— Nothing;
Nothing but rise, and take me in your Arms.
Thus brooding o'er you with a fruitful Joy,
I prophecy, by my Example led,
Such Love and Peace thro' all the World shall spread,
And *Roman* Arts that *British* Isle adorn,
Where *Helena* Deceas'd, and I was Born
While *Crispus* thus, to *Fausta*'s Love, I give:
And both for ever, in my Bosom live [*Ex.* Omn.

# EPILOGUE

Spoken by Mrs. *Cook*.

OUR Hero'*s happy in the Play's Conclusion:*
*The holy Rogue at last has met Confusion:*
*Though* Arius *all along appear'd a Saint,*
*The last Act shew'd him a true Protestant.*
Eusebius, (*for you know I read Greek Authors*)
*Reports, that after all these Plots and Slaughters,*
*The Court of* Constantine *was full of Glory,*
*And every* Trimmer *turn'd Addressing* Tory;
*They follow'd him in Herds as they were mad:*
*When* Clause *was King, then all the World was glad.*
Whigs *kept the Places they possest before,*
*And most were in a way of getting more,*
*Which was as much as saying, Gentlemen,*
*Here's Power and Mony to be Rogues again.*
*Indeed there were a sort of peaking Tools,*
*Some call them Modest, but I call 'em Fools,*
*Men much more Loyal, tho' not half so loud;*
*But these poor Devils were cast behind the Crowd*
*For bold Knaves thrive without one Grain of Sense,*
*But good Men starve for want of Impudence.*
*Besides all these, there's a sort of Wights,*
*(I think my Author calls them* Teckelites;)
*Such hearty Rogues against the King and Laws,*
*They favour'd even a Foreign Rebel's Cause.*

# PROLOGUE.

*, their own damn'd Design was quash'd and aw'd,*
*east they gave it their good Word abroad.*
*many a Man, who, for a quiet Life,*
*ds out his Bastard, not to noise his Wife.*
*o'er their Darling Plot these* Trimmers *cry;*
*though they cannot keep it in their Eye,*
*bind it Prentice to* Count Teckely.
*believe not the last Plot, may I be curst,*
*believe they e'er believ'd the first.*
*wonder their own Plot, no Plot they think;*
*Man that makes it, never smells the Stink.*
*now it comes into thy Head, I'll tell*
*these damn'd* Trimmers *lov'd the* Turks *so well.*
*Original* Trimmer, *though a Friend to no Man,*
*his Heart ador'd a pretty Woman:*
*ew that* Mahomet *laid up for ever,*
*Black-ey'd Rogues, for every true Believer:*
*which was more than mortal Man e'er tasted,*
*Pleasure that for threescore Twelve-months lasted:*
*rn for this, may surely be forgiven:*
*not be circumcis'd for such a Heav'n!*

# EDIPUS:

A

# TRAGEDY.

Written by

Mr. *DRYDEN* and Mr. *LEE.*

*Hi proprium decus & partum indignantur honorem*
*Ni teneant.*——— Virgil
*Vos exemplaria Græca,*
*Nocturna versate manu, versate diurna.* Horat.

Printed in the YEAR 1712.

THE

# PREFACE.

THOUGH it be dangerous to raise too great an Expectation, especially in Works of this Nature, where we are to please an satiable Audience, yet 'tis reasonable to prepos- s them in favour of an Author; and therefore h the *Prologue* and *Epilogue* inform'd you, that *Edipus* was the most celebrated Piece of all An- uity. That *Sophocles*, not only the greatest Wit, t one of the greatest Men in *Athens*, made it for e Stage, at the Publick Cost; and that it had the putation of being his Master-piece, not only a- ongst the Seven of his which are still remaining, t of the greater Number which are perish'd. *istotle* has more than once admir'd it in his Book Poetry; *Horace* has mentioned it; *Lucullus*, *lius Cæsar*, and other noble *Romans*, have itten on the same Subject, tho' their Poems are holly lost; but *Seneca*'s is still preserv'd. In our own

own Age, *Corneille* has attempted it, and it appea by his Preface, with great Succefs: But a judicio Reader will eafily obferve, how much the Copy inferior to the Original. He tells you himfelf, th he owes a great part of his Succefs to the hap Epifode of *Thefeus* and *Dirce*; which is the fam thing, as if we fhould acknowledge, that we a indebted for our good Fortune, to the Under pl of *Adraftus*, *Eurydice*, and *Creon*. The Truth he miferably failed in the Character of his Her If he defir'd that *OEdipus* fhould be pitied, fhould have made him a better Man. He forg that *Sophocles* had taken care to fhew him in h firft Entrance a juft, a merciful, a fuccefsful, a R ligious Prince, and in fhort a Father of his Cou try: Inftead of thefe, he has drawn him fufpicious, d figning, more anxious of keeping the *Theban* Crow than follicitous for the Safety of his People: Hecto by *Thefeus*, contemn'd by *Dirce*, and fcarce ma taining a fecond part in his own Tragedy. Th was an Error in the firft Concoction; and theref never to be mended in the fecond or the third introduc'd a greater Hero than *OEdipus* himfel for when *Thefeus* was once there, that Compa on of *Hercules* muft yield to none: The Poet w obliged to furnifh him with Bufinefs, to make h an Equipage fuitable to his Dignity; and by f lowing him too clofe, to lofe his other King *Brandford* in the Crowd. *Seneca* on the other f as if there were no fuch thing as Nature to minded in a Play, is always running after pomp Expreffions, pointed Sentences, and Philofophi Notions, more proper for the Study than the St The *Frenchman* followed a wrong Scent, and Roman was abfolutely at cold Hunting. All

co

ould gather out of *Corneille*, was, that an Episode must be, but not his way: And *Seneca* supply'd us with no new Hint, but only a Relation which he makes of his *Tiresias* raising the Ghost of *Lajus*, which is here perform'd in view of the Audience; the Rites and Ceremonies so far his, as he agreed with Antiquity, and the Religion of the *Greeks*; but he himself was beholden to *Homer*'s *Tiresias* in the *Odysses* for some of them; and the rest have been collected from *Helidore*'s *Ethiopiques*, and *Lucan*'s *Erictho*. *Sophocles*, indeed, is admirable every where; and therefore we have followed as close as possibly we cou'd: But the *Athenian* Theatre (whether more perfect than ours, is not now disputed) had a Perfection differing from ours. You see there in every Act a single Scene, (or two at most) which manage the Business of the Play; and after that succeeds the *Chorus*, which commonly takes up more Time in singing, than there has been employ'd in speaking. The principal Person appears almost constantly through the Play, but the inferior Parts seldom above once in the whole Tragedy. The Conduct of our Stage is much more difficult, where we are oblig'd never to lose any considerable Character which we have once presented. Custom likewise has obtain'd, that we must form an Under-Plot of Second Persons, which must be depending on the First, and their By Walks must be like those in a Labyrinth, which all of 'em lead into the great *Partere*, or like so many several Lodging-Chambers, which have their Out-lets into the same Gallery. Perhaps, after all, if we cou'd think so, the ancient Method, as 'tis the easiest, is also the most natural, and the best: For Variety, as 'tis manag'd, is too often subject to breed Distraction;

and

and while we would pleafe too many ways, fo
want of Art in the Conduct, we pleafe in non
But we have given you more already than was ne
ceffary for a Preface; and for ought we know, ma
gain no more by our Inftructions than that Politi
Nation is like to do, who have taught their En
mies to fight fo long, that at laft they are in
Condition to invade them.

PRO

# PROLOGUE.

WHEN Athens *all the* Græcian *State did guide,*
*And* Greece *gave Laws to all the World beside,*
*n* Sophocles *with* Socrates *did sit*
*time, in Wisdom one, and one in Wit:*
*d Wit from Wisdom differ'd not in those,*
*as 'twas sung in Verse, or said in Prose.*
*n* OEdipus *on Crowned Theatres,*
*w all admiring Eyes and list'ning Ears;*
*pleas'd Spectator shouted every Line,*
*noblest, manliest, and the best Design!*
*d every Critick of each learned Age*
*this just Model has reform'd the Stage.*
*w, should it fail, (as Heav'n avert our Fear!)*
*mn it in Silence, lest the World should hear.*
*were it known this Poem did not please,*
*might set up for perfect Salvages:*
*r Neighbours would not look on you as Men:*
*think the Nation all turn'd* Picts *again.*
*th as you manage Matters, 'tis not fit*
*should suspect your selves of too much Wit.*
*ve not the Jest too far, but spare this Piece·*
*d, for this once, be not more wise than* Greece
*twice! do not pell-mell to Damning fall,*
*e true-born* Britains, *who ne'er think at all:*
*y be advis'd, and though at* Mons *you won,*
*pointed Cannon do not always run.*
*h some respect to ancient Wit proceed,*
*take the four first Councils for your Creed.*
*when you lay Tradition wholly by,*
*d on the private Spirit alone rely,*
*turn Fanaticks in your Poetry.*
*otwithstanding all that we can say,*
*needs will have your pen'worths of the Play,*
*d come resolv'd to Damn, because you pay:*
*Record it, in memorial of the Fact,*
*The first Play bury'd since the Woollen Act.*

# Dramatis Personæ.

MEN

| | |
|---|---|
| OEdipus, | Mr. Bett[illegible] |
| Adraſtus, | Mr *Smith.* |
| Creon, | Mr. *Sanford* |
| Tireſias, | Mr *Harris.* |
| Hæmon, | Mr. *Crosby.* |
| Alcander, | Mr *William* |
| Diocles, | Mr. *Norris* |
| Pyracmon, | Mr. *Bow*[illegible] |
| Phorbas, | Mr. *Gillo.* |
| Dymas. | |
| Ægeon | |
| *Ghoſt of* Lajus, | Mr *William* |

WOMEN.

| | |
|---|---|
| Jocaſta, | Mrs. *Better*[illegible] |
| Eurydice, | Mrs. *Lee.* |
| Manto, | Mrs. *Evans.* |

*Prieſts*, *Citizens*, *Attendants*, &c.

SCENE *THEBE*[illegible]

OE[illegible]

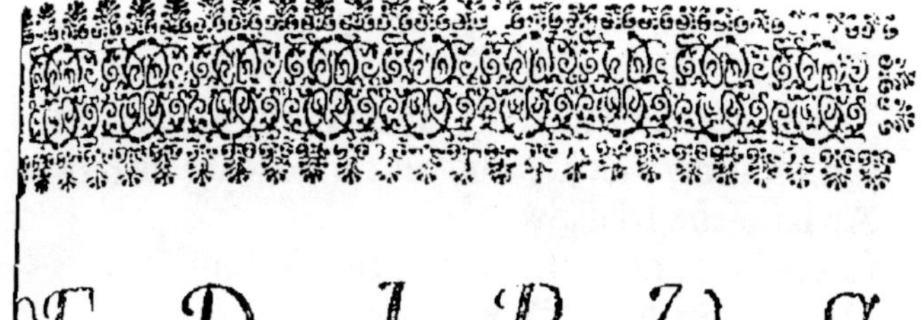

# ŒDIPUS.

## ACT I. SCENE I.

### SCENE *Thebes.*

*e Curtain rises to a plaintive Tune, representing the present Condition of* Thebes: *Dead Bodies appear at a distance in the Streets, some faintly go over the Stage, others drop.*

*Enter* Alcander, Diocles *and* Pyracmon.

*ALCANDER.*

Methinks we stand on Ruins; Nature shakes
About us, and the universal Frame
So loose, that it but wants another Push
To leap from off its Hinges.
*Dio.* No Sun to chear us, but a bloody Globe
at rowls above, a bald and beamless Fire,
s Face o'er-grown with Scurf. The Sun's sick too;
ortly he'll be an Earth.
*Pyr.* Therefore the Seasons
e all confus'd, and by the Heav'ns neglected,
rget themselves. Blind Winter meets the Summer
his Mid-way, and, seeing not his Livery,
s driv'n him headlong back: And the raw Damps
ith flaggy Wings fly heavily about,
attering their pestilential Colds and Rheums
rough all the lazy Air.

*Alc.* Hence Murrains follow,
On bleating Flocks, and on the lowing Herds:
At last, the Malady
Grew more domestick, and the faithful Dog
Dy'd at his Master's Feet.
*Dio.* And next his Master:
For all those Plagues which Earth and Air had brood
First on inferior Creatures try'd their Force,
And last they seiz'd on Man.
*Pyr* And then a thousand Deaths at once advanc'd
And every Dart took place; all was so sudden,
That scarce a first Man fell; one but began
To wonder, and strait fell a Wonder too.
A third, who stoop'd to raise his dying Friend,
Dropt in the pious Act Heard you that Groan?
[*Groan with*
*Dio* A Troop of Ghosts took flight together ther
Now Death's grown riotous, and will play no more
For single Stakes, but Families and Tribes
How are we sure we breath not now our last,
And that next Minute,
Our Bodies cast into some common Pit,
Shall not be built upon, and overlaid
By half a People?
*Alc* There's a Chain of Causes
Link'd to Effects; invincible Necessity
That whate'er is, could not but so have been,
That's my Security.
*Enter* Creon
*Cre* So had it need, when all our Streets lie cove
With dead and dying Men,
And Earth exposes Bodies on the Pavements
More than she hides in Graves!
Betwixt the Bride and Bridegroom have I seen
The Nuptial Torch do common Offices
Of Marriage and of Death.
*Dio* Now *Oedipus*,
(If he return from War, our other Plague)
Will scarce find half he left to grace his Triumph.
*Pyr.* A feeble Pæan will be sung before him

*Alc.* He would do well to bring the Wives and Chidren
Conquer'd *Argians* to renew his *Thebes.*
*Cre* May Funerals meet him at the City Gates
ith their detested Omen.
*Dio.* Of his Children.
*Cre* Nay, though she be my Sister, of his Wife
*Alc* Oh that our *Thebes* might once again behold
Monarch *Theban* born!
*Dio* We might have had one.
*Pyr* Yes, had the People pleas'd
*Cre* Come ye're my Friends.
e Queen, my Sister, after *Lajus'* Death,
r'd to lie single, and supply'd his Place
ith a young Successor.
*Dio.* He much resembles
r former Husband too.
*Alc* I always thought so. [black Locks
*Pyr* When twenty Winters more have grizzl'd his
will be a very *Lajus.*
*Cre* So he will.
n time she stands provided of a *Lajus*
re young and vigorous too, by twenty Springs.
ese Women are such cunning Purveyors!
k where their Appetites have once been pleas'd,
same Resemblance in a younger Lover
brooding in their Fancies the same Pleasures,
urges their Remembrance to desire.
*Dio.* Had Merit, not her Dotage, been consider'd,
n *Creon* had been King; but *Oedipus*,
tranger!
*Cre* That Word Stranger, I confess
nds harshly in my Ears
*Dio* We are your Creatures.
People prone, as in all general Ills,
sudden change, the King in Wars abroad,
Queen a Woman, weak and unregarded!
*dice* the Daughter of dead *Lajus*,
incess young and beauteous, and unmarried.
hinks from these disjointed Propositions
ething might be produc'd.

 *Cre.*

*Cre.* The Gods have done
Their part, by ſending this commodious Plague
But oh the Princeſs! her hard Heart is ſhut
By Adamantine Locks againſt my Love.
*Alc.* Your Claim to her is ſtrong, you are betroth'd.
*Pyr.* True! in her Nonage
*Alc.* But that Lett's remov'd.
*Dio.* I heard the Prince of *Argos*, your *Adraſtus*,
When he was Hoſtage here——
*Cre.* Oh name him not! the Bane of all my Hopes;
That hot-brain'd, headlong Warriour, has the Charms
Of Youth, and ſomewhat of a lucky Raſhneſs,
To pleaſe a Woman yet more Fool than he.
That thoughtleſs Sex is caught by outward Form
And empty Noiſe, and loves it ſelf in Man.
*Alc.* But ſince the War broke out about our Frontiers
He's now a Foe to *Thebes*!
*Cre.* But is not ſo to her; ſee ſhe appears,
Once more I'll prove my Fortune, you inſinuate
Kind Thoughts of me into the Multitude,
Lay load upon the Court; gull 'em with Freedom,
And you ſhall ſee 'em toſs their Tails, and gad,
As if the Breeze had ſtung 'em.
*Dio.* We'll about it.
[*Exeunt* Alcander, Diocles, Pyracmon.
*Enter* Eurydice.
*Cre.* Hail, Royal Maid, thou bright *Eurydice*!
A laviſh Planet reign'd when thou wert born,
And made thee of ſuch Kindred mold to Heav'n,
Thou ſeemeſt more Heav'ns than ours.
*Eu.* Caſt round your Eyes;
Where late the Streets were ſo thick ſown with Men,
Like *Cadmus*'s Brood they juſtled for the Paſſage
Now look for thoſe erected Heads, and ſee 'em
Like Pebbles paving all our publick Ways:
When you have thought on this, anſwer me this,
If theſe be Hours of Courtſhip.
*Cre.* Yes, they are,
For when the Gods deſtroy ſo faſt, 'tis time
We ſhou'd renew the Race.

*ur.* What, in the midst of horror!
*e* Why not then?
re's the more need of Comfort.
*ur* Impious *Creon*!
*,* Unjust *Eurydice*! can you accuse me
Love, which is Heav'ns Precept, and not fear
r Vengeance, which you say pursues our Crimes,
uld reach your Perjuries?
*ur* Still the old Argument.
d you cast your Eyes on other Men,
v cast 'em on your self. think what you are.
*e* A Man.
*ur.* A Man!
*e* Why doubt you? I'm a Man
*ur* 'Tis well you tell me so, I should mistake you
any other part o'th' whole Creation,
her than think you Man. hence from my sight,
u Poyson to my Eyes
*e* Twas you first poyson'd mine, and yet methinks
Face and Person shou'd not make you sport.
*ur.* You force me, by your Importunities,
shew you what you are.
*e* A Prince who loves you.
since your Pride provokes me, worth your Love,
at his highest Value.
*ur* Love for thee?
Love renounc'd thee ere thou saw'st the Light:
ure her self start back when thou wert born,
cry'd, The Work's not mine ——
Midwife stood agast, and when she saw
Mountain Back, and thy distorted Legs,
Face it self,
minted with the Royal Stamp of Man,
half o'ercome with Beast, stood doubting long,
ose Right in thee were more
knew not if to burn thee in the Flames,
re not the holier Work
*e* Am I to blame, if Nature threw my Body
o perverse a Mold? Yet when she cast
envious Hand upon my supple Joints,

Unable to resist, and rumpled 'em
On heaps in their dark Lodging, to revenge
Her bungled Work, she stampt my Mind more fair:
And as from *Chaos*, huddled and deform'd,
The Gods struck Fire, and lighted up their Lamps
That beautifie the Sky, so she inform'd
This ill-shap'd Body with a darling Soul·
And making less than Man, she made me more.

*Eur* No, thou art all one Error, Soul and Body;
The first young Tryal of some unskill'd Pow'r,
Rude in the making Art, an Ape of *Jove*.
Thy crooked Mind within, hunch'd out thy Back,
And wandred in thy Limbs To thy own kind
Make Love, if thou canst find it in the World,
And seek not from our Sex to raise an Off-spring,
Which mingled with the rest, would tempt the Gods
To cut off Human Kind.

*Cre* No; let em leave
The *Argian* Prince for you that Enemy
Of *Thebes* has made you false, and break the Vows
You made to me

*Eur.* They were my Mother's Vows,
Made when I was at Nurse.

*Cre* But hear me, Maid,
This Blot of Nature, this deform'd loath'd *Creon*,
Is Master of a Sword, to reach the Blood
Of your young *Minion*, spoil the Gods fine Work,
And stab you in his Heart

*Eur.* This when thou doest,
Then may'st thou still be curst with loving me·
And, as thou art, be still unpitied, loath'd,
And let his Ghost——No, let his Ghost have rest,
But let the greatest, fiercest, foulest Fury,
Let *Creon* haunt himself. [*Exit* Euryd.

*Cre.* 'Tis true, I am
What she has told me, an Offence to sight:
My Body opens inward to my Soul,
And lets in Day to make my Vices seen,
By all discerning Eyes, but the blind Vulgar.
I must haste, ere *Oedipus* return,

o snatch the Crown and her, for I still love,
t love with Malice, as an angry Cur
arles while he feeds, so will I seize and staunch
he hunger of my Love on this proud Beauty,
d leave the scraps for Slaves.

*Enter* Tiresias, *leaning on a Staff, and led by his Daughter* Manto

hat makes this blind prophetick Fool abroad?
ou'd his *Apollo* had him, he's too holy
r Earth and me; I'll shun his walk, and seek
y popular Friends. [*Exit* Creon.

*Tir.* A little farther, yet a little farther;
ou wretched Daughter of a dark old Man,
nduct my weary Steps, and thou who seest
r me and for thy self, beware thou tread not
ith Impious Steps upon dead Corps,——Now stay,
thinks I draw more open, vital Air.
here are we?

*Manto* Under Covert of a Wall:
e most frequented once, and noisie part
*Thebes*, now Midnight Silence reigns even here;
d Grass untrodden springs beneath our Feet.

*Tir.* If there be nigh this Place a Sunny Bank,
ere let me rest a while. A Sunny Bank!
, how can it be where no Sun shines!
a dim winking Taper in the Skies,
at nods, and scarce holds up its drowsie Head
glimer through the Damps

[*A Noise within, Follow, Follow, Follow. A* Creon, *A* Creon, *A* Creon!

k! a tumultuous Noise, and *Creon*'s Name
ice eccho'd

*Manto* Fly, the Tempest drives this way.

*Tir* Whither can Age and Blindness take their flight?
could fly, what could I suffer worse.
re of great Ill? [*Noise again*, Creon, Creon, Creon!

*ter* Creon, Diocles, Alcander, Pyracmon, *follow'd by the Crowd.*

*re* I thank ye, Countrymen, but must refuse
Honours you intend me, they're too great;

And

And I am too unworthy; think again,
And make a better Choice. [Life
1 *Cit* Think twice! I ne'er thought twice in all m[y]
That's double Work.
2 *Cit* My first Word is always my second, and there
fore I'll have no second Word, and therefore once ag[ain]
I say, a *Creon*.
*All*. A *Creon*, a *Creon*, a *Creon*
*Cre* Yet hear me, Fellow-Citizens.
*Dio* Fellow-Citizens! there was a Word of Kindne[ss]
*Alc*. When did *Oedipus* salute you by that famil[iar]
1 *Cit* Never, never; he was too proud. [Name
*Cre* Indeed he could not, for he was a Stranger
But under him our *Thebes* is half destroy'd.
Forbid it Heav'n the residue should perish
Under a *Theban* born
'Tis true, the Gods might send this Plague among yo[u]
Because a Stranger rul'd. But what of that?
Can I redress it now?
3 *Cit* Yes, you or none.
'Tis certain that the Gods are angry with us
Because he reigns
*Cre* *Oedipus* may return, you may be ruin'd
1 *Cit*. Nay if that be the matter, we are ruin'd alrea[dy]
2 *Cit* Half of us that are here present, were living M[en]
But Yesterday, and we that are absent do but drop and dr[op]
And no Man knows whether he be dead or living
Therefore, while we are sound and well, let us satisfie [our]
Consciences, and make a new King. [...]
3 *Cit* Ha, if we were but worthy to see another Coro[nation]
And then, if we must die, we'll go merrily together
*All*. To the Question, to the Question
*Dio* Are you content *Creon* should be your King?
*All* A *Creon*, a *Creon*, a *Creon*
*Tir*. Hear me ye *Thebans* And thou *Creon*, hear m[e]
1 *Cit* Who's that would be heard? We'll hear no Ma[n]
We can scarce hear one another
*Tir* I charge you by the Gods to hear me.
2 *Cit* Oh! 'tis *Apollo*'s Priest, we must hear him
the old blind Prophet that sees all things [Bet[...]
3 *Cit* He comes from the Gods too, and they are [...]

d therefore in good Manners we must hear him. Speak Prophet

*Cit* For coming from the Gods, that's no great matter; ey can all say that But he's a great Scholar, he can make amncks and he were put to't, and therefore I say hear him.

*Tir* When angry Heav'n scatters its Plagues among you, for Naught, ye *Thebans*? Are the Gods just in punishing? Are there no Crimes ich pull this Vengeance down?

*Cit* Yes, yes, no doubt there are some Sins stirring, at are the Cause of all.

*Cit.* Yes there are Sins, or we should have no Taxes.

*Cit* For my part, I can speak it with a safe Con-[science, 'er sin'd in all my Life.

*Cit* Nor I.

*Cit* Nor I. [our Doors

*Cit* Then we are all justified· The Sin lies not at

*Tir* All justifi'd alike, and yet all Guilty.
re every Man's False-dealing brought to light;
Envy, Malice, Lying, Perjuries,
Weights and Measures, th' other Man's Extortions,
th what Face could you tell offended Heav'n,
had not sin'd? [part, I never

*Cit* Nay, if these be Sins, the case is alter'd. For my ought any thing but Murder had been a Sin

*Tir* And yet, as if all these were less than nothing,
d Rebellion to 'em. Impious *Thebans*!
e you not sworn before the Gods, to serve
to obey this *Oedipus*, your King,
publick Voice elected? Answer me,
his be true

*Cit* This is true· But is't a hard World, Neighbours, Man's Oath must be his Master.

*re* Speak *Diocles*· All goes wrong.

*Dio* How are you Traitors, Countrymen of *Thebes*?
s holy Sir, who presses you with Oaths,
gets your first Were you not sworn before
*Lajus*, and his Blood?

*All* We were, we were.

*Dio.* While *Lajus* has a lawful Successor,

Your first Oath still must bind· *Eurydice*
Is Heir to *Lajus*, let her Marry *Creon*.
Offended Heav'n will never be appeas'd,
While *Oedipus* pollutes the Throne of *Lajus*,
A Stranger to his Blood.

*All.* We'll no *Oedipus*, no *Oedipus*.

1 *Cit* He puts the Prophet in a Mouse-hole

2 *Cit* I knew it would be so: the last Man ever speaks the best Reason

*Tir* Can Benefits thus die? Ungrateful *Thebans*!
Remember yet, when, after *Lajus*' Death,
The Monster *Sphynx* laid your rich Country waste,
Your Vineyards spoil'd, your labouring Oxen slew,
Your selves, for Fear, mew'd up within your Walls,
She, taller than your Gates o'er-look'd your Town,
But when she rais'd her Bulk to sail above you,
She drove the Air around her like a Whirl-wind,
And shaded all beneath; till stooping down,
She clap'd her Leathern Wing against your Tow'rs,
And thrust out her long Neck, ev'n to your Doors

*Dio Alc Pyr.* We'll hear no more.

*Tir.* You durst not meet in Temple,
T' invoke the Gods for Aid, the proudest he
Who leads you now, then crow'd like a dar'd Lark
This *Creon* shook for fear,
The Blood of *Lajus* cruddled in his Veins;
Till *Oedipus* arriv'd,
Call'd by his own high Courage, and the Gods;
Himself to you a God Ye offer'd him
Your Queen and Crown, (but what was then your Crown)
And Heav'n authoriz'd it by his Success.
Speak then, Who is your lawful King?

*All.* 'Tis *Oedipus*.

*Tir.* 'Tis *Oedipus*, your King more lawful
Than yet you dream, for something still there lies
In Heav'ns dark Volume, which I read through Mists
'Tis great, prodigious; 'tis a dreadful Birth
Of wondrous Fate, and now, just now disclosing.
I see, I see how terrible it dawns!
And my Soul sickens with it.

1 *Cit* How the God shakes him! [Triumph!
*Tir* He comes! he comes! Victory! Conquest!
it, oh! Guiltless and Guilty· Murder! Parricide!
cest! Discovery! Punishment ——— 'tis ended,
nd all your Sufferings o'er

*A Trumpet within, Enter* Hæmon,

*Hæm* Rouse up, ye *Thebans*; tune your *Io Pæans*
our King returns. The *Argians* are o'ercome;
heir warlike Prince in single Combat taken,
rd led in Bands by God-like *Oedipus*.
*All* *Oedipus*, *Oedipus*, *Oedipus*!
*Creon* Furies confound his Fortune! —— [*Aside*
aste, all haste [*To them*.
nd meet with Blessings our victorious King,
ecree Processions; bid new Holy Days;
rown all the Statues of our Gods with Garlands;
nd raise a Brazen Column, thus inscrib'd,
o *Oedipus*, now twice a Conqueror; Deliverer of his
ust me, I weep for Joy to see this Day. [*Thebes*.
*Tir* Yes, Heav'n knows how thou weep'st. ——Go
Country-men,
nd, as you us'd to supplicate your Gods,
meet your King, with Bays, and Olive-branches·
w down, and touch his Knees, and beg from him
End of all your Woes, for only he
n give it you [*Exit* Tiresias, *the People following*.

*Enter* Oedipus *in Triumph*, Adrastus *Prisoner*, Dymas, *Train*.

*Creon* All hail, great *Oedipus*,
ou mighty Conqueror, hail, welcome to *Thebes*,
thy own *Thebes*, to all that's left of *Thebes*
r half thy Citizens are swept away,
d wanting to thy Triumphs;
d we, the happy Remnant, only live
welcome thee, and die
*Oed*. Thus Pleasure never comes sincere to Man,
lent by Heav'n, upon hard Usury;
d while *Jove* holds us out the Bowl of Joy,
it can reach our Lips, 'tis dash'd with Gall
some Left-handed God. O mournful Triumph!

O

O Conquest gain'd abroad, and lost at home!
O *Argos*, now rejoice, for *Thebes* lies low;
Thy slaughter'd Sons now smile, and think they w
When they can count more *Theban* Ghosts than their

*Adr.* No; *Argos* mourns with *Thebes*, you temper'd
Your Courage while you fought, that Mercy seem'
The Manlier Virtue, and much more prevail'd.
While *Argos* is a People, think you *Thebes*
Can never want for Subjects. Every Nation
Will crowd to serve where *Oedipus* commands.

*Creon to Hæm.* How mean it shews, to fawn u
the Victor!

*Hæm.* Had you beheld him fight you had said ot
Come, 'tis brave Bearing in him, not to envy [W
Superior Virtue.

*Oed.* This, indeed, is Conquest,
To gain a Friend like you. Why were we Foes?

*Adr.* 'Cause we were Kings, and each disdain'd
I fought to have it in my Power to do [Fo
What thou hast done, and so to use my Conquest,
To shew thee Honour was my only Motive.
Know this, that were my Army at thy Gates,
And *Thebes* thus waste, I would not take the Gift,
Which, like a Toy drop'd from the Hands of For
Lay for the next Chance-comer.

*Oed. Embracing.* No more Captive,
But Brother of the War. 'Tis much more pleas
And safer, trust me, thus to meet thy Love,
Than when hard Gantlets clench'd our Warlike
And kept 'em from soft Use.

*Adr.* My Conqueror!

*Oed.* My Friend! That other Name keeps En
But longer to detain thee were a Crime:
To Love, and to *Eurydice*, go free:
Such Welcome as a ruin'd Town can give,
Expect from me; the rest let her supply.

*Adr.* I go without a Blush, though conquer'd tw
By you, and by my Princess. [*Exit* Adr.

*Creon. Aside.* Then I am conquer'd thrice;
*Oedipus*,

nd her, and even by him, the Slave of both.
ods, I am beholding to you for making me your Image
Would I could make you mine. [*Exit* Creon.

*Enter the People with Branches in their Hands holding them up, and kneeling: Two Priests before them*

*Oed* Alas my People!
What means this speechless Sorrow, down-cast Eyes,
nd lifted Hands? If there be one among you,
Whom Grief has left a Tongue, speak for the rest.

*Pri* O Father of thy Country!
o thee these Knees are bent, these Eyes are lifted,
to a visible Divinity,
Prince, on whom Heav'n safely might repose
e Business of Mankind: For Providence
ght on thy Bosom sleep secure,
d leave her Task to thee
where's the Glory of thy former Acts?
'n that's destroy'd when none shall live to speak it.
llions of Subjects shalt thou have, but mute.
People of the Dead, a crowded Desart:
Midnight-silence at the Noon of Day.

*Oed* Oh! were our Gods as ready with their Pity,
I with mine, this Presence should be throng'd
h all I left alive, and my sad Eyes
search in vain for Friends, whose promis'd Sight
ter'd my Toyls of War.

*Pri* Twice our Deliverer!

*Oed* Nor are now your Vows
ress'd to one who sleeps
en this unwelcome News first reach'd my Ears,
*as* was sent to *Delphos*, to enquire
Cause and Cure of this contagious Ill,
is this Day return'd. But since his Message
cerns the Publick, I refus'd to hear it,
n this general Presence. Let him speak

*ym* A dreadful Answer from the hallow'd Urn,
sacred *Tripous* did the Priestess give,
hese mysterious Words,

The

The Oracle. *Shed in a cursed Hour, by cursed Hand,*
*Blood-Royal unreveng'd, has curs'd the Land.*
*When* Lajus' *Death is expiated well,*
*Your Plague shall cease The rest let* Lajus *tell.*

*Oed* Dreadful indeed! Blood, and a King's Blood to
And such a King; and by his Subjects shed!
(Else, by this Curse on *Thebes!*) No wonder then
If Monsters, Wars and Plagues revenge such Crimes,
If Heav'n be just, its whole Artillery
All must be empty'd on us Not one Bolt
Shall err from *Thebes*, but more be call'd for, more
New-moulded Thunder, of a larger Size,
Driven by whole *Jove* What! Touch anointed Pow
Then Gods beware, *Jove* would himself be next,
Cou'd you but reach him too.

2 *Pri.* We mourn the sad Remembrance.

*Oed* Well you may
Worse than a Plague infects you· Ye're devoted
To Mother Earth, and to th' Infernal Pow'rs:
Hell has a Right in you I thank you Gods,
That I am no *Theban* born: How my Blood crudd
As if this Curse touch'd me! and touch'd me nearer
Than all this Presence!——Yes, 'tis a King's Blood
And I, a King, am ty'd in deeper Bonds
To expiate this Blood But where, from whom,
Or how must I attone it? Tell me, *Thebans*,
How *Lajus* fell, for a confus'd Report
Pass'd through my Ears, when first I took the Cr
But full of hurry, like a Morning-Dream,
It vanish'd in the Business of the Day.

1 *Pri* He went in private forth, but thinly follo
And ne'er return'd to *Thebes*

*Oed.* Nor any from him? Came there no Attend
None to bring News?

2 *Pri* But one; and he so wounded,
He scarce drew Breath to speak some few faint Wor

*Oed.* What were they? Something may be learnt
thence.

1 *Pri* He said a Band of Robbers watch'd their Pa
Who took Advantage of a narrow Way,

murder *Lajus* and the rest, himself
ft too for dead.

*Oed* Made you no Enquiry,
t took this bare Relation?

*Pri.* 'Twas neglected.
then the Monster *Sphynx* began to rage;
d present Cares soon buried the remote:
was it hush'd, and never since reviv'd.

*Oed* Mark, *Thebans*, mark!
then the *Sphynx* began to rage among you;
e Gods took hold ev'n of th' offending Minute,
d dated thence your Woes: Thence will I trace 'em.

*Pri* 'Tis just thou shouldst

*Oed.* Hear then this dread Imprecation, hear it:
laid on all, not any one exempt:
r witness, Heav'n, avenge it on the Perjur'd.
ny *Theban* born, if any Stranger
eal this Murder, or produce its Author;
*Attick* Talents be his just Reward:
if for Fear, for Favour, or for Hire,
Murder he conceal, the Curse of *Thebes*
heavy on his Head: Unite our Plagues,
Gods, and place 'em there: From Fire and Water,
erse, and all things common, be he banish'd.
for the Murderer's self, unfound by Man,
him, ye Pow'rs Celestial and Infernal;
the same Fate, or worse than *Lajus* met,
be his Lot, His Children be accurs'd;
Wife and Kindred, all of his be curs'd.

*Pri* Confirm it, Heav'n.

*Enter* Jocasta *attended by Women.*

At your Devotions 'Heav'n succeed your Wishes,
bring th' Effect of these your pious Pray'rs
ou, and me, and all.

Avert this Omen, Heav'n!

O fatal Sound! unfortunate *Jocasta!*
hast thou said! an ill Hour hast thou chosen
hose fore-boading Words: Why, we were cursing.

Then may that Curse fall only where you laid it.

*Oed* Speak no more;
For all thou say'st is ominous. We were cursing,
And that dire Imprecation hast thou fasten'd
On *Thebes*, and thee, and me, and all of us.
*Joc* Are then my Blessings turn'd into a Curse?
O unkind *Oedipus*! My former Lord
Thought me his Blessing, be thou like my *Lajus*.
*Oed* What, yet again! The third time hast thou cu
This Imprecation was for *Lajus*' Death; [
And thou hast wish'd me like him.
*Joc* Horror seizes me!
*Oed* Why dost thou gaze upon me? Prithee, Lo
Take off thy Eye; it burdens me too much.
*Joc.* The more I look, the more I find of *Lajus*.
His Speech, his Garb, his Action, nay, his Frown,
(For I have seen it,) but ne'er bent on me.
*Oed.* Are we so like?
*Joc.* In all thinks but his Love. [speak how w
*Oed* I love thee more: So well I love, Words can
No pious Son e'er lov'd his Mother more,
Than I my dear *Jocasta*.
*Joc* I love you too
The self-same way: And when you chid, methough
A Mother's Love start up in your Defence,
And bad me not be angry: Be not you:
For I love *Lajus* still as Wives shou'd love;
But you more tenderly, as Part of me:
And when I have you in my Arms, methinks
I lull my Child asleep
*Oed* Then we are bless'd:
And all these Curses sweep along the Skies,
Like empty Clouds, but drop not on our Heads.
*Joc* I have not joy'd an Hour since you departed,
For publick Miseries and for private Fears;
But this bless'd Meeting has o'er-pay'd 'em all.
Good Fortune, that comes seldom, comes more welco
All I can wish for now, is your Consent
To make my Brother happy.
*Oed.* How, *Jocasta*?

*Joc* By Marriage with his Neice *Eurydice*.
*Oed* Uncle and Neice! they are too near, my Love;
'Tis too like Inceſt; 'tis Offence to Kind.
Had I not promis'd, were there no *Adraſtus*,
No Choice but *Creon* left her of Mankind,
They ſhou'd not Marry. Speak no more of it;
The Thought diſturbs me.
*Joc.* Heav'n can never bleſs
A Vow ſo broken, which I made to *Creon*:
Remember he's my Brother.
*Oed* That's the Bar.
And ſhe thy Daughter: Nature would abhor
To be forc'd back again upon her ſelf,
And, like a Whirl-pool, ſwallow her own Streams.
*Joc* Be not diſpleas'd, I'll move the Suit no more.
*Oed* No, do not, for, I know not why, it ſhakes me
When I but think on Inceſt. Move me forward
To thank the Gods for my Succeſs, and pray
To waſh the Guilt of Royal Blood away. [*Exeunt.*

## ACT II. SCENE I.

SCENE *an open Gallery: A Royal Bedchamber being ſuppos'd behind. The Time Night, Thunder, &c.*

*Enter* Hæmon, Alcander, Pyracmon.

*Hæm* SURE 'tis the End of all things! Fate has torn
The Lock of Time off, and his Head is now
The ghaſtly Ball of round Eternity!
Call you theſe Peals of Thunder, but the Yawn
Of bellowing Clouds? By *Jove*, they ſeem to me
The World's laſt Groans, and thoſe vaſt Sheets of Flame
Are its laſt Blaze! The Tapers of the Gods,
The Sun and Moon, run down like waxen Globes;
The ſhooting Stars end all in Purple Jellies;
And *Chaos* is at hand.
*Pyr* 'Tis Midnight, yet there's not a *Theban* ſleeps,
But ſuch as ne'er muſt wake. All crowd about

The Palace, and implore, as from a God,
Help of the King, who, from the Battlement,
By the red Lightning's glare, descry'd far,
Atones the angry Powers.

*Ham.* Ha! *Pyracmon*, look;
Behold, *Alcander*, from yon' West of Heav'n,
The perfect Figures of a Man and Woman
A Scepter bright with Gems in each right Hand,
Their flowing Robes of dazling Purple made,
Distinctly yonder in that Point they stand,
Just West A bloody Red stains all the Place.
And see, their Faces are quite hid in Clouds

*Pyr.* Clusters of golden Stars hang o'er their Hea[ds]
And seem so crouded, that they burst upon 'em:
All dart at once their baleful Influence,
In leaking Fire.

*Alc.* Long-bearded Comets stick,
Like flaming Porcupines, to their left Sides,
As they would shoot their Quills into their Hearts

*Ham.* But see! the King, and Queen, and all the Co[urt]
Did every Day or Night shew ought like this?

[*Thunders ag*[ain]

*The* SCENE *draws and discovers the Prodigies*

*Enter* Oedipus, Jocasta, Eurydice, Adrastus, *all co*[me]
*forward with Amazement.*

*Oed* Answer, you Pow'rs Divine; spare all this N[oise]
This rack of Heav'n, and speak your fatal Pleasure,
Why breaks yon dark and dusky Orb away?
Why from the bleeding Womb of monstrous Nigh[t]
Burst forth such Miriads of abortive Stars?
Ha! my *Jocasta*, look! the Silver Moon!
A settling Crimson stains her beauteous Face!
She's all o'er Blood! and look, behold again,
What mean the mystick Heav'ns she journies on!
A vast Eclipse darkens the labouring Planet
Sound there, sound all your Instruments of War,
Clarions and Trumpets, Silver, Brass, and Iron,
And beat a thousand Drums to help her Labour

*Adr.* 'Tis vain, you see the Prodigies continue
Let's gaze no more, the Gods are humorous.

*Oed.* Forbear, rash Man——Once more I ask your
that the Glow-worm light of human Reason [Pleasure!
ight dare to offer at immortal Knowledge,
nd cope with Gods, why all this storm of Nature?
Why do the Rocks split, and why rowls the Sea?
Why these Portents in Heav'n, and Plagues on Earth?
Why yon' Gigantick Forms, Ethereal Monsters?
a! Is all this but to fright the Dwarfs
Which your own Hands have made? then be it so
if the Fates resolve some Expiation
r murder'd *Lajus*, Hear me, hear me, Gods!
ar me thus prostrate: Spare this groaning Land,
ve Innocent *Thebes*, stop the Tyrant Death;
this, and lo I stand up an Oblation
meet your swiftest and severest Anger;
oot all at once, and strike me to the Center.

*The Cloud draws that veil'd the Heads of the Figures in the Sky, and shews 'em Crown'd, with the Names of* Oedipus *and* Jocasta *written above in great Characters of Gold.*

*dr.* Either I dream, and all my cooler Senses
vanish'd with that Cloud that fleets away;
just above those two Majestick Heads,
, I read distinctly in large Gold,
*ipus* and *Jocasta*
*lc.* I read the same.
*dr* 'Tis wonderful, yet ought not Man to wade
far in the vast deep of Destiny.
[*Thunder, and the Prodigies vanish*
*oc* My Lord, my *Oedipus*, why gaze you now,
en the whole Heav'n is clear, as if the Gods
some new Monsters made! will you not turn,
bless your People, who devour each Word
breath?
*d* It shall be so.
I will die, O *Thebes*, to save thee!
w from my Heart my Blood, with more content
n e'er I wore thy Crown Yet, O *Jocasta*!
ll th' Indearments of miraculous Love,
ll our Languishings, our Fears in Pleasure,
ch oft have made us wonder, here I swear

On thy fair Hand, upon thy Breast I swear
I cannot call to mind, from budding Childhood
To blooming Youth, a Crime by me committed,
For which the awful Gods should doom my Death.
*Joc.* 'Tis not you, my Lord,
But he who murder'd *Lajus*, frees the Land:
Were you, which is impossible, the Man,
Perhaps my Poniard first should drink your Blood,
But you are Innocent, as your *Jocasta*,
From Crimes like those. This made me violent
To save your Life, which you unjust would lose;
Nor can you comprehend with deepest Thought,
The horrid Agony you cast me in,
When you resolv'd to die.
*Oed* Is't possible?
*Joc* Alas! why start you so? Her stiff'ning Grie
Who saw her Children slaughter'd all at once,
Was dull to mine. Methinks I should have made
My Bosom bare against the armed God,
To save my *Oedipus*
*Oed* I pray, no more
*Joc* You've silenc'd me, my Lord.
*Oed* Pardon me, dear *Jocasta*,
Pardon a Heart that sinks with Sufferings,
And can but vent it self in Sobs and Murmurs:
Yet to restore my Peace, I'll find him out
Yes, yes, you Gods! you shall have ample Venge
On *Lajus*' Murderer. O, the Traitor's Name!
I'll know it, I will: Art shall be conjur'd for it,
And Nature all unravel'd.
*Joc.* Sacred Sir ———
*Oed* Rage will have way, and 'tis but just, I'll f
Tho' lodg'd in Air upon a Dragon's Wing,
Tho' Rocks should hide him. Nay he shall be drag
From Hell, if Charms can hurry him along,
His Ghost shall be by sage *Tiresias*' Pow'r
(*Tiresias*, that rules all beneath the Moon)
Confin'd to Flesh, to suffer Death once more;
And then be plung'd in his first Fires again.

*Enter* Creon.

*Cre.* My Lord,
*resias* attends your Pleasure.
*Oed* Haste and bring him in.
my *Jocasta*, *Eurydice*, *Adrastus*,
*on*, and all ye *Thebans*, now the end
Plagues, of Madness, Murders, Prodigies,
aws on · This Battel of the Heav'ns and Earth
all by his Wisdom be reduc'd to Peace.

*ter* Tiresias *leaning on a Staff, led by his Daughter* Manto, *follow'd by other* Thebans.

thou, whose most aspiring Mind
ow'st all the Business of the Courts above,
ens the Closets of the Gods, and dares
mix with *Jove* himself and Fate at Council,
Prophet, answer me, declare aloud
e Traitor, who conspir'd the Death of *Lajus*.
be they more, who from malignant Stars
e drawn this Plague that blasts unhappy *Thebes*.
*ir* We must no more, than Fate commissions us
tell, yet something, and of Moment, I'll unfold,
hat the God would wake; I feel him now,
e a strong Spirit charm'd into a Tree,
at leaps, and moves the Wood without a Wind:
e rouz'd God, as all this while he lay
omb'd alive, starts and dilates himself:
struggles, and he tears my aged Trunk
th holy Fury, my old Arteries burst,
rivel'd Skin
e Parchment crackles at the hallow'd Fire;
all be young again: *Manto*, my Daughter,
ou hast a Voice that might have sav'd the Bard
*Thrace*, and forc'd the raging Bacchanals,
th lifted Prongs, to listen to thy Airs:
harm this God, this Fury in my Bosom,
l him with tuneful Notes, and artful Strings,
th pow'rful Strains; *Manto*, my lovely Child,
th the unruly God-head to be mild.

## SONG to *Apollo.*

Phœbus, *God belov'd by Men;*
*At thy dawn, every Beaſt is rouz'd in his Den;*
*At thy ſetting, all the Birds of thy Abſence complai*
*And we dye, all dye till the Morning comes again,*
Phœbus, *God belov'd by Men,*
*Idol of the Eaſtern Kings,*
*Awful as the God who flings*
*His Thunder round, and the Lightning wings;*
*God of Songs and* Orphean *Strings,*
*Who to this mortal Boſom brings,*
*All harmonous heav'nly Things*
*Thy drowzy Prophet to revive,*
*Ten thouſand thouſand Forms before him drive;*
*With Chariots and Horſes all o'fire awake him,*
*Convulſions, and Furies, and Propheſies ſhake him,*
*Let him tell it in Groans, tho' he bend with the L*
*Tho' he burſt with the weight of the terrible God.*

*Tir.* The Wretch, who ſhed the Blood of old *Lab*
Lives, and is great; [cus
But cruel Greatneſs ne'er was long·
The firſt of *Lajus*' Blood his Life did ſeize,
And urg'd his Fate,
Which elſe had laſting been and ſtrong.
The Wretch, who *Lajus* kill'd, muſt bleed, or fly;
Or *Thebes* conſum'd with Plagues in Ruin lye
*Oed.* The firſt of *Lajus*' Blood! pronounce the Perſ
May the God roar from thy prophetick Mouth,
That even the Dead may ſtart up to behold.
Name him, I ſay, that moſt accurſed Wretch,
For by the Stars he dies:
Speak, I command thee,
By *Phœbus*, ſpeak! for ſudden Death's his Doom:
Here ſhall he fall, bleed on this very ſpot;
His Name, I charge thee once more, ſpeak.
*Tir* 'Tis loſt,
Like what we think can never ſhun Remembrance,
Yet of a ſudden's gone beyond the Clouds.

Cr

*Oed* Fetch it from thence; I'll have't, where-e'er it be.
*Cre.* Let me intreat you, sacred Sir, be calm,
d *Creon* shall point out the great Offender.
, true, respect of Nature might injoyn
Silence at another time; but oh,
ch more the pow'r of my Eternal Love! [try——
at, that should strike me Dumb: Yet *Thebes*, my Coun-
break through all, to succour thee, poor City.
I must speak.
*Oed.* Speak then, if ought thou knowest:
much thou seem'd to know, delay no longer.
*Cre.* O Beauty! O Illustrious Royal Maid!
whom my Vows were ever paid till now,
d with such modest, chaste, and pure Affection,
e coldest Nymph might read 'em without blushing;
thou the Murdress then of wretched *Lajus*?
d I, must I accuse thee? O my Tears!
y will you fall in so abhor'd a Cause?
that thy beauteous, barbarous Hand destroy'd
Father (O monstrous Act!) both Gods
Men at once take Notice.
*Oed* Eurydice!
*Eur.* Traytor, go on; I scorn thy little Malice,
knowing more my perfect Innocence,
n Gods and Men, then how much more than thee,
o art their opposite, and form'd a Lyar.
us disdain thee! Thou once didst talk of Love,
ause I hate thy Love, thou dost accuse me.
*Adr* Villain, inglorious Villain
Traytor, double damn'd, who durst Blaspheme
spotless Virtue of the brightest Beauty;
u dy'st Nor shall the sacred Majesty
t guards this Place, preserve thee from my Rage.
[*Draws and wounds him*
*Oed.* Disarm 'em both: Prince, I shall make you know
t I can tame you twice. Guards, seize him.
*Adr.* Sir,
ust acknowledge in another Cause
entance might abash me, but I glory
this, and smile to see the Traytor's Blood

*Oed.*

*Oed.* *Creon*, you ſhall be ſatisfied at full.

*Cre.* My Hurt is nothing, Sir, but I appeal
To wiſe *Tireſias*, if my Accuſation
Be not moſt true. The firſt of *Lajus*' Blood
Gave him his Death. Is there a Prince before her?
Then ſhe is faultleſs, and I ask her Pardon
And may this Blood ne'er ceaſe to drop, O *Thebes*!
If pity of thy Sufferings did not move me
To ſhew the Cure, which Heav'n it ſelf preſcrib'd

*Eur.* Yes, *Thebans*, I will dye to ſave your Lives
More willingly than you can wiſh my Fate;
But let this Good, this Wiſe, this Holy Man
Pronounce my Sentence For to fall by him,
By the vile Breath of that prodigious Villain,
Would ſink my Soul, tho' I ſhould dye a Martyr.

*Adr.* Unhand me, Slaves O mightieſt of Kings,
See at your Feet a Prince not us'd to Kneel,
Touch not *Eurydice*, by all the Gods,
As you would ſave your *Thebes*, but take my Life
For ſhould ſhe periſh, Heav'n would heap Plagues
Rain Sulphur down, hurl kindled Bolts [Pl...
Upon your guilty Heads.

*Cre.* You turn to Gallantry, what is but Juſtice
Proof will be eaſie made. *Adraſtus* was
The Robber, who bereft th' unhappy King
Of Life, becauſe he flatly had deny'd
To make ſo poor a Prince his Son-in-Law.
Therefore twere fit that both ſhould periſh.

1 *Theb.* Both, let both dye

*All Theb.* Both, both, let 'em dye

*Oed.* Hence you wild Herd! For your Ring-leader
He ſhall be made an Example. *Hæmon*, take him.

1 *Theb.* Mercy, O Mercy.

*Oed.* Mutiny in my Preſence!
Hence, let me ſee that buſie Face no more. [R...

*Tir.* *Thebans*, what Madneſs makes you drunk
Enough of guilty Death's already acted:
Fierce *Creon* has accus'd *Eurydice*,
With Prince *Adraſtus*; which the God reproves
By inward Checks, and leaves their Fate in doubt

*ed* Therefore instruct us what remains to do,
suffer, for I feel a Sleep like Death
on me, and I sigh to be at rest
*Tir.* Since that the Pow'rs Divine refuse to clear
e mystick Deed, I'll to the Grove of Furies,
ere I can force th' Infernal Gods to shew
ir horrid Forms,
h trembling Ghost shall rise,
leave th ir grisly King without a Waiter:
Prince *Adrastus* and *Eurydice*,
Life's engag'd, I'll guard em in the Fane,
the dark Mysteries of Hell are done
low me, Princess, *Thebans*, all to Rest.
*Oedipus*, to-morrow —— but no more,
hat thy wakeful Genius will permit,
lge thy Brain this Night with softer Slumbers:
morrow, O to-morrow! ——— Sleep, my Son:
in prophetick Dreams thy Fate be shown
[*Ex* Thes. Adrast. Euryd Manto, Thebans.
*Manent* Oed Jocast Creon, Pyrac. Hæm Alcan.
*ed* To bed, my Fair, my Dear, my best *Jocasta*.
r the Toils of War, 'tis wondrous strange
Loves should thus be dash'd. One Moment's thought,
I'll approach the Arms of my belov'd
*c* Consume whole Years in Care, so now and then
y have leave to feed my famish'd Eyes
h one short passing Glance, and sigh my Vows.
s and no more, my Lord, is all the Passion
anguishing *Jocasta*. [*Exit*.
*ed* Thou softest, sweetest of the World! good Night.
, she is beauteous too, yet, mighty Love!
er offer'd to obey thy Laws,
an unusual Chillness came upon me;
unknown Hand still check'd my forward Joy,
'd me with Blushes, tho' no Light was near,
t ev'n the Act became a Violation.
*r* He's strangely Thoughtful [me?
*ed* Hark! who was that? Ha! *Creon*, didst thou call
*e* Not I, my gracious Lord, nor any here.

Oed.

*Oed.* That's ſtrange! Methought I heard a doleful Vo[ice]
Cry'd *Oedipus.*——The Prophet bad me Sleep,
He talkt of Dreams and Viſions, and to-morrow!
I'll muſe no more on't, come what will or can,
My Thoughts are clearer than unclouded Stars;
And with thoſe Thoughts I'll reſt; *Creon,* good Nig[ht.]
[*Ex. with* Hæ[mon.]

*Cre.* Sleep ſeal your Eyes, Sir, eternal Sleep.
But if he muſt ſleep and wake again, O all
Tormenting Dreams, wild Horrors of the Night,
And Hags of Fancy wing him through the Air
From Precipices hurl him headlong down,
*Charybdis* roar, and Death be ſet before him.

*Alc.* Your Curſes have already ta'en effect;
For he looks very ſad.

*Cre.* May he be rooted, where he ſtands, for ever,
His Eye-balls never move, Brows be unbent,
His Blood, his Entrails, Liver, Heart and Bowels,
Be blacker than the Place I wiſh him, Hell

*Pyr.* No more. You tear your ſelf, but vex not h[im]
Methinks 'twere brave this Night to force the Templ[e]
While blind *Tireſias* conjures up the Fiends,
And paſs the Time with nice *Eurydice.*

*Alc.* Try Promiſes and Threats, and if all fail,
Since Hell's broke looſe, why ſhould not you be m[ad?]
Raviſh and leave her Dead with her *Adraſtus*

*Cre* Were the Globe mine, I'd give a Province he[re]
For ſuch another Thought. Luſt and Revenge!
To ſtab at once the only Man I hate,
And to enjoy the Woman whom I love!
I ask no more of my auſpicious Stars,
The reſt as Fortune pleaſe, ſo but this Night
She play me fair, why let her turn for ever.

*Enter* Hæmon

*Hæm* My Lord, the troubled King is gone to reſt,
Yet, ere he ſlept, commanded me to clear
The Antichambers None muſt dare be near him

*Cre Hæmon,* do your Duty;—— [*Thun[der.]*
And we obey.——The Night grows yet more dreadf[ul.]
'Tis juſt that all retire to their Devotions

he Gods are angry: but to-morrow's dawn,
Prophets do not lye, will make all clear. [*As they go off,*
Oedipus *Enters, walking a-sleep in his Shirt, with a*
*Dagger in his right hand, and a Taper in his left*

*Oed* O, my *Jocasta*! 'tis for this the wet
rv'd Soldier lies all Night on the cold Ground,
r this he bears the Storms
Winter Camps, and freezes in his Arms:
be thus circled, to be thus embrac'd,
at I could hold thee ever! —— Ha! where art thou?
hat means this melancholly Light, that seems
e gloom of glowing Embers?
e Curtain's drawn, and see she's here again!
*asta*? Ha! what, fall'n asleep so soon?
w fares my Love? this Taper will inform me.
! Lightning blast me, Thunder
et me ever to *Prometheus*' Rock,
d Vulturs gnaw out my Incestuous Heart,
all the Gods! my Mother *Merope*!
Sword, a Dagger, Ha! who waits there? Slaves,
Sword What, *Hæmon*, dar'st thou, Villain, stop
me?
h thy own Ponyard perish. Ha! who's this?
is't a Change of Death? By all my Honours,
w Murder; thou hast slain old *Polybus*:
est and Parricide, thy Father's Murderer!
t thou Infernal Flame: Now all is dark,
blind and dismal: Most Triumphant Mischief!
d now, while thus I stalk about the Room,
allenge Fate to find another Wretch
e *Oedipus* [*Thunder, &c*

*ter* Jocasta, *attended with Lights, in a Night Gown*

*Oed* Night, Horrour, Death, Confusion, Hell and
ere am I? O *Jocasta*, let me hold thee [*Furies!*
us to my Bosom, Ages let me grasp thee:
hat the hardest temper'd weather'd Flesh,
h fiercest Human Spirit inspir'd, can dare
do, I dare But, O you Pow'rs, this was
infinite degrees too much for Man.
thinks my deafn'd Ears

Are burst; my Eyes, as if they had been knock'd
By some tempestuous Hand, shoot flashing Fire.
That Sleep should do this!

*Joc.* Then my Fears were true
Methought I heard a Voice, and yet I doubted
Now roaring like the Ocean, when the Winds
Fight with the Waves, now in a still small Tone
Your dying Accents fell, as racking Ships,
After the dreadful Yell, sink murmuring down,
And bubble up a Noise

*Oed* Trust me, thou fairest, best of all thy Kind,
None e'er in Dreams was tortur'd so before,
Yet what most shocks the Niceness of my Temper,
Ev'n far beyond the Killing of my Father,
And my own Death, is, that this horrid Sleep
Dash'd my sick Fancy with an Act of Incest
I Dreamt, *Jocasta*, that thou wert my Mother,
Which, though impossible, so damps my Spirits,
That I cou'd do a Mischief on my self,
Lest I should sleep, and Dream the like again

*Joc.* O *Oedipus*, too well I understand you!
I know the Wrath of Heav'n, the Care of *Thebes*,
The Cries of its Inhabitants, War's Toils,
And Thousand other Labours of the State,
Are all referr'd to you, and ought to take you
For ever from *Jocasta*.

*Oed* Life of my Life, and Treasure of my Soul!
Heav'n knows I love thee.

*Joc* Oh! You think me vile,
And of an Inclination so ignoble,
That I must hide me from your Eyes for ever
Be witness, Gods, and strike *Jocasta* dead,
If an immodest Thought, or low Desire
Inflam'd my Breast, since first our Loves were lighted.
[*Kneeling*

*Oed.* Oh, rise; and add not, by thy cruel Kindness,
A Grief more sensible than all my Torments.
Thou think'st my Dreams are forg'd. But, by thy Life,
The greatest Oath I swear, they are most true
But be they what they will, I here dismiss 'em:

gone *Chimera's*, to your Mother Clouds:
here a Fault in us? have we not search'd
e Womb of Heav'n, examin'd all the Entrails
Birds and Beasts, and tir'd the Prophet's Art?
t what avails? he, and the Gods together,
m, like Physicians, at a loss to help us:
erefore, like Wretches that have linger'd long,
'll snatch the strongest Cordial of our Love.
bed, my Fair.

*Ghost within* Oedipus!

*Oed.* Ha! Who calls?
'st thou not hear a Voice?

*Joc.* Alas! I did.

*Ghost.* *Jocasta*!

*Joc.* O my Love, my Lord, support me!

*Oed.* Call louder, till you burst your Airy Forms:
st on my Hand. Thus arm'd with Innocence,
face these babling *Dæmons* of the Air:
pight of Ghosts, I'll on.
ough round my Bed the Furies plant their Charms,
break 'em, with *Jocasta* in my Arms:
sp'd in the Folds of Love, I'll wait my Doom;
d act my Joys, though Thunder shake the Room. [*Exe.*

---

## ACT III. SCENE I.

### SCENE *A Dark Grove.*

*Enter* Creon *and* Diocles.

*Cre.* 'TIS better not to be, than to be unhappy.

*Dio.* What mean you by these Words?

*Cre.* 'tis better not to be, than to be *Creon*.
hinking Soul is Punishment enough:
when 'tis great, like mine, and wretched too,
en every Thought draws Blood.

*Dio.* You are not wretched.

*Cre.* I am: My Soul's ill married to my Body.
ould be young, be handsom, be belov'd:

Cou'd

Cou'd I but breath my ſelf into *Adraſtus*——
*Dio.* You rave; call home your Thoughts.
*Cre.* I prithee let my Soul take Air a while.
Were ſhe in *Oedipus*, I were a King;
Then I had kill'd a Monſter, gain'd a Battel,
And had my Rival Pris'ner: Brave, brave Actions!
Why have not I done theſe?
*Dio.* Your Fortune hinder'd.
*Cre.* There's it. I have a Soul to do 'em all,
But Fortune will have nothing done that's great,
But by young, handſom Fools. Body and Brawn
Do all her Work. *Hercules* was a Fool,
And ſtraight grew famous; a mad boyſterous Fool,
Nay worſe, a Woman's Fool.
Fool is the Stuff of which Heav'n makes a Hero.
*Dio.* A Serpent ne'er becomes a flying Dragon,
Till he has eat a Serpent.
*Cre.* Goes it there!
I underſtand thee, I muſt kill *Adraſtus*.
*Dio.* Or not enjoy your Miſtreſs:
*Eurydice* and he are Pris'ners here,
But will not long be ſo; this Tell-tale Ghoſt,
Perhaps will clear 'em both.
*Cre.* Well, 'tis reſolv'd.
*Dio.* The Princeſs walks this Way;
You muſt not meet her,
Till this be done.
*Cre.* I muſt.
*Dio.* She hates your Sight:
And more, ſince you accus'd her.
*Cre.* Urge it not.
I cannot ſtay to tell thee my deſign;
For ſhe's too near.

*Enter* Eurydice.

How, Madam, were your Thoughts employ'd?
*Eur.* On Death and thee.
*Cre.* Then were they not well ſorted: Life and [illegible]
Had been the better Match.
*Eur.* No, I was thinking
On two the moſt deteſted things in Nature;

d they are Death and thee.
ce. The thought of Death, to one near Death, is
, 'tis a fearful thing to be no more, [dreadful:
if to be, to wander after Death,
walk, as Spirits do, in Brakes all Day;
d when the Darkness comes, to glide in Paths
at lead to Graves, and in the silent Vault,
here lies your own pale Shrowd, to hover o'er it,
ving to enter your forbidden Corps;
d often, often, vainly breath your Ghost
o your lifeless Lips:
en, like a lone, benighted Traveller,
t out from Lodging, shall your Groans be answer'd
whistling Winds, whose every Blast will shake
r tender Form to Atoms.
ur. Must I be this thin Being? and thus wander!
Quiet after Death!
e None· You must leave
s beauteous Body, all this Youth and Freshness
t be no more the Object of Desire,
a cold Lump of Clay,
ich then your discontented Ghost will leave,
loath its former Lodging.
is the best of what comes after Death,
n to the best.
r What then shall be thy Lot?
nal Torments, Baths of boiling Sulphur;
ssitudes of Fires, and then of Frosts,
an old Guardian Fiend, ugly as thou art,
hollow in thy Ears at every Lash,
for *Eurydice*, these for her *Adrastus*
. For her *Adrastus*!
r. Yes, for her *Adrastus*:
Death shall ne'er divide us Death! What's Death?
You seem'd to fear it.
. But I more fear *Creon*:
ke that hunch-back'd Monster in my Arms;
Excrescence of a Man.
*to Cre.* See what you've gain'd.
Death only can be dreadful to the Bad:

To Innocence, 'tis like a Bug-bear, dreſs'd
To frighten Children. Pull but off his Maſque,
And he'll appear a Friend.

*Cre.* You talk too ſlightly
Of Death and Hell. Let me inform you better.

*Eur.* You beſt can tell the News of your own Countr[y]

*Dio.* Nay now you are too ſharp.

*Eur.* Can I be ſo to one, who has accus'd me
Of Murder, and of Parricide?

*Cre.* You provok'd me.
And yet I only did thus far accuſe you,
As next of Blood to *Lajus*: Be adviſ'd,
And you may live.

*Eur.* The Means?

*Cre.* 'Tis offer'd you.
The Fool *Adraſtus* has accus'd himſelf.

*Eur.* He has indeed, to take the Guilt from me.

*Cre.* He ſays, he loves you; if he does, 'tis well.
He ne'er cou'd prove it in a better time.

*Eur.* Then Death muſt be his Recompence for Lo[ve]

*Cre.* 'Tis a Fool's juſt Reward:
The Wiſe can make a better Uſe of Life.
But 'tis the Young Man's Pleaſure, his Ambition:
I grudge him not that Favour.

*Eur.* When he's dead,
Where ſhall I find his Equal?

*Cre.* Every where.
Fine empty things, like him,
The Court ſwarms with 'em.
Fine fighting things, in Camps they are ſo common,
Crows feed on nothing elſe. Plenty of Fools,
A glut of 'em in *Thebes*.
And Fortune ſtill takes care they ſhou'd be ſeen,
She places 'em aloft, o'th' topmoſt Spoke
Of all her Wheel. Fools are the daily Work
Of Nature; her Vocation. If ſhe form
A Man, ſhe loſes by't; 'tis too expenſive;
'Twoud make ten Fools. A Man's a Prodigy.

*Eur.* That is, a *Creon*. O thou black Detractor,
Who ſpitt'ſt thy Venom againſt Gods and Man!

Th[e]

Thou Enemy of Eyes!
Thou who lov'ſt nothing, but what nothing loves;
And that's thy ſelf! who haſt conſpir'd againſt
My Life and Fame, to make me loath'd by all,
And only fit for thee.
But for *Adraſtus'* Death, good Gods! his Death!
What Curſe ſhall I invent?

*Dio.* No more; he's here.

*Eur.* He ſhall be ever here.
He wou'd give his Life, give up his Fame——

*Enter* Adraſtus.

f all the Excellence of Womankind
Were mine,——No, 'tis too little all for him.
Were I made up of endleſs, endleſs Joys——

*Adr* And ſo thou art.
The Man who loves like me,
Wou'd think ev'n Infamy, the worſt of Ills,
ere cheaply purchas'd, were thy Love the Prize:
ncrown'd, a Captive, nothing left but Honour,
is the laſt thing a Prince ſhould throw away;
ut when the Storm grows loud, and threatens Love,
hrow ev'n that over-board, for Love's the Jewel,
nd laſt it muſt be kept.

*Cre. to Dio.* Work him, be ſure,
o Rage, he's paſſionate:
ake him th' Aggreſſor.

*Dio* O falſe Love! Falſe Honour!

*Cre* Diſſembled both, and falſe!

*Adr.* Dar'ſt thou ſay thus to me?

*Cre.* To you! Why, what are you, that I ſhould fear you?
m not *Lajus*: Hear me, Prince of *Argos*,
u give what's nothing, when you give your Honour;
is gone, 'tis loſt in Battel. For your Love,
ows made in Wine are not ſo falſe as that.
u kill'd her Father; you confeſs'd you did:
mighty Argument to prove your Paſſion to the Daughter!

*Adr aſide* Gods! Muſt I bear this Brand, and not retort
e Lie to his foul Throat!

*Dio.* Baſely, you kill'd him.

*Adr aside.* Oh, I burn inward; my Blood's all o fire:
*Alcides*, when the poyson'd Shirt sate closest,
Had but an Ague Fit to this my Fever.
Yet, for *Eurydice*, ev'n this I'll suffer,
To free my Love——Well then, I kill'd him basely.

*Cre.* Fairly, I'm sure you cou'd not.

*Dio.* Nor alone.

*Cre* You had your Fellow-Thieves about you, Prince;
They conquer'd, and you kill'd.

*Adr aside* Down, swelling Heart!
'Tis for thy Princess all.——O my *Eurydice*!——[To her.

*Eur to him.* Reproach not thus the Weakness of my Sex,
As if I could not bear a shameful Death,
Rather than see you burden'd with a Crime,
Of which I know you free.

*Cre* You do ill, Madam,
To let your head-long Love triumph o'er Nature.
Dare you defend your Father's Murderer?

*Eur* You know he kill'd him not.

*Cre* Let him say so.

*Dio* See, he stands mute

*Cre* O Pow'r of Conscience ev'n in wicked Men!
It works, it stings, it will not let him utter
One Syllable, one, no to clear himself
From the most base, detested, horrid Act
That e'er cou'd st in a Villain, not a Prince.

*Adr* Ha! Villain!

*Dio* Eccho to him, Groves: Cry Villain.

*Adr* Let me consider: Did I murder *Lajus*
Thus like a Villain?

*Cre.* Best revoke your Words,
And say, you kill'd him not

*Adr* Not like a Villain Prithee change me that,
For any other Lie.

*Dio* No, Villain, Villain

*Cre.* You kill'd him not! Proclaim your Innocence,
Accuse the Princess So I knew 'twou'd be.

*Adr* I thank thee, thou instruct'st me:
No matter how I kill'd him.

*Cre. aside.* Cool'd again.

*Eur.* Thou who usurp'st the sacred Name of Con- [science,
[...]d not thy own declare him Innocent?
[...]o me declare him so? the King shall know it
*Cre.* You will not be believ'd, for I'll forswear it.
*Eur* What's now thy Conscience?
*Cre* 'Tis my Slave, my Drudge, my supple Glove;
[...]y upper Garment, to put on, throw off,
[...] I think best. 'Tis my obedient Conscience.
*Adr.* Infamous Wretch!
*Cre* My Conscience shall not do me the ill Office
[...]o save a Rival's Life. When thou art dead,
[...]s dead thou shalt be, or be yet more base
[...]an thou think'st me,
[...] forfeiting her Life, to save thy own.)——
[...]ow this, and let it grate thy very Soul,
[...]e shall be mine; (she is, if Vows were binding.)
[...]rk me; the Fruit of all thy Faith and Passion,
[...]'n of thy foolish Death, shall all be mine.
*Adr.* Thine, say'st thou, Monster?
[...]ll my Love be thine?
[...], I can bear no more!
[...]y cunning Engines have with Labour rais'd
[...] heavy Anger, like a mighty Weight,
[...] fall, and push thee dead.
[...]here thy Nuptials, see, thou rash *Ixion*, [*Draws.*
[...]y promis'd *Juno* vanish'd in a Cloud,
[...]d in her room avenging Thunder rolls,
[...] blast thee thus —— Come both———
[...]e 'Tis what I wish'd. [*Both draw.*
[...]w see whose Arm can launch the surer Bolt,
[...] who's the better *Jove*——— [*Fight.*
[...]ur Help, Murder, help!
[...]ter Hæmon *and Guards, run betwixt them, and beat down their Swords*
[...]em. Hold, hold your Impious Hands. I think the [Furies,
[...]whom this Grove is hallow'd, have inspir'd you.
[...], by my Soul, the holiest Earth of *Thebes*
[...] have prophan'd with War. Nor Tree, nor Plant
[...]ws here, but what is fed with Magick Juice,
[...]ull of Human Souls, that cleave their Barks,

To dance at Midnight, by the Moon's pale Beams:
At least two hundred Years these reverend Shades
Have known no Blood, but of black Sheep and Oxen
Shed by the Priest's own Hand, to *Proserpine.*

*Adr* Forgive a Stranger's Ignorance: I knew not
The Honours of the Place.

*Ham* Thou, *Creon*, didst.
Not *Oedipus*, were all his Foes here lodg'd,
Durst violate the Religion of these Groves,
To touch one single Hair; but must, unarm'd,
Parl, as in Truce, or surlily avoid
What most he long'd to kill.

*Cre.* I drew not first;
But in my own Defence.

*Adr* I was provok'd
Beyond Man's Patience: All, Reproach cou'd urge,
Was us'd, to kindle one not apt to bear.

*Ham.* 'Tis *Oedipus*, not I, must judge this Act:
Lord *Creon*, you and *Diocles* retire;
*Tiresias*, and the Brotherhood of Priests,
Approach the Place. None at these Rites assist,
But you th' Accus'd; who by the Mouth of *Lajus*,
Must be absolv'd, or doom'd.

*Adr.* I bear my Fortune,

*Eur.* And I provok'd my Trial.

*Ham* 'Tis at Hand:
For see the Prophet comes, with Vervain crown'd,
The Priests with Yeugh; a venerable Band
We leave you to the Gods. [*Ex.* Hæm *with* Cre. *and* D.

*Enter* Tiresias, *led by* Manto. *The Priests follow, all Cloathed in long black Habits*

*Tir* Approach, ye Lovers;
Ill-fated Pair! whom seeing not, I know.
This Day your kindly Stars in Heav'n were join'd,
When (lo!) an envious Planet interpos'd,
And threaten'd both with Death. I fear, I fear.

*Eur.* Is there no God so much a Friend to Love,
Who can controul the Malice of our Fate?
Are they all deaf? Or have the Gyants Heav'n?

*Tir.* The Gods are just.——
ut how can Finite measure Infinite?
eason! alas, it does not know it self!
t Man, vain Man, wou'd with this short-lin'd Plummet,
athom the vast Abyss of Heav'nly Justice.
hatever is, is in its Causes just,
nce all things are by Fate. But purblind Man
es but a part o'th' Chain, the nearest Links;
is Eyes not carrying to that equal Beam
hat poizes all above.
*Eur.* Then we must die!
*Tir.* The Danger's imminent this Day.
*Adr.* Why then there's one Day less for Human Ills;
nd who would moan himself for suffering that,
hich in a Day must pass? Something, or nothing——
hall be what I was again, before
was *Adrastus.*——
nurious Heav'n! Canst thou not add a Night
o our one Day? Give me a Night with her,
nd I'll give all the rest.
*Tir.* She broke her Vow
rst made to *Creon.* But the Time calls on;
nd *Lajus'* Death must now be made more plain.
ow loth I am to have recourse to Rites
full of Horrour, that I once rejoyce
want the Use of Sight!——
*1 Pr* The Ceremonies stay.
*Tir.* Chuse the darkest part o'th' Grove,
ch as Ghosts at Noon-day love.
g a Trench, and dig it nigh
here the Bones of *Lajus* lie:
ars rais'd, of Turf or Stone,
ill th' Infernal Pow'rs have none.
swer me, if this be done?
*All Pr* 'Tis done.
*Tir* Is the Sacrifice made fit?
aw her backward to the Pit:
aw the barren Heyfer back,
rren let her be, and black;

Cut the curled Hair that grows
Full betwixt her Horns and Brows:
And turn your Faces from the Sun.
Anſwer me, if this be done?

*All Pr.* 'Tis done.

*Tir.* Pour in Blood, and Blood like Wine,
To Mother Earth, and *Proſerpine*:
Mingle Milk into the Stream,
Feaſt the Ghoſts that love the Steam;
Snatch a Brand from Funeral-pile;
Toſs it in to make 'em boil:
And turn your Faces from the Sun;
Anſwer me, if all be done?

*All Pr.* All is done

[*Peal of Thunder, and Flaſhes of Lightning; then groans below the Stage.*

*Manto.* O what Laments are thoſe?

*Tir.* The Groans of Ghoſts, that cleave the Earth with Pain.
And heave it up: they pant and ſtick half way.

[*The Stage wholly darken'd.*

*Manto.* And now a ſudden Darkneſs covers all.
True genuine Night. Night added to the Groves,
The Frogs are blown full in the Face of Heav'n

*Tir.* Am I but half obey'd. Infernal Gods,
Muſt you have Muſick too? then tune your Voices,
And let 'em have ſuch Sounds as Hell ne'er heard,
Since *Orpheus* brib'd the Shades. [*Muſick.*

SONG.

1. *Hear ye ſullen Pow'rs below;*
*Hear, ye Taskers of the dead.*
2 *You that boiling Cauldrons blow,*
*You that ſcum the molten Lead*
3 *You that pinch with red hot Tongs;*
1. *You that drive the trembling Hoſts*
*Of poor, poor Ghoſts,*
*With your ſharpen'd Prongs;*
2 *You that thruſt 'em off the brim.*
3. *You that plunge 'em when they ſwim:*

1. *Till they drown;*
*Till they go*
*On a row*
*Down, down, down,*
*Ten thousand thousand, thousand Fadoms low.*
Chorus. *Till they drown,* &c.
1. *Musick for a while*
*Shall your Cares beguile*
*Wondring how your Pains were eas'd*
2. *And disdaining to be pleas'd;*
3. *Till* Alecto *free the dead*
*From their eternal Bands;*
*Till the Snakes drop from her Head,*
*And whip from out her Hands,*
1. *Come away,*
*Do not stay,*
*But obey*
*While we play,*
*For Hell's broke up, and Ghosts have Holy-day.*
Chorus, *Come away,* &c.
[A flash of Lightning the Stage is made bright; and the Ghosts are seen passing betwixt the Trees.
1. *Lajus!* 2. *Lajus!* 3. *Lajus!*
1 *Hear!* 2. *Hear!* 3. *Hear!*
Tir *Hear and appear*
*By the Fates that spun thy thread;*
Cho. *Which are three*
Tir. *By the Furies fierce and dread;*
Cho. *Which are three*
Tir. *By the Judges of the dead,*
Cho *Which are three*
*Three times three.*
Ter. *By Hell's blue Flame,*
*By the* Stygian *Lake,*
*And by* Demogorgon's *Name*
*At which Ghosts quake,*
*Hear and appear*

*The Ghost of* Lajus *rises arm'd in his Chariot, as he was slain And behind his Chariot sit the three who were murder'd with him.*

*Ghost*

*Ghost.* Why hast thou drawn me from my Pains belo[w]
To suffer worse above; to see the Day,
And *Thebes* more hated? Hell is Heav'n to *Thebes*.
For Pity send me back, where I may hide,
In willing Night, this ignominious Head:
In Hell I shun the publick Scorn; and then
They hunt me for their Sport, and hoot me as I fly:
Behold ev'n now they grin at my gor'd Side,
And chatter at my Wounds.

*Tir.* I pity thee,
Tell but why *Thebes* is for thy Death accurst,
And I'll unbind the Charm.

*Ghost* O spare my Shame.

*Tir.* Are these two Innocent?

*Ghost.* Of my Death they are.
But he who holds my Crown, Oh, must I speak!
Was doom'd to do what Nature most abhors.
The Gods foresaw it; and forbad his Being,
Before he yet was born. I broke their Laws,
And cloath'd with Flesh his pre-existing Soul;
Some kinder Pow'r, too weak for Destiny,
Took pity, and indu'd his new-form'd Mass
With Temperance, Justice, Prudence, Fortitude,
And every Kingly Virtue; but in vain
For Fate, that sent him hood-wink'd to the World,
Perform'd its Work by his mistaking Hands.
Ask'st thou who murder'd me? 'twas *Oedipus*,
Who stains my Bed with Incest? *Oedipus*.
For whom then are you Curst, but *Oedipus*!
He comes, the Parricide. I cannot bear him.
My Wounds ake at him. O his Murd'rous Breath
Venoms my aiery Substance! hence with him,
Banish him; sweep him out; the Plague he bears
Will blast your Fields, and mark his way with Ruin.
From *Thebes*, my Throne, my Bed, let him be driv[en]
Do you forbid him Earth, and I'll forbid him Heav'n.

[*Ghost desce[nds]*

*Enter* Oedipus, Creon, Hæmon, *&c.*

*ed.* What's this! methought some pestilential Blast
ook me just entring, and some unseen Hand
uggled to push me backward Tell me why
Hair stands bristling up, why my Flesh trembles!
stare at me! then Hell has been among ye,
some lag Fiend yet lingers in the Grove.
*ir* What Omen saw'st thou entring?
*ed* A young Stork,
t bore his aged Parent on his Back;
weary with the weight, he shook him off,
Peck'd out both his Eyes.
*dr* Oh, *Oedipus*!
*ur* Oh, wretched *Oedipus*!
*ir* Oh, Fatal King!
*ed.* What mean these Exclamations of my Name?
nk the Gods, no secret Thoughts reproach me.
; I dare challenge Heav'n to turn me outward,
shake my Soul quite empty in your Sight.
n wonder not that I can bear unmov'd
e fix'd Regards, and silent Threats of Eyes:
enerous Fierceness dwells with Innocence,
conscious Virtue is allow'd some Pride.
*ir* Thou know'st not what thou say'st.
*ed* What mutters he! tell me, *Eurydice*:
u shak'st, thy Soul's a Woman. Speak, *Adrastus*,
boldly, as thou met'st my Arms in Fight;
'st thou not speak? why then 'tis bad indeed.
*as*, thee I summon by the Priest-hood,
me what News from Hell, where *Lajus* points,
who's the guilty Head?
*ir* Let me not Answer.
*ed* Be dumb then, and betray thy Native Soil
farther Plagues.
*r* I dare not name him to thee.
*ed* Dar'st thou converse with Hell, and canst thou [fear
human Name?
*r* Urge me no more to tell a thing, which known
u'd make thee more unhappy. 'twill be found
' I am silent.

*Oed.* Old and Obstinate! Then thou thy self
Art Author or Accomplice of this Murder,
And shun'st the Justice, which by publick ban
Thou hast incurr'd.

*Tir.* O! if the Guilt were mine,
It were not half so great: Know, wretched Man,
Thou only, thou art guilty; thy own Curse
Falls heavy on thy self.

*Oed.* Speak this again.
But speak it to the Winds, when they are loudest.
Or to the raging Seas, they'll hear as soon,
And sooner will believe.

*Tir* Then hear me Heav'n,
For blushing thou hast seen it; hear me Earth,
Whose hollow Womb could not contain this Murder,
But sent it back to Light, and thou Hell, hear me,
Whose own black Seal has 'firm'd this horrid Truth,
*Oedipus* murther'd *Lajus*.

*Oed* Rot the Tongue,
And blasted be the Mouth that spoke that Lye
Thou blind of Sight, but thou more blind of Soul.

*Tir* Thy Parents thought not so.

*Oed* Who were my Parents?

*Tir* Thou shalt know too soon.

*Oed.* Why seek I Truth from thee?
The Smiles of Courtiers, and the Harlots Tears,
The Tradesmens Oaths, and Mourning of an Heir,
Are Truths to what Priests tell.
O why has Priesthood Privilege to lye,
And yet to be believ'd!——Thy Age protects thee.

*Tir.* Thou canst not kill me, 'tis not in thy Fate,
As 'twas to kill thy Father; wed thy Mother,
And beget Sons, thy Brothers.

*Oed* Riddles, Riddles!

*Tir.* Thou art thy self a Riddle, a perplext
Obscure *Enigma*, which when thou unty'st,
Thou shalt be found and lost

*Oed* Impossible!
*Adrastus*, speak, and as thou art a King,
Whose Royal Word is sacred, clear my Fame.

*Adr* Wou'd I cou'd!

*Oed.* Ha, wilt thou not · Can the Plebeian Vice
f Lying mount to Kings! can they be tainted!
hen Truth is loft on Earth.

*Cre* The Cheat's too grofs:
*drastus* is his Oracle, and he,
e pious Jugler, but *Adraftus'* Organ.

*Oed* 'Tis plain the Prieft's fuborn'd to free the Pris'ner.

*Cre* And turn the Guilt on you.

*Oed* O honeft *Creon*, how haft thou been bely'd?

*Eur* Hear me.

*Cre.* She's brib'd to fave her Lover's Life.

*Adr.* If, *Oedipus*, thou think'ft——

*Cre.* Hear him not fpeak.

*Adr.* Then hear thefe holy Men

*Cre* Priefts, Priefts, all brib'd, all Priefts.

*Oed.* *Adraftus*, I have found thee.
e Malice of a vanquifh'd Man has feiz'd thee.

*Adr* If Envy and not Truth——

*Oed* I'll hear no more away with him.

[Hæmon *takes him off by force*, Cre. *and* Eur. *follow.*

*Oed to Tir* Why ftand'ft thou here, Impoftor!
old, and yet fo wicked——lye for Gain;
d Gain fo fhort as Age can promife thee!

*Tir* So fhort a time as I have yet to live
ceeds thy pointed Hour; remember *Lajus*;
more; if e'er we meet again, 'twill be
mutual Darknefs; we fhall feel before us
reach each others Hand, Remember *Lajus*.

[*Ex* Tirefias; *Priefts follow.*

*Oedipus Solus*

member *Lajus*! that's the Burthen ftill:
rther and Inceft! but to hear 'em nam'd
Soul ftarts in me. The good Sentinel
nds to her Weapons; takes the firft Alarm
guard me from fuch Crimes.——Did I kill *Lajus*?
en I walk'd fleeping, in fome frightful Dream,
Soul then ftole my Body out by Night,
d brought me back to Bed ere Morning-wake
cannot be ev'n this remoteft way,

But

But some dark hint would justle forward now;
And goad my Memory ——Oh my *Jocasta!*

*Enter* Jocasta.

*Joc* Why are you thus disturb'd?
*Oed* Why, would'st thou think it?
No less than Murder?
*Joc.* Murder? what of Murder?
*Oed* Is Murder then no more? add Parricide,
And Incest, bear not these a frightful Sound?
*Joc.* Alas!
*Oed.* How poor a Pity is Alas,
For two such Crimes!——Was *Lajus* us'd to lye?
*Joc.* Oh no; the most sincere, plain, honest Ma[n]
One who abhor'd a Lye
*Oed.* Then he has got that Quality in Hell.
He charges me——but why accuse I him?
I did not hear him speak it They accuse me,
The Priest, *Adrastus* and *Eurydice*,
Of Murdering *Lajus*—— Tell me, while I think o[n't]
Has old *Tiresias* practis'd long this Trade?
*Joc* What Trade?
*Oed.* Why this foretelling Trade.
*Joc* For many Years.
*Oed* Has he before this Day accus'd me?
*Joc.* Never.
*Oed* Have you ere this inquir'd, who did this M[ur-]
*Joc.* Often, but still in vain [der?]
*Oed* I am satisfy'd
Then 'tis an Infant-lye; but one day old
The Oracle takes place before the Priest;
The Blood of *Lajus* was to murder *Lajus*:
I'm not of *Lajus*' Blood.
*Joc* Ev'n Oracles
Are always doubtful, and are often forg'd:
*Lajus* had one, which never was fulfill'd,
Nor ever can be now!
*Oed* And what foretold it?
*Joc* That he shou'd have a Son by me, fore-doom['d]
The Murderer of his Father: True indeed,
A Son was born; but to prevent that Crime,

e wretched Infant of a guilty Fate,
'd through his untyr'd Feet, and bound with Cords,
a bleak Mountain, naked was expos'd:
e King himself liv'd many, many Years,
d found a different Fate; by Robbers murder'd,
here three Ways meet: Yet these are Oracles;
d this the Faith we owe 'em.

*Oed* Say'st thou, Woman?
Heav'n thou hast wakn'd somewhat in me,
at shakes my very Soul!

*Joc.* What, new disturbance?

*Oed.* Methought thou said'st,—(or do I dream
thou said'st it!)
is Murder was on *Lajus'* Person done,
here three Ways meet!

*Joc* So common Fame reports.

*Oed.* Wou'd it had ly'd

*Joc.* Why, good my Lord?

*Oed* No Questions:
s busie time with me; dispatch mine first;
where, where was it done?

*Joc* Mean you the Murder? [der?

*Oed* Could'st thou not answer, without naming Mur-

*Joc* They say in *Phocide*; on the Verge that parts it
m *Daulia* and from *Delphos*.

*Oed* So!——How long! when happen'd this?

*Joc* Some little time before you came to *Thebes*.

*Oed* What will the Gods do with me!

*Joc* What means that Thought?

*Oed.* Something but 'tis not your turn to ask:
w old was *Lajus*, what his Shape, his Stature,
Action and his Mien? quick, quick, your Answer—

*Joc.* Big made he was, and tall; his Port was fierce,
ct his Countenance; manly Majesty
e in his Front, and darted from his Eyes,
mmanding all he view'd; his Hair just grizled,
in a green old Age; bate but his Years,
u are his Picture.

*Oed.* *Aside* Pray Heav'n he drew me not. Am I his [Picture?

*Joc* So I have often told you.

*Oed.* True, you have;

Add

Add that to the rest. How was the King
Attended when he travell'd?
*Joc* By four Servants:
He went out privately.
*Oed* Well counted still,
One scap'd I hear, what since became of him?
*Joc.* When he beheld you first as King in *Thebes*,
He kneel'd, and trembling beg'd I wou'd dismiss him:
He had my leave; and now he lives retir'd.
*Oed.* This Man must be produc'd; he must, *Jocasta*.
*Joc* He shall——yet have I leave to ask you why?
*Oed* Yes, you shall know: for where should I repose
The Anguish of my Soul, but in your Breast!
I need not tell you *Corinth* claims my Birth,
My Parents *Polybus* and *Merope*,
Two Royal Names, their only Child am I.
It happen'd once, 'twas at a Bridal Feast,
One warm with Wine, told me I was a Foundling,
Not the King's Son, I, stung with this Reproach,
Struck him: My Father heard of it; the Man
Was made ask Pardon; and the business husht.
*Joc* 'Twas somewhat odd.
*Oed* And strangely it perplex'd me.
I stole away to *Delphos*, and implor'd
The God, to tell my certain Parentage.
He bad me seek no farther, 'twas my Fate
To kill my Father, and pollute his Bed,
By marrying her who bore me.
*Joc.* Vain, vain Oracles!
*Oed.* But yet they frighted me;
I lookt on *Corinth* as a Place accurst,
Resolv'd my Destiny should wait in vain;
And never catch me there.
*Joc.* Too nice a Fear.
*Oed* Suspend your Thoughts, and flatter not too soon:
Just in the Place you nam'd, where three Ways met,
And near that time, five Persons I encounter'd,
One was too like, (Heav'n grant it prove not him!)
Whom you describe for *Lajus*. Insolent
And fierce they were, as Men who liv'd on Spoil.

udg'd 'em Robbers, and by force repell'd
he force they us'd. In short, four Men I slew;
he fifth upon his Knees demanding Life,
y Mercy gave it ——— bring me comfort now,
I slew *Lajus*, what can be more wretched!
om *Thebes* and you my Curse has banish'd me.
om *Corinth*, Fate.
*Joc.* Perplex not thus your Mind;
y Husband fell by Multitudes opprest,
*Phorbas* said: This Band you chanc'd to meet;
d murder'd not my *Lajus*, but reveng'd him
*Oed.* There's all my hope: Let *Phorbas* tell me this,
d I shall live again ———
you good Gods, I make my last Appeal;
clear my Virtues or my Crime reveal:
wandring in the maze of Fate I run,
d backward trod the Paths I sought to shun,
pute my Errors to your own Decree,
Hands are guilty, but my Heart is free. [*Exeunt.*

---

## ACT IV. SCENE. I.

*Enter* Pyracmon *and* Creon

SOME business of import that Triumph wears
You seem to go with, nor is it hard to guess
hen you are pleas'd by a malicious Joy.
ose red and fiery Beams cast through your Visage
lowing Pleasure Sure you smile Revenge,
I cou'd gladly hear.
*e* Wouldst thou believe,
giddy hair-brain'd King, whom old *Tiresias*
Thunder-struck with heavy Accusation,
' conscious of no inward Guilt, yet fears;
ears *Jocasta*, fears himself, his Shadow;
ears the Multitude, and, which is worth
Age or laughter, out of all Mankind,
chuses me to be his Orator:
ars that *Adrastus*, and the lean-look'd Prophet,



Are

Are joint Conspirators, and wisht me to
Appease the raving *Thebans*; which I swore
To do.

*Pyr*. A dangerous Undertaking;
Directly opposite to your own Interest.

*Cre* No, dull *Pyracmon*; when I left his Presence,
With all the Wings with which Revenge could imp
My flight, I gain'd the midst o'th' City,
There, standing on a Pile of dead and dying,
I to the mad and sickly Multitude,
With interrupting Sobs, cry'd out, O *Thebes*,
O wretched *Thebes*, thy King, thy *Oedipus*,
This barbarous Stranger, thus Usurper, Monster,
Is by the Oracle, the wise *Tiresias*,
Proclaim'd the Murderer of the Royal *Lajus*
*Jocasta* too, no longer now my Sister,
Is found Comptroller in the horrid Deed
Here I renounce all tye of Blood and Nature,
For thee, O *Thebes*, dear *Thebes*, poor bleeding Th
And there I wept, and then the Rabble howl'd,
And roar'd, and with a thousand antick Mouths
Gabbled Revenge, Revenge was all the cry.

*Pyr*. This cannot fail. I see you on the Throne,
And *Oedipus* cast out.

*Cre* Then straight came on
*Alcander*, with a wild and bellowing Croud,
Whom when he had wrought, I whisper'd him to p
And head the Forces while the Heat was in 'em.
So to the Palace I return'd to meet
The King, and greet him with another Story.
But see, he enters

*Enter* Oedipus *and* Jocasta, *attended.*

*Oed*. Said you that *Phorbas* is return'd, and yet
Intreats he may return, without being ask'd
Of ought concerning what we have discover'd?

*Joc*. He started when I told him your Intent,
Replying, what he knew of that Affair
Would give no Satisfaction to the King;
Then, falling on his Knees, begg'd as for Life,
To be dismiss'd from Court; he trembled too,

ſf concluſive Death had ſeiz'd upon him,
ſtammer'd in his abrupt Pray'r ſo wildly,
t, had he been the Murderer of *Lajus*,
lt and Diſtraction could not have ſhook him more
*ed.* By your Deſcription, ſure as Plagues and Death
waſte our *Thebes*, ſome Deed that ſhuns the Light
t thoſe Fears: If thou reſpect'ſt my Peace,
re him, dear *Jocaſta*, for my Genius
nks at his Name.
*oc* Rather let him go·
y poor boding Heart would have it be,
hout a Reaſon
*d* Hark, the *Thebans* come!
efore retire; and, once more, if thou lov'ſt me,
*Phorbas* be retain'd.
You ſhall, while I
Life, be ſtill obey'd:
n you ſooth me with your ſoft Endearments,
ſet the faireſt Countenance to view,
gloomy Eyes, my Lord, betray a Deadneſs
nward languiſhing· That Oracle
like a ſubtile Worm, its venom'd Way,
on your Heart, and rots the noble Core,
e'er the beauteous Out ſide ſhews ſo lovely
*d* O, thou wilt kill me with thy Love's Exceſs!
ll is well, retire, the *Thebans* come. [*Ex.* Jocaſta.
*ſt Oedipus*!
*d* Ha! again that Scream of Woe!
e have I heard, thrice ſince the Morning dawn'd
low'd loud, as if my Guardian Spirit
from ſome vaulted Manſion, *Oedipus*!
it but the Work of Melancholly?
the Sun ſets, Shadows, that ſhew'd at Noon
nall, appear moſt long and terrible,
hen we think Fate hovers o'er our Heads,
Apprehenſions ſhoot beyound all Bounds,
Ravens, Crickets ſeem the Watch of Death,
e's worſt Vermine, ſcare her God-like Sons.
es, the very Leavings of a Voice,
babling Ghoſts, and call us to our Graves:

Each Mole-hill Thought swells to a huge *Olympus*,
While we fantastick Dreamers heave and puff,
And sweat with an Imagination's weight,
As if, like *Atlas*, with these mortal Shoulders
We could sustain the Burden of the World.
[Creon *comes from*

*Cre.* O Sacred Sir, my Royal Lord ——
*Oed* What now?
Thou seem'st affrighted at some dreadful Action,
Thy Breath comes short, thy darted Eyes are fix
On me for Aid, as if thou wert pursu'd
I sent thee to the *Thebans*, speak thy Wonder;
Fear not, this Palace is a Sanctuary,
The King himself's thy Guard.
*Cre.* For me, alas, [so
My Life's not worth a Thought, when weigh'd w
But fly, my Lord, fly as your Life is Sacred,
Your Fate is precious to your faithful *Creon*,
Who therefore, on his Knees, thus prostrate begs
You would remove from *Thebes* that vows your Ru
When I but offer'd at your Innocence,
They gather'd Stones, and menac'd me with Deat
And drove me through the Streets with Impreca
Against your Sacred Person, and those Traytors
Which justify'd your Guilt; which curs'd *Tiresias*
Told, as from Heav'n, was Cause of their Destruc
*Oed* Rise, worthy *Creon*, haste and take our G
Rank 'em in equal part upon the Square,
Then open every Gate of this our Palace,
And let the Torrent in Hark, it comes, [S
I hear 'em roar Be gone, and break down all
The Dams, that would oppose their furious Passag
[*Ex.* Creon *with* Gu

*Enter* Adrastus, *his Sword drawn*

*Adr* Your City
Is all in Arms, all bent to your Destruction:
I heard but now, where I was close confin'd,
A Thundering Shout, which made my Jaylors ru
Cry, Fire the Palace; where's the cruel King?
Yet, by th' Infernal Gods, those awful Pow'rs

t have accus'd you, which these Ears have heard,
these Eyes seen, I must believe you guiltless,
since I knew the Royal *Oedipus*,
ve observ'd in all his Acts such Truth
God-like Clearness. that to the last Gush
Blood and Spirits, I'll defend his Life,
here have sworn to perish by his Side.
*d.* Be witness, Gods, how near this Touches me,
hat Recompence can Glory make? [*Embracing him.*
*dr.* Defend your Innocence, speak like your self,
awe the Rebels with your dauntless Virtue.
hark! the Storm comes nearer.
*d.* Let it come.
force of Majesty is never known
n a general Wrack. Then, then is seen
difference 'twixt a Threshold and a Throne
*r* Creon, Pyracmon, Alcander, Tiresias, Thebans.
*c.* Where, where's this cruel King? *Thebans*, behold
e stands your Plague, the Ruin, Desolation
is Unhappy ——— speak, shall I kill him?
all he be cast out to Banishment?
*Theb* To Banishment, away with him.
Hence, you Barbarians, to your slavish Distance,
the Earth your sordid Looks; for he
stirs, dares more than Mad-men, Fiends, or Furies:
dares to face me, by the Gods, as well
brave the Majesty of thundering *Jove.*
for this relieve you when besieg'd
is fierce Prince, when coop'd within your Walls,
o the very Brink of Fate reduc'd,
lean-jaw'd Famine made more Havock of you,
does the Plague? But I rejoyce I know you,
the base Stuff that temper'd your vile Souls
Gods be prais'd, I needed not your Empire,
a greater, nobler of my own;
hall the Scepter of the Earth now win me
e such Brutes, so barbarous a People
Methinks, my Lord, I see a sad Repentance,
eral Consternation spread among 'em
My Reign is at an end; yet ere I finish ——

I'll do a Justice that becomes a Monarch,
A Monarch who i th' midst of Swords and Javelins,
Dares act as on his Throne encompast round
With Nations for his Guard *Alcander*, you
Are nobly born, therefore shall lose your Head.
[*Seizes* [illegible]
Here, *Hæmon*, take him, but for this, and this,
Let Cords dispatch 'em Hence, away with 'em.

*Ti* O Sacred Prince, pardon distracted *Thebes*,
Pardon her, if she acts by Heav'ns Award,
If that th' Infernal Spirits have declar'd
The Depth of Fate, and if our Oracles
May speak, O do not too severely deal,
But let thy wretched *Thebes*, at least complain·
If thou art guilty, Heav'n will make it known;
If Innocent, then let *Tiresias* dye [*Alca*[illegible]

*Oed* I take thee at thy Word Run, haste, and [illegible]
I swear the Prophet or the King shall dye.
Be witness, all you *Thebans*, of my Oath.
And *Phorbas* be the Umpire

*Tir* I submit [*Trumpets* [illegible]

*Oed* What mean those Trumpets?

*Enter* Hæmon *with* Alcander

*Hæm* From your Native Country,
Great Sir, the fam'd *Ægeon* is arriv'd,
That renown'd Favourite of the King your Fa[illegible]
He comes as an Ambassador from *Corinth*,
And sues for Audience

*Oed* Haste, *Hæmon*, fly, and tell him that I [illegible]
T'embrace him

*Hæm* The Queen, my Lord, at present holds [illegible]
In private Conference; but behold her here.

*Enter* Jocasta, Eurydice, &c

*Joc* Hail, happy *Oedipus*, happiest of Kings
Henceforth be blest blest as thou canst desire
Sleep without Fears the blackest Nights away,
Let Furies haunt thy Palace, thou shalt sleep
Secure, thy Slumbers shall be soft and gentle
As Infants Dreams

*Oed* What does the Soul of all my Joys intend?
And whither would this Rapture?

*Joc.* O, I could rave,
ull down those lying Fanes, and burn that Vault,
om whence resounded those false Oracles,
hat robb'd my Love of rest: If we must pray,
ear in the Streets bright Altars to the Gods,
t Virgins Hands adorn the Sacrifice,
nd not a grey-Beard forging Priest come near,
o pry into the Bowels of the Victim,
nd with his Dotage mad the gaping World.
ut see, the Oracle that I will trust,
rue as the Gods, and affable as Men

*Enter* Ægeon, *Kneels*

*Oed.* O, to my Arms, welcome, my dear *Ægeon*:
en thousand welcomes. O, my Foster-Father,
elcome as Mercy to a Man condemn'd!
elcome to me,
to a sinking Marriner
he lucky Plant, that bears him to the Shore!
t speak, O tell me what so mighty Joy
this thou bring'st, which so transports *Jocasta*?
*Joc.* Peace, peace *Ægeon*, let *Jocasta* tell him!
that I could for ever charm, as now,
y dearest *Oedipus* Thy Royal Father,
*lybus*, King of *Corinth*, is no more.
*Oed* Ha! can it be? *Ægeon*, answer me,
d speak in short, what my *Jocasta*'s Transport
y over-do
*Æge* Since in few Words, my Royal Lord, you ask
know the Truth; King *Polybus* is dead
*Oed* O all you Pow'rs, is't possible? What, dead!
that the Tempest of my Joy may rise
just degrees, and hit at last the Stars!
, how, how dy'd he? Ha! by Sword, by Fire,
Water? by Assassinates, or Poyson? speak·
did he languish under some Disease?
*Æge.* Of no Distemper, of no Blast he dy'd,
fell like Autumn-Fruit that melow'd long
n wonder'd at, because he dropt no sooner.
e seem'd to wind him up for fourscore Years;
freshly ran he on ten Winters more:

Till, like a Clock worn out with eating Time,
The Wheels of weary Life at last stood still.

*Oed.* O, let me press thee in my youthful Arms,
And smother thy old Age in my Embraces.
Yes *Thebans*, yes *Jocasta*, yes *Adrastus*,
Old *Polybus*, the King my Father's dead.
Fires shall be kindled in the midst of *Thebes*;
I' th' midst of Tumults, Wars, and Pestilence,
I will rejoyce for *Polybus* his Death.
Know, be it known to the limits of the World;
Yet farther let it pass yon dazling Roof,
The Mansion of the Gods, and strike 'em deaf
With everlasting Peals of thundring Joy.

*Tir.* Fate! Nature! Fortune! what is all this Wo[rld]

*Oed.* Now, Dotard; now, thou blind old wi[zard]
Prophet,
Where are your boding Ghosts, your Altars now,
Your Birds of Knowledge, that in dusky Air
Chatter Futurity, and where are now
Your Oracles, that call'd me Parricide?
Is he not dead? deep laid in's Monument?
And was not I in *Thebes* when Fate attackt him?
Avant, be gone, you Vizors of the Gods!
Were I as other Sons, now I should weep,
But as I am? I've reason to rejoyce:
And will, tho' his cold Shade should rise and blast m[e]
O, for his Death, let Waters break their Bounds,
Rocks, Valleys, Hills, with splitting *Io*'s ring:
*Io*, *Jocasta*, *Io pæan* sing.

*Tir.* Who would not now conclude an happy En[d]
But all Fate's Turns are swift and unexpected.

*Æge.* Your Royal Mother *Merope*, as if
She had no Soul since you forsook the Land,
Waves all the neighbouring Princes that adore her.

*Oed.* Waves all the Princes! Poor Heart! for what,
speak.

*Æge.* She, tho' in full-blown flow'r of glorious Beau[ty]
Grows cold, ev'n in the Summer of her Age:
And for your sake has sworn to die unmarry'd.

*Oed.* How! for my sake, die and not marry! O,
My Fit returns.

*Æge.* This Diamond, with a thousand Kisses blest,
ith a thousand Sighs and Wishes for your Safety,
e charg'd me give you, with the general Homage
our *Corinthian* Lords.
*Oed.* There's Magick in it, take it from my sight;
ere's not a Beam it darts, but carries Hell,
t flashing Lust, and Necromantick Incest·
ke it from my sick Eyes, O hide it from me.
, my *Jocasta*, tho' *Thebes* cast me out,
hile *Merope*'s alive, I'll ne'er return!
rather let me walk round the wide World
Beggar, than accept a Diadem
such abhor'd Conditions.
*Joc.* You make, my Lord, your own Unhappiness,
these extravagant and needless Fears.
*Oed.* Needless! O, all you Gods! by Heav'n I'd rather
mbrue my Arms up to my very Shoulders
the dear Entrails of the best of Fathers,
an offer at the execrable act
damned Incest, therefore no more of her.
*Æge.* And why, O sacred Sir, if Subjects may
sume to look into their Monarch's Breast,
hy should the chast and spotless *Merope*
use such Thoughts as I must blush to name?
*Oed.* Because the God of *Delphos* did forewarn me
ith thundering Oracles.
*Æge.* May I intreat to know 'em?
*Oed.* Yes, my *Ægeon*, but the sad Remembrance
ite blasts my Soul. See then the swelling Priest!
thinks I have his Image now in view;
mounts the *Tripos* in a Minute's Space,
clouded Head knocks at the Temple roof,
hile from his Mouth
ese dismal Words are heard·
Fly, Wretch, whom Fate has doom'd thy Father's
Blood to spill,
And with prepostrous Births thy Mother's Womb to fill.
*Æge.* Is this the Cause
y you refuse the Diadem of *Corinth*?
*Oed.* The Cause! why is it not a monstrous one?

*Æge.*

*Æge*. Great Sir, you may return, and tho' you sho
Enjoy the Queen (which all the Gods forbid)
The Act would prove no Incest.

*Oed* How, *Ægeon*?
Tho' I enjoy'd my Mother, not incestuous!
Thou rav'st, and so do I, and these all catcht
My Madness; look, they're dead with deep Distractio
Not Incest! what, not Incest with my Mother?

*Æge* My Lord, Queen *Merope* is not your Mothe

*Oed* Ha! did I hear thee right? not *Merope*
My Mother!

*Æge* Nor was *Polybus* your Father.

*Oed* Then all my Days and Nights must now be spe
In curious search, to find out those dark Parents
Who gave me to the World, speak then *Ægeon*,
By all the Gods Cœlestial and Infernal,
By all the Tyes of Nature, Blood and Friendship,
Conceal not from this rack'd despairing King
A Point or smallest Grain of what thou know'st
Speak then, O answer to my Doubts directly.
If Royal *Polybus* was not my Father,
Why was I call'd his Son?

*Æge* He, from my Arms,
Receiv'd you as the fairest Gift of Nature.
Not but you were adorn'd with all the Riches
That Empire could bestow in costly Mantles
Upon its Infant Heir

*Oed* But was I made the Heir of *Corinth*'s Crown,
Because *Ægeon*'s Hand presented me?

*Æge* By my Advice,
Being past all hope of Children,
He took, embrac'd, and own'd you for his Son

*Oed* Perhaps I then am yours; instruct me, Sir
If it be so, I'll kneel and weep before you,
With all th' Obedience of a penitent Child,
Imploring Pardon.
Kill me if you please,
I will not writh my Body at the Wound:
But sink upon your Feet with a last Sigh,
And ask Forgiveness with my dying Hands.

*Æge.* O rise, and call not to this aged Cheek
The little Blood which should keep warm my Heart,
You are not mine, nor ought I to be blest
With such a Godlike Offspring. Sir, I found you
Upon the Mount *Cithæron.*
*Oed.* O speak, go on, the Air grows sensible
Of the great things you utter, and is calm:
The hurry'd Orbs, with Storms so rack'd of late,
Seem to stand still, as if that *Jove* were talking.
*Cithæron!* speak, the Valley of *Cithæron!*
*Æge.* Oft times before I thither did resort,
Charm'd with the Conversation of a Man
Who led a rural Life, and had Command
O'er all the Shepherds, who about those Vales
Tended their numerous Flocks; in this Man's Arms
I saw you smiling at a fatal Dagger,
Whose Point he often offer'd at your Throat;
But then you smil'd, and then he drew it back,
Then lifted it again, you smil'd again
Till he at last in Fury threw it from him,
And cry'd aloud, the Gods forbid thy Death:
Then I rush'd in, and, after some Discourse,
To me he did bequeath your innocent Life;
And I, the welcome Care to *Polybus.*
*Oed.* To whom belongs the Master of the Shepherds?
*Æge.* His Name I knew not, or I have forgot,
That he was of the Family of *Lajus,*
I well remember.
*Oed.* And is your Friend alive? For if he be,
I'll buy his Presence, tho' it cost my Crown.
*Æge.* Your menial Attendants best can tell
Whether he lives, or not, and who has now
His Place.
*Joc.* Winds bear me to some barren Island,
Where Print of Human Feet was never seen,
O'er-grown with Weeds of such a monstrous height,
Their baleful Tops are wash'd with bellowing Clouds,
Beneath whose venomous Shade I may have vent
For Horrour, that would blast the barbarous World.
*Oed.* If there be any here that knows the Person
Whom

Whom he describ'd, I charge him on his Life
To speak; Concealment shall be sudden Death:
But he who brings him forth, shall have Reward
Beyond Ambition's lust.

*Tir* His Name is *Phorbas*:
*Jocasta* knows him well; but if I may
Advise, rest where you are, and seek no farther.

*Oed.* Then all goes well, since *Phorbas* is secur'd
By my *Jocasta* Haste and bring him forth:
My Love, my Queen, give Orders Ha' what means
These Tears, and Groans, and Strugling? speak my Fa[ir]
What are thy Troubles?

*Joc* Yours; and yours are mine:
Let me conjure you take the Prophet's Counsel,
And let this *Phorbas* go.

*Oed* Not for the World.
By all the Gods, I'll know my Birth, tho' Death
Attends the search · I have already past
The middle of the Stream, and to return
Seems greater Labour than to venture o'er.
Therefore produce him

*Joc.* Once more, by the Gods,
I beg, my *Oedipus*, my Lord, my Life,
My Love, my all, my only utmost Hope,
I beg you banish *Phorbas*: O, the Gods!
I kneel that you may grant this first Request,
Deny me all things else, but for my sake,
And as you prize your own Eternal Quiet,
Never let *Phorbas* come into your Presence

*Oed.* You must be rais'd, and *Phorbas* shall appear,
Tho' his dead Eyes were *Basilisks* · Guards, haste,
Search the Queen's Lodgings, find and force him hither

[*Exeunt Guard[s]*.

*Joc* O, *Oedipus*, yet send,
And stop their Entrance, ere it be too late:
Unless you wish to see *Jocasta* rent
With Furies, slain out-right with meer Distraction,
Keep from your Eyes and mine the dreadful *Phorbas*.
Forbear this search, I'll think you more than Mortal:
Will you yet hear me?

Oed

*Oed* Tempests will be heard,
d Waves will dash, tho' Rocks their basis keep——
r see, they enter. If thou truly lov'st me,
ther forbear this Subject, or retire

*Enter* Hæmon, *Guards*, *with* Phorbas.

*Joc* Prepare then, wretched Prince, prepare to hear
Story, that shall turn thee into Stone:
uld there be hewn a monstrous Gap in Nature,
Flaw made through the Center by some God,
rough which the Groans of Ghosts might strike thy Ears,
ey would not wound thee, as this Story will.
rk! hark! a hollow Voice calls out aloud,
*asta* yes, I'll to the Royal Bed,
here first the Mysteries of our Loves were acted,
d double dye it with Imperial Crimson;
ar off this curling Hair,
gorg'd with Fire, stab every vital Part,
d when at last I'm slain, to Crown the Horrour
y poor tormented Ghost shall cleave the Ground,
try if Hell can yet more deeply Wound.

*Oed* She's gone, and as she went, methought her Eyes
ew larger, while a thousand Frantick Spirits
ething, like rising Bubbles, on the Brim,
ep'd from the Watry Brink, and glow'd upon me.
leck no more; but hush my Genius up
at throws me on my Fate.——— Impossible!
wretched Man! whose too too busie Thoughts
de swifter than the galloping Heav'ns round,
th an Eternal hurry of the Soul
y there's a time, when ev'n the rowling Year
ms to stand still, dead Calms are in the Ocean,
hen not a Breath disturbs the drowzy Waves:
Man, the very Monster of the World,
e'er at rest, the Soul for ever wakes:
me then, since Destiny thus drives us on,
's know the bottom. *Hæmon*, you I sent:
ere is that *Phorbas*?

*Hæm.* Here, my Royal Lord

*Oed* Speak first, *Ægeon*, say, is this the Man?

*Æge.* My Lord it is: tho' Time has plough'd that Face

With

With many Furrows since I saw it first;
Y[illegible] too well acquainted with the Ground, quite
*Oed.* Peace, stand back a while. [forget
Come hither Friend; I hear thy Name is *Phorbas*
Why dost thou turn thy Face? I charge thee answer
To what I shall enquire. Wert thou not once
The Servant of King *Lajus* here in *Thebes*?
*Phor.* I was, great Sir, his true and faithful Servant
Born and bred up in Court, no Forreign Slave.
*Oed* What Office hadst thou? what was thy Em-
ployment?
*Phor.* He made me Lord of all his Rural Pleasures
For much he lov'd 'em. oft I entertain'd
With sporting Swains, o'er whom I had Command
*Oed.* Where was thy Residence? to what part o'th'
Didst thou most frequently resort? [Country
*Phor* To Mount *Cithæron*, and the pleasant Vallies
Which all about lye shadowing its large Feet.
*Oed* Come forth *Ægeon.* Ha! why starts thou *Phorbas*
Forward, I say, and Face to Face confront him,
Look wistly on him, through him if thou canst,
And tell me on thy Life, say, dost thou know him?
Didst thou e'er see him? converse with him,
Near Mount *Cithæron*?
*Phor.* Who, my Lord, this Man?
*Oed* This Man, this old, this venerable Man?
Speak, didst thou ever meet him there?
*Phor.* Where, Sacred Sir?
*Oed* Near Mount *Cithæron*; answer to the purpose
'Tis a King speaks; and Royal Minutes are
Of much more worth than thousand Vulgar Years
Didst thou e'er see this Man near *Cithæron*?
*Phor.* Most sure, my Lord, I have seen Lines like these
His Visage bears; but know not where, nor when
*Æge* Is't possible you should forget your antient Friend
There are perhaps
Particulars which may excite your dead remembrance.
Have you forgot I took an Infant from you,
Doom'd to be murder'd in that gloomy Vale?
The Swadling-bands were Purple, wrought with Gold
Ha

ve you forgot too how you wept, and begg'd
at I should breed him up, and ask no more?

*Phor.* What e'er I begg'd; thou, like a Dotard, speak'st
re than is requisite And what of this?
hy is it mention'd now? and why, O why
st thou betray the Secrets of thy Friend?

*Æge.* Be not too rash. That Infant grew at last
King; and here the happy Monarch stands

*Phor* Ha! Whither would'st thou! O what hast thou utter'd!
what thou hast said, Death strike thee dumb for ever.

*Oed.* Forbear to curse the Innocent; and be
urst thy self, thou shifting Traitor, Villain,
n'd Hypocrite, equivocating Slave

*Phor.* O Heav'ns! wherein, my Lord, have I offended?

*Oed* Why speak you not according to my Charge?
g forth the Rack, since Mildness cannot win you,
ments shall force.

*Phor* Hold, hold, O dreadful Sir!
will not rack an Innocent old Man.

*Oed* Speak then

*Phor* Alas! what would you have me say?

*Oed* Did this old Man take from your Arms an Infant?

*Phor.* He did: and, oh! I wish to all the Gods,
I had perish'd in that very moment

*Oed* Moment! Thou shalt be Hours, Days, Years a [dying
, bind his Hands, he dallies with my Fury.
shall find a way————

*Phor.* My Lord, I said I gave the Infant to him.

*Oed* Was he thy own, or given thee by another?

*Phor.* He was not mine, but given me by another

*Oed* Whence? and from whom? what City? of what House?

*Phor.* O Royal Sir, I bow me to the Ground,
ld I could sink beneath it, by the Gods,
conjure you to enquire no more.

*Oed* Furies and Hell! *Hæmon*, bring forth the Rack,
hither Cords, and Knives, and sulphurous Flames,
all be bound, and gash'd, his Skin flead off,
burnt alive.

*Phor.* O spare my Age.

*Oed.*

*Oed* Rise then, and speak.

*Phor.* Dread Sir, I will.

*Oed* Who gave that Infant to thee?

*Phor* One of King *Lajus'* Family.

*Oed* O, you immortal Gods! but say, who was't,
Which of the Family of *Lajus* gave it?
A Servant; or one of the Royal Blood?

*Phor* O wretched State! I dye, unless I speak,
And, if I speak, most certain Death attends me!

*Oed* Thou shalt not dye. Speak then, who was it, spe
While I have Sense to understand the Horror;
For I grow cold.

*Phor.* The Queen *Jocasta* told me
It was her Son by *Lajus*

*Oed* O you Gods! But did she give it thee?

*Phor.* My Lord, she did. [He

*Oed.* Wherefore? for what?——O break not yet
Tho' my Eyes burst, no matter: Wilt thou tell me,
Or must I ask for ever? For what end?
Why gave she thee her Child?

*Phor.* To murder it

*Oed* O more than savage! Murder her own Bowe
Without a Cause!

*Phor.* There was a dreadful one,
Which had foretold that most unhappy Son
Should kill his Father, and enjoy his Mother.

*Oed.* But one thing more:
*Jocasta* told me thou wert by the Chariot
When the old King was slain: Speak, I conjure the
For I shall never ask thee ought again,
What was the number of the Assassinates?

*Phor.* The dreadful Deed was acted but by one
And sure that one had much of your Resemblance.

*Oed.* 'Tis well! I thank you Gods! 'tis wondrous w
Daggers and Poyson, O there is no need
For my Dispatch; and you, you merciless Pow'rs,
Hoard up your Thunder-stones, keep, keep your Bo
For Crimes of little note. [Fa

*Adr.* Help, *Hæmon*, help, and bow him gently forwa
Chafe, chase his Temples: How the mighty Spirit
H

alf strangled with the damp his Sorrows rais'd,
uggle for vent! But see, he breaths again,
d vigorous Nature breaks through all opposition.
ow fares my Royal Friend?

*Oed.* The worse for you
barbarous Men! and oh the hated Light!
hy did you force me back to curse the Day;
o curse my Friends; to blast with this dark Breath
e et untainted Earth and circling Air;
o raise new Plagues, and call new Vengeance down?
hy did you tempt the Gods, and dare to touch me?
ethinks there's not a Hand that grasps this Hell,
t should run up like Flax all blazing Fire.
nd from this spot, I wish you as my Friends,
d come not near me, least the gaping Earth
allow you too————Lo, I am gone already.

*aws and claps his Sword to his Breast, which* Adrastus *rikes away with his Foot.*

*Adr.* You shall no more be trusted with your Life.
en, *Alcander*, *Hamon* help to hold him.

*Oed.* Cruel *Adrastus*! Wilt thou, *Hamon* too?
e these the Obligations of my Friends?
worse than worst of my most barbarous Foes!
r, dear *Adrastus*, look with half an Eye
my unheard of Woes, and judge thy self,
be fit that such a Wretch should live!
by these melting Eyes, unus'd to weep,
th all the low Submissions of a Slave,
o conjure thee give my Horrors way!
k not of Life, for that will make me rave:
well thou may'st advise a tortur'd Wretch,
mangled o'er from Head to Foot with Wounds,
his Bones broke, to wait a better Day.

*Adr.* My Lord, you ask me things impossible;
I with Justice should be thought your Foe,
leave you in this Tempest of your Soul.
' banish'd *Thebes*, in *Corinth* you may Reign;
Infernal Pow'rs themselves exact no more
n then your Rage, and once more seek the Gods.

*Oed.* I'll have no more to do with Gods, nor Men.

Hence from my Arms, avant. Enjoy thy Mother!
What, violate with Bestial Appetite
The sacred Veils that wrapt thee yet unborn!
This is not to be born, hence! off, I say!
For they who let my Vengeance, make themselves
Accomplices in my most horrid Guilt.

*Adr* Let it be so, we'll fence Heav'ns Fury from yo
And suffer altogether: This perhaps,
When Ruin comes, may help to break your Fall.

*Oed.* O that, as oft I have at *Athens* seen
The Stage arise, and the big Clouds descend,
So now in very Deed I might behold
The pond'rous Earth, and all yon marble Roof
Meet, like the Hands of *Jove*, and crush Mankind.
For all the Elements, and all the Pow'rs
Celestial, nay, Terrestrial and Infernal,
Conspire the Rack of out-cast *Oedipus*:
Fall Darkness then, and everlasting Night
Shadow the Globe; may the Sun never dawn,
The Silver Moon be blotted from her Orb,
And for an universal Rout of Nature
Through all the inmost Chambers of the Sky,
May there be not a Glimpse, one Starry Spark,
But Gods meet Gods and justle in the Dark
That Jars may rise, and Wrath divine be hurl'd,
Which may to Atoms shake the solid World. [*Ex*

## ACT V. SCENE I.

*Enter* Creon, Alcander *and* Pyracmon

*Cre* THEBES is at length my own; and all my Wi
(Which sure were great as Royalty e'er for
Fortune and my auspicious Stars have crown'd.
O Diadem, thou Center of Ambition,
Where all its different Lines are reconcil'd,
As if thou wert the Burning-glass of Glory!

*Pyr.* Might I be Counsellor, I wou'd intreat you

o cool a little, Sir;
nd out *Eurydice*;
d with the Resolution of a Man
ark'd out for Greatness, give the fatal choice
f Death or Marriage.
*Alc* Survey curs'd *Oedipus*,
one who, tho' unfortunate, 's belov'd,
ought innocent, and therefore much lamented
all the *Thebans*; you must mark him dead:
ce nothing but his Death, not Banishment,
n give Assurance to your doubtful Reign.
*Cre.* Well have you done to snatch me from the Storm
racking Transport, where the little Streams
Love, Revenge, and all the under Passions,
Waters are by sucking Whirl-pools drawn,
re quite devour'd in the vast Gulph of Empire:
erefore *Pyracmon*, as you boldly urg'd,
*ydice* shall dye, or be my Bride.
*ander*, summon to their Master's Aid
menial Servants, and all those whom Change
State, and Hope of the new Monarch's Favour
win to take our part. Away: What now? [*Ex.* Alc.

*Enter* Hæmon.

en *Hæmon* weeps, without the help of Ghosts,
y foretell there is a fatal Cause.
*Hæm* Is't possible you should be ignorant
what has happen'd to the desperate King?
*e* I know no more, but that he was conducted
his Closet, where I saw him fling
trembling Body on the Royal Bed.
left him there, at his desire, alone:
sure no Ill, unless he dy'd with Grief,
d happen, for you bore his Sword away.
*Hæm* I did: and, having lock'd the Door, I stood;
through a Chink I found, not only heard,
saw him, when he thought no Eye beheld him:
irst, deep Sighs heav'd from his woful Heart,
murs and Groans, that shook the outward Rooms.
art thou still alive, O Wretch! he cry'd:
n groan'd again, as if his sorrowful Soul

Had crack'd the Strings of Life, and burst away.

*Cre.* I weep to hear, how then should I have griev'd
Had I beheld this wondrous heap of Sorrow!
But, to the fatal period.

*Hæm* Thrice he struck,
With all his force, his hollow groaning Breast,
And thus, with out-cries, to himself complain'd.
But thou canst weep then, and thou think'st 'tis well
These Bubbles of the shallowest emptiest Sorrow,
Which Children vent for Toys, and Women rain
For any Trifle their fond Hearts are set on;
Yet these thou think'st are ample Satisfaction
For bloodiest Murder, and for burning Lust
No, Parricide, if thou must weep, weep Blood;
Weep Eyes, instead of Tears O! by the Gods,
'Tis greatly thought, he cry'd, and fits my Woes.
Which said, he smil'd revengfully, and leapt
Upon the Floor; thence gazing at the Skies,
His Eyes-balls fiery red, and glowing Vengeance,
Gods, I accuse you not, tho' I no more
Will view your Heav'n, 'till with more durable Glass
The mighty Soul's immortal Perspectives,
I find your dazling Beings· Take, he cry'd,
Take, Eyes, your last, your fatal farewel view.
When with a Groan that seem'd the Call of Death,
With horrid force lifting his impious Hands,
He snatch'd, he tore, from forth their bloody Orbs,
The Balls of Sight, and dash'd 'em on the Ground

*Cre* A Master-piece of Horror! new and dreadful

*Hæm* I ran to succour him; but, oh! too late,
For he had pluck'd the remnant Strings away
What then remains, but that I find *Tiresias*,
Who, with his Wisdom may allay those Furies
That haunt his gloomy Soul?

*Cre* Heav'n will reward
Thy Care, most honest, faithful, foolish *Hæmon*.
But see, *Alcander* enters, well attended.

*Enter* Alcander *attended.*

I see thou hast been diligent.

*Alc.* Nothing these

r Number to the Crouds that soon will follow.
resolute,
d call your utmost Fury to revenge.
*Oe.* Ha! thou hast given
' Alarm to Cruelty; and never may
ese Eyes be clos'd, till they behold *Adrastus*
etch'd at the Feet of false *Eurydice*

*Enter* Adrastus *and* Eurydice *attended.*

*Adr.* Alas! *Eurydice*, what fond rash Man,
hat inconsiderate and ambitious Fool,
at shall hereafter read the Fate of *Oedipus*,
ill dare, with his frail Hand, to grasp a Scepter?
*Eur.* 'Tis true, a Crown seems dreadful, and I wish
at you and I, more lowly plac'd, might pass
r softer Hours in humble Cells away:
t but I love you to that infinite height,
ould (O wondrous Proof of fiercest Love!)
greatly wretched in a Court with you.
*Adr.* Take then this most lov'd Innocence away,
from tumultuous *Thebes*,
m Blood and Murder,
from the Author of all Villanies,
pes, Death, and Treason, from that Fury *Creon*;
uchsafe that I, o'erjoy'd, may bear you hence,
d at your Feet present the Crown of *Argos*

[Creon *and Attendants come up to him*

*Cre.* I have o'er-heard thy black Design, *Adrastus*
d therefore, as a Traytor to this State,
ath ought to be thy Lot: Let it suffice
at *Thebes* surveys thee as a Prince, abuse not
proffer'd Mercy, but retire betimes;
t she repent, and hasten on thy Doom
*Adr* Think not, most abject,
st abhorr'd of Men,
*astus* will vouchsafe to answer thee;
*bans*, to you I justifie my Love:
ve address'd my Prayers to this fair Princess.
, if I ever meant a Violence,
thought to Ravish, as that Traytor did,
at humblest Adorations could not win,

Brand me, you Gods, blot me with foul Dishonour,
And let Men curse me by the Name of *Creon*

*Eur.* Hear me, O *Thebans*, if you dread the Wr
Of her whom Fate ordain'd to be your Queen,
Hear me, and dare not, as you prize your Lives,
To take the part of that Rebellious Traitor.
By the Decree of Royal *Oedipus*,
By Queen *Jocasta*'s Order, by what's more,
My own dear Vows of everlasting Love,
I hear resign to Prince *Adrastus*' Arms
All that the World can make me Mistress of.

*Cre* O perjur'd Woman!
Draw all, and when I give the word, fall on.
Traytor, resign the Princess, or this moment
Expect, with all those most unfortunate Wretches,
Upon this spot straight to be hewn in pieces.

*Adr* No, Villain, no;
With twice those odds of Men,
I doubt not in this Cause
To Vanquish thee,
Captain, remember to your Care I give
My Love, Ten thousand thousand times more dear
Than Life, or Liberty.

*Cre* Fall on, *Alcander*.
*Pyracmon*, you and I must wheel about
For nobler Game, the Princess

*Adr.* Ah! Traytor, dost thou shun me?
Follow, follow,
My brave Companions; see, the Cowards fly.

[*Exit fighting*· Creon's *Party beaten off by* Adrast.

*Enter* Oedipus.

*Oed* O, 'tis too little this' thy loss of Sight,
What has it done? I shall be gaz'd at now
The more, be pointed at, There goes the Monster!
Nor have I hid my Horrors from my self;
For tho' corporeal Light be lost for ever,
The bright reflecting Soul, through glaring Opticks
Presents in larger size her black Idea's
Doubling the bloody Prospect of my Crimes,
Holds Fancy down, and makes her act again,

Wi

ith Wife, and Mother, Tortures, Hell, and Furies.
' now the baleful Off-spring's brought to light!
horrid Form they rank themselves before me;
hat shall I call this Medly of Creation?
re one, with all th' Obedience of a Son,
rrowing *Jocasta's* Look, kneels at my Feet,
d calls me Father, there are a sturdy Boy,
sembling *Lajus* just as when I kill'd him,
ars up, and with his cold Hand grasping mine,
ies out, how fares my Brother *Oedipus*?
hat, Sons and Brothers! Sisters and Daughters too?
y all, begone, fly from my whirling Brain;
nce, Incest, Murder; hence you ghastly Figures!
Gods! Gods, answer; is there any mean?
t me go mad, or dye.

*Enter* Jocasta.

*Joc.* Where, where is this most wretched of Mankind,
is stately Image of Imperial Sorrow,
hose Story told, whose very Name but mention'd,
ould cool the Rage of Feavers, and unlock
e Hand of Lust from the pale Virgins Hair,
d throw the Ravisher before her Feet?

*Oed* By all my fears, I think *Jocasta's* Voice!
nce, fly, begone. O thou far worse than worst
damning Charmers! O abhorr'd, loath'd Creature!
, by the Gods, or by the Fiends, I charge thee,
as the East, West, North or South of Heav'n,
t think not thou shalt ever enter there:
e Golden Gates are barr'd with Adamant,
inst thee, and me, and the Celestial Guards,
l as we rise, will dash our Spirits down.

*Joc.* O wretched Pair! O greatly wretched we!
o Worlds of Woe!

*Oed* Art thou not gone then? Ha!
w dar'st thou stand the Fury of the Gods!
com'st thou in the Grave to reap new Pleasures?

*Joc* Talk on, 'till thou mak'st mad my rowling Brain,
oan still more Death: and may those dismal Sources
l bubble on, and pour forth Blood and Tears.
thinks at such a Meeting, Heav'n stands still;

The Sea nor ebbs, nor flows; this Mole-hill Earth
Is heav'd no more; the busie Emmets cease;
Yet hear me on—— ——

*Oed.* Speak then, and blast my Soul

*Joc.* O my lov'd Lord, tho' I resolve a Ruin
To match my Crimes, by all my Miseries,
'Tis Horror, worse than thousand thousand Deaths,
To send me hence without a kind Farewel.

*Oed* Gods? how she shakes me!---stay thee, O *Jocasta*,
Speak something ere thou goest for ever from me

*Joc.* 'Tis Woman's Weakness that I would be pity'd
Pardon me then, O greatest, tho' most wretched,
Of all thy Kind, my Soul is on the brink,
And sees the boiling Furnace just beneath.
Do not thou push me off, and I will go
With such a willingness, as if that Heav'n
With all its Glories glow'd for my reception.

*Oed* O, in my Heart, I feel the Pangs of Nature!
It works with kindness o'er. Give, give me way,
I feel a melting here, a tenderness,
Too mighty for the Anger of the Gods:
Direct me to thy Knees, yet oh forbear!
Lest the dead Embers should revive,
Stand off——and at just Distance
Let me groan my Horrors———here
On the Earth, here below my utmost Gale,
Here sob my Sorrows, 'till I burst with sighing·
Here gasp and languish out my wounded Soul

*Joc* In spight of all those Crimes, the cruel Gods
Can charge me with, I know my Innocence,
Know yours· 'tis Fate alone that makes us wretch[ed]
For you are still my Husband.

*Oed* Swear I am,
And I'll believe thee, steal into thy Arms,
Renew Endearments, think 'em no Pollutions,
But chast as Spirits Joys gently I'll come,
Thus weeping blind, like Dewy-Night, upon thee,
And fold thee softly in my Arms to Slumbers.

*The Ghost of* Lajus *ascends by degrees pointing at* Jocasta

*Joc.* Be gone, my Lord! alas! what are we do[ing]

ly from my Arms! Whirl-winds, Seas, Continents,
nd Worlds, divide us! O thrice happy thou,
Who hast no use of Eyes; for here's a Sight
Would turn the melting Face of Mercy's self
To a wild Fury.

*Oed* Ha! what seest thou there?

*Joc* The Spirit of my Husband! O the Gods!
ow wan he looks!

*Oed.* Thou rav'st, thy Husband's here.

*Joc* There, there he mounts,
 circling Fire, amongst the blushing Clouds!
nd see, he waves *Jocasta* from the World!

*Ghost. Jocasta, Oedipus.* [*Vanish with Thunder.*

*Oed.* What wouldst thou have?
Thou know'st I cannot come to thee, detain'd
 Darkness here, and kept from means of Death.
ve heard a Spirit's Force is wonderful,
t whose Approach when starting from his Dungeon,
he Earth does shake, and the old Ocean groans,
ocks are remov'd, and Towers are thundred down;
nd Walls of Brass, and Gates of Adamant,
re passable as Air, and fleet like Winds.

*Joc.* Was that a Raven's Croak or my Son's Voice?
o matter which; I'll to the Grave and hide me:
arth open, or I'll tear thy Bowels up.
ark! he goes on, and blabs the Deed of Incest.

*Oed* Strike then, Imperial Ghost, dash all at once
This House of Clay into a thousand Pieces:
That my poor lingring Soul may take her Flight
o your Immortal Dwellings.

*Joc* Haste thee then,
 I shall be before thee. See, thou canst not see;
hen I will tell thee that my Wings are on:
l mount, I'll fly, and with a Port Divine
lide all along the gaudy Milky Soil,
o find my *Lajus* out; ask every God
 his bright Palace, if he knows my *Lajus*,
y murder'd *Lajus*!

*Oed* Ha! how's this, *Jocasta*?
ay, if thy Brain be sick, then thou art happy.

Joc.

*Joc.* Ha! will you not? shall I not find him out!
Will you not show him? are my Tears despis'd?
Why, then I'll thunder: yes, I will be mad,
And fright you with my Cries: yes, cruel Gods!
Tho' Vultures, Eagles, Dragons tear my Heart,
I'll snatch Celestial Flames, fire all your Dwellings,
Melt down your Golden Roofs, and make your Doors
Of Crystal fly from off their Diamond Hinges;
Drive you all out from your Ambrosial Hives,
To swarm like Bees about the Field of Heav'n,
This will I do unless you shew me *Lajus*,
My dear, my murder'd Lord. O *Lajus! Lajus! Lajus!*
[*Ex.* Jocasta.

*Oed.* Excellent Grief! why, this is as it should be:
No Mourning can be suitable to Crimes
Like ours, but what Death makes, or Madness forms.
I cou'd have wish'd methought for Sight again,
To mark the Gallantry of her Distraction:
Her blazing Eyes darting the wandring Stars,
T'have seen her mouth the Heav'ns and mate the Gods,
While with her thund'ring Voice she menac'd high,
And every Accent twang'd with smarting Sorrow,
But what's all this to thee? thou Coward yet
Art living, canst not, wilt not find the Road
To the great Palace of magnificent Death;
Tho' thousand Ways lead to his thousand Doors,
Which Day and Night are still unbarr'd for all.
[*Clashing of Swords, Drums and Trumpets without.*
Hark! 'tis the noise of clashing Swords! the Sound
Comes near: O, that a Battel would come o'er me!
If I but grasp a Sword, or wrest a Dagger,
I'll make a Ruin with the first that falls.

*Enter* Hæmon, *with Guards.*

*Hæm.* Seize him, and bear him to the Western Tower.
Pardon me, Sacred Sir; I am inform'd
That *Creon* has Designs upon your Life:
Forgive me then, if, to preserve you from him,
I order your Confinement.

*Oed* Slaves unhand me.
I think thou hast a Sword: 'twas the wrong side.

t, cruel *Hæmon*, think not I will live;
that could tear his Eyes out, sure can find
me desperate way to stifle his curst Breath:
if I starve! but that's a lingring Fate;
if I leave my Brains upon the Wall!
e Airy Soul can easily o'er-shoot
ose Bounds with which thou striv'st to pale her in:
, I will perish in despight of thee,
d, by the Rage that stirs me, if I meet thee
th' other World I'll curse thee for this Usage [*Ex.*
*Hæm* *Tiresias*, after him, and with your Counsel
vise him humbly, charm, if possible,
le Feuds within while I without extinguish,
perish in th' Attempt, the Furious *Creon*,
a Brand which sets our City in a Flame.
*Tir* Heav'n prosper your Intent, and give a Period
all your Plagues · what old *Tiresias* can,
ll strait be done. Lead, *Manto*, to the Tow'r.
[*Ex.* Tir. Manto.
*Hæm.* Follow me all, and help to part this Fray,
[*Trumpets again.*
fall together in the bloody Broil. [*Ex.*
*Enter* Creon *with* Eurydice, Pyracmon *and his Party giving Ground to* Adrastus
*Cre.* Hold, hold your Arms, *Adrastus*, Prince of *Argos*,
r, and behold: *Eurydice* is my Prisoner.
*Adr.* What would'st thou, Hell-hound?
*Cre* See this brandish'd Dagger ·
ego th' advantage which thy Arms have won,
by the Blood, which trembles through the Heart
her whom more than Life I know thou lov'st,
bury to the Haft in her fair Breast,
s Instrument of my Revenge.
*Adr* Stay thee, damn'd Wretch, hold, stop thy bloody Hand.
*Cre* Give order then, that on this Instant now,
s Moment, all thy Soldiers strait disband.
*Adr* Away my Friends, since Fate has so allotted;
one, and leave me to the Villain's Mercy
*Eur.* Ah, my *Adrastus*! call 'em, call 'em back!
d there, come back! O, cruel barbarous Men!
Could

Could you then leave your Lord, your Prince, your Ki
After so bravely having fought his Cause,
To perish by the Hand of this base Villain?
Why rather rush you not at once together
All to his Ruin? drag him through the Streets,
Hang his contagious Quarters on the Gates;
Nor let my Death affright you.
*Cre.* Die first thy self then.
*Adr.* O, I charge thee, hold.
Hence, from my Presence all; he's not my Friend
That disobeys: See, art thou now appeas'd?
[*Ex. Attenda*
Or is there ought else yet remains to do
That can attone thee? slake thy thirst of Blood
With mine; but save, O save that innocent Wretch
*Cre* Forego thy Sword, and yield thy self my Priso
*Eur.* Yet while there's any Dawn of Hope to save
Thy precious Life, my dear *Adrastus*,
What-e'er thou dost, deliver not thy Sword,
With that thou may'st get off, tho' Odds oppose th
For me, O, fear not, no, he dares not touch me;
His horrid Love will spare me Keep thy Sword;
Lest I be ravish'd after thou art slain.
*Adr* Instruct me, Gods! What shall *Adrastus* do
*Cre* Do what thou wilt, when she is dead, my Sold
With numbers will o'er-power thee. Is't thy Wish
*Eurydice* should fall before thee?
*Adr* Traitor, no:
Better, that thou and I, and all Mankind
Should be no more.
*Cre* Then cast thy Sword away
And yield thee to my Mercy, or I strike.
*Adr* Hold thy rais'd Arm · give me a moment's p
My Father, when he blest me, gave me this;
My Son, said he, let this be thy last Refuge:
If thou forego'st it, Misery attends thee;
Yet Love now charms it from me; which in all
The Hazards of my Life I never lost.
'Tis thine, my faithful Sword, my only Trust;
Tho' my Heart tells me that the Gift is fatal.

*Cre.* Fatal! Yes, foolish Love-sick Prince, it shall:
y Arrogance, thy Scorn,
Wounds Remembrance,
nall at once the fatal Point upon thee.
*amon*, to the Palace, dispatch
King · hang *Hæmon* up, for he is Loyal,
d will oppose me: Come, Sir, are you ready?
*dr.* Yes, Villain, for whatever thou canst dare.
*Eur* Hold *Creon*, or thro' me, thro' me you wound:
*dr.* Off, Madam, or we perish both, behold
not unarm'd, my Ponyard's in my Hand:
erefore away.
*Eur* I ll guard your Life with mine.
*re.* Die both then; there is now no time for dallying.
[*Kills* Eurydice.
*Eur.* Ah, Prince, farewel! farewel, my dear *Adrastus.*
[*Dies.*
*dr.* Unheard of Monster! eldest born of Hell!
wn, to thy Primitive Flames. [*Stabs* Creon.
*re* Help, Soldiers, help:
enge me
*dr* More, yet more: a thousand Wounds!
amp thee still, thus, to the gaping Furies.
[Adrastus *falls, kill d by the Soldiers.*
*ter* Hæmon, *Guards with* Alcander, *and* Pyracmon
*bound the Assassins are driven off.*
*Hæmon*, I am slain, nor need I name
nhuman Author of all Villanies;
re he lies gasping.
*e* If I must plunge in Flames,
first my Arm; base Instrument, unfit
t the Dictates of my daring Mind,
burn for ever, O weak Substitute
hat, the God, Ambition. [*Dies.*
*dr.* She's gone, O deadly Marks-man, in the Heart!
in the Pangs of Death she grasps my Hand:
Lips too tremble, as if she would speak
last Farewel. O *Oedipus*, thy Fall
eat; and nobly now thou goest attended.
y talk of Heroes, and Celestial Beauties,

And

And wondrous Pleasures in the other World;
Let me but find her there, I ask no more. [L

*Enter a Captain to* Hæmon; *with* Tiresias *and* Man

*Cap* O, Sir, the Queen *Jocasta*, swift and wild,
As a robb'd Tygress bounding o'er the Woods,
Has acted Murders that amaze Mankind:
In twisted Gold I saw her Daughters hang
On the Bed Royal, and her little Sons
Stabb'd through the Breasts upon the bloody Pillow

*Hæm.* Relentless Heav'ns! is then the Fate of *La*
Never to be Atton'd? How sacred ought
Kings Lives be held, when but the Death of one
Demands an Empire's Blood for Expiation?
But see! the furious mad *Jocasta*'s here.

SCENE *draws, and discovers* Jocasta *held by her men, and stabb'd in many places of her Bosom, her disbevel'd, her Children slain upon the Bed.*

Was ever such a sight of so much Horror,
And Pity, brought to view!

*Joc.* Ah, cruel Women!
Will you not let me take my last Farewel
Of those dear Babes? O let me run and seal
My melting Soul upon their bubbling Wounds!
I'll print upon their Coral Mouths such Kisses,
As shall recall their wandring Spirits Home.
Let me go, let me go, or I will tear you piece-mea
Help, *Hæmon*, help.
Help, *Oedipus*, help, Gods; *Jocasta* dies.

*Enter* Oedipus *above.*

*Oed* I've found a Window, and I thank the God
'Tis quite unbarr'd: sure by the distant Noise,
The Height will fit my fatal Purpose well.

*Joc* What hoa, my *Oedipus*, see where he stand
His groping Ghost is lodg'd upon a Tow'r,
Nor can it find the Road. Mount, mount my Sou
I'll wrap thy shivering Spirit in Lambent Flames! a
But see! we're landed on the happy Coast, [we'll
And all the golden Strands are cover'd o'er
With glorious Gods that come to try our Cause.
*Jove*, *Jove*, whose Majesty now sinks me down;

who himself burns in unlawful Fires,
ll judge, and shall acquit us. O, 'tis done!
fixt by Fate, upon Record Divine!
l Oedipus shall be now ever mine. [Dies.
ed Speak, Hamon, what has Fate been doing there?
at dreadful Deed has mad Jocasta done?
Ham. The Queen her self, and all your wretched Off-
by her Fury slain. [spring,
ed By all my Woes,
has out-done me, in Revenge and Murder;
I should envy her the sad Applause.
oh! my Children! oh! what have they done?
was not like the Mercy of the Heav'ns,
et her Madness on such Cruelty:
stirs me more than all my Sufferings,
with my last Breath I must call you Tyrants.
em What mean you, Sir?
d Jocasta! Lo! I come.
Lajus, Labdacus, and all you Spirits
he Cadmean Race, prepare to meet me,
weeping rang'd along the gloomy Shore;
nd your Arms t'embrace me, for I come;
l the Gods too from their Battlements
'd, and wonder at a Mortal's daring;
when I knock the Goal of dreadful Death,
and applaud me with a Clap of Thunder:
more, thus wing'd by horrid Fate, I come
s a falling Meteor; lo! I fly,
thus go downwards, to the darker Sky.
hunder, he flings himself from the Window, the Thebans gather about his Body.
m. O Prophet, Oedipus is now no more!
'd effect of the most deep Despair!
Cease your Complaints, and bear his Body hence:
dreadful Sight will daunt the drooping Thebans,
m Heav'n decrees to raise with Peace and Glory.
y these terrible Examples warn'd,
sacred Fury that alarms the World,
one, tho' ne'er so Virtuous, Great and High,
g'd entirely blest before they dye. [Exeunt.

EPI-

# EPILOGUE

WHAT Sophocles *could undertake alone,*
*Our Poets found a Work for more than One;*
*And therefore Two lay tugging at the Piece,*
*With all their force, to draw the pondrous Mass from* Gre
*A Weight that bent even* Seneca's *strong Muse,*
*And which* Corneille's *Shoulders did refuse.*
*So hard it is th'* Athenian *Harp to string!*
*So much Two Consuls yield to one just King.*
*Terror and Pity this whole Poem sway;*
*The mightiest Machines that can mount a Play.*
*How heavy will those vulgar Souls be found,*
*Whom Two such Engines cannot move from Ground?*
*When* Greece *and* Rome *have smil'd upon this Birth,*
*You can but damn for one poor Spot of Earth.*
*And when your Children find your Judgment such,*
*They'll scorn their Sires, and wish themselves born* Dutc
*Each haughty Poet will infer with Ease,*
*How much his Wit must under-write to please.*
*As some strong Churle would brandishing advance*
*The monumental Sword that conquer'd* France;
*So you by judging this, your Judgments teach*
*Thus far you like, that is, thus far your reach.*
*Since then the Vote of full two thousand Years*
*Has Crown'd this Plot, and all the Dead are theirs;*
*Think it a Debt you pay, not Alms you give,*
*And in your own Defence, let this Play live.*
*Think 'em not vain, when* Sophocles *is shown,*
*To praise his Worth, they humbly doubt their own.*
*Yet as weak States each others Pow'r assure,*
*Weak Poets by Conjunction are secure:*
*Their Treat is what your Palats relish most,*
*Charm! Song! and Show! a Murder and a Ghost!*
*We know not what you can desire or hope,*
*To please you more, but burning of a* Pope.

# THE

# DUKE

OF

# GUISE.

A

# TRAGEDY.

---

Written by

Mr. *DRYDEN* and Mr. *LEE*.

---

ἰλότιμοι φύσεις ἐν ταῖς πολιτείαις τὸ ἄγαν μὴ φυλαξάμεναι, τοῦ ἀγαθοῦ μεῖζον τὸ κακὸν ἔχουσι Plutarch in Agesilao

---

Printed in the YEAR 1712.

To the Right Honourable

# LAWRENCE,

## EARL of *Rochester*, &c.

*My* LORD,

THE Authors of this Poem present it humbly to your Lordship's Patronage, if you shall think it worthy of that Honour. It has already been a Confessor, and was almost made a Martyr r the Royal Cause. But having stood two Tryals m its Enemies, one before it was acted, another the Representation, and having been in both acuited, 'tis now to stand the Publick Censure in the ding. Where since, of necessity, it must have e same Enemies, we hope it may also find the ne Friends; and therein we are secure not only the greater Number, but of the more Honest d Loyal Party. We only expected bare Justice the Permission to have it Acted; and that we had, r a severe and long Examination, from an Upht and Knowing Judge, who having heard both des, and examin'd the Merits of the Cause in a ict Perusal of the Play, gave Sentence for us, t it was neither a Libel, nor a Parallel of parular Persons. In the Representation it self, it s persecuted with so notorious Malice by one , that it procur'd us the Partiality of the other;

ſo that the Favour more than recompenc'd the P
judice And 'tis happier to have been ſav'd (i
we were) by the Indulgence of our good and fai
ful Fellow-Subjects, than by our own Deſerts,
cauſe thereby the Weakneſs of the Faction is
ſcover'd, which in us, at that time, attack'd
Government; and ſtood combin'd, like the M
bers of the Rebellious League, againſt the Law
Sovereign Authority. To what Topique will t
have recourſe, when they are manifeſtly be
from their chief Poſt, which has always been
pularity, and Majority of Voices? They will
us, That the Voices of a People are not to be
ther'd in a Play-Houſe; and yet even there,
Enemies as well as Friends have free Admiſſ
but while our Argument was ſerviceable to t
Intereſts, they cou'd boaſt that the Theaters w
True Proteſtant, and came inſulting to the Pl
where their own Triumphs were repreſented.
let them now aſſure themſelves, that they cann
the major part of no Aſſembly, except it be a M
*ing-Houſe*. Their Tide of Popularity is ſpent,
the natural Current of Obedience is, in ſpigh
them, at laſt prevalent. In which, *my Lord*, a
the merciful Providence of God, the unſhaken
ſolution, and prudent Carriage of the King, and
inviolable Duty, and manifeſt Innocence of
Royal Highneſs, the prudent Management of
Miniſters, is alſo moſt conſpicuous. I am not
ticular in this Commendation, becauſe I am
willing to raiſe Envy to your Lordſhip, who
too juſt not to deſire that Praiſe ſhou'd be com
nicated to others, which was the common En
vour and Co-operation of all. 'Tis enough
*Lord*, that your own Part was neither obſcu

nor unhazardous. And if ever this excellent Go-
nment, so well establish'd by the Wisdom of our
efathers, and so much shaken by the Folly of
Age, shall recover its ancient Splendor, Poste-
cannot be so ungrateful, as to forget those, who
he worst of Times, have stood undaunted by
ir King and Country, and for the Safeguard of
h, have expos'd themselves to the Malice of false
riots, and the Madness of an headstrong Rabble.
since this glorious Work is yet unfinish'd, and
ugh we have reason to hope well of the Success,
the Event depends on the unsearchable Pro-
ence of Almighty God; 'tis no time to raise Tro-
es, while the Victory is in dispute: But every
n by your Example, to contribute what is in
Power, to maintain so just a Cause, on which
ends the future Settlement and Prosperity of
ree Nations. The Pilot's Prayer to *Neptune*
not amiss, in the middle of the Storm: *Thou*
*st do with me*, O Neptune, *what thou pleasest*,
*I will be sure to hold fast the Rudder.* We
to trust firmly in the Deity, but so as not to
get, that he commonly works by second Causes,
admits of our Endeavour with his Concurrence.
our own Parts, we are sensible as we ought,
little we can contribute with our weak Assist-
e The most we can boast of, is, that we are
so inconsiderable as to want Enemies, whom
have rais'd to our selves on no other account,
n that we are not of their number: And since
'tis their Quarrel, they shall have daily occasion
hate us more 'Tis not, *my Lord*, that any
n delights to see himself pasquin'd and affronted
their inveterate Scriblers, but on the other side
ought to be our Glory, that themselves believe

X 3 not

not us what they write: Reasonable Men a well satisfy'd for whose sakes the Venom of the Party is shed on us, because they see that at th same time, our Adversaries spare not those to who they owe Allegiance and Veneration. Their De spair has push'd them to break those Bonds; an 'tis observable, that the lower they are driven, th more violently they write: As *Lucifer* and h Companions were only proud when Angels, b grew malicious when Devils. Let them rail, since 't the only Solace of their Miseries, and the only R venge, which, we hope, they now can take. The grea est and the best of Men are above their reach, and f our Meanness, though they assault us like Foot pa ders in the dark, their Blows have done us litt harm; we yet live, to justifie our selves in op Day, to vindicate our Loyalty to the Governme and to assure your Lordship, with all Submissi and Sincerity, that we are

*Your Lordship's*

*most Obedient, Faithful Servants,*

John Dryden, Nat. Le

PRO

# PROLOGUE.

## Vritten by Mr. *Dryden.* Spoken by Mr. *Smith.*

*OUR Play's a Parallel: The Holy League*
*Begot our Cov'nant:* Guisard's *got the Whigg:*
*hate'er our hot-brain'd Sherifs did advance,*
*s, like our Fashions, first produc'd in* France:
*d, when worn out, well scourg'd, and banish'd there,*
*nt over, like their godly Beggars here*
*u'd the same Trick, twice play'd, our Nation gull?*
*looks as if the Devil were grown dull;*
*serv'd us up, in scorn, his broken Meat,*
*d thought we were not worth a better Cheat.*
*fulsome Cov'nant, one wou'd think in Reason,*
*d giv'n us all our Belly's-full of Treason:*
*t yet, the Name but chang'd, our nasty Nation*
*ews its own Excrement, th' Association.*
*is true, we have not learn'd their pois'ning way,*
*r that's a Mode but newly come in play;*
*sides, your Drug's uncertain to prevail;*
*t your true Protestant can never fail,*
*ith that compendious Instrument, a Flail.*
*o on; and bite, ev'n though the Hook lies bare;*
*ce in one Age expel the Lawful Heir:*
*ce more decide Religion by the Sword:*
*d purchase for us a new Tyrant Lord.*
*ay for your King; but yet your Purses spare;*
*ke him not Two-pence richer by your Prayer.*
*shew you love him much, chastise him more;*
*d make him very Great, and very Poor*
*sh him to Wars, but still no Pence advance;*
*t him lose* England, *to recover* France.
*y Freedom up with Popular noisie Votes:*
*d get enough to cut each others Throats.*
*p all the Rights that fence your Monarch's Throne;*
*r fear of too much Pow'r, pray leave him none.*
*Noise was made of Arbitrary Sway;*
*t in Revenge, you Whiggs, have found a way,*
*n Arbitrary Duty now to pay.*
*t his own Servants turn, to save their stake;*
*ean from his Plenty, and his Wants forsake.*

X 4 But

# PROLOGUE.

*But let some* Judas *near his Person stay,*
*To swallow the last Sop, and then betray.*
*Make* London *independant of the Crown:*
*A Realm apart, the Kingdom of the Town.*
*Let* Ignoramus *Juries find no Traytors:*
*And* Ignoramus *Poets scribble Satyrs*
*And, that your Meaning none may fail to scan,*
*Do, what in Coffee-houses you began;*
*Pull down the Master, and Set up the Man.*

---

# Dramatis Personæ.

## MEN.

| | |
|---|---|
| THE King, | Mr *Kynaston.* |
| Duke of *Guise*, | Mr. *Betterton* |
| Duke of *Mayenne*, | Mr. *Jevon.* |
| Grillon, | Mr. *Smith.* |
| The Cardinal of *Guise*, | Mr. *Wiltshire.* |
| Archbishop of *Lyons*, | Mr. *Perin.* |
| Alphonso Corso, | Mr. *Monfert* |
| Polin, | Mr. *Bowman.* |
| Aumale, | Mr. *Carlile.* |
| Bussy, | Mr. *Saunders.* |
| The Curate of St *Eustace*, | Mr *Underhill.* |
| Malicorne, | Mr. *Percival.* |
| Melanax, *a Spirit*, | Mr. *Gillo.* |
| Two Sheriffs, | *Bright* and *Samson* |
| Citizens and Rabble, *&c.* | |

## WOMEN.

| | |
|---|---|
| Queen-Mother, | Lady *Slingsby* |
| Marmoutier, | Mrs. *Barry.* |

## SCENE *PARIS.*

THE

# )UKE of *GUISE.*

## ACT I. SCENE I.

*CENE the Council of Sixteen Seated. An empty Chair prepar'd for the Duke of* Guise.

Bussy *and* Polin, *two of the Sixteen.*

*BUSSY.*

Ights there! more Lights; what, burn the Tapers dim,
When glorious *Guise*, the *Moses*, *Gideon*, *David*,
*The Saviour of the Nation*, makes approach?
*Pol.* And therefore are we met; the whole Sixteen,
at sway the Crowd of *Paris*, guide their Votes,
mge their Purses, Persons, Fortunes, Lives,
mount the *Guise*, where Merit calls him, high;
d give him a whole Heav'n, for room to shine.

*Enter*

*Enter Curate of St.* Eustace.

*Buſ.* The Curate of St. *Euſtace* comes at laſt;
But, Father, why ſo late?

*Cur.* I have been taking godly Pains, to ſatisfie ſo[me] Scruples rais'd amongſt weak Brothers of our Par[ty,] that were ſtaggering in the Cauſe

*Pol.* What cou'd they find t object?

*Cur* They thought to Arm againſt the King w[as]

*Buſ* I hope you ſet 'em right? [Treaſ[on.]

*Cur* Yes, and for Anſwer, I produc'd this Book,
A Calviniſt Miniſter of *Orleans*
Writ this, to juſtifie the Admiral
For taking Arms againſt the King deceas'd:
Wherein he proves that irreligious Kings
May juſtly be depos'd, and put to Death

*Buſ* To borrow Arguments from Heretick Books
Methinks was not ſo prudent.

*Cur.* Yes, from the Devil, if it would help our Cau[ſe;]
The Author was indeed a Heretick;
The Matter of the Book is good and pious.

*Pol.* But one prime Article of our Holy League,
Is to preſerve the King, his Pow'r and Perſon.

*Cur.* That muſt be ſaid, you know, for Decency;
A pretty Blind to make the Shoot ſecure.

*Buſ* But did the Primitive Chriſtians e'er rebell,
When under Heathen Lords? I hope they did

*Cur.* No ſure, they did not, for they had not Pow['r;]
The Conſcience of a People is their Pow'r.

*Pol.* Well, the next Article in our Solemn Coven[ant]
Has clear'd the Point again.

*Buſ* What is't? I ſhou'd be glad to find the King
No ſafer than needs muſt. [ſoever-

*Pol.* That in caſe of Oppoſition from any Perſon wh[at]

*Cur.* That's well, that's well; then the King is [not]
excepted, if he oppoſe us———

*Pol.* We are oblig'd to join as one, to puniſh
All, who attempt to hinder or diſturb us.

*Buſ.* 'Tis a plain Caſe; the King's included in [the]
Puniſhment, in caſe he rebell againſt the People.

*Pol.* But how can he rebell?

*Cur.* I'll make it out: Rebellion is an Insurrection a-
inst the *Government*, but they that have the Power
actually the Government. Therefore if the People
e the Power, the Rebellion is in the King
*Buss* A most convincing Argument for Faction.
*Cur* For Arming, if you please, but not for Faction.
still the Faction is the fewest number,
what they call the lawful Government,
now the Faction, for the most are ours
*Pol* Since we are prov'd to be above the King, I
u'd gladly understand whom we are to obey, or whe-
r we are to be all Kings together?
*Cur* Are you a Member of the League, and ask that
Question?
ere's an Article, that, I may say, is as necessary as any
the Creed. Namely, that we, the said Associates, are
orn to yield ready Obedience, and Faithful Service,
that Head which shall be deputed.
*Buss* 'Tis most manifest, that by Virtue of our Oath
e are all Subjects to the Duke of *Guise* The King's
Officer that has betray'd his Trust; and therefore we
ve turn'd him out of Service.
*Omnes* Agreed, agreed.
*er the Duke of* Guise; *Cardinal of* Guise, Aumale:
*Torches before them* *The Duke takes the Chair.*
*Buss* Your Highness enters in a lucky Hour,
unanimous Vote you heard, confirms your Choice,
Head of *Paris*, and the Holy League
*Curd.* I say *Amen* to that.
*Pol* You are our Champion, Buckler of our Faith.
*Card.* The King, like *Saul*, is Heav'ns repented Choice;
his Anointed one, on better Thought
*Guise* I'm what you please to call me: Any thing,
utenant General, Chief, or Constable,
od Decent Names, that only mean your Slave
*Buss* You chas'd the *Germans* hence, exil'd *Navarre*,
d rescu'd *France* from Hereticks and Strangers.
*Aum.* What he and all of us have done, is known.
hat's our Reward? Our Offices are lost,
rn'd out like labour'd Oxen, after Harvest,
the bare Commons of the wither'd Field.

*Buſ.* Our Charters will go next; because we Sheriffs
Permit no Juſtice to be done on thoſe
The Court calls Rebels, but we call them Saints
*Gui.* Yes, we are all involv'd, as Heads, or Parties,
Dipt in the noiſie Crime of State, call'd Treaſon
And Traitors we muſt be, to King, or Country.
*Buſ* Why then my Choice is made.
*Pol.* And mine.
*Cr. n* And all.
*Card* Heav'n is it ſelf Head of the holy League,
And all the Saints are Cov'nanters, and *Guiſards.*
*Gui.* What ſay you, Curate?
*Cur.* I hope well, my Lord.
*Card.* That is, he hopes you mean to make him Abbot
And he deſerves your care of his Preferment,
For all his Prayers are Curſes on the Government,
And all his Sermons Libels on the King
In ſhort, a Pious, Hearty, Factious Prieſt.
*Gui* All that are here my Friends, ſhall ſhare my Fortunes
There's Spoil, Preferments, Wealth enough in *France*
'Tis but deſerve and have. The *Spaniſh* King
Conſigns me fifty thouſand Crowns a Week
To raiſe and to foment a Civil-War.
'Tis true, a Penſion from a Foreign Prince
Sounds Treaſon in the Letter of the Law,
But good Intentions juſtifie the deed
*Cur.* Heav'n's good, the Cauſe is good, the Money good,
No matter whence it comes.
*Buſ* Our City Bands are twenty thouſand ſtrong,
Well diſciplin'd, well arm'd, well ſeaſon'd Traitors,
Thick rinded Heads, that leave no room for Kernel,
Shop Conſciences, of proof againſt an Oath,
Preach'd up, and ready tin'd for a Rebellion.
*Gui* Why then the Noble Plot is fit for birth,
And Labouring *France* cries out for Midwife hands
We miſs'd ſurprizing of the King at *Blois*,
When laſt the States were held, 'twas Over-ſight
Beware we make not ſuch another Blot
*Card* This Holy time of *Lent* we have him ſure;
He goes unguarded, mix'd with whipping Fryars,

that Proceſſion, he's more fit for Heav'n
What hinders us to ſeize the Royal Penitent,
nd cloſe him in a Cloyſter?
*Cur* Or diſpatch him I love to make all ſure.
*Gui* No, guard him ſafe,
hin Diet will do well, 'twill ſtarve him into Reaſon,
ill he exclude his Brother of *Navarre*,
nd graft Succeſſion on a worthier Choice.
o favour this, five hundred Men in Arms
hall ſtand prepar'd to enter at your Call,
nd ſpeed the Work St *Martin's Gate* was nam'd:
ut the *Sheriff Conty*, who commands that Ward,
efus'd me Paſſage there
*Buſ.* I know that *Conty*.
Sniveling, Conſcientious, Loyal Rogue:
e'll Peach, and ruin all.
*Card* Give out he's Arbitrary; a *Navarriſt*;
Heretick, diſcredit him betimes,
nd make his Witneſs void.
*Cur* I'll ſwear him Guilty.
ſwallow Oaths as eaſie as Snap-dragon,
ork-Fire that never burns.
*Gui* Then *Buſſy*, be't your care t'admit my Troops,
t *Porte* St. *Honore* [*riſes*] Night wears apace,
nd Day-light muſt not peep on dark Deſigns.
will my ſelf to Court, pay Formal Duty;
ake leave, and to my Government retire:
patient to be ſoon recall'd, to ſee
he King Impriſon'd, and the Nation free.
[*Exe.*

*Enter* Malicorn *ſolus.*

*Mal* Each diſmal Minute when I call to Mind
he Promiſe that I made the Prince of Hell,
one and twenty Years to be his Slave,
which near twelve are gone, my Soul runs back,
he Wards of Reaſon rowl into their Spring.
horrid Thought! but one and twenty Years,
nd twelve near paſt, then to be ſteep'd in Fire,
ſh'd againſt Rocks, or ſnatch'd from molten Lead,
eking and dropping, piece-meal born by Winds,

And

And quench'd ten thousand Fathom in the Deep!
[*Knocking at the D*

But hark! he comes, see there, my Blood stands, ...
My Spirits start an end for *Guises* Fate.

*A Devil rises.*

*Mal* What Counsel does the Fate of *Guise* requ...

*Dev* Remember with his Prince there's no delays,
But, the Sword drawn, to fling the Sheath away,
Let not the fear of Hell his Spirit grieve,
The Tomb is still whatever Fools believe;
Laugh at the Tales which wither'd Sages bring,
Proverbs and Morals, let the Waxen King
That rules the Hive, be born without a Sting,
Let *Guise* by Blood resolve to mount to Pow'r,
And he is great as *Mecha*'s Emperor;
He comes, bid him not stand on Altar Vows,
But then strike deepest, when he lowest bows,
Tell him Fate's aw'd when an Usurper Springs,
And joyns to crowd out Just Indulgent Kings [*Van...*

*Enter the Duke of* Guise, *and Duke of* Mayen.

*May* All Offices and Dignities he gives
To your profest and most inveterate Foes;
But if he were inclin'd, as we could wish him,
There is a Lady Regent at his Ear,
That never Pardons

*Gui* Poyson on her Name,
Take my Hand on't, that Cormorant *Dowager*
Will never rest, till she has all our Heads
In her Lap I was at *Bayon* with her,
When She, the King, and Grisly *d' Alva* met,
Methinks I see her listening now before me,
Marking the very Motion of his Beard,
His op'ning Nostrils and his Dropping Lids,
I hear him Croak too to the Gaping Council,
Fish for the great Fish, take no care for Frogs,
Cut off the Popy-Heads, Sir, *Madam*, charm
The Winds but fast, the Billows will be still.

*May* But Sir, how comes it you should be thus w...
Still pushing Councils when among your Friends,

t at the Court cautious, and cold as Age,
ur Voice, your Eyes, your Meen so different,
ou seem to me two Men?

*Gui.* The Reason's plain:
' with my Friends, because the Question giv'n,
start the Judgment right where others drag.
his is the effect of Equal Elements,
d Atoms justly pois'd; nor should you wonder
ore at the strength of Body than of Mind,
is equally the same to see me plunge
eadlong into the *Seine* all over Arm'd,
d Plow against the Torrent to my Point,
'twas to hear my Judgment on the *Germans*,
is to another Man wou'd be a brag,
at the Court among my Enemies,
be as I am here quite off my Guard,
ould make me such another thing as *Grillon*,
blunt, hot, honest, downright, valiant Fool.

*May.* Yet this you must allow a Failure in you;
u love his Neece, and to a Politician,
Passion's bane, but Love directly Death

*Gui.* False, false, my *Mayen*, thou'rt but half *Guise* again;
ere she not such a wondrous Composition,
Soul so flush'd as mine is with Ambition,
acious and so nice, must have disdain'd her;
she was made when Nature was in humour,
a *Grillon* got her on the Queen,
here all the honest Atoms fought their way,
k a full Incture of the Mother's Wit,
left the dregs of Wickedness behind.

*May.* Have you not told her what we have in hand?

*Gui.* My utmost aim has been to hide it from her,
there I'm short, by the long Chain of Causes
has scan'd it, just as if she were my Soul:
d though I flew about with Circumstances,
als, Oaths, Improbabilities;
through the Histories of our Lives, she look'd,
saw, she overcame.

*May.* Why then, we're all undone.

*Gui.* Again you err.

Chast

Chast as she is, she wou'd as soon give up
Her Honour, as betray me to the King:
I tell thee, she's the Character of Heav'n.
Such an habitual over-womanly Goodness,
She dazles, walks meer Angel upon Earth
But see, she comes, call the Cardinal *Guise*,
While *Malicorn* attends for some Dispatches,
Before I take my farewell of the Court.

*Enter* Marmoutire.

*Mar.* Ah, *Guise*, you are undone

*Gui.* How, Madam?

*Mar.* Lost,
Beyond the possibility of Hope.
Despair, and die

*Gui.* You menace deeply, Madam,
And should this come from any Mouth but yours,
My Smile should answer how the Ruin touch'd me

*Mar* Why do you leave the Court?

*Gui.* The Court leaves me

*Mar* Were there no more but weariness of State,
Or cou'd you, like great *Scipio*, retire,
Call *Rome* ungrateful, and sit down with that,
Such inward Gallantry would gain you more,
Than all the sullied Conquest you can boast.
But oh, you want that *Roman* Mastery,
You have too much of the tumultuous Times,
And I must mourn the Fate of your Ambition.

*Gui.* Because the King disdains my Services,
Must I not let him know I dare be gone?
What when I feel his Council on my Neck,
Shall I not cast 'em backward if I can;
And at his Feet make known their Villany?

*Mar.* No, *Guise*, not at his Feet, but on his He[ad]
For there you strike.

*Gui.* Madam, you wrong me now,
For still what-e'er shall come in Fortune's whim,
His Person must be safe.

*Mar* I cannot think it.
However, your last Words confess too much.
Confess, what need I urge that Evidence,

W[...]

When every Hour I see you court the Crowd,
When with the Shouts of the rebellious Rabble,
I see you born on Shoulders to Cabals,
Where with the Traiterous Council of Sixteen,
You sit and Plot the Royal *Henry*'s Death.
Cloud the Majestick Name with Fumes of Wine,
Infamous Scrowls, and Treasonable Verse,
While, on the other side, the Name of *Guise*,
By the whole Kennel of the Slaves, is rung:
Pamphleteers, Balladmongers, sing your Ruin,
While all the Vermin of the vile *Parisians*
Toss up their greasie Caps where-e'er you pass,
And hurl your dirty Glories in your Face.
*Gui.* Can I help this?
*Mar.* By Heav'n, I'd Earth my self,
Rather than live to act such black Ambition:
But, Sir, you seek it with your Smiles and Bows,
This side, and that side congeing to the Crowd;
You have your Writers too, that cant your Battels,
That stile you the New *David*, Second *Moses*,
Prop of the Church, Deliverer of the People.
Thus from the City, as from the Heart, they spread
Thro' all the Provinces, alarm the Countries,
Where they run forth in Heaps, bellowing your Wonders,
Then cry, The King, the King's a *Hugonot*,
And, spight of us, will have *Navarre* succeed,
Spight of the Laws, and spight of our Religion:
But we will pull 'em down, down with 'em, down. [*Kneels.*
*Gui.* Ha, Madam! Why this Posture?
*Mar.* Hear me, Sir:
Yet, if 'tis possible, my Lord, I'll move you.
Look back, return, implore the Royal Mercy,
Ere 'tis too late, I beg you by these Tears,
These Sighs, and by th' ambitious Love you bear me;
By all the Wounds of your poor groaning Country,
That bleeds to Death, O seek the best of Kings,
Kneel, fling your stubborn Body at his Feet:
Your Pardon shall be sign'd, your Country sav'd,
Virgins and Matrons all shall sing your Fame,
And every Babe shall bless the *Guise*'s Name.

*Gui.* O riſe, thou Image of the Deity;
You ſhall prevail, I will do any thing;
You have broke the very Gall of my Ambition,
And all my Powers now float in Peace again:
Be ſatisfy'd that I will ſee the King,
Kneel to him, ere I Journey to *Champagn*,
And beg a kind Farewel.

*Mar* No, no, my Lord;
I ſee thro' that, you but withdraw a while,
To Muſter all the Forces that you can,
And then rejoyn the Council of Sixteen.
You muſt not go.

*Gui* All the Heads of the League
Expect me, and I have engag'd my Honour. [ſar

*Mar.* Would all thoſe Heads were off, ſo yours we
Once more, O *Guiſe*, the weeping *Marmoutire*
Entreats you do not go

*Gui.* Is't poſſible
That *Guiſe* ſhould ſay, in this he muſt refuſe you?

*Mar.* Go then, my Lord. I late receiv'd a Lett
From one at Court, who tells me the King loves me
Read it, there is no more than what you hear.
I have Jewels offer'd too, perhaps may take 'em.
And if you go from *Paris*, I'll to Court.

*Gui.* But Madam, I have often heard you ſay,
You lov'd not Courts.

*Mar.* Perhaps I have chang'd my Mind:
Nothing as yet could draw me, but a King,
And ſuch a King, ſo good, ſo juſt, ſo great,
That at his Birth the Heavenly Council paus'd,
And then at laſt cry'd out, This is a Man.

*Gui.* Come, 'tis but Counterfeit; you dare not go

*Mar.* Go to your Government, and try.

*Gui.* I will.

*Mar.* Then I'll to Court, nay, to the King.

*Gui.* By Heav'n
I ſwear, you cannot, ſhall not, dare not ſee him

*Mar.* By Heav'n I can, I dare, nay, and I will:
And nothing but your Stay ſhall hinder me;
For now, methinks, I long for't.

*Gui.* Possible!

*Mar.* I'll give you yet a little time to think:
t if I hear you go to take your leave,
meet you there, before the Throne I'll stand,
y, you shall see me kneel, and kiss his Hand [*Ex*.

*Gui.* Furies and Hell! She does but try me: Ha!
is is the Mother-Queen and *Espernon*,
bot *Delbene*, *Alphonso Corso* too,
packt to plot, and turn me into Madness.
[*Reading the Letter.*

*ter Cardinal* Guise, *Duke of* Mayen, Malicorn, &c

! can it be! *Madam, the King loves you.* [*Reads.*
Vengeance I will have; to pieces, thus,
pieces with 'em all. [*Tears the Letter.*

*ard* Speak lower.

*ui.* No;
all the Torments of this galling Passion,
hollow the Revenge I vow, so loud,
Father's Ghost shall hear me up to Heav'n.

*rd* Contain your self, this Outrage will undo us.

*ui.* All things are ripe, and Love new points their Ruin.
my good Lords, what if the murd'ring Council
re in our Power, should they escape our Justice?
by each Man's laying of his Hand
n his Sword, you swear the like Revenge.
me, I wish that mine may both rot off——

*rd* No more.

*ay* The Council of Sixteen attend you

*ui.* I go——That Vermin may devour my Limbs,
I may die like the late puling *Francis*,
r the Barbers Hands, Imposthumes choak me,
hile alive I cease to chew their Ruin;
*onso Corso*, *Grillon*, Priest, together,
ang 'em in Effigie, nay, to tread,
, stamp, and grind 'em, after they are dead. [*Exeunt*,

## ACT II. SCENE I.

*Enter* Queen-Mother, *Abbot* Delbene, Polin

*Q M* PRAY mark the Form of the Conspiracy
*Guise* gives it out he Journeys to *Champag*
But lurks indeed at *Lagny*, hard by *Paris*,
Where every Hour he hears, and gives Instructions
Mean time the Council of Sixteen assure him
They have twenty thousand Citizens in Arms.
Is it not so, *Polin*?

*Pol* True, on my Life;
And if the King doubts the Discovery,
Send me to the *Bastile* till all be prov'd.

*Q M.* Call Colonel *Grillon*, the King would spe
with him. [*Exit* Pol

*Ab* Was ever Age like this?

*Q M* *Polin* is honest:
Beside, the whole Proceeding is so like
The hair-brain'd Rout, I guess'd as much before.
Know then, it is resolv'd to seize the King,
When next he goes in Penitential Weeds,
Among the Friars, without his usual Guards,
Then, under shew of Popular Sedition,
For Safety, shut him in a Monastery,
And sacrifice his Favourites to their Rage.

*Ab* When is this Council to be held again?

*Q M* Immediately upon the Duke's Departure.

*Ab* Why sends not then the King sufficient Gua
To seize the Fiends, and hew 'em into Pieces?

*Q M* 'Tis in Appearance easie, but th' Effect
Most hazardous, for straight, upon th' Alarm,
The City would be sure to be in Arms
Therefore to undertake, and not to compass,
Were to come off with Ruin and Dishonour.
You know th' *Italian* Proverb, *Bisogna Copriersi*
He that will venture on a Hornet's Nest,
Should Arm his Head, and Buckler well his Breast.

*Ab.* But wherefore seems the King so unresolv'd?
*Q. M.* I brought *Polin*, and made the Demonstration,
old him Necessity cry'd out to take
Resolution to preserve his Life,
nd look on *Guise* as a reclaimless Rebel.
ut through the natural Sweetness of his Temper,
nd dangerous Mercy, coldly he reply'd,
adam, I will consider what you say.
*Ab.* Yet after all, could we but fix him.
*Q. M.* Right,
he Business were more firm for this Delay,
or Noblest Natures, tho' they suffer long,
hen once provok'd, they turn the Face to Danger.
ut see, he comes, *Alphonso Corso* with him
us withdraw, and when 'tis fit, rejoyn him. [*Ex.*

*Enter* King, Alphonso Corso.

*King. Alphonso Corso.*
*Alph.* Sir.
*King.* I think thou lov'st me.
*Alph.* More than my Life.
*King.* That's much; yet I believe thee.
y Mother has the Judgment of the World,
d all things move by that: But my *Alphonso*,
has a cruel Wit.
*Alph.* The Provocation, Sir.
*King.* I know it well
it thou'dst have my Heart within thy Hand,
Conjurations blot the Name of Kings.
hat Honours, Interest, were the World to buy him,
ll make a brave Man smile, and do a Murder?
erefore I hate the Memory of *Brutus*,
ean the latter, so cry'd up in Story.
ar did ill, but did it in the Sun,
d foremost in the Field, but sneaking *Brutus*,
om none but Cowards and white-liver'd Knaves
ould dare commend, lagging behind his Fellows,
Dagger in his Bosom, stabb'd his Father.
is is a Blot which *Tully*'s Eloquence
ill ne'er wipe off, tho' the mistaken Man

## ACT II. SCENE I.

*Enter* Queen-Mother, *Abbot* Delbene, Polin

*Q. M.* PRAY mark the Form of the Conspiracy:
*Guise* gives it out he Journeys to *Champag*
But lurks indeed at *Lagny*, hard by *Paris*,
Where every Hour he hears, and gives Instructions.
Mean time the Council of Sixteen assure him
They have twenty thousand Citizens in Arms.
Is it not so, *Polin*?

*Pol.* True, on my Life;
And if the King doubts the Discovery,
Send me to the *Bastile* till all be prov'd.

*Q. M.* Call Colonel *Grillon*, the King would spe
with him. [*Exit* Poli

*Ab.* Was ever Age like this?

*Q. M.* *Polin* is honest.
Beside, the whole Proceeding is so like
The hair-brain'd Rout, I guess'd as much before.
Know then, it is resolv'd to seize the King,
When next he goes in Penitential Weeds,
Among the Friars, without his usual Guards,
Then, under shew of Popular Sedition,
For Safety, shut him in a Monastery,
And sacrifice his Favourites to their Rage.

*Ab.* When is this Council to be held again?

*Q. M.* Immediately upon the Duke's Departure.

*Ab.* Why sends not then the King sufficient Gua
To seize the Fiends, and hew 'em into Pieces?

*Q. M.* 'Tis in Appearance easie, but th' Effect
Most hazardous, for straight, upon th' Alarm,
The City would be sure to be in Arms.
Therefore to undertake, and not to compass,
Were to come off with Ruin and Dishonour.
You know th' *Italian* Proverb, *Bisogna Coprirsi*.
He that will venture on a Hornet's Nest,
Should Arm his Head, and Buckler well his Breast.

*Ab.* But wherefore ſeems the King ſo unreſolv'd?
*Q. M* I brought *Polin*, and made the Demonſtration,
old him Neceſſity cry'd out to take
Reſolution to preſerve his Life,
nd look on *Guiſe* as a reclaimleſs Rebel
ut through the natural Sweetneſs of his Temper,
nd dangerous Mercy, coldly he reply'd,
adam, I will conſider what you ſay.
*Ab.* Yet after all, could we but fix him.
*Q M* Right,
he Buſineſs were more firm for this Delay;
or Nobleſt Natures, tho' they ſuffer long,
hen once provok'd, they turn the Face to Danger.
t ſee, he comes, *Alphonſo Corſo* with him.
t us withdraw, and when 'tis fit, rejoyn him. [*Ex.*

*Enter* King, Alphonſo Corſo.

*King.* *Alphonſo Corſo.*
*Alph.* Sir.
*King.* I think thou lov'ſt me.
*Alph.* More than my Life.
*King* That's much; yet I believe thee
y Mother has the Judgment of the World,
d all things move by that. But my *Alphonſo*,
e has a cruel Wit.
*Alph* The Provocation, Sir.
*King* I know it well
it thou'dſt have my Heart within thy Hand,
Conjurations blot the Name of Kings.
hat Honours, Intereſt, were the World to buy him,
ll make a brave Man ſmile, and do a Murder?
erefore I hate the Memory of *Brutus*,
ean the latter, ſo cry'd up in Story.
ar did ill, but did it in the Sun,
d foremoſt in the Field; but ſneaking *Brutus*,
hom none but Cowards and white-liver'd Knaves
ould dare commend, lagging behind his Fellows,
Dagger in his Boſom, ſtabb'd his Father
is a Blot which *Tully*'s Eloquence
uld ne'er wipe off, tho' the miſtaken Man

Makes bold to call those Traytors Men Divine;

*Alph* *Tully* was wise, but wanted Constancy.

*Enter* Queen-Mother, *Abbot* Delbene.

*Q. M* Good-even Sir; 'tis just the time you order'd

To wait on your Decrees.

*King* Oh Madam.

*Q. M.* Sir,

*King* Oh Mother, but I cannot make it way;

Chaos and Shades, 'tis huddled up in Night.

*Q. M.* Speak then, for Speech is Morning to the Mind

It spreads the beauteous Images abroad,

Which else lye furl'd and clouded in the Soul.

*King* You would embark me in a Sea of Blood.

*Q. M.* You see the Plot directly on your Person;

But give it o'er, I did but state the Case.

Take *Guise* into your Heart, and drive your Friends;

Let Knaves in Shops prescribe you how to sway,

And when they read your Acts, with their vile Bre[ath]

Proclaim aloud, they like not this or that;

Then in a drove come Lowing to the *Louvre*,

And cry they'll have it mended, that they will,

Or you shall be no King.

*King* 'Tis true, the People

Ne'er know a Mean, when once they get the Power

But O, if the Design we lay should fail,

Better the Traytors never should be touch'd,

If Execution cries not out 'tis done

*Q. M.* No Sir; you cannot fear the sure Design,

But I have liv'd too long since my own Blood

Dares not confide in her that gave him Being.

*King* Stay Madam, stay, come back, forgive my Fe[ars]

Where all our Thoughts should creep like deepest strea[ms]

Know then, I hate aspiring *Guise* to Death,

Whor'd *Margerite* Plots upon my Life,

And shall I not Revenge?

*Q. M* Why this is *Harry*;

*Harry* at *Moncontour*, when in his Bloom

He saw the Admiral *Colligny*'s Back

*King* O this Whale *Guise*, with all the *Lorain* F[ry]

Might I but view him after his Plots and Plunges,

S[it]

Struck on those cowring Shallows that await him,
This were a *Florence* Master-piece indeed.

*Q. M.* He comes to take his leave.

*King.* Then for *Champagn*;
But lies in wait till *Paris* is in Arms.
Call *Grillon* in, all that I beg you now,
Is to be hush'd upon the Consultation,
As Urns that never blab.

*Q. M.* Doubt not your Friends;
Love 'em, and then you need not fear your Foes.

*Enter* Grillon.

*King.* Welcome my Honest-Man, my old try'd Friend
Why dost thou fly me *Grillon*, and retire?

*Grill.* Rather let me demand your Majesty,
Why fly you from your self? I've heard you say,
You'd arm against the League, why do you not?
The Thoughts of such as you, are Starts Divine,
And when you mould with second Cast the Spirit,
The Air, the Life, the golden Vapour's gone.

*King.* Soft, my old Friend, *Guise* plots upon my Life,
I'll shall tell thee more, hast thou not heard
Th' unsufferable Affronts he daily offers,
War without Treasure on the *Hugonots*,
While I am forc'd against my bent of Soul,
Against all Laws, all Custom, Right, Succession,
To cast *Navarre* from the Imperial Line

*Grill.* Why do you, Sir? Death, let me tell the Traytor.

*King* Peace, *Guise* is going to his Government,
You are his Foe of old: Go to him, *Grillon*,
Visit him as from me, to be employ'd
In this great War against the *Hugonots*,
And prethee tell him roundly of his Fauls;
No farther, honest *Grillon*.

*Grill.* Shall I fight him?

*King* I charge thee not.

*Grill* If he provokes me, strike him?
You'll grant me that?

*King* Not so, my honest Soldier.
Yet speak to him.

*Grill.* I will by Heav'n to th' purpose,

And if he force a beating, who can help it? [*Ex.* Gri
*King* Follow *Alphonso*, when the Storm is up,
Call me to part 'em
*Q. M.* *Grillon* to ask him Pardon,
Will let *Guise* know, we are not in the Dark.
*King* You hit the Judgmemt; yet, O yet, there's mor
Something upon my Heart, after these Counsels,
So soft, and so unworthy to be nam'd.
*Q. M.* They say that *Grillon*'s Niece is come to Cou
And means to kiss your Hand. [*Exit* Q. Moth
*King* Could I but hope it.
O my dear Father, pardon me in this,
And then enjoin me all that Man can suffer;
But sure the Powers above will take our Tears
For such a fault, Love is so like themselves. [*Exeu*

## SCENE II. *The Louvre.*

*Enter* Guise *attended with his Family*, Marmoutier *mee-*
*ting him New Drest, attended*, &c.

*Gui* Furies, she keeps her Word, and I am lost;
Yet let not thy Ambition shew it to her,
For after all she does it but to try me,
And foil my vow'd Designs. Madam, I see
You're come to Court; the Robes you wear become y
Your Air, your Meen, your Charms, your every Gra
Will kill at east your thousand in a Day. [*Tu*
*Mar* What, a whole Day, and kill but one poor tho
An Hour you mean, and in that Hour ten thousand?
Yes, I wou'd make with every Glance a Murder
Mend me this Curl.
*Gui* Woman!
*Mar* You see my Lord,
I have my Followers, like you: I swear
The Court's a Heav'nly Place, but O my Hear,
I know not why that Sigh should come uncall'd,
Perhaps 'twas for your going, yet I swear
I never was so mov'd, O *Guise*, as now;
Just as you enter'd, when from yonder Window

aw the King.

*Gui.* Woman, all over Woman.

he World confesses, Madam, *Henry*'s Form

Noble and Majestick.

*Mar.* O you grudge

n extorted Praise, and speak him but by halfs.

*Gui.* Priest, *Corso*, Devils! how she carries it!

*Mar.* I see, my Lord, you are come to take your leave;

nd were it not to give the Court Suspicion,

would oblige you, Sir, before you go,

o lead me to the King.

*Gui.* Death and the Devil!

*Mar.* But since that cannot be, I'll take my leave

f you, my Lord, Heav'n grant your Journey safe,

arewel once more. Not stir? Does, this become you?

oes your Ambition swell into your Eyes?

ealousie, by this Light. Nay then, proud *Guise*,

ell you, you're not worthy of the Grace,

t I will carry't, Sir, to those that are,

nd leave you to the Curse of Bosom War. [*Exit.*

*May.* Is this the Heav'nly?

*Gui.* Devil, Devil, as they are all;

'Tis true, at first she caught the Heav'nly Form,

t now Ambition sets her on her Head,

Hell, I see the cloven Mark upon her:

! *Grillon* here! some new Court Trick upon me.

*Enter* Grillon.

*Grill.* Sir, I have business for your Ear.

*Gui.* Retire. [*Exeunt his Followers.*

*Grill.* The King, my Lord, commanded me to wait [you,

d bid you welcome to the Court.

*Gui.* The King

ill loads me with new Honours, but none greater

an this the last.

*Grill.* There is one greater yet,

ur High Commission against the *Hugonots*;

nd my Family shall shortly wait you,

d 'twill be Glorious Work.

*Gui.* If you are there,

here must be Action.

*Grill.*

*Grill.* O, your Pardon, Sir,
I'm but a Stripling in the Trade of War;
But you, whose Life is one continued Broyl,
What will not your Triumphant Arms accomplish!
You, that were form'd for Mastery in War;
That, with a start, cry'd to your Brother *Mayenne*,
To Horse, and slaughter'd forty thousand *Germans*.
*Gui.* Let me beseech you, Colonel, no more.
*Grill.* But, Sir, since I must make at least a Figure
In this great Business, let me understand
What 'tis you mean, and why you force the King
Upon so dangerous an Expedition.
*Gui.* Sir, I intend the Greatness of the King,
The Greatness of all *France*, whom it imports
To make their Arms their Business, Aim, and Glory
And where so proper, as upon those Rebels
That cover'd all the State with Blood and Death?
*Grill* Stor'd Arsenals and Armories, Fields of H[illegible]
Ordnance, Munition, and the Nerve of War,
Sound Infantry, not harras'd and diseas'd,
To meet the fierce *Navarre*, should first be thought
*Gui.* I find, my Lord, the Argument grows wa[illegible]
Therefore, thus much, and I have done I go
To joyn the holy League in this great War,
In which no Place of Office, or Command,
Not of the Greatest, shall be bought or sold;
Whereas too often Honours are confer'd
On Soldiers, and no Soldiers, this Man Knighted
Because he Charg'd a Troop before his Dinner,
And sculk'd behind a Hedge i'th' Afternoon
I will have strict Examination made
Betwixt the Meritorious and the Base [&c.]
*Grill.* You have Mouth'd it bravely, and there[illegible]
Your Deeds would answer well your haughty Wor[ds]
Yet let me tell you, Sir, there is a Man,
Curse on the Hearts that hate him, that wou'd be[illegible]
Better than you, or all your puffy Race,
That better would become the Great Battalion;
That when he Shines in Arms, and Suns the Field,
Moves, Speaks, and Fights, and is himself a War

*Gui.* Your Idol, Sir, you mean the Great *Navarre*;
t yet——
*Grill.* No Yet, my Lord of *Guise*, no Yet,
Arms, I bar you that; I swear, No Yet,
r never was his like, nor shall again,
o' voted from his Right by your Curs'd League.
*Gui.* Judge not too rashly of the Holy League,
t look at Home.
*Grill.* Ha! dar'st thou justify
ose Villains?
*Gui* I'll not justify a Villain
re than your self; but if you thus proceed,
every heated Breath can puff away,
each surmise, the Lives of Free-born People,
hat need that Awful General Convocation,
e Assembly of the States? Nay let me urge,
hus they villifie the Holy League,
hat may their Heads expect?
*Grill.* What, if I cou'd,
ey should be certain of, whole piles of Fire.
*Gui* Collonel, 'tis very well I know your Mind,
hich without fear or flattery to your Person,
tell the King, and then, with his Permission,
claim it for a warning to our People.
*Grill* Come, you're a Murderer your self within,
Traitor
*Gu* Thou a—— hot old Hair-brain'd Fool
*Grill* You were Complotter with the Cursed League,
e black Abettor of our *Harry*'s Death.
*Gui* 'Tis false.
*Grill* 'Tis true, as thou art double hearted:
ou double Traitor, to Conspire so basely,
d when found out, more basely to deny't.
*Gui.* O Gracious *Harry*, let me sound thy Name,
ll this old rust of War, this knotty Trifler
ould raise me to Extreams.
*Grill* If thou'rt a Man,
t did'st refuse the Challenge of *Navarre*,
me forth.
*Gui.* Go on, since thou'rt resolv'd on Death,

I'll

I'll follow thee, and rid thy shaking Soul.

*Enter* King, Queen-Mother, Alphonso, Abbot, &c.

But see, the King: I scorn to ruin thee,
Therefore go tell him, tell him thy own Story.

*King* Ha, Colonel, is this your Friendly Visit?
Tell me the truth, how happen'd this Disorder?
Those ruffled Hands, red Looks, and port of Fury?

*Grill* I told him, Sir, since you will have it so,
He was the Author of the Rebel League,
Therefore a Traitor, and a Murderer.

*King* Is't possible?

*Gui.* No matter, Sir, no matter;
A few hot Words, no more upon my Life;
The old Man rous'd and shook himself a little:
So if your Majesty will do me Honour,
I do beseech you let the business die.

*King. Grillon*, submit your self, and ask his Pardon.

*Grill.* Pardon me! I cannot do't.

*King.* Where are the Guards?

*Gui.* Hold, Sir, come Colonel, I'll ask Pardon for you.
This Soldierly Embrace makes up the Breach,
We will be sorry, Sir, for one another.

*Grill.* My Lord, I know not what to answer you,
I'm Friends, and I am not, and so farewell. [Ex.

*King.* You have your Orders, yet before you go,
Take this Embrace. I court you for my Friend,
Tho' *Grillon* wou'd not.

*Gui.* I thank you on my Knees.
And still while Life shall last, will take strict care
To justifie my Loyalty to your Person. [Ex.

*Q. M.* Excellent Loyalty, to lock you up!

*King* I see even to the bottom of his Soul.
And, Madam, I must say the *Guise* has Beauties,
But they are set in Night, and foul Design.
He was my Friend when young, and might be still.

*Abbot.* Mark'd you his hollow Accents at the parting?

*Q. M.* Graves in his Smiles.

*King.* Death in his bloodless Hands.
O *Marmoutiere*! now I will haste to meet thee;
The Face of Beauty, on this rising Horror,

Lec

ooks like the midnight Moon upon a Murder;
gilds the dark design that stays for Fate,
nd drives the Shades that thicken from the State.
[*Exeunt.*

---

## ACT III. SCENE. I.

*Enter* Grillon *and* Polin.

*Grill* HAVE then this Pious Council of Sixteen
Scented your late Discovery of the Plot?

*Pol* Not as from me, for still I kennel with them,
nd bark as loud as the most deep-mouth'd Traytor,
gainst the King, his Government and Laws;
Whereon immediately there runs a Cry
t, Seize him on the next Procession, seize him,
d clap the *Chilperick* in a Monastry,
us it was fixt, as I before discover'd:
when, against his Custom, they perceiv'd
King absented, straight the Rebels met,
d roar'd, they were undone.

*Grill* O, 'tis like 'em,
like their Mungrel Souls; Flesh 'em with Fortune,
d they will worry Royalty to Death:
it some crabbed Virtue turn and pinch 'em,
rk me, they'll run, and yelp, and clap their Tails,
ke Curs, betwixt their Legs, and howl for Mercy.

*Pol* But *Malicorn*, sagacious on the point,
r'd, Call the Sheriffs, and bid 'em arm their Bands;
yet to this, to raise you above hope,
*Guise* my Master will be here to day.
r, on bare guess of what has been reveal'd,
e wing'd a Messenger to give him notice;
t spight of all this Factor of the Fiends
'd urge, they slunk their Heads like Hinds in Storms:
t see, they come.

*Enter Sheriffs with the Populace.*

*Grill* Away, I'll have amongst 'em;
y to the King, warn him of *Guise*'s coming,
hat he may straight dispatch his strict Commands

To

To ſtop him.

1 *Sher.* Nay, this is Colonel *Grillon*,
The Blunderbuſs o'th' Court, away, away;
He carries Ammunition in his Face.

*Grill.* Hark you, my Friends, if you are not in haſte,
Becauſe you are the Pillars of the City,
I wou'd inform you of a General Ruin.

2 *Sher.* Ruin to the City! marry, Heav'n forbid!

*Grill.* Amen, I ſay; for look you, I'm your Friend.
'Tis blown about you've plotted on the King,
To ſeize him, if not kill him; for who knows,
When once your Conſcience yields, how far 'twill ſtretch?
Next, quite to daſh your firmeſt hopes in pieces,
The Duke of *Guiſe* is dead.

1 *Sher.* Dead, Colonel!

2 *Sher.* Undone, undone!

*Grill.* The World cannot redeem you;
For what, Sirs, if the King, provok'd at laſt,
Should joyn the *Spaniard*, and ſhould fire your City,
*Paris* your Head, but a moſt Venomous one,
Which muſt be blooded?

1 *Sher.* Blooded, Colonel!

*Grill.* Ay, blooded, thou moſt infamous Magiſtrate,
Or you will blood the King, and burn the *Louvre*:
But, ere that be, fall million miſcreant Souls,
Such Earth-born Minds as yours; for mark me, Slaves,
Did you not Ages paſt conſign your Lives,
Liberties, Fortunes, to Imperial Hands,
Made 'em the Guardians of your ſickly Years,
And now you're grown up to a Boobies Greatneſs,
What, wou'd you reſt the Scepter from his Hand?
Now, by the Majeſty of Kings I ſwear,
You ſhall as ſoon be ſav'd for packing Juries.

1 *Sher.* Why, Sir, mayn't Citizens be ſav'd?

*Grill.* Yes, Sir,
From drowning, to be hang'd, burnt, broke o'th' wheel.

1 *Sher.* Colonel, you ſpeak us plain.

*Grill.* A Plague confound you,
Why ſhould I not? what is there in ſuch Raſcals,
Should make me hide my Thought, or hold my Tongue?

Not

ow, in the Devils Name, what make you here,
wbing the Inside of the Court like Snails,
ming out Walls, and pricking out your Horns?
hear, I warrant, what the King's a doing,
d what the Cabinet-Council, then to th' City,
spread your monstrous Lyes, and sow Sedition?
ld-fire choak you.

*1 Sher.* Well, we'll think of this,
d so we take our leaves.

*Grill* Nay, stay, my Masters;
r I'm a thinking now just whereabouts
ow the two tallest Trees in *Arden* Forest.

*1 Sher.* For what, pray Colonel, if we may be so bold?

*Grill* Why to hang you upon the highest Branches;
re God it will be so; and I shall laugh
see you dangling to and fro i'th' Air,
ith the honest Crows pecking your Traytors Limbs.

*All.* Good Colonel!

*Grill* Good Rats, my precious Vermin,
u moving Dirt, you rank stark Muck o'th' World,
u Oven-Bats, you things so far from Souls,
e Dogs you're out of Providence's reach,
d only fit for hanging; but be gone,
d think of Plunder ——— You right Elder Sheriff,
ho Carv'd our *Henry*'s Image on a Table,
your Club-Feast, and after stabb'd it through?

*Sher.* Mercy, good Colonel.

*Grill* Run with your Nose to Earth,
n Blood-hound, run, and scent out Royal Murder.
u second Rogue, but equal to the first,
nder, go hang, nay take your tackling with you
these shall hold you fast, your Slaves shall hang you
the mid Region in the Sun [*Exeunt Sheriffs, and People.*
nder, be gone Vipers, Asps, and Adders.

*Enter* Malicorn.

but here comes a Fiend that soars above,
ince o'th' Air, that sets the Mud a moving.

*Mal.* Colonel, a word.

*Grill* I hold no speech with Villains

*Mal.* But, Sir, it may concern your Fame and Safety.

*Grill.*

*Grill* No matter, I had rather dye traduc'd,
Than live by ſuch a Villain's help as thine.
*Mal.* Hate then the Traytor, but yet love the Tre
*Gill* Why, are not you a Villain,
*Mal* 'Tis confeſs'd
*Grill.* Then in the Name of all thy Brother De
What would'ſt thou have with me?
*Mal* I know you're honeſt,
Therefore it is my buſineſs to diſturb you.
*Grill* Fore God I'll beat thee, if thou urge me fa
*Mal* Why tho' you ſhou'd, yet if you hear me
The pleaſure I ſhall take in your Vexation,
Will heal my Bruiſes
*Grill.* Wert thou definite Rogue,
I'faith, I think that I ſhould give thee hearing,
But ſuch a boundleſs Villany as thine,
Admits no Patience.
*Mal.* Your Niece is come to Court,
And yields her Honour to our *Henry*'s Bed.
*Grill.* Thou ly'ſt, damn'd Villain. [*Strikes*
*Mal.* So, why this I look'd for·
But yet I ſwear by Hell, and my Revenge,
'Tis true, as you have wrong'd me.
*Grill* Wrong'd thee, Villain!
And name Revenge! O wert thou *Grillon*'s Match
And worthy of my Sword, I ſwear by this
One had been paſt an Oath; but thou'rt a Worm,
And if I tread thee dar'ſt not turn again.
*Mal.* 'Tis falſe, I dare like you, but cannot act;
There is no force in this Enervate Arm
Blaſted I was ere born, Curſe on my Stars,
Got by ſome Dotard in his pithleſs Years,
And ſent a wither'd Saplin to the World
Yet, I've Brain, and there is my Revenge;
Therefore I ſay again theſe Eyes have ſeen
Thy Blood at Court bright as a Summers Morn,
When all the Heav'n is ſtreak'd with dappled Fires
And fleck'd with Bluſhes like a rifled Maid,
Nay, by the Gleamy Fires that melted from her,
Faſt Sighs and Smiles, ſwoln Lips and heaving Bre

Soul presages *Henry* has enjoy'd her.

*Mal.* Again thou ly'st, and I will crumble thee,
Thou bottled Spider, into thy Primitive Earth,
Unless thou swear thy very Thought's a Lye.

*Mal.* I stand in Adamant, and thus defie thee,
Draw, draw, and with the edge betwixt my Lips,
Even while thou rak'st it through my Teeth, I'll swear
What I have said is true, as thou art honest,
And I a Villain.

*Grill.* Damn'd infamous Wretch,
So much below my Scorn, I dare not kill thee:
And yet so much my Hate, that I must fear thee.
But should it be as thou hast said, not all
The Trophies of my Lawrell'd Honesty
Should bar me from forsaking this bad World,
I'd never draw my Sword for *Henry* more.

*Mal.* Ha, 'tis well, and now I am Reveng'd
...in hopes thou would'st have utter'd Treason,
And forfeited thy Head to pay me fully.

*Grill.* Hast thou Compacted for a Lease of Years
With Hell, that thus thou ventur'st to provoke me?

*Mal.* Perhaps I have: (How right the Blockhead hits.)
Once more to rack thy Heart, and break thy Brain,
Thy Neice has been before the *Guise*'s Mistress.

*Grill.* Hell-hound, avant.

*Mal.* Forgive my honest Meaning. [*Exit.*

*Grill.* 'Tis hatch'd beneath, a Plot upon mine Honour,
And thus he lays his Baits to catch my Soul.
...but the Presence opens; who comes here!
...Heav'n my Neice, led by *Alphonso Corso*!
...*Malicorn*, is't possible, Truth from thee!
...plain, and I in justifying Woman
...done the Devil wrong.

*Usher.* Madam, the King,
...you to sit, will instantly attend you.

*Grill.* Death, Hell, and Furies! ha, she comes to seek him;
...ostitute! and on her prodigal Flesh
...has lavish'd all the Diamonds of the *Guise*
...set her off, and sell her to the King.

*Mar.* O Heav'ns! did ever Virgin yet attempt

An Enterprise like mine? I that resolv'd
Never to leave those dear delightful Shades,
But act the little part that Nature gave me,
On the green Carpets of some guiltless Grove,
And having finish'd it forsake the World,
Unless sometimes my Heart might entertain
Some small Remembrance of the taking *Guise*
But that far, far from any dark'ning Thought,
To cloud my Honour, or eclipse my Virtue.

*Grill* Thou ly'st, and if thou hadst not glanc'd asid[e]
And spy'd me coming, I had had it all

*Mar* By Heav'n, by all that's good ——

*Grill* Thou hast lost thy Honour.
Give me thy Hand, this Hand by which I caught th[ee]
From the bold Ruffian in the Massacre,
That would have stain'd thy almost Infant Honour,
With Lust, and Blood; dost thou remember it?

*Mar* I do, and bless the Godlike Arm that sav'd m[e]

*Grill* 'Tis false, thou hast forgot my gen'rous Actio[n]
And now thou laugh'st to think how thou hast chea[ted]
For all his Kindness, this old grisled Fool.

*Mar.* Forbid it Heav'n!

*Grill* But oh that thou hadst dy'd
Ten thousand Deaths, ere blasted *Grillon*'s Glory,
*Grillon*, that sav'd thee from a barb'rous World,
Where thou hadst starv'd, or sold thy self for Bread,
Took thee into his Bosom, foster'd thee
As his own Soul, and lapp'd thee in his *Heart-strings*;
And now for all my Cares, to serve me thus!
O 'tis too much, ye Powers! double Confusion
On all my Wars; and oh, out, shame upon thee,
It wrings the *Tears* from *Grillon*'s *Iron Heart*,
And melts me to a *Babe*.

*Mar* Sir, Father, hear me;
I come to Court, to save the Life of *Guise*.

*Grill.* And prostitute thy Honour to the King.

*Mar.* I have look'd, perhaps, too nicely for my S[ex]
Into the dark Affairs of fatal State;
And to advance this dangerous Inquisition,
I listen'd to the Love of daring *Guise*.

*Grill.* By Arms, by Honesty, I swear thou lov'st him.

*Mar* By Heav'n that gave those Arms Success, I swear
I do not, as you think, but take it all
I've heard the *Guise*, not with an Angel's Temper,
Something beyond the tenderness of Pity,
And yet, not Love.
Now, by the Powers that fram'd me, this is all;
Nor should the World have wrought this close Confession,
But to rebate your Jealousie of Honour.

*Grill* I know not what to say, nor what to think;
There's Heav'n still in thy Voice, but that's a Sign
Virtue's departing, for thy better Angel
Still makes the Woman's Tongue his rising Ground,
Wags there a while, and takes his flight for ever.

*Mar* You must not go.

*Grill.* Tho' I have Reason, plain
As Day, to judge thee false, I think thee true:
By Heav'n, methinks I see a Glory round thee;
There's something says thou wilt not lose thy Honour:
Death, and the Devil, that's my own Honesty·
My foolish open Nature, that would have
All like my self, but off, I'll hence, and Curse thee.

*Mar* O stay!

*Grill* I won't

*Mar* Hark, the King's a coming.
Let me conjure you, for your own Soul's Quiet,
And for the everlasting Rest of mine,
Stir not till you have heard my Heart's design.

*Grill* Angel, or Devil, I will——nay, at this rate
She'll make me shortly bring him to her Bed
And Ward for him? No, he shall make me run my Head
Into a Cannon, when 'tis Firing, first.
That's honourable Sport; but I'll retire,
And if she plays me false, here's that shall mend her.

[Marmoutiere *Sits* *Song and Dance.*

*Enter the King*

*King.* After the breathing of a Love-sick Heart,
Upon your Hand, once more, nay twice, forgive me.

*Mar* I discompose you, Sir.

*King* Thou dost, by Heav'n;

But with such Charming Pleasure,
I love, and tremble, as at Angels view.
*Mar.* Love me, my Lord?
*King.* Who shou'd be lov'd, but you?
So lov'd, that even my Crown, and self are vile,
While you are by, try me upon despair,
My Kingdom at the stake, Ambition starv'd,
Revenge forgot, and all great Appetites
That whet uncommon Spirits to aspire;
So once a day I may have leave———
Nay, Madam, then you fear me
*Mar.* Fear you, Sir? what is there dreadful in you?
You've all the Graces that can crown Mankind
Yet wear 'em so, as if you did not know 'em.
So stainless, fearless, free in all your Actions,
As if Heav'n lent you to the World to Pattern
*King.* Madam, I find you're no Petitioner,
My People would not treat me in this sort,
Tho' 'twere to gain a part of their Design:
But to the *Guise* they deal their faithless Praise
As fast, as you your Flattery to me;
Tho' for what end I cannot guess, except
You come, like them, to mock at my Misfortunes.
*Mar.* Forgive you, Heav'n! that Thought. No, mighty Monarch,
The Love of all the Good, and Wonder of the Great,
I swear, by Heav'n, my Heart adores and loves you.
*King* O, Madam, rise
*Mar.* Nay, were you, Sir, unthron'd
By this Seditious Rout that dare despise you,
Blast all my days, ye Powers, torment my Nights,
Nay, let the Misery invade my Sex,
That cou'd not for the Royal Cause, like me,
Throw all their Luxury before your Feet,
And follow you like Pilgrims through the World
*Grill* Sound Wind and Limb, fore-God a gall Girl. [*A*
*King.* What shall I answer to thee, O thou Balm
To heal a broken, yet a Kingly Heart,
For, so I swear I will be to my last:
Come to my Arms, and be thy *Harry*'s Angel,

Sh

Shine through my Cares, and make my Crown sit easie

*Mar.* O never, Sir.

*King.* What said you, *Mormoutiere*?
Why dost thou turn thy Beauties into Frowns?

*Mar.* You know, Sir, 'tis impossible, no more

*King.* No more---and with that stern resolv'd Behavi-
By Heav'n, were I a dying, and the Priest [our.
Shou'd urge my last Confession, I'd cry out,
Oh *Marmoutiere*! and yet thou say'st No more.

*Mar.* 'Tis well, Sir, I have lost my Aim, farewell.

*King.* Come back, O stay, my Life flows after you.

*Mar.* No, Sir, I find I am a trouble to you.
You will not hear my Suit.

*King.* You cannot go,
You sha'not——O your Suit, I kneel to grant it,
I beg you take whatever you demand

*Mar* Then, Sir, thus low, or prostrate, if you please,
Let me intreat for *Guise*

*King* Ha, Madam, what!
For *Guise*! for *Guise*! that stubborn arrogant Rebel,
That laughs at proffer'd Mercy, slights his Pardon,
Mocks Royal Grace, and plots upon my Life?
Ha! and do you protect him? then the World
Is sworn to *Henry*'s Death: Does Beauty too,
And Innocence it self, conspire against me?
Then let me tamely yield my Glories up,
Which once I vow'd with my drawn Sword to wear
To my last drop of Blood. Come, *Guise*, come Cardinal,
All you lov'd Traitors, come——I strip to meet you;
Sheath all your Daggers in curst *Henry*'s Heart.

*Mar* This I expected, but when you have heard
How far I would intreat your Majesty,
Perhaps you'll be more calm.

*King* See, I'm hush'd;
Speak then, how far, Madam, would you command?

*Mar* Not to proceed to last Extremities,
Before the Wound is desperate; think alone,
For no man Judges like your Majesty,
Take your own Methods, all the Heads of *France*
Cannot so well advise you, as your self:
Therefore resume, my Lord, your Godlike Temper,

Yet do not bear more than a Monarch should:
Believe it Sir, the more your Majesty
Draws back your Arm, the more of Fate it carries.

*King* Thou Genius of my State, thou perfect Mode
Of Heav'n it self, an Abstract of the Angels,
Forgive the late disturbance of my Soul;
I'm clear by Nature, as a rockless Stream,
But they dig through the Gravel of my Heart,
Therefore let me conjure you do not go,
'Tis said the *Guise* will come, in spight of me;
Suppose it possible, and stay to advise me.

*Mar.* I will, but on your Royal Word, no more.

*King.* I will be easie
To my last Gasp, as your own Virgin Thoughts,
And never dare to breath my Passion more;
Yet you'll allow me now and then to sigh
As we discourse, and Court you with my Eyes.

*Enter* Alphonso.

Why do you wave your Hand,
And warn me hence?
So looks the poor condemn'd,
When Justice beck'ns, there's no hope of Pardon.
Sternly, like you, the Judge his Victim eyes,
And thus, like me, the Wretch despairing dies

[*Exit with* A[illegible]

*Enter* Grillon.

*Grill* O rare, rare Creature! by the Power that m[illegible]
Wer't possible we cou'd be damn'd again
By some new *Eve*, such Virtue might relieve us;
O I cou'd clasp thee, but that my Arms are rough,
Till all thy Sweets were broke with my Embraces,
And kiss thy Beauties to a dissolution

*Mar* Ah Father, Uncle, Brother, all the Kin,
The precious Blood that's left me in the World,
Believe, dear Sir, whate'er my Actions seem,
I will not lose my Virtue for a Throne.

*Grill.* Why, I will carve thee out a Throne m[illegible]
I'll hew down all the Common-wealths in *Christend[om]*
And seat thee on their Necks, as high as Heav'n

En[illegible]

*Enter* Abbot Delbene.

*Ab* Colonel, your Ear.

*Mar* By these whispering Councils,
My Soul presages that the *Guise* is coming:
If he dares come, were I a Man, a King,
I'd sacrifice him in the City's sight.
O Heav'ns! what was't I said? Were I a Man,
I know not that, but as I am a Virgin,
If I wou'd offer thee, too lovely *Guise*,
It shou'd be kneeling to the Throne of Mercy.
Ha! then thou lov'st, that thou art thus concern'd;
Down, rising Mischief, down, or I will kill thee,
Even in thy Cause, and strangle new-born Pity.
Yet, if he were not married! ha, what then?
His Charms prevail, no, let the Rebel die.
I faint beneath this strong Oppression here,
Reason and Love rend my divided Soul,
Heav'n be the Judge, and still let Virtue conquer;
Love to his Tune my jarring Heart wou'd bring,
But Reason over-winds and cracks the String. [*Ex.*

*Ab* The King dispatches Order upon Order,
With positive Command to stop his coming.
Yet there is Notice given to the City;
Besides *Bellieure* brought but a half account,
How that the *Guise* reply'd he would obey
His Majesty in all, yet if he might
Have leave to justify himself before him,
He doubted not his Cause.

*Grill* The Ax, the Ax.
Rebellion's pamper'd to a Plurisie,
And it must bleed. [*Shouts within.*

*Ab* Hark, what a Shout was there!
I'll to the King, it may be 'tis reported
On purpose thus Let there be Truth or Lies
In this mad Fame, I'll bring you instant word [*Ex* Ab.

*Manet* Grillon · *Enter* Guise, Cardinal Mayen, Malicorn, *Attendants*, &c *Shouts again.*

*Grill.* Death, and thou Devil *Malicorn*, is that
Thy Master?

*Gui* Yes, *Grillon*, 'tis the *Guise*,

One that wou'd court you for a Friend.

*Grill.* A Friend!
Traitor, thou mean'st, and so I bid thee welcome,
But since thou art so insolent, thy Blood
Be on thy Head, and fall by me unpitied. [*Exi*

*Gui.* The Bruises of his Loyalty have craz'd him.
[*Shouts louder*

*Spirit within Sings.*

*Malicorn, Malicorn, Malicorn, ho!*
*If the* Guise *resolves to go,*
*I charge, I warn thee let him know,*
*Perhaps his Head may lye too low.*

*Gui.* Why, *Malicorn*?

*Mall* [*starting.*] Sir, do not see the King.

*Gui* I will.

*Mal* 'Tis dangerous

*Gui.* Therefore I will see him,
And so report my Danger to the People
Halt to your Judgment, let him, if he dare;
But more, more, more, why, *Malicorn*, again?
I thought a Look with us had been a Language,
I'll talk my Mind on any point but this
By Glances; ha, not yet, thou mak'st me blush
At thy delay; why, Man, 'tis more than Life,
Ambition, or a Crown.

*Mal.* What, *Marmoutiere*!

*Gui.* Ay, there a General's Heart beat like a Drum
Quick, quick, my Reins, my Back, and Head and Brea
Ake, as I'd been a Horse-back forty hours.

*Mal* She has seen the King.

*Gui* I thought she might. A trick upon me, we

*Mal* Passion o' both sides.

*Gui.* His, thou meanest.

*Mal.* On hers.
Down on her Knees.

*Gui* And up again, no matter

*Mal* Now all in Tears, now smiling, sad at partin

*Gui.* Dissembled, for she told me this before,

'Tw

'Twas all put on that I might hear, and rave.

*Mal* And so, to make sure work on't, by Consent
Of *Grillon*, who is made their Bawd———

*Gui* Away.

*Mal* She's lodg'd at Court.

*Gui.* 'Tis false, they do bely her.

*Mal* But, Sir, I saw the Apartment.

*Gui* What, at Court?

*Mal* At Court, and near the King; 'tis true by Heav'n.
I never play'd you foul, why should you doubt me?

*Gui* I wou'd thou hadst, ere thus unmann'd my Heart,
Blood, Battels, Fire, and Death! I run, I run
With this last Blow, he drives me like a Coward;
May let me never win a Field again,
If with the Thought of these irregular Vapours,
The Blood han't burst my Lips.

*Card* Peace, Brother.

*Gui* By Heav'n, I took thee for my Soul's Physician,
And dost thou vomit me with this loath'd Peace,
This contradiction; no, my peaceful Brother,
I'll meet him now, tho' Fire-arm'd Cherubins
Shou'd cross my way. O Jealousie of Love!
Greater than Fame; thou eldest of the Passions,
Or rather, all in one, I here invoke thee,
Where e'er thou'rt Thron'd, in Air, in Earth, or Hell,
Bring me to my Revenge, to Blood, and Ruin.

*Card.* Have you no Temper?

*Gui* Pray, Sir, give me leave,
A moment's Thought, ha, but I sweat and tremble,
My Brain runs this and that way, 'twill not fix
On ought but Vengeance, *Malicorn*, call the People
[*Shouts within.*
Or hark, they shout again, I'll on and meet 'em,
Nay, head 'em to his Palace as my Guards,
Yet more, on such exalted Causes born,
I'll wait him in his Cabinet alone,
And look him pale, while in his Courts without
The People shout him dead with their Alarms,
And make his Mistress tremble in his Arms. [*Exeunt.*

SCENE

## SCENE III.

*Enter King and Council.*

[*Shouts witho*

*King* What mean these Shouts?
*Ab* I told your Majesty,
The Sheriffs have puff'd the Populace with hopes
Of their Deliverer [*Shouts aga*
*King* Hark, there rung a Peal
Like Thunder, see, *Alphonso*, what's the Cause.
*Enter* Grillon.
*Grill.* My Lord, the *Guise* is come.
*King* Is't possible! ha! *Grillon*, said'st thou, come
*Grill.* Why droops the Royal Majesty? O Sir—
*King.* O Villain, Slave, wert thou my late-born H
Giv'n me by Heav'n, ev'n when I lay a dying;
But Peace, thou festring Thought, and hide thy Wou
Where is he?
*Grill* With her Majesty, your Mother;
She has taken Chair, and he walks bowing by her,
With thirty thousand Rebels at his Heels.
*King.* What's to be done? No pall upon my Sp
But he that loves me best, and dares the most
On this nice point of Empire, let him speak.
*Alph.* I would advise you, Sir, to call him in,
And kill him instantly upon the Spot
*Ab.* I like *Alphonso*'s Counsel, short, sure Work
Cut off the Head, and let the Body walk.
*Enter* Queen-Mother.
*Q M* Sir, the *Guise* waits.
*King.* He enters on his Fate.
*Q. M.* Not so, forbear, the City's up in Arms
Nor doubt, if in their heat you cut him off,
That they will spare the Royal Majesty.
Once, Sir, let me advise, and rule your Fury.
*King* You shall, I'll see him, and I'll spare him
*Q M* What will you say?
*King.* I know not;

Col

...lonel *Grillon*, call the Archers in,
...uble your Guards, and strictly charge the *Swits*
...nd to their Arms, receive him as a Traitor. [*Ex.* Grill.
... Heart has set thee down, O *Guise* in Blood,
...o', Mother, Blood, ne'er to be blotted out
*Q. M.* Yet you'll relent, when this hot fit is over.
*King.* If I forgive him, may I ne'er be forgiven,
..., if I tamely bear such Insolence,
...hat act of Treason will the Villain stop at?
...e me, they've sworn, Imprison me's the next,
...rhaps Arraign me, and then doom me dead,
...ere I suffer that, fall all together,
... rather, on their slaughter'd Heaps erect
... Throne, and then proclaim it for Example,
... born a Monarch; which implies alone
... wield the Scepter, and depend on none. [*Exeunt.*

---

## ACT IV. SCENE I.

### SCENE *The Louvre.*

*...hair of State plac'd; the King appears sitting in it; a ...able by him, on which he leans, Attendance on each side ...f them amongst the rest,* Abbot, Grillon, *and* Bellieure. *The* Queen-Mother *enters led by the Duke of* Guise, *who ...akes his approach with three Reverences to the King's ...hair; after the third, the King rises, and coming for-...ward, speaks*

*King.* I Sent you word you should not come
*Gui.* Sir, that I came——
*King.* Why, that you came I see.
...e more, I sent you word, you should not come.
*Gui.* Not come to throw my self with all Submission,
...eath your Royal Feet, to put my Cause
...d Person in the Hands of Soveraign Justice!
*King.* Now 'tis with all Submission, that's the Preface,
...d still you came against my strict Command,
...u dissobey'd me, *Duke*, with all Submission.
*Gui.* Sir, it was the last Necessity that drove me

To clear my ſelf of Calumnies, and Slanders,
Much urg'd, but never prov'd againſt my Innocence;
Yet had I known it was your expreſs Command,
I ſhou'd not have approach'd.

*King* 'Twas as expreſs, as Words could ſignifie,
Stand forth *Bellieure*, it ſhall be prov'd you knew it.
Stand forth, and to this falſe Man's Face declare
Your Meſſage, Word for Word.

*Bell.* Sir, thus it was; I met him on the way,
And plain as I could ſpeak, I gave your Orders,
Juſt in theſe following Words———

*King* Enough, I know you told him;
But he has us'd me long to be contemn'd,
And I can ſtill be patient, and forgive.

*Guiſe* And I can ask Forgiveneſs when I err;
But let my Gracious Maſter, pleaſe to know
The true Intent of my miſ-conſtru'd Faith
Should I not come to vindicate my Fame,
From wrong Conſtructions? And ———

*King* Come, Duke, you were not wrong'd, your Con-
ſcience knows,
You were not wrong'd; were you not plainly told
That if you dar'd to ſet your Foot in *Paris*,
You ſhou'd be held the Cauſe of all Commotions,
That ſhou'd from thence enſue? and yet you came

*Guiſe* Sir, will you pleaſe with Patience but to hear

*King* I will, and wou'd be glad, my Lord of Gu
To clear you to my ſelf.

*Guiſe* I had been told
There were in agitation here at Court,
Things of the higheſt note againſt Religion,
Againſt the common Properties of Subjects,
And Lives of honeſt well-affected Men;
I therefore judg'd———

*King.* Then you it ſeems are Judge
Betwixt the Prince and People, Judge for them,
And Champion againſt me?

*Guiſe* I fear'd it might be repreſented ſo,
And came reſolv'd———

*King.* To head the factious Crowd.

G

*Guise* To clear my Innocence.
*King* The means for that,
...d been your Absence from this hot brain'd Town——
...here you, not I, are King ———
...eel my Blood kindling within my Veins,
...e Genius of the Throne knocks at my Heart;
...ome what may come, he dies.
*Q. M. stopping the King.* What mean you, Sir?
...ou tremble and look pale, for Heav'ns sake think,
...'tis your own Life you venture, if you kill him.
*King* Had I ten thousand Lives, I'd venture all.
...e me way, Madam.
*Q. M.* Not to your Destruction.
...e whole *Parisian* Herd is at your Gates;
...Crowd's a Name too small, they are a Nation,
...mberless, arm'd, enrag'd, one Soul informs 'em.
*King* And that one Soul's the *Guise*, I'll rend it out,
...d damn the Rabble all at once in him
*Guise (aside)* My Fate is now i'th' Ballance, Fool within,
...ank thee for thy Foresight.
*Q. M.* Your Guards oppose 'em.
*King* Why not? a Multitude's a Bulky Coward.
*Q. M.* By Heav'n there are not Limbs in all your Guards
...every one a Morsel.
*King* *Cæsar* quell'd 'em,
...with a Look and Word.
*Q. M.* So *Galba* thought.
*King* But *Galba* was not *Cæsar*.
*Guise.* I must not give 'em time for Resolution [*Aside*.
...Journey, Sir, has discompos'd my Health. [*To the King*.
...mbly beg your leave I may retire,
...your Commands recall me to your Service. [*Ex* Guise.
*Manent* King, Queen Mother, Grillon, Abbot.
*King* So, you have counsell'd well, the Traytor's gone
...mock the Meekness of an injur'd King. [*To* Q. M.
...y did not you, who gave me part of Life,
...se my Father stronger in my Veins?
...when you kept me coop'd within your Womb,
...pall'd his generous Blood with the dull Mixture

Of

Of your *Italian* Food, and milk'd slow Arts
Of Womanish Tameness in my Infant Mouth;
Why stood I stupid else, and miss'd a Blow,
Which Heav'n and daring Folly made so fair.

*Q. M* I still maintain 'twas wisely done to spare hi

*Grill* A pox o'this unseasonable Wisdom;
He was a Fool to come; if so, then they
Who let him go, were somewhat

*King* Th' Event, th' Event will shew us what we w
For like a blazing Meteor hence he shot,
And drew a sweeping Fiery Train along.
O *Paris*, *Paris*, once my Seat of Triumph;
But now the Scene of all thy King's Misfortunes,
Ungrateful, Perjur'd, and Disloyal Town,
Which by my Royal Presence I have warm'd
So long, that now the Serpent hisses out,
And shakes his forked Tongue at Majesty.
While I——

*Q. M.* While you lose time in idle Talk,
And use no means for Safety and Prevention.

*King* What can I do! O Mother, *Abbot*, *Grillon*
All dumb! nay, then 'tis plain my Cause is desperat
Such an o'er-whelming Ill makes Grief a Fool,
As if Redress were past

*Grill* I ll go to the next Sheriff,
And beg the first Reversion of a Rope;
Dispatch is all my business, I'll hang for you.

*Abb.* 'Tis not so bad, as vainly you surmise,
Some space there is, some little space, some steps
Betwixt our Fate and us, our Foes are powerful,
But yet not arm'd, nor martiall'd into Order,
Believe it, Sir, the *Guise* will not attempt,
'Till he have rowl'd his Snow-ball to a heap.

*King* So then, my Lord, we're a Day off from D
What shall to-morrow do?

*Abb* To-morrow, Sir,
If Hours between slide not too idle by,
You may be Master of their Destiny,
Who now dispose so loftily of yours.
Not far without the Suburbs there are quarter'd

T

hree thousand *Swisse*, and two *French* Regiments.
*King* Wou'd they were here, and I were at their Head.
*Q M* Send Mareschal *Byron* to lead 'em up
*King* It shall be so, by Heav'n there's Life in this,
he wrack of Clouds is driving on the Winds,
d shows a break of Sun-shine.
, *Grillon*, give my Orders to *Byron*,
d see your Soldiers well dispos'd within,
r safeguard of the *Louvre*.
*Q M* One thing more,
e *Guise* (his bus'ness not yet fully ripe)
'treat at least for show of Loyalty;
, him be met with the same Arts he brings.
*King* I know he'll make exorbitant Demands,
here your part of me will come in play,
'*Italian* Soul shall teach me how to sooth:
n *Jove* must flatter with an empty Hand,
time to thunder, when he gripes the Brand. [*Ex.*

*A Night* SCENE

*Enter* Malicorn *solus*

*Mal* Thus far the Cause of God. But God's or Devil's,
ean my Master's Cause, and mine succeed:
at shall the *Guise* do next? [*A flash of Lightning.*

*Enter the Spirit* Melanax.

*Mel* First seize the King, and after murder him
*Mal* Officious Fiend, thou com'st uncall'd to Night.
*Mel* Always uncall'd, and still at hand for Mischief.
*Mal* ——But why in this Fanatick Habit, Devil?
u look'st like one that preaches to the Crowd,
pel is in thy Face, and outward Garb,
Treason on thy Tongue.
*Mel.* Thou hast me right,
thousand Devils more are in this Habit,
ship and Zeal are still our best disguise·
mix unknown with the hot thoughtless Crowd,
quoting Scriptures, which too well we know,
h impious Glosses ban the holy Text,
make it speak Rebellion, Schism, Murder,
urn the Arms of Heav'n against it self.
*Mal.* What makes the Curate of St. *Eustace* here?
*Mel.* Thou art mistaken, Master, 'tis not he,

But 'tis a zealous, godly, canting Devil,
Who has aſſum'd the Churchman's lucky Shape,
To talk the Croud to Madneſs and Rebellion.
*Mal.* O true Enthuſiaſtick Devil, true;
For lying is thy Nature, even to me
Didſt thou not tell me, if my Lord the *Guiſe*
Enter'd the Court, his Head ſhou'd then lie low?
That was a Lye, he went, and is return'd.
*Mel* 'Tis falſe; I ſaid, perhaps it ſhould lie low,
And, but I chill'd the Blood in *Henry*'s Veins,
And cram'd a thouſand ghaſtly, frightful Thoughts,
Nay, thruſt 'em foremoſt in his lab'ring Brain,
Even ſo it wou'd have been.
*Mal* Thou haſt deſerv'd me,
And I am thine, dear Devil; what do we next?
*Mel.* I ſaid, Firſt ſeize the King.
*Mal.* Suppoſe it done,
He's clapt within a Convent, ſhorn a Saint,
My Maſter mounts the Throne.
*Mel* Not ſo faſt, *Malicorn*;
Thy Maſter mounts not, till the King be ſlain.
*Mal* Not when depos'd?
*Mel* He cannot be depos'd.
He may be kill'd, a violent Fate attends him;
But at his Birth there ſhone a Regal Star.
*Mal.* My Maſter had a ſtronger.
*Mel.* No, not a ſtronger, but more Popular!
Their Births were full oppos'd, the *Guiſe* now ſtrong
But if th' ill Influence paſs o'er *Harry*'s Head,
As in a Year it will, *France* ne'er ſhall boaſt
A greater King than he, now cut him off,
While yet his Sars are weak
*Mal.* Thou talk'ſt of Stars·
Canſt thou not ſee more deep into Events,
And by a ſurer way?
*Mel* No, *Malicorne*,
The ways of Heav'n are broken ſince our Fall,
Gulph, beyond Gulph, and never to be ſhot·
Once we cou'd read our mighty Maker's Mind,
As in a Chryſtal Mirror, ſee th' Idea's

Of things that always are, as he is always.
Now shut below in this dark Sphere,
By Second Causes dimly we may guess,
And peep far off on Heav'ns revolving Orbs,
Which cast obscure Reflections from the Throne.
*Mal.* Then tell me thy Surmises of the future.
*Mel.* I took the Revolution of the Year,
Just when the Sun was entering the Ram:
Th' ascending Scorpion poison'd all the Sky,
A sign of deep Deceit and Treachery.
Full on his Cusp his angry Master sate,
Conjoyn'd with *Saturn*, baleful both to Man:
Of secret Slaughters, Empires overturn'd,
Strife, Blood, and Massacres expect to hear,
And all th' Events of an ill-omen'd Year.
*Mal.* Then flourish Hell, and mighty Mischief reign,
Mischief to some, to others must be good;
But hark, for now tho' 'tis the dead of Night,
When Silence broods upon our darkned World,
Methinks I hear a murmuring hollow Sound,
Like the deaf Chimes of Bells in Steeples touch'd.
*Mel.* 'Tis truly guess'd.
Know, 'tis from no nightly Sexton's hand,
There's not a damned Ghost, nor Hell-born Fiend,
That can from Limbo scape, but hither flies,
With leathern Wings they beat the dusky Skies.
To sacred Churches all in swarms repair,
Some crowd the Spires, but most the hallow'd Bells,
And softly Toll for Souls departing Knells;
Each Chime thou hear'st, a future Death foretells.
Now there they perch to have 'em in their Eyes,
Who shall go loaded to the Neather Skies.
*Mal.* To-morrow then.
*Mel.* To-morrow let it be:
If thou deceiv'st those hungry, gaping Fiends,
Then *Beelzebub* will rage.
*Mal.* Why *Beelzebub*? hast thou not often said,
That *Lucifer*'s your King?
*Mel.* I told thee true:
But *Lucifer*, as he who foremost fell,

So now lies lowest in th' Abyss of Hell.
Chain'd till the dreadful Doom, in place of whom
Sits *Beelzebub*, Vicegerent of the damn'd,
Who listning downward hears his roaring Lord,
And executes his Purpose· But no more,
The Morning creeps behind yon Eastern Hill;
And now the Guard is mine, todrive the Elves
And foolish Fairies from their Moon-light Play,
And lash the Laggers from the sight of Day. [*Desc*

*Enter* Guise, Mayenne, Cardinal, *and* Archbishop

*May* Sullen, methinks, and slow the Morning bre
As if the Sun were listless to appear,
And dark designs hung heavy on the Day.

*Gui.* Y are an old Man too soon, y'are superstitio
I'll trust my Stars, I know 'em now by proof,
The Genius of the King bends under mine
Inviron'd with his Guards, he durst not touch me
But aw'd and craven'd as he had been spell'd,
Would have pronounc'd, Go kill the *Guise*, and durs

*Card.* We have him in our power, coopt in his C
Who leads the first Attack? Now by yon Heav'n
That blushes at my Scarlet Robes, I'll doff
This Womanish Attire of Godly Peace,
And cry, Lie there, Lord *Cardinal* of *Guise*.

*Gui* As much too hot, as *Mayenne* too cool,
But 'tis the manlier Fault o'th' two.

*Arcbb* Have you not heard the King, preventing
Receiv'd the Guards into the City Gates,
The jolly *Swisses* marching to their Fifes?
The Crowd stood gaping, heartless, and amaz'd,
Shrunk to their Shops, and left the Passage free.

*Gui.* I would it should be so, 'twas a good hon
First let 'em fear for Rapes, and ransack'd Houses
That very fright, when I appear to head 'em,
Will harden their soft City Courages:
Cold Burghers must be struck, and struck like Fli
Ere their hid Fire will sparkle.

*Arcbb.* I am glad the King has introduc'd these G

*Car.* Your Reason

*Arcbb.* They are too few for us to fear,

Our Numbers in old martial Men are more,
The City not cast in, but the pretence
That hither they are brought to bridle *Paris*,
Will make this rising pass for just defence.

*May*. Suppose the City should not rise

*Gui*. Suppose as well the Sun should never rise:
He may not rise, for Heav'n may play a trick,
But he has risen from *Adam*'s time to ours.
Is nothing to be left to Noble Hazard?
No Venture made, but all dull Certainty;
By Heav'n I'll tug with *Harry* for a Crown,
Rather than have it on tame terms of yielding.
I scorn to poach for Power.

*Enter a Servant, who whispers* Guise.

A Lady, say'st thou, Young, and Beautiful,
Brought in a Chair?
Conduct her in———— [*Exit Serv.*

*Card* You wou'd be left alone?

*Gui* I wou'd Retire.

*Re-enter Servant with* Marmoutier, *and Exit*

Is't possible, I dare not trust my Eyes [*Starting back.*
You are not *Marmoutier*!

*Mar*. What am I then?

*Gui* Why, any thing but she·
What should the Mistress of a King do here?

*Mar* Find him, who wou'd be Master of a King.

*Gui* I sent not for you, Madam.

*Mar* I think, my Lord, the King sent not for you.

*Gui* Do you not fear your Visit will be known?

*Mar* Fear is for guilty Men, Rebels and Traytors;
Where-e'er I go, my Virtue is my Guard.

*Gui* What Devil has sent thee here to plague my Soul?
O that I cou'd detest thee now as much
As ever I have lov'd, nay, even as much
As yet in spight of all thy Crimes I love:
But 'tis a Love so mixt with dark Despair,
The Smoke and Soot smother the rising Flame,
And make my Soul a Furnace: Woman, Woman,
What can I call thee more? if Devil, 'twere less.
But thine's a Race was never got by *Adam*,

But *Eve* play'd false, engend'ring with the Serpent,
Her own part worse than his.

*Mar* Then they got Traytors.

*Gui* Yes, Angel-Traytors, fit to shine in Palaces,
Fork'd into ills, and split into deceits;
Two in their very frame, 'twas well, 'twas well,
I saw not thee at Court, thou Basilisk;
For if I had, those Eyes, without his Guards,
Had done the Tyrant's work.

*Mar* Why then, it seems,
I was not false in all; I told you, *Guise*,
If you left *Paris*, I wou'd go to Court:
You see I kept my Promise.

*Gui* Still thy Sex.
Once true in all thy Life, and that for Mischief.

*Mar* Have I said I lov'd you?

*Gui* Stab on, Stab,
'Tis plain you love the King

*Mar* Nor him, nor you,
In that unlawful way you seem to mean.
My Eyes had once so far betray'd my Heart,
As to distinguish you from common Men,
Whate'er you said, or did, was Charming all

*Gui* But yet, it seems, you found a King more Charmin

*Mar.* I do not say more Charming, but more Nob
More truly Royal, more a King in Soul,
Than you are now in Wishes.

*Gui.* May be so.
But Love has oyl'd your Tongue to run so glib,
Curse on your Eloquence.

*Mar.* Curse not that Eloquence, that sav'd your Li
For when your wild Ambition, which defy'd
A Royal Mandat, hurried you to Town,
When over-weening Pride of Popular Power,
Had thrust you headlong in the *Louvre* Toils,
Then had you dy'd. For know, my haughty Lord,
Had I not been, offended Majesty
Had doom'd you to the Death you well deserv'd

*Gui.* Then was't not *Henry*'s Fear preserv d my Li

*Mar.* You know him better, or you ought to know hi

H

He's born to give you Fear, not to receive it.

*Gui* Say this again, but add you gave not up
Your Honour as the Ransom of my Life;
For if you did, 'twere better I had dy'd

*Mar.* And so it were.

*Gui* Why said you, So it were?
For tho' 'tis true, methinks 'tis much unkind

*Mar.* My Lord, we are not now to talk of Kindness,
If you acknowledge I have sav'd your Life,
Be grateful in return, and do an Act
Your Honour, though unask'd by me, requires.

*Gui* By Heav'n, and you whom next to Heav'n I love,
(If I said more, I fear I should not lie,)
I'll do whate'er my Honour will permit.

*Mar* Go throw your self at *Henry*'s Royal Feet,
And rise not, 'till approv'd a Loyal Subject

*Gui.* A duteous Loyal Subject I was ever.

*Mar.* I'll put it short, my Lord, depart from *Paris.*

*Gui.* I cannot leave
My Country, Friends, Religion, all at stake,
Be wise, and be before-hand with your Fortune;
Prevent the turn, forsake the ruin'd Court,
Stay here, and make a Merit of your Love.

*Mar* No, I'll return, and perish in those Ruins,
I find thee now, Ambitious, faithless *Guise*
Farewel the basest, and the last of Men

*Gui.* Stay or---O Heav'n! I'll force you Stay——

*Mar* I do believe
So ill of you, so villainously ill
That if you durst you would
Honour you've little, Honesty you've less;
But Conscience you have none.
Yet there's a thing call'd Fame, and Mens Esteem,
Preserves me from your force, once more Farewel·
Look on me *Guise*, thou seest me now the last,
Tho' Treason urge not Thunder on thy Head,
This one departing Glance shall flash thee dead. [*Ex.*

*Gui* Ha, said she true? have I so little Honour?
Why then a Prize so easie, and so fair,
Had never scap'd my Gripe, but mine she is,

For that's ſet down as ſure as *Harry*'s Fall:
But my Ambition, that ſhe calls my Crime:
Falſe, falſe, by Fate, my Right was born with me,
And Heav'n confeſt it in my very Frame,
The Fires that would have form'd ten thouſand Ange
Were cram'd together for my ſingle Soul.

*Enter* Malicorne.

*Mal.* My Lord, you trifle precious hours away,
The Heav'ns' look gaudily upon your Greatneſs,
And the crown'd Moments court you as they fly,
*Briſack* and fierce *Aumale* have pent the *Swiſſe*,
And folded 'em like Sheep in holy Ground,
Where now with order'd Pikes, and Colours furl'd,
They wait the Word that dooms 'em all to die·
Come forth and bleſs the Triumph of the day.

*Gui.* So ſlight a Victory requir'd not me:
I but ſate ſtill, and nodded like a God
My World into Creation; now tis time
To walk abroad, and careleſly ſurvey
How the dull Matter does the form obey.

[*Exit with* Malicor

*Enter Citizens, and* Melanax *in his Fanatick Habit at the Head of 'em.*

*Mel.* Hold, hold a little, Fellow-Citizens, and Gentlemen of the Rabble, a word of Godly Exhor tion to ſtrengthen your hands, ere you give the On

1 *Cit* Is this a time to make Sermons? I wou'd hear the Devil now, tho' he ſhould come in God's na to Preach Peace to us.

2 *Cit* Look you, Gentlemen, Sermons are not to deſpis'd, we have all profited by godly Sermons t promote Sedition, Let the Precious Man Hold forth

*Omnes.* Let him Hold forth, let him Hold forth.

*Mel* To promote Sedition is my Buſineſs· It been ſo before any of you were born, and will be when you are all dead and damn'd; I have led on Rabble in all Ages.

1 *Cit* That's a Lye, and a loud one. He has led Rabble both Old and Young, that's all Ages: A heav ſweet Man, I warrant him, I have ſeen him ſomewh in a Pulpit.

M

*Mel* I've ſown Rebellion every where.

1 *Cit.* How every where? That's another Lye How have you travell'd, Friend?

*Mel.* Over all the World.

1 *Cit* Now that's a Rapper

2 *Cit.* I ſay, No· For, look you Gentlemen, if he has [...]n a Traveller, he certainly ſays true, for he may lye Authority.

*Mel* That the Rabble may depoſe their Prince, has [...]ll Times, and in all Countries, been accounted Lawful.

1 *Cit.* That's the firſt true Syllable he has utter'd: [...]t as how, and whereby, and when may they depoſe [...]n?

*Mel.* Whenever they have more Power to Depoſe, [...]n he has to Oppoſe, and this they may do upon the [...]ſt occaſion.

1 *Cit* Sirrah, you mince the Matter; you ſhould ſay, [...] may do it upon no occaſion, for the leſs the better.

*Mel.* *Aſide.* Here's a Rogue now will out-ſhoot the [...]vil in his own Bow

[...] *Cit.* Some Occaſion, in my mind, were not amiſs: [...], look you Gentlemen, if we have no occaſion, then [...]ereby we have no occaſion to depoſe him, and [...]refore either Religion or Liberty, I ſtick to thoſe [...]aſions: For when they are gone, Good-night to [...]dlineſs, and Freedom.

*Mel* When the moſt are of one Side, as that's our [...]e, we are always in the Right; for they that are in [...]wer will ever be the Judges So that if we ſay, White [...]lack, poor White muſt loſe the Cauſe, and put on [...]urning, for White is but a Single Syllable, and we [...]a whole Sentence· Therefore go on boldly, and lay [...]reſolutely, for your Solemn League and Covenant, [...] if here be any ſqueamiſh Conſcience who fears to [...]t againſt the King, though I that have known you [...]izens theſe Thouſand Years ſuſpect not any, let ſuch [...]erſtand, That his Majeſty's Politick Capacity is to be [...]nguiſh'd from his Natural; and though you murder [...] in one, you may preſerve him in the other; and ſo [...]ch for this time, becauſe the Enemy is at hand

2 *Cit* [*Looking out*] Look you, Gentlemen, 'tis *Grillo*
the fierce Colonel, he that devours our Wives, and ra
vishes our Childern

1 *Cit.* He looks so grum, I don't care to have to d
with him; wou'd I were safe in my Shop behind th
Counter.

2 *Cit.* And wou'd I were under my Wife's Petticoats
Look you, Gentlemen.

*Mel* You, Neighbour, behind your Counter Yester
day, paid a Bill of Exchange in Glass *Lousdors*, an
you, Friend, that cry, Look you Gentlemen, this ver
Morning was under another Woman's Petticoats, an
not your Wife's

2 *Cit.* How the Devil does he know this?

*Mel* Therefore fight lustily for the Cause of Heav'n
and to make even Tallies for your Sins, which th
you may do with a better Conscience, I absolve yo
both, and all the rest of you Now go on merrily, fo
those that escape shall avoid killing, and those who d
not escape, I will provide for in another World

[*Cry within on the other Side of the Stage*, Viv
le Roy, Vive le Roy

*Enter* Grillon, *and his Party*

*Grill.* Come on, Fellow-Soldiers, *Commilitones*, that
my Word, as 'twas *Julius Cæsar*'s of *Pagan* Memory
'fore God I am no Speech-maker, but there are th
Rogues, and here's Bilbo, that's a Word and a Blow
we must either cut their Throats, or they cut ou
that's pure Necessity for your comfort: Now if a
Man can be so unkind to his own Body, for I medd
not with your Souls, as to stand still like a good Christia
and offer his Weeson to a Butcher's Whittle, I say
more, but that he may be sav'd, and that's the b
can come on him.

[*Cry on both Sides*, Vive le Roy, Vive Guise *They Fig*

*Mel.* Hey for the Duke of *Guise* and Property,
with Religion and the Cause, and down with th
Arbitrary Rogues there Stand to't, you Associat
Cuckolds. [*Citizens go ba*

Rogues, O Cowards, Damn these half-strain'd Shop-keepers, got between Gentlemen and City-Wives, how naturally they quake, and run away from their own Fathers? twenty Souls a Penny were a dear Bargain of 'em

*They all run off*, Melanax *with them, the* 1 *and* 2 *Cit taken.*

*Grill.* Possess your selves of the Place, *Maubert*, And hang me up those two Rogues for an Example.

1 *Cit.* O spare me, sweet Colonel, I am but a young Beginner, and new set up.

*Grill.* I'll be your Customer, and set you up a little better, Sirrah,
Go hang him at the next Sign-post·
What have you to say for your self, Scoundrel?
Why were you a Rebel?

2 *Cit.* Look you, Colonel, 'twas out of no ill Meaning to the Government, all that I did, was pure Obedience to my Wife.

*Grill.* Nay, if thou hast a Wife that wears the Breeches,
Thou shalt be condemn'd to live.
Get thee home for a Hen-peck'd Traitor———
What, are we encompass'd? Nay, then Faces this way;
We'll sell our Skins to the fairest Chapmen.

*Enter* Aumale *and Soldiers on the one Side, Citizens on the other.* Grillon *and his Party are disarm'd.*

1 *Cit* Bear away that bloody-minded Colonel,
And hang him up at the next Sign-post:
Sir, when I am in Power, I can make Examples too.

*Omnes* Tear him piece-meal, tear him piece-meal. [*Pull and hale him.*

*Grill.* Rogues, Villains, Rebels, Traitors, Cuckolds, Zounds what do you make of a Man? Do you think Legs and Arms are strung upon a Wire, like a Jointed-Baby?
Carry me off quickly, you were best, and hang me decently, according to my first Sentence.

2 *Cit* Look you, Colonel, you are too bulky to be carried off all at once, a Leg or an Arm is one Man's Burden. Give me a little Finger for a Sample of him, whereby

whereby I'll carry it for a Token to my Sovereign Lady

*Grill.* 'Tis too little, in all Conſcience, for her; Take a bigger Token, Cuckold. *Et tu Brute* whom I ſav'd O the Conſcience of a Shop keeper!

2 *Cit.* Look you, Colonel, for your ſaving me, I thank you heartily, whereby that Debt's paid, but for your ſpeaking Treaſon againſt my anointed Wife, that's new Reckoning between us.

*Enter* Guiſe *with a General's Staff in his Hand*, Mayenne, *Cardinal*, *Archbiſhop*, Malicorn, *and Attendants*

*Omnes.* Vive *Guiſe*.

*Gui.* I thank you Country-men, the Hand of Heav'n [*Bowing and Bareheaded*
In all our Safeties has appear'd this Day,
Stand on your Guard, and double every Watch,
But ſtain your Triumph with no Chriſtian Blood,
*French* we are all, and Brothers of a Land.

*Card* What mean you, Brother, by this Godly Talk
Of ſparing Chriſtian Blood? why theſe are Dogs;
Now by the Sword that cut off *Malchus* Ear,
Meer Dogs that neither can be ſav'd nor damn'd.

*Archb* Where have you learnt to ſpare inveterate Foes

*Gui.* You know the Book.

*Archb.* And can expound it too·
But Chriſtian Faith was in the Nonage then,
And *Roman* Heathens lorded o'er the World;
What Madneſs were it for the Weak and Few,
To fight againſt the Many and the Strong?
*Grillon* muſt die, ſo muſt the Tyrant's Guards,
Leſt gathering Head again, they make more Work

*Mal.* My Lord, the People muſt be fleſh'd in Blood
To teach 'em the true Reliſh, dip 'em with you—
Or they'll perhaps repent

*Gui.* You are Fools, to kill'em were to ſhew I fear'd 'em
The Court diſarm'd, diſheartned, and beſieg'd,
Are all as much within my Power, as if
I grip'd 'em in my Fiſt.

*May.* 'Tis rightly judg'd:
And let me add, who heads a Popular Cauſe,
Muſt proſecute that Cauſe by Popular Ways:

, whether you are merciful or no,
ou must affect to be.

*Gui.* Dismiss those Prisoners; *Grillon*, you are free,
do not ask your Love, be still my Foe

*Grill.* I will be so: But let me tell you, *Guise*,
this was greatly done, 'twas proudly too;
ll give you back your Life when next we meet,
ill then I am your Debtor

*Gui* That's till Dooms-Day.

[Grillon *and his Exeunt one way, Rabble the other.*

lise, Brother, draw out fifteen thousand Men,
round the *Louvre*, lest the Prey should 'scape.
know the King will send to treat,
e'll set the Dice on him in high Demands,
o less than all his Offices of Trust,
shall be par'd, and canton'd out, and clipt,
long he shall not pass.

*Card* What do we talk
paring, clipping, and such tedious Work,
e those that hang their Noses o'er a Potion,
d Qualm, and Keck, and take it down by Sips?

*Archb.* Best make advantage of this Popular Rage,
in th'o'erwhelming Tide on *Harry*'s Head.
that promiscuous Fury who shall know,
ong a thousand Swords, who kill d the King.

*Mal.* O my dear Lord, upon this only Day
ends the Series of your following Fate:
ink your good Genius has assum'd my Shape
this prophetick Doom

*Gui* Peace, croaking Raven,
seize him first, then make him a led Monarch;
be declar'd Lieutenant-General
idst the three Estates that represent
glorious, full, majestick Face of *France*,
ich in his own despight the King shall call:
et him Reign my Tenant during Life,
Brother of *Navarre* shut out for ever,
ded with Heresie, and barr'd from Sway,
t when *Valois* consum'd in Ashes lies,
*Phœnix* Race of *Charlemain* may rise. [*Exeunt.*

SCENE

## SCENE *The Louvre.*

*Enter* King, Queen-Mother, Abbot, Grillon

*King* Dismist with such Contempt?
*Grill* Yes, Faith, we past like beaten *Romans* und
neath the Fork.
*King* Give me my Arms.
*Grill.* For what?
*King* I'll lead you on.
*Grill* You are a true Lion, but my Men are Shee
If you run first, I'll swear they'll follow you
*King* What, all turn'd Cowards? Not a Man in *Fra*
Dares set his Foot by mine, and perish by me.
*Grill.* Troth I cant find 'em much inclin'd to perish
*King* What can be left in danger, but to dare?
No matter for my Arms, I'll go bare-fac'd,
And seize the first bold Rebel that I meet
*Ab.* There's something of Divinity in Kings
That sits between their Eyes, and guards their Liv
*Grill.* True, *Abbot*, but the Mischief is, you Chur
Can see that something further than the Crowd, [n
These Musquet Bullets have not read much Logick,
Nor are they given to make your nice Distinctions
[*One Enters, and gives the Queen a Note, she re*
One of 'em possibly may hit the King
In some one part of him that's not Divine;
And so the mortal part of his Majesty wou'd draw
The Divinity of it into another World, sweet Abb
*Q. M.* 'Tis equal Madness to go out or stay,
The Reverence due to Kings is all transferr'd
To haughty *Guise*, and when new Gods are made,
The old must quit the Temple; you must fly.
*King* Death, had I Wings, yet I would scorn to
*Grill* Wings, or no Wings, is not the Questior
If you won't fly for't, you must ride for't,
And that comes much to one.
*King* Forsage my regal Town!
*Q M* Forsake a Bedlam:

[Th]is Note informs me, Fifteen thousand Men
[Ar]e marching to enclose the *Louvre* round.

*Alb.* The Business then admits no more dispute;
[Y]ou, Madam, must be pleas'd to find the *Guise*,
[S]eem easie, fearful, yielding, what you will,
[Bu]t still prolong the Treaty all you can,
[T]o gain the King more time for his Escape.

*Q. M.* I'll undertake it——Nay, no thanks, my Son,
[M]y Blessing shall be given in your Deliverance;
[Th]at once perform'd, their Web is all unravel'd,
[An]d *Guise* is to begin his Work again. [*Exit Q. M.*

*King* I go this Minute.

*Enter* Marmoutier.

[Na]y then, another Minute must be given.
[O] how I blush, that thou shouldst see thy King
[D]o this low Act that lessens all his Fame.
[De]ath, must a Rebel force me from my Love!
[Bu]t must be——

*Mar* It must not, cannot be.

*Grill* No, nor shall not Wench, as long as my Soul wears a Body.

*King* Secure in that, I'll trust thee, Shall I trust thee?
[Th]e Conquerors have Charms, and Women Frailty:
[Far]ewel, thou may'st behold me King again,
[M]y Soul's not yet depos'd, why then Farewel,
[Sa]y't as comfortably as I can:
[B]ut O curs'd *Guise*, for pressing on my Time,
[An]d cutting off Ten thousand more Adieus.

*Mar* The Moments that retard your Flight are Traytors.
[Ma]ke haste my Royal Master to be safe,
[An]d save me with you, for I'll share your Fate.

*King* Wilt thou go too?

[Th]en I am reconcil'd to Heav'n again.
[W]elcome thou good Angel of my Way,
[Th]ou Pledge and Omen of my safe Return;
[No]t *Greece*, nor hostile *Juno* cou'd destroy
[Th]e Hero that abandon'd burning *Troy*,
[E]scap'd the Dangers of the dreadful Night,
[Wh]en loaded with his Gods he took his Flight
[*Ex. King, leading her.*

ACT

# ACT V. SCENE I.

## SCENE The Castle of Blois.

*Enter* Grillon, *and* Alphonso Corso.

*Grill* WElcome, Colonel, welcome to *Blois*.
*Alph* Since last we parted at the Barricad
The World's turn'd upside down
*Grill* No, Faith, 'tis better, now 'tis downside u
Our part o'th' the Wheel is rising, tho' but slowly,
*Alph.* Who look'd for an Assembly of the States
*Grill.* When the King was escaped from *Paris*, got out of the Toils, 'twas time for the *Guise* to 'em down, and pitch others: That is, to treat for Calling of a Parliament, where being sure of the jor part, he might get by Law, what he had m by Force.
*Alph* But why should the King assemble the St to satisfie the *Guise* after so many Affronts?
*Grill.* For the same Reason that a Man in a Duel he has received Satisfaction, when he is first Woun and afterwards disarm'd.
*Alph.* But why this Parliament at *Blois* and not at P
*Grill* Because no Barricado's have been made at B
This *Blois* is a very little Town, and the King can it after him.
But *Paris* is a damn'd unweildly Bulk, and when Preachers draw against the King, a Parson in a P is a Devillish Fore-horse.
Besides, I found in that Insurrection, what dang Beasts these Townsmen are; I tell you, Colonel, a had better deal with Ten of their Wives, than with Zealous Citizen:
O your inspir'd Cuckold is most inplacable.
*Alph.* Is there any seeming kindness between the and the Duke of *Guise*?
*Grill* Yes most wonderful: They are as dear to another, as an old Usurer, and a rich young Heir

Mortgage The King is very Loyal to the *Guise*, and the *Guise* is very gracious to the King: Then the Cardinal of *Guise*, and the Archbishop of *Lions*, are the Two Perdants, that are always hanging at the Royal Ear · They ease his Majesty of all the Spiritual Business, and the *Guise* of all the Temporal, so that the King is certainly the happiest Prince in *Christendom*, without any Care upon him: So yielding up every thing to his Loyal Subjects, that he's infallibly in the way of being the greatest and most Glorious King in all the World.

*Alph.* Yet I have heard, he made a sharp reflecting Speech upon their Party at the opening of the Parliament, admonish'd Men of their Duties, pardon'd what was past, but seem'd to threaten Vengeance if they persisted for the future.

*Grill* Yes, and then they all took the Sacrament together · He promising to unite himself to them, and they to obey him, according to the Laws; yet the very next Morning they went on, in pursuance of their old Common-wealth Designs, as violently as ever.

*Alph.* Now I am dull enough to think they have broken their Oaths.

*Grill* Ay but you are but one private Man, and they are the Three States, and if they Vote that they have not broken their Oaths, who is to be Judge?

*Alph.* There's one above.

*Grill* I hope you mean in Heav'n, or else you are a bolder Man than I am in Parliament-time, but here comes the Master, and my Neice.

*Alph.* Heav'n preserve him, if a Man may pray for him without Treason

*Grill.* O yes, you may pray for him; the Preachers on the *Guise*'s side do that most formally: Nay, you may be suffer'd civilly to drink his Health, be of the Court, and keep a Place of Profit under him: For, in short, 'tis a judg'd Case of Conscience, to make your Profit of the King, and to side against him.

*Enter* King *and* Marmoutier.

*King.* *Grillon*, be near me,
There's something for my Service to be done,

Your

Your Orders will be ſudden, now withdraw.

*Grill aside* Well, I dare truſt my Neice, even thoug ſhe comes of my own Family; but if ſhe Cuckolds m good Opinion of her Honeſty, there's a whole Sex fall under a general Rule without one Exception.

[*Exeunt* Grill *and* Alp

*Mar.* You bid my Uncle wait you.

*King* Yes

*Mar.* This Hour.

*King* I think it was.

*Mar.* Something of Moment hangs upon this Hour

*King* Not more on this, than on the next and nex
My time is all ta'en up on Uſury;
I never am before-hand with my Hours,
But every one has work before it comes

*Mar.* There's ſomething for my Service to be don
Thoſe were your Words.

*King.* And you deſire their Meaning.

*Mar.* I dare not ask, and yet perhaps may gueſs.

*King* 'Tis ſearching there where Heav'n can only p
Not Man, who knows not Man but by ſurmiſe;
Nor Devils, nor Angels of a purer Mould,
Can trace the winding Labyrinths of Thought.
I tell thee, *Marmoutier*, I never ſpeak
Not when alone, for fear ſome Fiend ſhould hear,
And blab my Secrets out.

*Mar.* You hate the *Guiſe*

*King* True, I did hate him.

*Mar.* And you hate him ſtill.

*King.* I am reconcil'd.

*Mar* Your Spirt is too high;
Great Souls forgive not Injuries, till Time
Has put their Enemies into their Power,
That they may ſhew Forgiveneſs is their own;
For elſe 'tis fear to puniſh that forgives·
The Coward, not the King.

*King* He has ſubmitted.

*Mar* In ſhow, for in effect he ſtill inſults.

*King.* Well, Kings muſt bear ſometimes.

*Mar.* They muſt, till they can ſhake their Burden

nd that's, I think, your aim.

*King.* Mistaken still.
ll Favours, all Preferments, pass through them,
m pliant, and they mould me as they please.

*Mar.* These are your Arts to make 'em more secure,
ust so your Brother us'd the Admiral.
rothers may think, and act like Brothers too.

*King* What said you, ha! what mean you, *Marmoutier*?

*Mar* Nay, what mean you? That Start betray'd you, Sir.

*King* This is no Vigil of St. *Bartholomew*.
or is *Blo's Paris*.

*Mar.* 'Tis an open Town.

*King* What then?

*Mar.* Where you are strongest.

*King.* Well, what then?

*Mar.* No more, but you have Power, and are pro- [vok'd.

*King* O! thou hast set thy Foot upon a Snake,
t quickly off, or it will sting thee dead.

*Mar* Can I unknow it?

*King* No, but keep it secret.

*Mar.* Think, Sir, your Thoughts are still as much your [own,
when you kept the Key of your own Breast:
t since you let me in, I find it fill'd
ith Death and Horror; you would murder *Guise*.

*King.* Murder! what Murder! use a softer Word,
d call it Sovereign Justice.

*Mar.* Wou'd I cou'd:
Justice bears the Godlike shape of Law,
d Law requires Defence, an equal Plea
wixt th' Offender, and the Righteous Judge.

*King* Yes, when th' Offender can be judg'd by Laws,
when his Greatness overturns the Scales,
n Kings are Justice in the last Appeal,
d forc'd by strong Necessity may strike:
which indeed they assert the Publick Good,
like sworn Surgeons, lop the gangreen'd Limb:
pleasant wholsom Work.

*Mar.* If this be needful.

*King* Ha, didst not thou thy self, in fathoming
depth of my Designs, drop there the Plummet?

Didst thou not say Affronts, so great, so publick,
I ne'er could forgive?

*Mar.* I did, but yet——

*King.* What means, But yet? 'Tis Evidence so full,
If the last Trumpet sounded in my Ears,
Undaunted I should meet the Saints half way,
And in the Face of Heav'n maintain the Fact.

*Mar.* Maintain it then to Heav'n, but not to me.
Do you love me?

*King.* Can you doubt it?

*Mar.* Yes, I can doubt it, if you can deny:
Love begs once more this great Offender's Life:
Can you forgive the Man you justly hate,
That hazards both your Life and Crown to spare him
One whom you may suspect I more than pity,
(For I wou'd have you see that what I ask,
I know is wond'rous difficult to grant)
Can you be thus extravagantly good?

*King.* What then? For I begin to fear my firmness
And doubt the soft destruction of your Tongue.

*Mar.* Then in return, I swear to Heav'n, and you
To give you all the preference of my Soul:
No Rebel Rival to disturb you there,
Let him but live, that he may be my Convert.

[*King walks a while, then wipes his Eyes, and spea*

*King.* You've conquer'd, all that's past shall be forgiv
My lavish Love has made a lavish Grant:
But know this Act of Grace shall be my last.
Let him repent, yes, let him well repent,
Let him desist, and tempt Revenge no farther
For by yon Heav'n, that's conscious of his Crimes,
I will no more by Mercy be betray'd.

[*Deputies appearing at the D*

The Deputies are ent'ring. You must leave me
Thus Tyrant Business all my Hours usurps,
And makes me live for others. [Re

*Mar.* Now Heav'n reward you with a prosper
And grant you never may be good in vain. [*E*

*E*

*nter Deputies of the three States, Cardinal of* Guise *and Archbishop of* Lyons *at the Head of 'em*

*King* Well, my good Lords, what Matters of Impor-
mploy'd the States this Morning? [tance
*Archb.* One high Point
as warmly canvas'd in the Commons House,
nd will be soon resolv'd
*King* What was't?
*Card* Succession.
*King* That's one high Point indeed, but not to be
warmly canvas'd, or so soon resolv'd
*Card* Things necessary must sometimes be sudden.
*King* No sudden Danger threatens you, my Lord.
*Archb.* What may be sudden, must be counted so:
e hope, and wish your Life; but Yours, and ours,
e in the Hand of Heav'n.
*King* My Lord, they are:
in a Natural way I may live long,
Heav'n and you my Loyal Subjects please.
*Archb* But since good Princes, like your Majesty,
ke care of Dangers meerly possible,
hich may concern their Subjects, whose they are,
d for whom Kings are made——
*King* Yes, we for them,
d they for us, the Benefits are mutual,
d so the Ties are too.
*Card* To cut things short,
Commons will decree to exclude *Navarre*
m the Succession of the Realm of *France*.
*King.* Decree, my Lord! What, one Estate decree!
ere then are the other two, and what am I?
Government is cast up somewhat short,
Clergy and Nobility cashier'd,
hundred popular Figures on a Row,
l my self that am, or should be King,
o'er-grown Cypher set before the Sum:
at Reasons urge our Sovereigns for th' Exclusion?
*Archb* He stands suspected, Sir, of Heresie.
*King.* Has he been call'd to make his just Defence?
*Card.* That needs not, for 'tis known.

*King* To whom?

*Card.* The Commons

*King.* What is't those Gods the Commons do not [know?

But Heresie, you Church-men teach us Vulgar,
Supposes obstinate and still persisting
In Errors prov'd, long Admonitions made,
And all rejected, has this course been us'd?

*Archb.* We grant it has not, but——

*King* Nay give me leave,
I urge from your own grant it has not been:
If then in process of a petty sum,
Both Parties having not been fully heard,
No Sentence can be giv'n·
Much less in the Succession of a Crown,
Which after my Decease, by Right Inherent,
Devolves upon my Brother of *Navarre.*

*Card.* The Right of Souls is still to be preferr'd,
Religion must not suffer for a Claim.

*King.* If Kings may be excluded, or depos'd,
Whene'er you cry Religion to the Crowd,
That Doctrine makes Rebellion Orthodox,
And Subjects must be Traytors to be sav'd.

*Archb.* Then Heresie's entail'd upon the Throne.

*King* You would entail Confusion, Wars and Slaughter
Those Ills are certain, what you name Contingent.
I know my Brother's Nature, 'tis sincere,
Above Deceit, no crookedness of Thought,
Says what he means, and what he says, performs·
Brave, but not rash, successful, but not proud
So much acknowledging, that he's uneasie,
Till every petty Service be o'er-paid.

*Archb* Some say revengeful.

*King* Some then libel him
But that's what both of us have learnt to bear.
He can forgive, but you disdain Forgiveness.
Your Chiefs are they no Libel must profane:
Honour's a Sacred thing in all but Kings;
But when your Rhimes assassinate our Fame,
You hug your nauseous, blund'ring Ballad-wits,

A

And pay 'em as if Nonsence were a Merit,
If it can mean but Treason
*Archb.* Sir, we have many Arguments to urge—
*King.* And I have more to answer, let 'em know
My Royal Brother of *Navarre* shall stand
Secure by Right, by Merit, and my Love
God, and good Men will never fail his Cause,
And all the bad shall be constrain'd by Laws.
*Archb.* Since gentle means t'exclude *Navarre* are vain,
To morrow in the States 'twill be propos'd,
To make the Duke of *Guise* Lieutenant-General;
Which Power most graciously confirm'd by you,
Will stop this headlong Torrent of Succession,
That bears Religion, Laws, and all before it.
I hope you'll not oppose what must be done.
We wish you, Sir, a long and prosperous Reign.
[*Exeunt omnes but the* King
*King.* To-morrow *Guise* is made Lieutenant-General,
Why then to-morrow I no more am King,
'Tis time to push my slacken'd Vengeance home,
To be a King, or not to be at all
The Vow that manackled my Rage is loos'd,
When Heav'n is wearied with repeated Crimes,
Till lightning flashes round to guard the Throne,
And the curb'd Thunder grumbles to be gone.
*Enter* Grillon *to him.*
*Grill.* 'Tis just the pointed hour you bid me wait.
*King.* So just, as if thou wert inspir'd to come;
As if the Guardian Angel of my Throne,
Who had o'erslept himself so many Years,
Just now was rouz'd, and brought thee to my Rescue.
*Grill.* I hear the *Guise* will be Lieutenant-General.
*King.* And canst thou suffer it?
*Grill.* Nay, if you will suffer it, then well may I
Kings will be so civil to their Subjects, to give up all
things tamely, they first turn Rebels to themselves, and
'tis a fair Example for their Friends, 'Slife Sir, 'tis a
dangerous matter to be Loyal on the wrong side, to serve
a Prince in spite of him; if you'll be a Royalist your
self, there are Millions of honest Men will fight for you;

but if you wo'nt, there are few will hang for you.

*King* No more I am resolv'd.
The course of things can be with-held no longer
From breaking forth to their appointed end.
My Vengeance, ripen'd in the womb of time,
Presses for birth, and longs to be disclos'd.
*Grillon*, the *Guise* is doom'd —— to sudden death.
The Sword must end him, Has not thine an Edge?

*Grill* Yes, and a Point too, I'll challenge him

*King* ——I bid thee kill him [*Walk*

*Grill* ——So I mean to do.

*King* ——Without thy hazard.

*Grill.* Now I understand you, I shou'd murder hi
I am your Soldier, Sir, but not your Hangman

*King* ———Dost thou not hate him?

*Grill* ——Yes.

*King* 'Hast thou not said,
That he deserves it?

*Grill* Yes, but how have I
Deserv'd to do a Murder?

*King.* 'Tis no Murder
'Tis Soveraign Justice urg'd from Self-Defence.

*Grill* 'Tis all confest, and yet I dare not do't.

*King* Go, thou art a Coward.

*Grill* You are my King

*King* Thou say'st thou dar'st not kill him.

*Grill* Were I a Coward, I had been a Villain,
And then I durst ha' don't.

*King* Thou hast done worse in thy long course of A
Hast thou ne'er kill'd a Man?

*Grill* Yes, when a Man wou'd have kill'd me

*King* Hast thou not plunder'd from the helpless P
Snatch'd from the sweating Labourer his Food?

*Grill* Sir, I have eaten and drunk in my own def
When I was hungry and thirsty
I have plunder'd,
When you have not paid me———
I have been content with a Farmer's Daughter,
When a better Whore was not to be had.
As for Cutting off a Traytor, I'll execute him law

In my own Function, when I meet him in the Field;
But for your Chamber-practice, that's not my Talent.
*King* Is my Revenge Unjust, or Tyrannous?
Heav'n knows, I love not Blood
*Grill* No, for your Mercy is your only Vice.
You may dispatch a Rebel lawfully,
But the mischief is, that Rebel
Has given me my Life at the Barricadoes,
And till I have return'd his Bribe,
I am not upon even Terms with him.
*King* Give me thy hand, I love thee not the worse.
Make much of Honour, 'tis a Soldier's Conscience.
Thou shalt not do this Act, thou'rt e'en too good;
But keep my Secret, for that's Conscience too.
*Grill.* When I disclose it, think I am a Coward.
*King* No more of that, I know thou art not one:
Call *Lognac* hither straight, and St. *Malin*,
Bid *Larchant* find some unsuspected means
To keep Guards doubled at the Council-door,
That none pass in or out, but those I call
The rest I'll think on further, so farewel.
*Grill.* Heav'n bless your Majesty! [kill'd;
Tho I'll not kill him for you, I'll defend you when he's
For the honest part of the Jobb let me alone

[*Exeunt severally*

The SCENE *opens, and discovers Men and Women at a Banquet*, Malicorn *standing by*

*Mal* This is the Solemn Annual Feast I keep,
'Tis this day Twelve Years on this very Hour
I sign'd the Contract for my Soul with Hell;
I barter'd it for Honours, Wealth, and Pleasure,
Three things which mortal Men do covet most.
And, Faith, I over-sold it to the Fiend:
What, One and twenty Years, Nine yet to come,
How can a Soul be worth so much to Devils?
O how I hug my self, to out-wit these Fools of Hell!
And yet a sudden damp, I know not why,
Has seiz'd my Spirits, and like a heavy weight
Hangs on their active Springs: I want a Song
To rouze me, my Blood freezes: Musick there!

A SONG and Dance

Shepherdess *Tell me*, Thirsis, *tell your Anguish,*
*Why you Sigh, and why you Languish,*
*When the Nymph whom you Adore,*
*Grants the Blessing of possessing.*
*What can Love and I do more?*

Shepherd. *Think it's Love beyond all measure,*
*Makes me faint away with Pleasure;*
*Strength of Cordial may destroy,*
*And the Blessing of possessing*
*Kills me with excess of Joy.*

Shepherdess Thirsis, *how can I believe you?*
*But confess, and I'll forgive you;*
*Men are false, and so are you;*
*Never Nature fram'd a Creature*
*To enjoy, and yet be true.*

Shepherd *Mine's a Flame beyond expiring,*
*Still possessing, still desiring*
*Fit for Love's Imperial Crown,*
*Ever shining, and refining,*
*Still the more 'tis melted down*

[Loud knocking at the Do

*Enter Servant*

*Mal* What Noise is that?
*Serv* An ill look'd surly Man,
With a hoarse Voice, says he must speak with you
*Mal* Tell him I dedicate this Day to Pleasure,
I neither have, nor will have Business with him [*Ex Se*
What louder yet, what sawcy Slave is this? [*Knocks loud*

*Re-enter Servant.*

*Serv* He says you have, and must have Business wi him;
Come out, or he'll come in, and spoil your Mirth.
*Mal.* I wo'nt.

Se

*Serv.* Sir, I dare not tell him so.
[*Knocks again more fiercely.*
My Hair stands up in Bristles when I see him:
The Dogs run into Corners; the Spade-Bitch
Bayes at his Back, and howls.
*Mal.* Bid him enter, and go off thy self [*Exit Serv.*
[*Scene closes upon the Company.*
*Enter* Melanax, *an Hour-glass in his hand almost empty.*
How dar'st thou interrupt my softer hours?
By Heav'n I'll ramm thee in some knotted Oak,
Where *thou shalt sigh and groan to whistling Winds*
Upon the lonely Plain. [the Sands,
Or I'll confine thee deep in the Red Sea grov'ling on
Ten thousand Billows rowling o'er thy Head.
*Mel.* Hoh, hoh, hoh.
*Mal* Laugh'st thou, malicious Fiend?
I'll ope my Book of bloody Characters,
Shall rumple up thy tender airy Limbs,
Like Parchment on a flame.
*Mel* Thou canst not do't,
Behold this Hour-glass.
*Mal* Well. and what of that?
*Mel.* See'st thou these ebbing Sands?
They run for thee, and when their Race is run,
Thy Lungs, the Bellows of thy mortal Breath,
Shall sink for ever down, and heave no more.
*Mal.* What, resty Fiend?
Nine Years thou hast to serve.
*Mel.* Not full nine Minutes.
*Mal* Thou ly'st, look on thy Bond, and view the date.
*Mel.* Then wilt thou stand to that without Appeal?
*Mal.* I will, so help me Heav'n.
*Mel* So take thee Hell. [*Gives him the Bond.*
Here, Fool, behold, who lyes, the Devil or thou?
*Mal.* Ha! One and twenty Years are shrunk to twelve.
Do my Eyes dazle?
*Mel.* No, they see too true.
They dazled once, I cast a Mist before 'em,
So what was figur'd Twelve, to thy dull sight
Appear'd full Twenty one.

*Mal.*

*Mal.* There's Equity in Heav'n for this, a Cheat.
*Mel.* Fool, thou hast quitted thy Appeal to Heav
To stand to this.
*Mal.* Then I am lost for ever
*Mel* Thou art
*Mal* O why was I not warn'd before?
*Mel.* Yes to repent, then thou hadst cheated me.
*Mal* Add but a day, but half a day, an hour:
For sixty Minutes I'll forgive nine Years
*Mel* No not a Moments Thought beyond my time
Dispatch, 'tis much below me to attend
For one poor single Fate.
*Mal* So pitiless?
But yet I may command thee, and I will:
I love the *Guise* even with my latest Breath,
Beyond my Soul, and my lost hopes of Heav'n·
I charge thee by my short-liv'd Power, disclose
What Fate attends my Master.
*Mal.* If he goes
To Council when he next is call'd, he dyes.
*Mal* Who waits?

*Enter Servant.*

Go, give my Lord my last adieu,
Say I shall never see his Eyes again·
But if he goes when next he's call'd to Council,
Bid him believe my latest breath, he dies. [*Exit S*
The Sands run yet, O do not shake the Glass
[*The Devil shakes the Gl*
I shall be thine too soon, cou'd I repent,
Heav'n's not confin'd to Moments, Mercy, Mercy.
*Mel* I see thy Prayers disperst into the Winds,
And Heav'n has puft 'em by
I was an Angel once of foremost Rank,
Stood next the shining Throne, and wink'd but ha
So almost gaz'd I Glory in the Face
That I could bear it, and star'd farther in,
'Twas but a moment's Pride, and yet I fell,
For ever fall, but Man, base Earth-born Man,
Sins past a Sum, and might be Pardon'd more·
And yet 'tis just, for we were perfect Light,

And saw our Crimes, Man in his Body's Mire,
Half-soul, Half-clod, sinks blindful into Sin,
Betray'd by Frauds without, and Lusts within.
*Mal.* Then I have hope
*Mel.* Not so, I preach'd on purpose
To make thee lose this Moment of thy Prayer,
Thy Sand creeps low, Despair, Despair, Despair.
*Mal.* Where am I now? Upon the brink of Life,
The Gulph before me, Devils to push me on,
And Heav'n behind me closing all its Doors.
A thousand Years for ev'ry Hour I've past,
O cou'd I 'scape so cheap! But Ever, Ever,
Still to begin an endless round of Woes,
To be renew'd for Pains, and last for Hell?
Yet can Pains last, when Bodies cannot last?
Can earthy Substance endless Flames endure?
Or when one Body wears, and flits away,
Do Souls thrust forth another Crust of Clay?
To fence and guard their tender Forms from Fire——
I feel my Heart-strings rend, I'm here, I'm gone:
Thus Men too careless of their future State,
Dispute, know nothing, and believe too late.
[*A Flash of Lightning, they sink together.*

*Enter Duke of* Guise, *Cardinal*, Aumale.

*Card.* A dreadful Message from a dying Man,
A Prophecy indeed!
For Souls just quitting Earth, peep into Heav'n,
Make swift Acquaintance with their Kindred Forms,
And Partners of immortal Secrets grow.
*Aum.* 'Tis good to lean on the securer side
When Life depends, the mighty Stake is such,
Fools fear too little, and they dare too much.

*Enter Archbishop*

*Guise.* You have prevail'd, I will not go to Council,
I have provok'd my Sov'raign past a Pardon,
It but remains to doubt if he dare kill me.
Then if he dares but to be just, I dye,
'Tis too much odds against me, I'll depart,
And finish Greatness at some safer time.
*Arch.* By Heav'n 'tis *Harry*'s Plot to fright you hence,
That,

That, Coward-like, you might forsake your Friends.
*Gui.* The Devil foretold it dying *Malicorne.*
*Archb.* Yes, some Court-Devil, no doubt:
If you depart, consider, good my Lord,
You are the Master-spring that move our Fabrick,
Which once remov'd, our Motion is no more.
Without your Presence, which buoys up our Hearts
The League will sink beneath a Royal Name:
Th' inevitable Yoke prepar'd for Kings,
Will soon be shaken off, things done, repeal'd;
And things undone, past future Means to do
*Card* I know not, I begin to taste his Reasons.
*Archb* Nay, were the danger certain of your stay,
An Act so mean would lose you all your Friends,
And leave you single to the Tyrant's Rage:
Then better 'tis to hazard Life alone,
Than Life, and Friends, and Reputation too.
*Gui* Since more I am confirm'd, I'll stand the shoc
Where-e'er he dares to call, I dare to go.
My Friends are many, faithful and united,
He will not venture on so rash a Deed;
And now I wonder I should fear that Force,
Which I have us'd to Conquer and Contemn

*Enter* Marmoutier

*Archb.* Your Tempter comes, perhaps, to turn the Sc
And warn you not to go.
*Gui* O fear her not,
I will be there. [*Exeunt Archbishop and Cardin*
What can she mean, Repent?
Or is it cast betwixt the King and her
To sound me? Come what will, it warms my Heart
With secret Joy, which these my ominous Statesmen
Left dead within me, Ha! she turns away.
*Mar* Do you not wonder at this Visit, Sir?
*Gui* No, Madam, I at last have gain'd the Point
Of mightiest Minds, to wonder now at nothing.
*Mar.* —Believe me *Guise*, 'twere gallantly resolv'd,
If you cou'd carry't on the inside too.
Why came that Sigh uncall'd? For Love of me
Partly perhaps, but more for thirst of Glory,

Wh

hich now again dilates it ſelf in Smiles,
if you ſcorn'd that I ſhould know your purpoſe
*Gui.* I change, 'tis true, becauſe I Love you ſtill;
e you, O Heav'n, ev'n in my own deſpight,
ll you all even at that very Moment,
now you ſtraight betray me to the King.
*Mar* O *Guiſe*, I never did, but, Sir, I come
tell you, I muſt never ſee you more.
*Gui* The King's at *Blois*, and you have reaſon for't,
refore what am I to expect from Pity,
m yours, I mean, when you behold me ſlain?
*Mar.* Firſt anſwer me, and then I'll ſpeak my Heart;
re you, O *Guiſe*, ſince your laſt ſolemn Oaths,
d firm to what you ſwore? Be plain, my Lord,
run it o'er awhile, becauſe again
l you I muſt never ſee you more.
*Gui.* Never! She's ſet on by the King to ſift me.
y by that Nerve then, all I have ſworn
rue, as that the King deſigns to end me.
*Mar.* Keep your Obedience, by the Saints you live.
*Gui* Then mark, 'tis judg'd by Heads grown white in Council,
s very Day he means to cut me off.
*Mar* By Heav'n then you're forſworn, you've broke your Vows
*Gui* ——By you, the Juſtice of the Earth, I have not.
*Mar* By you, Diſſembler of the World, you have;
ow the King
*Gui* ——I do believe you, Madam.
*Mar* ——I have try'd you both.
*Gui* -- Not me, the King you mean
*Mar* —— Do theſe o'erboiling Anſwers ſuit the *Guiſe*?
go to Council, Sir, there ſhew your truth,
u are innocent you're ſafe, but O
hou'd chance to ſee you ſtretch'd along,
r Love, O *Guiſe*, and your Ambition gone,
venerable Aſpect pale with Death,
ſt conclude you merited your End. [der.
*Gui.*——You muſt, you will, and ſmile upon my Mur-
*Mar* Therefore if you are conſcious of a Breach,
fs it to me, lead me to the King, He

He has promis'd me to conquer his Revenge,
And place you next him; therefore if you're right,
Make me not fear it by Asseverations:
But speak your Heart, and O resolve me truly.

*Gui.*——Madam, I ha' thought, and trust you with my Soul,
You saw but now my parting with my Brother,
The Prelate too of *Lyons*, 'twas debated
Warmly against me that I should go on.

*Mar.*——Did I not tell you, Sir?

*Gui.*——True, but in spight
Of those Imperial Arguments they urg'd,
I was not to be work'd from second Thought;
There we broke off, and, mark me, if I live,
You are the Saint that makes a Convert of me.

*Mar* Go then O Heav'n! why must I still suspect you
Why heaves my Heart? And why o'erflow my Eyes?
Yet if you live, O *Guise*, there, there's the Cause,
I never shall converse, nor see you more.

*Gui* O say not so, for once again I'll see you,
Were you this very Night to lodge with Angels,
Yet say not never, for I hope by Virtue
To merit Heaven, and wed you late in Glory.

*Mar* This Night, my Lord, I'm a Recluse for ever

*Gui* Ha! Stay till Morning Tapers are too dim,
Stay till the Sun rises to salute you,
Stay till I lead you to that dismal Den
Of Virgins, buried quick, and stay for ever

*Mar.* Alas! your Suit is vain, for I have vow'd it:
Nor was there any other way to clear
Th' imputed Stains of my suspected Honour

*Gui.* Hear me a Word, one Sigh, one Tear at parting
And one last Look, for, O my Earthly Saint,
I see your Face pale, as the Cherubims
At *Adam*'s Fall.

*Mar* O Heav'n! I now confess
My Heart bleeds for thee, *Guise*.

*Gui* Why, Madam, why?

*Mar.* Because by this disorder,
And that sad Fate that bodes upon your Brow,
I do believe you love me more than Glory. G

*Gui.* Without an Oath I do, therefore have Mercy,
nd think not Death cou'd make me tremble thus·
pitiful to those Infirmities
hich thus Unman me, stay till the Council's o'er;
you are pleas'd to grant an Hour or two
o my last Prayer, I'll thank you as my Saint;
you refuse me, Madam, I'll not murmur.
*Mar.* Alas, my *Guise!* O Heav'n what did I say?
t take it, take it, if it be too kind,
nour may pardon it, since it is my last.
*Gui.* O let me crawl, vile as I am, and kiss
ur sacred Robe. Is't possible, your Hand!
[*She gives him her Hand.*
hat it were my last expiring Moment,
, I shall never taste the like again.
*Mar.* Farewel, my Proselyte, your better Genius
atch your Ambition.
*Gui.* I have none but you;
st I ne'er see you more?
*Mar.* I have sworn you must not:
ich Thought thus roots me here, melts my Resolves, [*Weeps.*
d makes me loyter when the Angels call me.
*Gui.* O ye Celestial Dews! O Paradise!
Heav'n! O Joys! Ne'er to be tasted more.
*Mar.* Nay, take a little more, cold *Marmoutier*,
temperate, devoted *Marmoutier*
gone, a last Embrace I must bequeath you.
*Gui.* And O let me return it with another. [part,
*Mar.* Farewel for ever, Ah, *Guise*, though now we
he bright Orbs prepar'd us by our Fates,
r Souls shall meet---Farewel----and *Io*'s sing above,
ere no Ambition, nor State-Crime, the happier Spirits prove,
all are blest, and all enjoy an everlasting Love [*Exit* Mar.

Guise *solus*

*Gui.* Glory, where art thou? Fame, Revenge, Ambition,
here are you fled? There's Ice upon my Nerves.
Salt, my Mettal, and my Spirit's gone,

Pall'd

Pall'd as a S[illegible] that's [illegible] with an Ague,
I wish my Flesh were off— What now! Thou bleed'st
Three and no more! What not run? And why what then
But just Three Drops! And why not just Three Drops
As well as Four or Five, or Five and twenty?

*Enter Page.*

*Page* My Lord, your Brother and the Archbisho[p] wait you.

*Gui* I come; down Devil, Ha! must I stumble too
Away ye Dreams, what if I thunder'd now?
Or if a Raven cross'd me in my way,
Or now it comes, because last Night I dreamt
The Council-Hall was hung with Crimson round,
And all the Cieling plaister'd o'er with Black.
No more, blue Fires, and ye dull rowling Lakes,
Fathomless Caves, ye Dungeons of old Night,
Fantoms be gone, if I must die, I'll fall
True Politician, and defy you all.

## SCENE *The Court before the Council-Ha[ll]*

Grillon, Larchant, *Souldiers plac'd, People crowding.*

*Grill* Are your Guards doubled, Captain?

*Larch* Sir, They are

*Grill.* When the *Guise* comes, remember your Petitio[n]
Make way there for his Eminence. Give back,
Your Eminence comes late

*Enter Two Cardinals, Counsellors, the Cardinal of* Guise
*Archbishop of* Lyons, *last the* Guise

*Gui* Well, Colonel, are we Friends?

*Grill.* Faith, I think not.

*Gui* Give me your Hand

*Grill* No, for that gives a Heart.

*Gui* Yet we shall clasp in Heav'n.

*Grill.* By Heav'n we shall not,
Unless it be with Gripes.

*Gui.* True *Grillon,* still.

*Larch* My Lord.

*Gui.* Ha, Captain, you are well attended,

If I mistake not, Sir, your Number's doubled.

*Larch.* All these have serv'd against the Hereticks,
And therefore beg your Grace you would remember
Their Wounds, and lost Arrears.

*Gui.* It shall be done.
Again my Heart, there is a Weight upon thee,
But I will sigh it of · Captain, Farewel.

[*Exeunt* Cardinal, Guise, &c.

*Grill.* Shut the Hall-door, and bar the Castle-gates:
March, March there, closer yet, Captain, to the Door.

[*Exit.*

## SCENE *The Council-Hall.*

*Gui* I do not like my self to day.

*Archb.* ———A Qualm, he dares not.

*Card* ———That's one Man's thought, he dares, and that's anothers.

*Enter* Grillon,

*Gui.* O *Marmoutier*, Ha, never see thee more!
Peace my tumultuous Heart, why jolt my Spirits
this unequal Circling of my Blood?
I stand it while I may; O mighty Nature!
Why this Alarm, why dost thou call me on
to fight, yet rob my Limbs of all their use? [*Swoons.*

*Card.* Ha! he's fall'n, chafe him. He comes again.

*Gui* I beg your Pardons, Vapours, no more.

*Grill* Th' Effect
last Night's Lechery with some working Whore.

*Enter* Revol.

*Rev* My Lord of *Guise*, the King would speak with [you.

*Gui.* O Cardinal, O *Lyons!* but no more,
one word more, thou hast a Privilege

[*To the Cardinal.*

to speak with a Recluse, O therefore tell her,
never thou behold'st me breath again,
her I sigh'd it last, — O *Marmoutier.* [*Exit bowing.*

*Card* You will have all Things your own way, my Lord,
Heav'n, I have strange horror on my Soul.

*Archb* I say again, that *Henry* dares not do't.

*Card* Beware your Grace of Minds that bear like him
I know he scorns to stoop to mean Revenge;
But when some mightier Mischief shocks his Tour,
He shoots at once with Thunder on his Wings,
And makes it Air; but hark, my Lord, 'tis doing.

*Gui within.*] Murderers Villains!

*Archb.* I hear your Brother's Voice; run to the Door

*Card* Help, help, the *Guise* is murder'd.

*Archb* Help, help.

*Grill* Cease your vain Cries, you are the King's Pri
Take 'em, *Dugast*, into your Custody. [soners

*Card.* We must obey, my Lord, for Heav'n calls us [Ex

*The* SCENE *draws, behind it a Traverse.*

*The* Guise *is assaulted by Eight · They stab him in all Part but most in the Head.*

*Gui* O Villains! Hell-hounds! Hold:
Murder'd, O basely, and not draw my Sword!

[*Half draws his Sword, is hel*

Dog, *Logniack*, but my own Blood choaks me,
Down, Villain, down, I'm gone. O *Marmoutier*!

[*Flings himself upon him——Die*

*The Traverse is drawn The King rises from his Chair, com forward with his Cabinet Council*

*King* Ope the Closet, and let in the Council,
Bid *Dugast* execute the Cardinal,
Seize all the Factious Leaders, as I order'd,
And every one be answer'd on your Lives.

*Enter* Queen-Mother, *followed by the Counsellors*

O, Madam, you are welcome, how goes your Health

*Q M* A little mended, Sir; what have you done?

*King* That which has made me King of *France*, for the
The King of *Paris* at your Feet lies dead.

*Q. M.* You have cut out dangerous Work, but ma
it up
With speed and resolution.

*King* Yes, I'll wear
The Fox no longer, but put on the Lion;
And since I cou'd resolve to take the Heads

Of this great Insurrection, you the Members
Look to't, beware, turn from your Stubborness;
And learn to know me, for I will be King.

*Grill* 'Sdeath, how the Traytors lowre, and quake, and droop,
And gather to the Wing of his Protection,
As if they were his Friends, and fought his Cause.

*King.* Be witness, Heav'n, I gave him treble Warning;
[*Looking upon* Guise.
He's gone, no more, disperse, and think upon't,
Beware my Sword, which if I once unsheath,
By all the Reverence due to Thrones and Crowns;
Nought shall atone the Vows of speedy Justice,
Till Fate to Ruin every Traytor brings,
That dares the Vengeance of Indulgent Kings. [*Exeunt.*

---

# EPILOGUE.

Written by Mr. *Dryden.* Spoken by Mrs. *Cook.*

*MUCH Time and Trouble this poor Play has cost;*
*And, Faith, I doubted once the Cause was lost.*
*Yet no one Man was meant; nor Great nor Small,*
*Our Poets, like frank Gamesters, threw at all.*
*They took no single Aim:——*
*But like bold Boys, true to their Prince and hearty,*
*Huzza'd and fir'd Broad-sides at the whole Party.*
*Duels are Crimes; but when the Cause is right,*
*In Battel, every Man is bound to fight.*
*For what shou'd hinder me to sell my Skin*
*Dear as I cou'd, if once my Hand were in?*
*Se* Defendendo *never was a Sin.*
*'Tis a fine World, my Masters, right or wrong,*
*The Whiggs must talk, and Tories hold their Tongue.*
*They must do all they can——*
*But we, Forsooth, must bear a Christian Mind;*
*And fight, like Boys, with one Hand ty'd behind;*
*Nay, and when one Boy's down, 'twere wond'rous wise,*
*To cry, Box fair, and give him time to rise.*

# EPILOGUE.

*When Fortune favours, none but Fools will dally.*
*Wou'd any of you Sparks, if* Nan *or* Mally
*Tip you th' inviting Wink, stand shill I, shall I?*
*A* Trimmer *cry'd, (that heard me tell his Story)*
*Fie, Mistress* Cook! *Faith you're too rank a Tory!*
*Wish not Whiggs hang'd, but pity their hard Cases,*
*You Women love to see Men make wry Faces.*
*Pray, Sir, said I, don't think me such a* Jew;
*I say no more, but give the Devil his due.*
*Lenitives, says he, suit best with our Condition*
Jack Ketch, *says I, 's an excellent Physician*
*I love no Blood——Nor I, Sir, as I breath;*
*But hanging is a fine dry kind of Death.*
*We* Trimmers *are for holding all things even:*
*Yes——just like him that hung 'twixt Hell and Heav'n.*
*Have we not had Mens Lives enow already?*
*Yes sure:——but you're for holding all things steady*
*Now since the Weight hangs all on one side, Brother,*
*You* Trimmers *shou'd, to poize it, hang on t'other.*
*Damn'd Neuters, in their middle way of steering,*
*Are neither Fish, nor Flesh, nor good Red-Herring.*
*Not Whiggs nor Tories they; nor this, nor that;*
*Not Birds, nor Beasts; but just a kind of Bat:*
*A Twilight Animal, true to neither Cause,*
*With Tory Wings, but Whiggish Teeth and Claws.*

# THE MASSACRE OF *PARIS.*

## A TRAGEDY.

Printed in the YEAR 1712.

# PROLOGUE.

By Mr. *Mountfort*

*THIS Day we shew you the most Bloody Rage*
*That ever did Religious Fiends engage,*
*A Reconcilement, with a Wedding-Feast,*
*While Murder was the Treat for ev'ry Guest*
*Which well may prove, to Ages yet to come,*
*The Faith of* France, *the Charity of* Rome.
France, *by the most detestable Perjury,*
*Enslav'd its Subjects, who by Laws were free.*
*No Sacrament can this Great Hero bind,*
*Oaths are weak Shackles for his mighty Mind,*
*And worse than Heathens does he Persecute.*
*His Priests want Sense and Learning to dispute,*
*But weak Divines by strong Dragoons confute:*
*And who-e're doubts of any Priestly Maggot,*
*The Heretick Dog must be convinc'd by Faggot.*
*With* Rome's *Religion and* French *Government,*
*What Slave so abject as to be content?*
*Now, idle Malecontent, what is't you'd have?*
*Would you be an Idolater or Slave?*
*What d'you murmur for, because you're free,*
*And this bless'd Isle enjoys its Liberty?*
*Cross but the Narrow Seas, and you will find*
*Slavery and Superstition to your Mind*
*Take with you all your Friends that grumble too,*
*The Land will happily be rid of You,*
*Then all as one with our Great Prince combin'd,*
*And his Allies by Sacred Union joyn'd,*
*Will such false Bloody Tyrants still oppose,*
*Till none shall dare to own the Name of Foes*

# Dramatis Personæ.

## MEN

| | |
|---|---|
| King *Chales* IX. | Mr. *Mountfort* |
| Duke of *Guise*. | Mr. *Williams*. |
| Cardinal of *Lorrain*. | Mr. *Kynaston* |
| Duke of *Anjou*. | Mr. *Pruet*. |
| *Alberto* Gondi. | Mr. *Harris* |
| *Lignoroles*. | Mr. *Bowen*. |
| Admiral of *France*. | Mr. *Betterton* |
| *Cavagnes*. | Mr. *Freeman*. |
| *Langoiran*. | Mr. *Alexander* |

## WOMEN.

| | |
|---|---|
| Queen Mother. | Mrs. *Betterton* |
| *Marguerite*. | Mrs. *Barry*. |
| Queen of *Navarre*. | Mrs. *Knight*. |
| *Antramont* Wife to the Admiral. | Mrs. *Jorden*. |
| *Genius*. | Mr. *Bowman* |

## SCENE *PARIS*.

TH

# THE
# MASSACRE of *PARIS.*

## ACT I. SCENE I.

*The Duke of* Guiſe, *Cardinal of* Lorraine, Marguerite.

*GUISE.*

JUST from your Arms, by this great Guardian rais'd,
Call'd to the Council of a wary King,
On whom depends the Fortune of *Lorraine*,
O, *Marguerite*, yet to drag at this,
After ſuch full Poſſeſſion thus to languiſh.
f this be not to love thee, ſay what is!
eaſe then the rolling Torrent of thy Tears,
hich when I ſtrive to climb the Hill of Honour,
aſhes my hold away, and drives me down
eneath Man's Scorn, into the vale of Ruin.

*Mar.* Hear, hear him, O you Powers! becauſe I love [him
bove my Life, beyond all Joys on Earth,
e ſays I am his Ruin; to my Face,
ith a Court Metaphor, he vows he loaths me,
or all Men hate their Ruin. Nay, 'tis true,
find your Falſhood, 'tis the trick of great Ones,
ike Beaſts of Strength, to prey upon the Weakeſt.

*Gui.*

*Gui* I swear———

*Mar* O do not, dear, Ambitious *Guise*;
For Perjury so necessary seems
To great Mens Oaths, thou must of course be damn'd
Yet as I am, thus plung'd in this Dishonour,
Like a fall'n Angel roll'd through all my Hells,
I cannot hate thee, *Guise*, but sighing far,
Far from the shining Clime where I was born,
I beg those cruel Fates that hurl'd me down
To pity thee, and keep thee from my Ruin:
For I'm so curs'd, I do not wish my Foe,
Much less the Man I love above the World

*Gui* As I love thee, and O be Witnesses
My Brain and Soul, there's not an Artery
That runs through all the Body of thy *Guise*,
But beats where-e'er it pass *Marguerite*,
Yet this is nothing haste away, my Lord,
Go tell the King and Council I am sick,
For I'll to Bed again, or on a Couch
Sit gazing in her beauteous Eyes all day,
And let the business of a grave World pass.

*Mar*. No more, my Lord; you shall, you shall Council:
I see 'tis necessary; but I find
My Soul presages Mischief, if not Murder;
For if you should prove false, Crowns, Kingdoms, Empir
Worlds should not save poor *Marguerite* from the Gra
Ah, *Guise*, ah venerable *Lorrain*, view me,
Behold me on the Earth, I swear I love
As never Woman lov'd, I'm all a Brand,
With, or without you, I am ne'er at rest:
Farewel, this Fever of my furious Passion
Burns me to Madness, yet I say, farewel

*Gui* Farewel Yet why farewel, when e'er the Even
I shall again rush to eternal Sweets,
This bosom of the Spring'

[Marguerite *going o*

Mar. [*returning*] What, no Endearments at so sad a p
Alas perhaps I ne'er shall see you more. [tin
You bow'd, you kiss'd, but did not press my Hand;
Y

You shou'd, like me, have stagger'd when you left me,
And eat your *Marguerite* with your hungry Eyes;
But you are cold and pall'd, a lukewarm Lover,
Must to the business of the cursed State,
Which will not let you think of dying *Marguerite*,
Who to her last gasp will remember you
But see, I rave again, my Fits return
Yet pity me, for oh, I burn, I burn. [*Exit.*

*Car.* I think I never heard so fierce a Passion:
She's all Convulsion, and she gazes on you,
As you would do on him that kill'd your Father
What have you done, my Lord, to make her thus?

*Gui.* Causes are endless for a Woman's loving
Perhaps she has seen me break a Lance on Horse-back,
Or, as my Custom is, all over Arm'd,
Plunge in the *Seine* or *Loire*; and where 'tis swiftest
Plow to my Point against the headlong Stream.
Tis certain, were my Soul of that soft Make
Which some believe, she has Charms, my Heav'nly Uncle,
Beyond the Art and Wit of *Cleopatra:*
Such was not she stretch'd in her Golden Barge,
As *Marguerite* was last Night in Bed,
Who, as she mourn'd at my unkind delay,
Hung all the Chambers round with Black, her Bed,
Her Coverings, nay, her Sarsnet Sheets were Black——

*Car* Fy, fy, my Lord.

*Gui.* And, for the Weather's heat,
Were roll'd beneath the Beauties of her Breast,
Which with a White, more pure than new fall'n Snow,
Would sure have tempted Hermites from their Orgies,
To nod and smile a little at the wonder.

*Car.* Come, come, my Lord, you anger me indeed,
Not for the Sin, that's as the Conscience makes it,
I had rather you should Whore a thousand Women,
Than love but one, tho' in a lawful way.
Shew me through all Memorials of Great Men,
Except the Partner of the *Roman* Empire,
Drooping *Antonius*, and the fam'd *Decemvir*,
One that e'er bow'd before this little Idol!

*Gui.* First know your Man, before your Application:

I

I love, 'tis true; but most for my Ambition;
Therefore I thought to marry *Marguerite*;
But oh, that *Cassiopeia* in the Chair,
The Regent Mother, and that Dog *Anjou*;
Cross Constellations blast my Plots ere born:
The King too frowns upon me; for last Night,
Hearing a Ball was promis'd by the Queen,
I came to help the Show; when at the Door
The King, who stood himself the Centry, stopt me,
And ask'd me what I came for? I reply'd,
To serve his Majesty: He, sharp and short,
Retorted thus; He did not need my Service.

*Car* 'Tis plain, you must resolve, my Lord, to quit her
For I am charg'd to tell you, she's design'd
To be the Wife of *Henry* of *Navarre*
'Tis the main Beam in all that Mighty Engin,
Which now begins to move so dreadfully
Against the Heads of the Rebellious Faction

*Gui.* I have it, and methinks it looks like *D' Alva*,
I see the very motion of his Beard,
His opening Nostrils, and his dropping Lids,
I hear him Croak too, to the King and Queen,
In *Biscay*'s *Bay*, at *Bayonne*,
Fish for the great Fish, take no care for Frogs:
Cut off the Poppy-heads, lay the Winds fast,
And straight the Waves (the People) will be still.

*Car.* Then you will leave her?

*Gui* Hurl her to the Sea!
The Air, the Earth, or Elemental Fire,
So I may see *Castilion* in the Net.
Oh that Whale-Admiral: might I but view him,
After his thousand Fetches, Plots, and Plunges,
Struck on those Scouring Shallows which await him,
Furies and Hell, and I, stand by to gall him;
Were *Marguerite* all one World of Pleasure,
I'd sell her, and my Soul, for such Revenge.

*Car.* Speak lower.

*Gui.* What, upon my Father's Death?
O Glorious *Guise*, be calm upon thy Murder!
No, I will hollow my Revenge so loud,

That

That his great Ghost shall hear me up to Heav'n,
In height of Honours; oh, to fall so basely,
When *Orleance* was block'd up, and Conquests crown'd
By damn'd *Poltrot* so villainously slain, [thee,
*Poltrot*, by *Beza*, and this curs'd Admiral,
Set on with hopes of infinite Rewards,
Here and hereafter, so to blast thy Glory!
O, I could pull my bursting Eye-balls forth,
But that they may one day prove Basilisks
To that detested Head of all these Broils;
Then Tortures, Racks and Death shall close thy Wound,
Kill him in Riots, Pride, and Lust of Pleasures,
That I may add Damnation to the rest,
And foil his Soul and Body both together.

*Car* Behold your Brother, and the Duke *Delbeuf*,
*Mercour* too comes, this Outrage will undo us.

*Gui* No, not at all; for 'tis in general terms.
O my good Lords, what if the Admiral
Stood here before you; should he scape our Justice?
I see by each Man's laying of his hand
Upon his Sword, you vow the like Revenge:
For me, I wish that both mine may rot off———

*Car* No more, away, my Lords: the King calls for you.

*Gui* I go. That Vermin may devour my Limbs,
That I may die like the late puling King
Under the Barber's hands, Imposthumes choak me,
If while alive I cease to chew his Ruin,
To hang him in Effigie, nay to tread,
Drag, stamp, and grind him, after he is dead. [*Exeunt*.

## SCENE II. *The Cabinet Council.*

*Table with Lights on it.* [*A Chamber beyond it*]

Queen Mother, Anjou *asleep*.

*Q M* O my *Anjou*, the Wheels of this new Ruin
Go wrong, for want of one that knows to drive;
He sits too light upon the whirling Throne,
And totters, with the dismal Prospect, down:
Young *Charles*, a smart suspicious doubtful Boy,

But,

But, *Charles*, you must be rul'd in this dark Road,
Or with the Lightning of my fatal Power,
Which never cracks and claps, I'll melt thee down,
For ever lost amongst the Mass of Things,
That thou, the darling of my doating Soul,
The Prince of my Eternal Thought, may'st mount
Like *Nero*, tho' at *Aggrippina*'s Ruin.
But see the King with the new Count of *Retz*.
Let us withdraw; it may be worth our hearing.

*Enter King with* Alberto Gondi.

*King* *Alberto Gondi.*

*Alb* Sir!

*King* I think thou lov'st me.

*Alb* More than my Life.

*King*. That's much; yet I believe thee.
My Mother has the Judgment of the World,
And all things move by that; but my *Alberto*,
She has a cruel Wit, and, let me tell thee,
Thus to destroy the Soldiers of the Kingdom,
Famous as ever fought for *Rome* or *Greece*,
Under a shadow of a thousand Oaths,
'Tis Barbarous, *Alberto*, is it not?
And seems to be unworthy of a King.

*Alb* The Provocation, Sir.

*King* I know it well.
But if thou'dst have my Heart within thy Hand,
I swear, Conspiraces of that foul Nature
For ever blot the Memory of Kings.
What Honours, Interest, with the World to buy him
Shall make a brave Man smile and do a Murder?
Therefore I hate the Treachery of *Brutus*,
I mean the latter, so cry'd up in Story.
Whom none but Cowards and white-liver'd Knaves
Would dare commend, lagging behind his Fellows,
His Dagger in his Bosom, stabb'd his Father.
This is a blot, the *Ciceronian* Stile
Could ne'er wipe off, tho' the mistaken Man
(Mistaken in his Love, for *Brutus* scorn'd him)
Makes bold to call those Traitors Men Divine.

*Alb*. *Tully* was wise, but wanted Constancy.

*Ki*

*King* He did, *Alberto.* Hark, but one thing more,
or much I love thee, and would fain unburden
My Soul of half her Cares on such a Man,
o good

*Alb* My ever dear and honour'd Master.

*King.* No more of that I'll tell thee then: Last Night,
, I lay tossing in a Feverish Dream,
call'd for Drink; when streight my Mother brought it;
ut as she reach'd it to my trembling Lips,
ethought her Eyes roll'd ghastly upon me,
Palsey shook her Hand; yet I resolv'd,
ook off the Draught, when streight a fainting seiz'd me,
My Eyes wept Blood, my Ears, my Nose and Mouth
ur'd forth whole Streams, and all my Sweat was Blood,
y Hair and Nails dropt off as *Autumn* Leaves,
hen Tempests rise, fall from the wither'd Trees:
h, oh, the Fancy seems so much unnatural,
I think no more on't; yet I thought to tell thee,
cause she is a Woman whom no Art
or Wisdom of the World can ever fathom.

*Alb* O my gracious Lord,
ge not the Queen by Dreams, and vain Chimæra's;
member, Sir, how often in your Nonage
e manag'd with her Wit the Weight of Empire,
ontending with th' Effects of blind Religion,
he Contumacy of Rebellious Subjects,
he deep Dissimulation of the Court,
he want of Treasure, baffling with her Prudence
he utmost strength Ambition rais'd to gain her.

*King* O Count of *Rhetz*, thou lead'st me through the Garden
every Grace, but dar'st not point her Weeds:
she not of a most deceitful Soul;
rfidious, even to violating Vows?
she not greedy too of Human Blood?
Wit so wasteful in destroying Lives,
hat she will turn a City to a Wild? [order'd,

*Q M* Good Morrow, Sir! 'Tis just the time you
hink the second Watch, and we are met
o wait on your Decrees.

*King.*

*King* O Mother, Mother,
You have imbark'd me in a Sea of Blood;
And sure so damnable an Enterprise
Was never fram'd by Man.

*Q M* If, Sir, you fear it,
Why give it o'er, and let the Admiral reign,
Call in the *Hugonots*, drive out your Friends,
Banish your Blood, and the establish'd Peers,
Forget the long Succession of your Fathers,
The Throne of Kings, forget the Laws, Religion,
Cut off the noble Spirits from your Council,
And from the Dregs of this Heretical Faction
Compose a Bastard Cabinet Election,
Let Knaves in Shops prescribe you how to Sway,
They read your Acts, and with their hardned Thumb
Erase 'em out, or with their stinking Breath
Proclaim aloud they like not this or that;
Then in a drove come lowing to the *Louvre*,
And say, they'll have it mended, that they will,
Or you shall be no King.

*King*. 'Tis true the People
Ne'er know a Mean, when once they get the Power.

*Q. M*. Did you not late dispatch by *Lodowick*
Thus to the Admiral, with Vows of Honour,
That young *Navarre* should streight espouse your Siste[r]
So to root up all Seeds of least Suspicion,
And that those Nuptials should be solemniz'd
At *Paris*, to be bound with deepest Oaths?

*King* Yet, Madam, I must fear, for, should it fa[il]
We should be less than our worst Foes could wish us
The Poultron Court, the Scorn, the Laughing-stock
Of all the Christian and the Barbarous World

*Q M* No, Sir, you cannot fear the sure Design,
But you're in fear of those that are about you:
You fear ev'n me; but I have liv'd too long,
Since my own Bowels, nay, my very Heart-Strings,
(For so I always lov'd and priz'd my Children)
Dare not confide in her that gave 'em Being.

*King* Stay, Madam, stay, come back, forgive my Fear
Forgive my sifting Soul her narrow Searches,

Whe

Where all our Thoughts should creep like deepest Streams;
For know, I hate the haughty Admiral,
And all his curst Accomplices to Death.

*Q M* What brings the Cardinal of *Lorrain* from *Rome*?

*King* That the new Pope is fully satisfy'd,
I sent the Legate too that Diamond Ring,
With this close Motto writ within the Gold:
By this, my solid Zeal I own;
And Blood can never melt it down.

*Anj* A murd'ring Sentence for the *Hugonots*

*King* And which so clear'd the matter, that the Pope
Order'd a Dispensation for the Marriage.

*Q M* Behold the Duke of *Guise*, and Cardinal:
'Twere fit you send his Eminence to *Rochel*,
T'acquaint the Admiral of a War with *Spain*,
And that the Plot we form'd for the *Low-Countries*
Against the Catholick King, should strait be acted

*King* O Mother, oh, what's this that rends my Heart,
That rides my Nights, and clouds my Days with horror?
Is it not Conscience? which sometimes appears
Like a She Wolf, in *Jane* of *Albert*'s Shape,
And drags me on the Floor; now in the Form
Of that old Lyon Admiral, it comes,
And grins, and roars, just gaping to devour me.

*Q M* Why, let him, when his Throat is cut we'll trust him
Clear up your furrow'd Brow. Believe me, Sir,
You'll see him shortly where you need not fear him;
For, should he stay behind the Queen and Princess,
Doubting the Marriage, fill'd with boding Fears,
The War with *Spain* will so bewitch his Glory,
And lull his proud Ambition, that should Fate,
Which awes him now, leap up more terrible,
He'll follow with a speed shall make him foremost,
And scorn a Grave.

*King* O, tis a dreadful Image;
But when his Brains are pash'd I shall be still.
The Morning rises, yet I cannot rest;
Like those eternal Lamps that wink above;
Methinks, O Mother, I could watch for ever

Once more let me conjure you, all be hush'd,
Be secret on this horrid Consultation,
As Urns and Monuments, that never blab.
*Gui.* Therefore let's lye like Furies on the watch,
As if it were an Ambush for the World. ['em
*King.* With Claws lock'd in, like Lions, couch to tea
Our Mother, thou so fierce upon the slaughter,
Direct thy Brood, we will not stir nor breath·
But when thou giv'st the Word, then start away,
Rush from the Shade, and make 'em all our Prey.
[*Exeun*

## ACT II. SCENE I.

*Enter* Admiral, Cavagnes, *and* Langoiran.

*Adm.* YOur Reasons are to all appearance fair,
Like *Eden*'s Fruit, the Tempter hangs 'em fort
But there's a canker-Queen within the Core,
That eats *Colignie*'s firmest hopes away·
Like Paradise, she paves my spacious walk,
But oh, *Cavagnes* and *Langoiran*, look,
Do you not find her lurking in the Flowers?
With soft indented glides behold she comes,
I see the forked Tongue betwixt her Teeth,
Hissing us from the Stage of Life and Honour
O, she's a Serpent equal to the first,
And has the Will to damn another World;
Therefore I'm positive, till I'm convinc'd
The King foregoes her Counsel, I'll not stir:
I'll not to Court.
*Cav* Thus far I can make good,
She is believ'd, through all the Courts of *Europe*,
A most transcendent Wit, and absolute Woman.
*Adm.* That is an absolute Murderer and Dissembl
Who that proceeds on such black Principles,
That thinks there is no God above Ambition,
But may accomplish all that he intends?
Where's then the Art, the Reach, the Policy

Of this transcendent and most absolute Woman!
Is it not easie to Assassinate,
To Lie, and Swear you love the Man you hate,
Train him into the dark, and murder him?
I urge again, unless the King resolve
To rule alone, I will not come to Court.
*Lang.* *Cavagnes* is a Master in Court Secrets;
For me, I ruin'd the bus'ness of the War.
*Adm.* Perswade me while the Queen is at his Ear,
That if he were made up of Worlds of Mercy,
He ever would forgive me! pray look back
Into the former times, and see who sow'd
Those glowing Grains which shot up to a War,
Who blew the Coals of *Calvin's* kindled Doctrine,
And earth'd the little Sect at *Hugo's* Gate,
Was it not I that form'd 'em to a Body?
*Lang.* Stick to your self, Sir, follow your own methods.
*Adm.* Who therefore, while the pangs of Rage were on [her,
Proclaim'd me in all Languages a Traitor,
Dragg'd my Effigies through the Streets of *Paris*,
Hung up my Statue on the common Gallows,
Set, by Court Officers, my Goods to sale,
My Houses raz'd, or burnt 'em to the Ground.
*Cav.* I must confess that start of open Vengeance,
Not common to the Nature of the Queen.
*Adm.* And why all this, not for a private Grudge?
I judg'd 'twas time to view the ghastly flaws
Of that Religion that would rend the World,
That sticks not at the slaughter of whole States,
Blowing up Senates, nor at murdering Kings.
Driv'n with this Thought, I push'd the War yet farther;
And, though we lost the Fight at *Moncontour*,
Yet speak, *Cavagnes*, did I fail in ought?
*Cav.* I was not there.
*Adm.* Then give me leave to say,
I fought my self the Protestant Cause alone,
When in the Head of our remaining Horse,
I met the Elder *Rhinegrave* hand to hand,
Shot him i'th' Face, and left him on the Ground;
Then seeing all our Army quite defeated,

My Jaw-bone shatter'd, and my Voice quite spent,
I fled, with hopes to rise more terrible,
As it succeeded, to th' astonishment
Of all the Christian Word.

*Enter* Colombier *with a Paper in his Hand*

*Col.* My Lord the Cardinal of *Lorrain*'s arriv'd,
To swear and sign the Articles of Peace,
The Queen at present holds him in Discourse;
Mean time commends this Paper to your view,
Sent to her Majesty from the King of *France.*

Adm. reads. *Madam, as you demanded, you have powe o'er all the County suddenly of* Armagnac. *Tell the grea Admiral I seek his Friendship. Ask of* Lorrain *the rest who knows my Heart*

Perhaps, my Friends, it may be thus indeed,
That, quite tir'd out with infinite Distractions,
He may at last resolve to Rule alone,
Come from his Page-ship, and put off the Mother,
Not lose his Youth, the pleasure of his Bloom
Among grey Senators, and withering Councils.
If it were so, but hold, there's something here
Forbids that Thought, it rises like a Vapour,
A strange Misgiving, such as Women swoon at,
And Men themselves may fear But see, the Queen.

*Enter the Queen of* Navarre, *Prince of* Navarre, *and Prince of* Conde

*Q. Nav* I come, Sir, to forestall the Cardinal,
Who from the King offers these terms of Peace.
He adds to what Count *Lodwick* brought before,
His Mother's Policy shall sway no longer;
That he'll submit his Genius to your Conduct,
Confirms your being Captain General
In that most glorious Enterprize on *Spain*,
Allows you fifty for your Person's Guard;
Therefore, for sealing this Eternal Bond,
And for the former weighty Consultations,
He begs you instantly to come to Court.

*Adm* What has your Majesty resolv'd to do?

Q. N

*Q. Nav.* To go with both the Princes ſtraight to *Paris*,
And ſee the Nuptials of my young *Navarre*.
I know not what your Lordſhip does intend;
But I have ſent already to the King
My Anſwer by *Byron*, and will attend him.
*Adm.* Then 'tis too late to think of going back;
You have lanch'd me now indeed, and I muſt plunge
In this Abyſs, tho' it be deep as Hell.
No, Madam, ſpite of all the Augurs here,
Since you are thus reſolv'd, I'll go the foremoſt.
'Twas for your ſake, and in the Prince's Cauſe,
For Liberty of Conſcience and Religion,
That I thus long did propagate the War,
And ſhall I now not follow where you lead me?
*Lan.* Why ſhould you, if it goes againſt your Mind?
*Adm.* Peace, Peace, *Langoman*, ſince the Main's produc'd,
I mean, the Reſolution of the Queen,
My Fate cries out, we muſt, we muſt away.
Therefore, my Friend, go gather my Dependants,
Bid 'em prepare for *Paris*. Tell my Wife,
My deareſt *Martia*, we muſt bid farewell,
Tell her, I'm forc'd to ſwim againſt the Stream;
Say, that her *Cato's* bound for *Utica*,
From whence perhaps he never ſhall return.

*Enter Cardinal of* Lorrain.

*Car.* Conqueſt, Proſperity, and ſmooth Succeſs
Be ever ſtrow'd before our General's Feet.
Thus, Sir, the King ſalutes you, with Commiſſion
To turn the Torrent of your Arms on *Spain*.
*Adm.* My Lord, I glory in the great Employ.
[illegible]ear beſide, the King will rule alone,
[illegible], Sir, whate'er the Wit of Women be,
[illegible]m War and Councils let 'em be remov'd.
[illegible] again, with my old Bluntneſs, Sir,
To have a Female Finger in the State,
[illegible] blaſting to the Prince's Memory.
Let him but be ſincere, and leave the Mother,
Old as I am, I will put on my Arms,
And with this hand, not wither'd yet in War,
Bear to th' *Eſcurial* his Imperial Standard.

*Car*. My Lord, for the Sincerity of the King,
That he intends his Dear and Great *Chastillon*,
(The very words that did express his Love)
All Honours, Titles, Greatness, all Advancement,
Nay, to the curbing of his Mother's Will,
For the performance of each Article,
Without a pious Catch, or trick of State;
Without the smallest Mental Reservation,
Equivocation, or the least Reserve,
In the King's Name, as I am Priest profess'd,
As I am sent from Heav'n, to teach Salvation,
I pawn the truth of my immortal Soul.

*Adm.* He then, to whom our Hearts are free and open,
Be judge betwixt his Majesty and me.

*Car.* O Sir, O Madam, oh, you make me weep,
Viewing by this the frailty of the World,
For if the Mind of Man be so suspicious
On such clear Demonstration of Affection,
How can you e'er believe the Love Divine?

*Q. Nav.* My Lord, you may return with our Obedience,
And tell the King, the Admiral, the Princes,
My self, and all his humble faithful Subjects,
Will haste to throw our Bodies at his Feet.

*Adm.* My Lord, farewell, I must not doubt your Oaths,
But with implicite Faith believe the King,
At whose Tribunal I must shortly kneel,
For Pardon and Forgiveness. [*Ex.*

Admiral *returns with* Cavagnes.

*Adm.* Hark, my *Cavagnes*, write to Count *Lodowic*,
The *Sieurs de Genlis*, and *La-Nove*, to haste,
And suddenly to make Surprise of *Mons*.

*Cav.* My Lord———

*Adm.* Nay, write I say; I'll have it done,
On my *Parisian* Entrance, I'm resolv'd
To see into the Heart of this young *Charles*,
And force him thus upon a War with *Spain*;
For tho' this Cardinal swear, and damn his Soul
As deep as Heav'n's high, yet if his Bowels
Be like the rest of that Blood-colour'd Robe,
And laughs at Ghosts, where's then the Admiral?

Caught

Caught by this perjur'd jugling Man of God!
What, for the Cabinet Murderers to play with,
To toſs *Chaſtillon*'s Fate from one to t'other,
And grin my Life and Honour from the World!
But now for *Paris*: Call *Colonbier*,
The Count *la Rochfoucalt*, Marquis *de Renel*,
*Piles*, *Pluviah*, *Pardillan*, and *Lavardine*,
*Randane*, and all my Gallants of the War:
For *Paris* bid 'em haſte.

*Enter* Antramont, *with* Langoiran.

*Ant.* Stay, ſtay, my Lord;
I charge you ſtay, for *Martia* does arreſt you,
And ſays, you ſhall not go to *Utica*.
*Martia* reſolves to hinder this Self-Murder.

*Adm.* Self-Murder, *Martia*!

*Ant.* Yes, you turn the Sword
Upon your ſelf, which *Charles* and that falſe Queen
Brandiſh againſt you, going thus to Court
Againſt your will; for ſo you ſent me word.
Is not this running it in your own Bowels?
Is it not, *Cato*? but you ſhall not leave me:
You're now Betroth'd, and in this ſad Condition,
Thus fraught with your clear Image, like a Bark
Too richly laden, with an over Ballaſt,
Leave me not *Gaſpar*, to a flood of Tears,
A Sea of Paſſion, and a Storm of Sorrow.

*Adm.* Beg me not, *Martia*, 'tis impoſſible
To ſtay me now, my Honour is engag'd,
My Word is paſt.

*Ant.* Yet ſtay, Sir, ſtay ſo long,
So long at leaſt, as may preſerve your Likeneſs;
For if I yield you now to thoſe Court-Murderers,
My boding Fears will blaſt it ere 'tis born,
As ſure as *Cæſar*'s Butchery was perform'd
At *Rome*, your Murder is contriv'd at *Paris*:
*Calphurnia*'s bloody Dream, and Scent of Slaughter
Are nothing, Sir, to my Prophetick Spirit;
Which not by Viſions, Fantoms of the Night,
But by day Arguments, and certain Reaſon,

Will give such Evidence for your Undoing,
As you, your self being Judge, shall say are true.

*Adm* O, *Antramont*, away, why dost thou thus
Unman me with thy Tears? Tho' certain Death,
With all the dagger'd Council, stood to wait me,
Ev'n in my view, I swear I would among 'em.

*Ant* Then you are caught indeed, they hate you, Sir;
Your Wife, with this poor Innocent unborn,
With all your other Orphans, are undone:
The Glory of the Earth is laid along.
I see the Vine that spreads his Arms to Heav'n,
With all his Clusters rotting on the Ground,
Blasted with Lightning from a clouded Council,
By her that is the *Juno* of your Fate,
That Murd'ring Sorceress, that dry Hag of *Florence*,
That Midnight *Hecate* of ten thousand forms,
That varies with all Shapes, that tries all Spirits,
Selling her Soul to each, and all together,
To make your Fate inevitably sure.

*Adm.* Give me your hand, and take this farewel Kiss,
If thou wouldst have me think thou lov'st old *Gaspar*
Reply no more, but leave me and be dumb.

*Ant* I'm all Obedience, let me speak but once,
And whisper't in your Ear: By all my hopes
Of Earth and Heav'n, you shall not die alone,
I'll gather all the Branches of your Body,
The little Arms, the Sprouts of him that was
Yes, with that precious Fardel, bound together
By Cords of Hair, cemented with my Tears,
And wreath'd about till Death with my Embraces,
I'll follow you to Court: I will, my Lord,
And since you'll have it so, we'll burn together [*Exit*

*Enter Commanders*

*Adm* O, my brave Friends! my dear *la Rochfoucalt*
Your hand, and yours, my rough *Colombiere*;
My Gallant *Piles*, and thine, my plain *Langoiran*:
But say, how stand you to this Expedition,
This new Exploit, this dangerous Court Adventure?

*Lang* My Lord, I'll answer for 'em; there's not one
But has resolv'd to follow, tho' they had rather

Run

Run the most violent Shock of Glorious War,
Than stand one Complemental Death at Court.

*Adm.* Then our Opinions jump. But to the purpose;
Since 'tis resolv'd that we must go to *Paris*,
Because you're Strangers to the King and Queen,
I would instruct you in the Royal Tempers,
Draw the Queen Mother's Face in Minature,
For there the watch and ward of all our Caution
Must lye, if possible to wave the Ruin.

*Lang.* Fore-warn'd, fore-arm'd, fear not, we shall re-[member.

*Adm.* Imagine then the King, like *Adam* laid
Among the Sweets of Pardise to rest,
While to his listning Soul this second *Eve*,
Full of the Devil, and design'd to damn us,
Thus breaths her Counsels fatal to the World:
What ever Paths you trod before your Reign,
'Tis Blood and Terror must your Throne maintain:
Scorn then thy Slaves; nor to thy Vassalls bow;
Fix the Gold Circle to thy bended Brow,
By Murders, Massacres, no matter how.
For Conscience, and Heav'ns Fear, Religion's Rules,
They're all State-Bells, to toll in pious Fools. [*Exeunt.*

---

## ACT III. SCENE I.

*Enter Queen Mother, and* Marguerite.

*Mar.* IS *Guise* then false? or do you try me, Madam,
And search my Heart, to know how much I love him?
If it be so, I will resolve you quickly,
I'll swear to you by Heav'n, by all things sacred,
By all that's great and lovely upon Earth,
By him, by *Guise*, by all the blessed Moments
Of that dear Life, which single I prefer
To Millions of my own, I love him more
Than you love Glory, Vengeance, and Ambition.

*Q. M.* Then thou art lost, a Wretch, an out-cast Fool,
Not worthy of my Care, nor worth my seeking,

For,

For, by my best Desires, I know he scorns thee,
And to my certain Knowledge, is betroth'd
To *Catharine Cleve*, the Prince of *Porcien*'s Widow.

*Mar.* 'Tis false, he's not, he shall not, nor he cannot:
You hate me, Madam, and you forge this Matter,
To make me die, to kill your *Marguerite*;
For, if you did respect me as your Blood,
Why should you tear my Heart in thousand pieces?
Why should you make me rave with Jealousie?
For, oh, I love beyond all former Passion:
Die for him! that's too little; I could burn
Piece-meal away, or bleed to Death by drops,
Be flead alive, then broke upon the Wheel,
Yet with a Smile endure it all for *Guise*.
And when let loose from Torments, all one Wound,
Run with my mangled Arms, and crush him dead.

*Q. M.* Farewell, thou'rt mad indeed. I'll find the King,
And send him to convince you of the Truth.

*Mar.* The Truth! O Heav'n, nay, stay, and I'll believe you.
But is he false! is't possible in Nature?
Is *Guise* then, like his Kindred Savages,
True Man, an upright, bold, and hearty Villain?

*Q. M.* I tell thee, as I love thy Life and Honour,
Tho' much I fear the latter is past hope,
Their Marriage will be solemniz'd to-morrow,
The Cardinal of *Lorrain* must joyn their hands.

*Mar.* What, he that keeps the Tye, the sacred Contract!
I'll warrant too he'll be a Witness for him.
Why then, for ever throw off Modesty,
If thus Religion cheats us: let us haste,
With *Messalina*, to the common Stews,
Where Bauds are honester than *Roman* Church-men.

*Q. M.* Think no more on't, but with a generous Fury
Resolve to cast him from your Soul for ever.
Prepare your self for what the King commands,
Without delay, to wed the young *Navarre*.

*Mar.* To wed my Tomb, to dwell in Dust below,
Where we shall see no more deceitful Men,
Hear no more Flattery, nor no damning Vows;
Where I shall never start from my cold Bed,
Nor walk with folded Arms about the Room,

With

With Eyes, like Rivers, ever running down;
While with my over-watching, I mistake
The rustling Wind, and every little Noise
For *Guise*'s coming; which not finding true,
I weep again, till all my Face is drown'd;
And groan, as if there were no end of Sorrow.

*Q. M.* Then I must find some other Instruments,
That have the power to rule you. So farewel. [*Exit.*

*Mar.* Stay, Madam, stay. She's gone, and leaves me here!
To do a mischief on my Life. False *Guise*!
Perfidious *Guise*! but I will find thee out,
And wreck the Miseries of my Soul upon thee;
Ay, I'll allarm the Priest that makes thee wicked;
Priests, that like Devils, laugh at humane Pains,
And Souls ne'er reckon, so they count their Gains. [*Exit.*

## SCENE II. *A Palace.*

*Enter Duke of* Guise, *and Cardinal of* Lorrain.

*Gui.* But are you sure he'll come?

*Car.* Most certain, Sir.

*Gui.* Why then, I will not eat till I behold him.
O, I could pine my self into a Ghost,
So I at last might thrust my hungry Sword
Into the curs'd Carcass of this *Admiral*,
And glut my greedy Vengeance with his Heart.

*Car.* The Queen too of *Navarre*, the Heretick Princes,
Gentlemen and Commanders, Knights, Barons, Counts,
With all the Combination of the Rebels,
Come to the Wedding of the young *Bearnois*.

*Gui.* Why, what an Oglio will the Devil have?
A Feast for Hell, to cram it to the mouth,
A Massacre of Souls. Methinks I see
The glutton Death gorg'd with devouring Lives,
And stretching o'er the City his swoln bulk,
As he would vomit up the Dead.

*Car.* My Lord,
How brooks your Heart the Marriage of *Navarre*?

*Gui.* Why, faith, Sir, as we must necessity

The

The King resolves it; urging to my Face,
The Man that dar'd to contradict his Pleasure,
Should make that opposition with his Ruin:
On this I turn'd my Court to *Porcien*'s Widow.
But O, *Lorrain*, Love mourn'd at the mistake,
As conscious of the cruel Change he made.
Take then the prospect of a Summer's Morn,
The gaudy Heav'n all streak'd with dappled Fires,
And fleck'd with Blushes like a rising Bride,
With Sweets so pour'd from such a lavish Spring,
That it must begger all the Years to come:
From this bright view, from *Marguerite*'s Form,
Now turn thy Eye upon the yellow Autumn,
On *Porcien*'s Wife, the Widow of the Seasons.

*Car.* You speak, methinks, as if you lov'd the Princess.

*Gui.* How e'er I bragg'd before, I do confess it,
Spite of my Glory, spite of my Ambition,
And all the vow'd Resolves of my Revenge,
Had she not poorly yielded to the Marriage,
I would have turn'd my Widow to the Common:
But I am satisfy'd, 'tis now the talk
Of the whole Court, how she in secret likes it;
Hears too, no doubt, of my design on *Cleve*,
Yet (Curses on that changeable Stuff her Soul)
Regards it not. But see, she comes: a Tempest

*Enter* Marguerite.

Ruffles her Face! the Mother taught this cunning;
And she has catch'd the Plague of that Dissembler
So right, methinks I see the tokens on her.

*Mar.* Look in my Face,

*Gui.* I do.

*Mar.* Nay, in my Eyes.

*Gui.* I view 'em as I would the setting Sun,
Were I to die at Midnight.

*Mar.* Come, you dare not.

*Gui.* What, dare not die?

*Mar.* Thou dar'st not one, nor t'other:
At least thou shouldst not, for thou art so wicked,
So gone in Sin, Damnation must attend thee.

*Gui.* Why, then the Devil is sure of one great Man.

*Mar.* Of one! of all; at Court he's no Retailer,

Bu

But deals in Grofs, and takes you by the Lump.
In Country-Fields he's forc'd to sit all Day,
With Patience, angling down the guiltless Stream,
Yet rarely catches one for all his labour;
But when he comes to Court, the Sea of Pleasures,
He throws his Drag-Net in from side to side,
Where none of all the Fry escape Perdition:
There may you see Whales plunging in the Meash,
Disgorging streams, like Drunkards on the Ground,
The Sword-fish, like the Souldier, fast in hold;
The floundering Priest, like Sharks, that gape for prey;
Fat Porcpise Bauds, the Mermaids too of Honour,
The Minim Pages, all the twinkling Host
So fill'd, the Snare of Hell must crack to hold you.
*Gui.* No, there's another Cause for this fine Satyr,
Too well digested for a sudden Thought,
An Argument at home, there in your Heart,
Tho' you have learnt discretion thus to turn it.
*Mar.* O Heav'ns! What means he?
*Gui.* D'ye seem amaz'd?
I say again, however you upbraid me,
You bear the Guilt, who bring the Accusation:
Ye, *Marguerite*, thou hast plaid me foul.
Nay, do not start, nor gaze, nor make false Steps.
Come, Princess, these are Tricks too stale for *Guise*,
Shew 'em your little Creatures, bid your Mother
Fetch something quainter from the Schools of *Florence*,
Where she has learnt the Art of honest-dealing.
*Mar.* O, all ye Pow'rs of Heav'n, of Earth and Hell,
Where would he, whither, and when will he end?
*Gui.* Madam, I've done already, but least you should
Forget coherence, through your World of Passion,
Tell you, you are false, your Vows, your Tears,
Your Languishings, your very height of Pleasures,
Your grasping Joys are false, for even then
When you cry out, There can be nothing farther,
All your Perjuries, you wish 'em more.
*Mar.* Furies and Devils! shall he bear it thus!
What with his Lip! his Eye! his ev'ry Scorn,
Walk thus before me, and defie me thus!
O *Guise*! disloyal, faithless, perjur'd Wretch!

Thou

Thou art more damn'd, than any Fiend in Hell:
Impostor!
*Gui.* Woman.
*Mar* Traitor.
*Gui.* Woman.
*Mar.* Villain.
*Gui.* Woman still.
*Mar.* Hark *Guise*, hear Monster, hear and mark me:
While to thy Conscious Soul I sound the Name
Of *Porcien*.
*Gui.* Of *Navarre*.
*Mar.* *Porcien*, I swear.
*Gui.* *Navarre*, *Navarre*.
*Mar.* Thou ly'st, thou ly'st · *Porcien*, the Widow
*Porcien*.
O, I could cut my Face! what, for a Widow!
Leave me, for *Porcien*! O thou dull, dull *Guise*!
Wilt thou sit down to the refuse of Meals!
A Widow! what, the Monument of Man!
The Tomb, Grave-Vault, the very Damp of Nature!
For this, I hate thee more than e'er I lov'd thee,
And from my Presence banish thee for ever.
*Gui.* No, I will banish this detested *Guise*
My self; you shall not buy him to your Presence:
For, know, I hate more perfectly than you;
Yours is a gust, a puff of Woman's Fury;
But mine a manly, constant settled Hate,
Which, ever since you made your better choice,
Of young *Navarre*, took root within my Heart.
*Mar.* 'Tis false, 'tis false, a Treason fetch'd from Hell
But where! speak out; where was this Lie invented?
*Gui* Thus then in short, and so farewel for ever:
The King and Queen, with all particulars
Avow'd it to me; and in general
The Court You may perceive the Choice
I made of *Cleve*, was more to be reveng'd,
Than want of Constancy: but yours was weigh'd;
*Navarre* has Youth, and may be King of *France*,
Tickling Variety for Love and Glory,
For the false Appetite of luxurious Woman,
Woman, damn'd Woman; but I waste breath to name her

M

My Lord *Lorrain*, I charge you by your Friendship
Give me the Contract
*Mar.* Hold, my Lord.—— For what?
*Gui* That I may tear it to as many pieces
As she has done her Vows. What Faith in Women!
The very fragments of the whole Creation,
Whose sever'd Souls, like many parted Mirrors,
Reflect the Face of all Mankind at once;
Who with their weeping Smiles, and laughing Tears,
Were they allow'd a Heav'n, as sure they are not,
Would tempt the Angels to a Second Fall.
But I grow wild, give me the Contract, Sir.
Nay, Madam, off; I swear you must unhand me.
*Mar* I will not. O my Heart! Ah *Guise, Guise, Guise*!
You have got the Conquest, and you shall maintain it,
Tho' at th' expence of *Marguerite*'s Death.
'Tis true, my Mother mention'd such a Marriage;
But if I did not loath it, scorn, detest it,
O, if this be not true as thou art false,
(Forgive me, for I meant to say unkind)
Banish poor *Marguerite* from those Eyes
That feed her Life, let me no more approach you,
But take, O take this Ponyard from my Hand,
And stick it in my Heart, that Heart that loves you,
That when 'tis injur'd dares not stand before you,
But owns you for the Tyrant of my Days.
*Gui* No, *Marguerite*, no,
You've found the way to Temper me indeed,
Nay, turn it upon me, who am a Traitor,
Because I dar'd to counterfeit a Falshood
Against such perfect Love, to seem t'affect
The hated *Porcien*.
*Mar* Did you then dissemble?
Did you not love her in your Heart, indeed?
*Gui* I swear by Heav'n.
*Mar* O let me then embrace you
Yet closer O that I could get within you!
*Gui.* My Life!
*Mar.* My Soul!
*Gui.* My Heart!
*Car.* My Lord, the Duke of *Anjou* moves this way.

*Gui.*

*Gui* Farewel. And till I hear that thou art Marry'd,
The Heart of *Guise* is riveted to thine:
Which all the Hammers in thy Mother's Brain
Shall never loose.

*Mar.* They may compel my Body;
But till I hear thee say thy self, Thou'rt false,
Death shall not force my Soul to wed *Navarre*.
[*Exit* Marguerite.

*Enter* Anjou, *and* Ligneroles.

*Gui* I'll stand the shock of this Imperious Duke,
This *Anjou*, that has got a Name in War,
I know not how, because his Horse was shot
At *Moncontour*. You see, by what ensu'd,
Nature design'd him for a Reveller.

*Anj* O *Ligneroles*, thou Partner of my Soul,
Be secret, for if once the King should know
What I have told thee through excess of Love,
The World could not redeem thee from the Grave.
Ha! *Guise*! But soft, my Soul. My Lord *Lorrain*,
'Tis said, the Admiral, and *Hugonot* Princes
Are scarce a League from *Paris*.

*Car.* Yes, my Lord,
I hear so too. the Duke of *Guise* was going.

*Anj.* I hope he will not move for fear of me.

*Gui.* You're right, my Lord, nor will not stay for love.

*Anj.* What, not a Woman's Love! Love of a Princess?

*Gui.* No, nor a Boy's, your Sister may do much

*Anj.* Haste *Ligneroles*, go bear the King this Packet.
My Lord of *Guise*, 'tis not impossible [*Exit* Ligneroles.
But *Anjou* one day may be King of *France*;
Mark me, if then I find *Valois* dishonour'd,
I will not leave a *Guise* to gape at Power. [*Exit.*

*Gui.* 'Tis so. By all the Mysteries of Empire,
By the Eternal Fates, his Mother's Poison
Boils in the Brains of the young drooping King,
And speeds him to make way for curs'd *Anjou*.
*Charles* has Religion, which she wonders at,
And scarce believes him her's; laughs at his Pity,
Calls his Remorse the Colick of the Mind,
His starts and fears, the gripes and checks of Conscience.

Enter

*Enter King, Queen Mother,* Ligneroles.

But see, the King! mark, mark, my Dear *Lorrain!*
Mark how she tempers him betwixt her hands.
He has it in his Veins, the lingring draught
That moulders him away. Let's tell him of it:
By my Ambition, and my vow'd Revenge,
I'll do't.

*Car* Away; you shall not: are you mad?
Where is your Temper? Walk a little off,
And lay these Fumes.

*Gui* Lead then the blind away;
Yet, if I meet him in the dark, I'll crush him.

[*Ex.* Lor. *and* Gui.

*King* Was ever such an Insolence? Read there.
My Brother has Intelligence from *Rochel,*
The Admiral has order'd his Adherents
To seize on *Mons,* as he arrives at *Paris,*
So to assure the kindling of a War
O, Mother, now I feel thy Flames inspire me;
Yes by the injur'd Majesty of Kings,
I'll fetch this soaring Rebel from his height:
Traitor, Imperious, Saucy, Arrogant Slave!

*Lig.* Why should your Majesty thus shock your Peace
With needless Fury, since the time draws on
When he, and all those Rebel *Hugonots,*
Shall never grieve you more?

*King* Your Meaning, Sir.

*Lig.* When, as your Royal Justice has decreed,
They shall be Massacred.

*King* A vain Surmise.
Go, Sir, and bid the Count of *Rhets* attend me.

[*Ex* Lig.

*Q. M* Well, Sir, what think you now?

*King* Death, and Destruction,
We're all undone, the Secret of the World,
Th'eternal Care of my contriving Soul,
Which has so many Moons, with constant watching,
Reduc'd me to this state, is blab'd by you,
Divulg'd, and made the Prattle of a Boy.

*Q. M.* No, no, my Lord; I am not to be taught
By you, to keep a Secret Look at home,

Collect, if in your late tempestuous Passion
You did not give suspicion of the Truth.

*King.* Suspicion? no, 'tis more; we are betray'd.
He told me to my Face he knew the matter,
How that the Admiral, and the *Hugonots*
Should straight be Massacred. O, I could rave!
Our Hearts are Rebels to our Bosom-Councils.

*Enter* Alberto Gondi.

But see, perhaps this Villain gave it Air.
Ah, Traitor! ah perfidious false *Alberto*!
Have I not rais'd thee from the dregs of baseness,
And lodg'd thee in the bosom of thy Master?
Nay, rise, and speak, where didst thou git the daring
T'unravel the close Web of my sworn Councils,
And trust 'em to the giddy *Ligneroles*?
Confess; nay, hide not what thou hast reveal'd,
Or Racks, Blood, Blood and Fire, and lasting Torments
Shall force thee, speak.

*Alb.* Then let the Rack be brought:
Methinks I long to give a noble proof
How much I can endure in such a Cause.

*King* I know not what to say, whom to accuse,
Or where to turn my self. Call hither *Guise*,
And Cardinal of *Lorrain*. But see my Brother.

*Enter* Anjou.

It must be so. 'tis he, 'tis he, false Man!
I had forgot! this Boy's his only Minion,
The very Turn-key of his Cabinet-thoughts.
But speak, *Anjou*; how didst thou dare to trust
So strong a Secret, such Important Counsels,
That from the Book of Fate must wipe for ever
A hundred thousand Lives, or quash the Throne?
O, I'm not able to contain the Transport!
Why didst thou trust a Business of such weight
To *Ligneroles*?

*Enter* Cardinal *and* Guise.

*Anj.* 'Tis true, my Lord, I did;
But I'll engage my Life he'll ne'er divulge it.

*King.* No, Sir; I pass my Word he never shall.

*Anj.* My Lord, I beg——

*King.* Speak not, stir not hence.

N

My Lord of *Guise*, I must engage your Service.
*Q. M.* Think no more of him, lest the violent King,
Whom yet I never saw so strangely mov'd,
Should turn his Rage on you.
*Gui.* My Lord, 'tis done
Two of my Train there are that bear him grudge.
*King.* When he's dispatch'd, let your Friends go to
To put a little Varnish on his Blood, [Prison,
Then you, or some that have the seeming Power,
Beg for their Pardon, and it shall be sign'd.

*Enter* Alberto.

*Alb.* My Lord, the Admiral's arriv'd.
*King.* O, Madam,
Give me your Hand, and yours and yours
To prop me,
Now we must shew a Master-piece indeed,
To meet the Man whom we would make an end of,
Ev'n at that time when mortal Wars within,
When the Blood boils and flushes to be at him,
Yet then to shew the signs of heartiest Love,
To cringe, to fawn, to smile, to weep, and swear,
Are Masks for Women, not for Men to wear. [*Exeunt.*

## SCENE III.

*Enter* Admiral, *Queen of* Navarre, *the* Princes, Commanders, Gentlemen, &c.

*Adm.* *Cavagnes* would'st thou think it possible,
I scarce have Breath to tell thee I'm not well?
*Cav.* Why should you fear?
*Adm.* Because it goes against me
Upon the way, my sad presaging Heart
At the first view of *Paris* sunk within me,
I stopt, and start, and answer'd without Thought,
Like one that breaks his Sleep with his own brawl,
As if my Genius shock'd me with a question,
And ask'd me, whither I was bound for Death?
But it must be, *Cavagnes*: nay, what's more
Than Death it self, confess my self a Traitor,
Ev'n in the Theatre of all the Kingdom:

Do Penance for the glorious Wars I made,
In view of those that have so bravely back'd me.

*Enter the* King, Queen Mother, Anjou, Alberto Gondi, *Cardinal of* Lorrain. *All the* Hugonots *kneel.*

*King* Madam, you're welcome, this the Prince your Son
Most welcome, this the Prince of *Conde*, welcome;
Welcome to *Paris*, welcome to the Court:
The Heart of *Charles* bids welcome to you all.
Who's that upon the Earth! the great *Chastillon*,
The glorious Admiral, the fam'd *Coligni*,
The Scourge of Kingdoms! O, my Father, rise;
Or, by the Majesty of Age, the Reverence
Due to these Hairs, the King himself shall kneel.

*Adm* O Sir, is't possible! can this be real!
Can you forgive this Out-law; this Offender,
Who has so often turn'd your Subjects Arms
Against their Lawful Soveraign, made whole wilds
Of Populous Towns, and brav'd the Lions Fury!
Now you have drawn me quite unarm'd to Court,
Can you so far be Master of your Temper
As not to hew me in a thousand pieces?

*King.* Can you, who had the Power to make me tremble,
Can you, my awful Subject, be so good
To kneel before my Feet, and ask my Pardon,
And shall I be so barbarous to refuse it!
No, mighty Warrior, in the heat of Broils,
When thou so terribly becam'st the Field,
Had'st thou thus sought me, by those Saints we worship,
I had receiv'd thee with a Breast of Mercy

*Adm.* Forgive me, Sir, my Heart so rises in me,
I cannot speak

*King* Let then the World be witness,
All that is Honest, Sacred, Good, and Just,
Be Witnesses the Powers of Heav'n and Earth,
With this Embrace I pardon thee thy Errors,
I bid thee welcome, as my better Angel:
Thou shalt direct in all my Bosom Councils;
My Genius; O! and while I hold thee thus,
Methinks I press my Father in my Arms. [Heart

*Adm* O! Sir, what have you done? you've burst the
Of your old *Gasper*, with this Flood of Goodness

And

And see, it gushes from my Aged Eyes.
*King* No more.
*Adm* I must, I must make way, my Lord,
For this dear Load that makes me sore within:
But haste, employ my Arm, let Fortune raise
Some Foe that's worthy of *Chastillon's* Sword:
Nay I shall quarrel with the Fates themselves
Unless they rouze me up some brave occasion,
To signalize my Loyalty, my Conduct,
And constant Zeal for your Immortal Glory.
*King* Your Friendship to the Queen, who courts it too,
Will more oblige me than your Wars abroad
*Adm.* For all past Faults thus low I ask her Pardon
*Q M.* Rise, rise, my Lord: let us forgive each other
May I, when dying, miss the Throne of Mercy,
If when I saw the King and you embrace,
My wounded Heart did not weep Blood for Joy
*King.* Come, come, my Lord, since you're so fierce to serve me,
I'll find your Sword Employment. Rest a while,
And then for *Flanders*, where the Duke of *Alva*
Will hold you to't.
*Adm.* I long, my Lord, to try him
He who so curses the reform'd Religion.
I wish that, with some thousands I could raise
Of those poor Protestants whom he disdains,
I could but face him on the dusty Plain,
Tho' to his Aid he call'd his Catholick Master,
With thousand Arms held up to thousand Saints,
Ev'n with this handful of my old Commanders
Heading the well truss'd Body of our Men,
We'd on, to make the Mytred Armies yield,
And drive the trembling Crosiers from the Field.
[*Exeunt.*

## ACT IV. SCENE I.

*The Scene draws; the King, the Queen Mother, the Duke of* Anjou *Duke of* Guise, *Cardinal of* Lorrain *The Body of* Ligneroles *held up all bloody.*

*Anj.* AH, Traitor *Guise*! but I will have thy Life—
*Gui.* Let go your hand; or by the Majesty
That governs here, I'll send you to your Boy.
*King.* Tear 'em asunder.
*Anj.* I'll have Satisfaction.
*King.* Remove the Body. You my Lord of *Guise*,
Say how this Murder hapned.
*Gui.* Thus, my Lord.
*Charles* Count of *Mansfeild*, and the Count of *Guercby*,
When with this Morning's hunt, the Hills, and Groves,
The Skies and Fountains seem'd one mutual Cry,
Riding in company, with this bold Spirit,
On fiery Coursers, chanc'd to discompose him:
He frown'd, they laugh'd, and so the beaten road
Of Quarrels, hot Words rose, then Blows and Thrusts,
The Youth betwixt 'em fell, I know not how,
And there's an end of him.
*Anj.* Traitor, thou ly'st. Thou know'st the Cause.
*King.* No, Sir, it was my Order.
Now, as you have respect to your own Safety,
No more of this. Had you not blush'd in Blood,
In the Heart-blood of him you dearest lov'd,
By my dead Father's Soul, by my Revenge,
You should your self have mourn'd so gross a failing.
*Q. M.* Sir, he repents.
*King.* He does but what he ought.
Now to the Business.
Since then the Cloud that holds our horrid Vengeance
Comes nearer racking o'er the *Hugonots* Heads,
Let's help the fall, and stir not from this place
Till we have fixt the Plat-form of their Ruin.
First, for the Queen, *Jane Albert* of *Navarre*,
Because a Woman, and of Royal Blood,

My

My Mother judg'd that ſhe ſhould die by Poiſon

*Q. M.* Diſpatch'd with Sweets Paſs to the reſt; ſhe's dead.

*King* Yet not without ſuſpicion of the Princes,
Who therefore, by my Order, were deſir'd
To ſee her Body open'd; which was done
Before the chief of all the *Hugonots*;
Only her Head was ſpar'd, as I appointed,
Out of a ſeeming Reverence, but indeed,
Leſt that the Poiſon, tho' it paſs'd unſeen,
Like a cloſe Murderer, through the Lanes of Life,
Might yet at laſt be taken where it lodg'd.
With this, in part, I ſatisfy'd their Murmurs,

*Q. M.* Therefore you muſt confer more Favours ſtill
Upon the Admiral, lull him with Honours,
Strike him but in the Throat of his Ambition,
You have him ſure yet let him play a while,
And roll at random down the ſtream of Glory
My Lord of *Guiſe*, you have not yet convers'd him,
Therefore, while this Suſpicion on the death
Of the late Queen flies warm about his Ears,
Viſit him, as commanded by the King,
But ſo as if enforc'd and by degrees,
Proceed to half a Quarrel, that the King,
Being made the Judge, as coming there by chance,
May give it quite againſt you in appearance,
And force you to ſubmit your ſelf for Pardon

*Guiſ* It ſhall be ſo And fear not, I'll provoke him;
I will eaſe my Heart a little, with keen words
To right my Father's Wrongs, and ſhed the Venom
That ſwells me all within

*King.* On this proceed
To the intended Marriage of *Navarre*,
Which once perform'd, as if that were the Lightning
To the ſure Peal of Horror that muſt follow,
Begin our Vengeance with the Admiral's Death.

*Anj* Firſt, Sir, it would be known how *Guiſe* approves
The Marriage of *Navarre* with *Marguerite.*

*King.* I know the Duke approves what I reſolve,
And on ſo great a puſh, would forfeit both
A *Legneroles* and *Marguerite* too

E e 4 Q. M.

*Q. M.* Come, come, it's monstrous but to make a Scru-
To stand on Pets, Intrigues, and foolish Passions, [ple,
When such a Fate is now upon the Bolt,
As ne'er perhaps yet Thunder'd with Success,
Since first the World began.
*Gui.* My Lord, I yield,
And take Prince *Porcien*'s Widow for my Wife.
*King* I sent the Count of *Rhets* to bring her hither.
My Lord *Lorrain*, pray let me view the Contract.
This, by the hand of *Guise*, must first be torn,
And then presented her.
*Gui* Excuse me, Sir. [not;
*King.* If Prayers or Threats can bend her, Sir, you shall
But, if those fail, my Lord, without more words,
I charge you for your Honour, and my own,
To act as I command: or, by my Blood,
Nor you, nor I shall never see her more.
*Gui.* That's a home thrust indeed Sir, I obey,
And wait your farther Order.
*King.* My Lord *Lorrain*,
Attend the Duke while I examine *Marguerite*,
Wait till I stamp, and when thy trouble's over,
Make to the Admiral; and I will follow.
*Enter* Alberto *with* Marguerite.
How, *Marguerite* weeping? all in Tears!
Sure then the Count of *Rhets* mistook the Message.
I sent to give thee Joy, to tell my Sister
She must be marry'd
*Mar* And I come, my Lord,
To shew my Heart before your Majesty,
To beg your Favour, Mercy, and your Pardon;
For O, my Lord, I cannot, if I would,
Be marry'd to *Navarre*
*King* You cannot? Rise,
And tell me why I'll hear you out with patience
*Mar* Ah, Sir, how shall I speak your Sister's Frailty?
How shall I, but thus drown'd with Tears and Blushes,
Confess the fault of Duty? I am marry'd,
Betroth'd, my Lord.
*King.* To whom?

*Mar.*

*Mar.* Alas, you're angry;
But I must own the Truth, tho' on your Brow
A thousand Deaths sat menacing my Soul:
Yes, Sir, I'm marry'd to the Duke of *Guise.*

*King.* Not marry'd, *Marguerite*; but contracted:
And so far I'll forgive thy heedless Youth,
But on Condition that, without more noise,
Thou raze the haughty *Guise* from thy Remembrance,
Or, by the violation of our Name,
I will not spare to drain thy tainted Blood,
Till I have mounted thee by Death a Victim
To the great Memory of the wrong'd *Valois*

*Mar.* Call then, my Lord, call forth your fierce Tor-[mentors,
Propose to *Marguerite* Flames and Wounds,
And all the cruel Arts of thoughtful Fury,
See your poor Sister's Spirit parch'd away
By ling'ring Fires, to make my Death more dreadful;
Yet, Sir, with my last Breath I must avow
My Love to *Guise*, and Hatred to *Navarre.*

*King.* No; I have thought on't better; I'll proclaim [thee,
A Prostitute; thou shalt no more be Royal:
Poor, and abandon'd, with thy Shame upon thee,
I'll turn thee forth a Beggar to the World.

*Mar* Do, do, my Lord, rather than wed *Navarre*,
And make it Death for any to relieve me,
Set the mad Multitude like Dogs upon me,
To tear, to worry me like common Flesh,
To drag me to a Ditch, and leave me gasping;
Yet with my last Sighs I will groan to Heav'n,
'Tis easier this, than to be false to *Guise*

*King* But, *Marguerite*, was there ever Love,
Without brave Revenge on Provocation?
Yet, Wretch, thou lov'st without being lov'd again:
Since in my Presence *Guise* now past his Word
To leave thee, and to wed the Widow *Porcien*

*Mar* No, no, my Lord; that Art was us'd before,
Yet, Sir, you make me tremble, for methinks
There's something more resolv'd, more stern in you,
Than in my Mother yet my Heart's confirm'd
Not to believe ev'n you, O therefore cease,
Or rather execute your former Rage,

And

And give me up to those Tormentors Hands
That wait your Call.
*King*. But if I bring the Duke
Before thy Face, that Contract in his Hand,
Which past betwixt you, and he tears it here
Openly, in the Presence of us all;
Wilt thou then quit him, with resolv'd Revenge,
And wed *Navarre*?
*Mar*. Why should you ask me, Sir?
Prove me but half as much, but half that Falshood,
That Impudence, that Treason to the Throne
Of our crown'd Loves, and I will wed a Slave:
There's not a thing so loath'd upon the Earth,
But you shall bind me to it for my Life,
To Age, Deformity, to all that's hateful,
Blasting, and deadly.——Ha! what's this he tears?
The Contract? O, it is the cursed Contract!
Then I'll tear too Death, Furies, Hell, and Devils!
But call him, Sir, call back the perjur'd Traitor;
Let your Guards hold him, you shall see, my Lord,
How well I hate him. Give me but a Dagger,
And I will gore his Heart with thousand Wounds,
Nay, if 'twere possible, I'd stab his Soul,
Fill it so full, brimfull of Woman's Gall,
That, tho' he were an Angel it should damn him;
But he's a Devil, Devil, Devil, Devil.
*King* Give me your Hand, you shall along with me
To a young King, that will be proud to serve you.
*Mar*. O, Sir, I know not what to say, or do,
But fling this load of Misery at your Feet:
You have my Promise; but with all my Blood
I would retrieve it; for since *Guise* is false,
Whom I believ'd the worthiest of the World,
Since he has prov'd himself so damn'd a Villain,
O, give me leave, Sir, give me leave to shun,
To hate, to loath, to curse all Humane Kind.
*King* I'll have no more delay; I claim your Promise:
Come then; or, by my Crown, I'll have thee drag'd,
What hoa? without there.

Enter

*Enter Attendants.*

*Mar.* Mother, pity me.
Have Patience, Sir, a little time, my Lord,
To vent these bursting Sighs, and I will go
Let me but dry my Eyes, and I will go.
This remnant of a wretched Royal Woman,
This stain to all your Blood, O cruel Heav'n!
This curs'd, forlorn, unhappy Bride, shall go
Thus to the Altar where my Fate's decreed;
But like a Victim that is doom to bleed [*Exeunt.*

## SCENE II.

*Enter* Admiral, Antramont, Cavagnes, Langoiran.

*Ant.* Poison'd; the Royal dead *Navarre* was poison'd;
'Tis the first Thunder-clap of that vast Storm
That seems already breaking o'er your Head.
Why are you senseless then, and deaf to warning;
When, wheresoe'er you cast your Eyes, the Storm
Looks blacker yet? Why stays the Duke of *Guise*?
Why does he summon all his Blood to Court,
With Barons, Knights, that hold the Catholick Party,
With Foreign Gentry living on his Pensions,
And therefore ready upon all occasions,
With hazard of their Lives to act his Pleasure?
*Adm.* Peace, *Antramont.*
*Ant.* Alas, my Lord, I cannot.
Why should the Visdam *Chartres*, Count *Mongomery*,
Resolve to lodge themselves beyond the *Sein*,
Unless their Minds presage some dreadful Mischief!
'Tis coming, O, with deeper Policies
The King and Queen delude your easie Soul
With fatal Praises, and undoing Honours
O, they have caught you! my Prophetick Soul
Sees the red Tempest thunder down in Blood,
In Blood of you, of me, of all about you
*Adm.* O, *Antramont*, you foil me now indeed;
Yet I shall answer, if your Passion please.
First, for the Queen, I saw her Body open'd,

The

The Parts whereof were found, untouch'd by Poison,
And by our own Physicians 'twas concluded
She dy d a natural Death. Then for the *Guises*,
Some little Satisfaction must be given,
As to permit their Presence at the Marriage;
But, for the management of State-Affairs,
Or Favour from the King, they're lost for ever·
Nor shall it keep my dauntless Powers awake,
Tho' *Chartres* and *Mongomery* will not come.
But, to forbear the Subject, leave me here
With my *Cavagnes*

*Ant* I am commanded, Sir;
Yet, for the safety of your innocent Babes,
Beware my Lord, be cautious, O prevent [*Ex* Ant

*Adm* Fear not, Farewel, be gone, I will beware.
Why should I fear, *Cavagnes*, when the King
Inclines his Heart to the Reform'd Religion,
When the whole Management of Home-affairs,
With all Confederacies made abroad,
Are left to me, as Judge and Arbitrator,
The Genius and the Oracle of *France*?
But, if the Will of Heav'n has set it down,
That all this Trust is deep Dissimulation,
That there's no Faith nor Credit to be given
To the inviolable Royal Word,
O, my *Cavagnes*, if 'tis possible,
If this be so, I yield, I yield to die·
I am contented for the Protestant Faith
Here to be hewn into a thousand pieces,
And made the Martyr of so good a Cause.

*Lang* My Lord, I take my leave, and am resolv'd
To leave the Court.

*Adm* *Cavagnes*, prethee speak,
It is not worth our Smile But why *Langoiran*,
Why dost thou leave the Maker of thy Fortune?
Is it not worth the hazard?

*Lang* No, my Lord.
I'm sorry, Sir, to see you made so much of:
And so farewel For my part, I'm content
To save my self with Fools; rather than perish
With those that are too wise. [*Exit.*

Enter

*Enter a Servant.*

*Serv.* My Lord the Duke of *Guise.*

[*Exeunt* Cavag. *and Serv.*

*Enter* Guise

*Gui* The King, my Lord, commanded me to wait you,
And bid you welcome to the Court.

*Adm.* The King
Still loads me with new Honours; but none greater
Than this the last.

*Gui* There is one greater yet,
Your high Commission for the War with *Spain*:
I, and my Family, are charg'd to serve you,
And 'twill be glorious Work.

*Adm.* If you are there,
There must be Action.

*Gui.* O, your Pardon, Sir;
I'm but a Stripling in the Trade of War:
But you, whose Life is one continu'd Battel,
What will not your Triumphant Arms accomplish?
Who, as your self confess'd, or Fame is false,
Have quite out-gone the Memory of the Ancients,
Of *Alexander*, and of *Julius Cæsar*,
For they in all their Actions had Success;
But you, in spite of your malicious Fortune,
After the loss of four most signal Battels,
Still rose more fierce and dreadful to your Foes:
And last, when all Men thought you had no way
To save your Life, but wander through the World;
You forc'd the King to grant your own Conditions,
More proper for a Conqueror, than one
That was o'ercome.

*Adm* No more of that, my Lord.

*Gui* But, Sir, since I must make a little one
In this great Business, let me understand
What 'tis you mean, and why you put the King
Upon so dangerous an Expedition?

*Adm.* Know, I intend the Greatness of the King,
The Greatness of all *France*, whom it imports
To make their Arms their Aim and Occupation:
Since then the Genius of the Kingdom's rouz'd,
I'll turn the Feaver of those Civil Broils

To

To wholsome Exercise, to War with Strangers
*Gui* Stor'd Arsenals, and Armories, and Fields of Horse,
Ordnance, Ammunition, and the Nerve of War,
Sound Infantry, not harrass'd and diseas'd,
To meet a Veteran Army, should be thought of;
Nor ought you to rely on Protestants,
Those Mercenaries that must come, for he
Who, thus resolv'd, depends on such, shall spread
His Feathers now, but mew 'em all to Morrow.
*Adm.* I find, my Lord, the Argument grows warm,
Therefore thus much, and I have done. The King
Intends to send an Army into *Flanders*,
A powerful one, and under my Command
First then, altho' the Wars of latter Ages
Are, in respect of former, made i'th' dark,
*Chastillon* will not steal a Victory
*Gui.* The Phrase of *Alexander* at *Arbela*!
*Adm* No place of Honour, Office, or Command
Through the whole Series of this glorious War,
For Profit, Favour, or for Interest,
Not of the greatest, shall be bought or sold:
Whereas too, for th' incouragement of Fighters,
There are degrees promiscuously conferr'd
On Souldiers, and no Souldiers, this Man Knighted,
Because he charg'd a Troop before his Dinner,
And sculk'd behind a hedge in th' Afternoon;
I will have strict Examination made
Betwixt the Meritorious and the Base;
And, since I am entrusted as I wish,
I'll spoil the Traffick of this Brandy Court,
And vye Rewards for Merit with old *Rome*
*Guy* You will, my good Lord Admiral?
*Adm.* Sir, I will
Upon the very Spot of Victory
For Gallant Men ——
Erect their Trophies, Funeral Laudatives,
And Monuments for those that dy'd in War,
Crowns of Distinction, Garland Personal,
All but the Stile of Emperor, which the King
Of the whole Universe did after borrow;
That for my Master: and perhaps for me

The Triumph of their Generals on return.

*Gui* You have mouth'd it bravely; and there is no doubt
Your deeds would answer well such haughty words.
Yet, let me tell you, Sir, there was a Man
(Curse on the hand that sped him) that would better,
Better than you, or all the bragging Generals,
That when he shone in Arms and sunn'd the Field,
That better would become the great Battallion,
Mov'd, spoke, and fought, and was himself a War.

*Adm* The Noble *Guise*, your Father, Sir you mean,
But yet, my Lord———

*Gui* No yet, my Lord, no yet:
By Arms, I bar you that,
For never was his like, nor shall again,
Till murder'd by *Poltrot*, curs'd, damn'd *Poltrot*,
Whose Soul now gluts the Maw of *Lucifer*.

*Adm* Speak with more Charity

*Gui* Ha! Charity!
Damnation on the Soul that harbours it.
Were I in Heav'n, and saw him scorch'd in Flames,
I would not spit my Indignation down,
Lest I should cool his Tongue. For *Beza* too,
That set him on, with the rewards of Heav'n,
To act so black, so deep, so damn'd a Murder.
O why will *Charles* thus sheath the Sword of Justice,
Till he has rooted up this Sect of Villains,
And collar'd to the Stake that canting Slave,
That preach'd my God like Father from the World?

*Adm* Come, come, my Lord, hear with a little patience,
And you shall find 'tis not the Protestant way
To stab, and bear the Brains out in the dark:
Look home, my Lord, go to the *Vatican*,
See in all those polish'd Decretales,
There be not one Red-letter'd Page for killing.

*Gui* Ha, Admiral! then durst thou justify
The Villain, whom my Vengeance marks for Death?

*Adm* My Lord, I will not justify a Villain
More than your self. But if you thus proceed,
If that a great Man's Breath can puff away
On every Pet the Lives of free-born People,
What need that awful General Convocation,

The

Th' Assembly of the States? nay, let me urge,
If thus you threat the Venerable *Beza*,
Wh t may the rest expect?
*Gui* What, if I could,
They should be certain of, whole Piles of Fire.
*Adm* 'Tis very well my Lord, I know your Mind,
Which without fear or flatt'ry to your Person,
I'll tell the King, and then, with his Permission,
Proclaim it for a Warning to our People.
*Gui* Come, you're a Murd'rer your self.
*Adm.* Away
*Gui.* You were Complotter with that Villain *Beza*,
The black Abbeter of my Father's Murder.
*Adm.* This wou'd sound well, my Lord, in Front-Battle,
But here upon a Visit from the King
It looks not like the *Guise*
*Gui* My Father's Murder? bid me not stand on points
When that's remember'd!
But track me to the Forest with thy Sword,
Thus Man to Man, bark'd with all thy People,
Follow me, or I will proclaim thee Traitor, Coward
*Adm.* O King, King, King! still let me sound thy Name,
Lest this Fool-hardy Boy, this knotty Trifler,
This Spawn of Words, this Urchin of the War,
Should rule my Anger past the pulling down.

*Enter* King, Queen Mother, Alberto, Anjou, *and* Morvile.

But see He's here, I scorn to ruin thee:
Therefore go tell him, tell him thy own Story
*King.* What now, my Lord of *Guise*? is this your Visit?
I charge you on your Life, without reserve,
Tell me the Truth; how hapned this Disorder?
These ruffled hands, red looks, and port of Fury?
*Gui* I told him, Sir, since you resolve to have it,
He was the Murderer of my Noble Father;
Therefore a Traitor, Villain and a Coward.
*King* Is't possible?
*Adm.* No matter, Sir, no matter;
The old Man rouz'd, and shook himself, my Lord,
A few hot words; no more, upon my Life.
So, if your Majesty will do me Honour,
I do beseech you, let the business die.

King

*King.* *Guise*, go, submit your self, and ask his Pardon.
*Gui.* My Lord, I cannot speak.
*King.* Where are our Guards?
*Adm.* Hold there Come, Sir, I will interpret for you.
My Lord, this close Embrace makes up the breach:
We will be sorry, Sir, for one another.
*Gui* You have out-done me, Sir; but you'll excuse me,
'Twas a great Rack that screw'd me to this Folly.
*Adm.* More than enough, we're riveted the faster.
*King* My Lord of *Guise*
*Q M* My good Lord Admiral,
Now use your Power, and quite oblige the Court:
*Villandry* has provok'd the King at Play,
In such a nature, that he's doom'd to die;
My Son refus'd my Intercession for him;
Therefore, when he has done his Check to *Guise*,
For your Affront; pray, my good Lord, intreat him.
*King.* The Marriage stays within; which past, resolve
His Execution sudden as you can.
*Gui* *Morvele*
*Mor.* My Lord?
*Gui* I, by the King's Commission, have Command
To take the Admiral's Life.
*Mor.* I'll shoot him.
*Gui.* Right:
As he returns from Court.
*Mor* From some Out-Lodging
I'll watch him, till I execute your Order.
*Adm* I am a Suitor to your Majesty
For poor *Villandry*'s Life
*King.* Haste, bring him forth.
I think, my Lord, if you should ask my Heart,
My yielding Breast would open to your Hand.
But, Father, let's away; the Cardinal
Stays for *Navarre.*
*Adm* We'll wait your Majesty. [*Ex.* King *with Court.*
O, my *Cavagnes*, where's *Langoiran* now?
Where's *Antramont*? but haste, and tell her all;
Tell her th' extravagant Kindness of the King;
Tell her —— but stay, why such repeated Oaths?
That's to be thought on; Hollow was his Aspect,

Graves in his Smiles; Death in his bloodless Hands.
O, *Antramont*! I'll haste to meet thy Eyes.
The Face of Beauty on these rising Horrors,
Looks like the Midnight Moon upon a Murder:
It drives the Shades that thicken from the State,
And gilds the dark design that's ripe for Fate. [*Exe.*

## ACT V. SCENE I.

*The* King *rises from a Couch.*

FROM Amber Shrouds I see the Morning rise,
Her Rosy Hand begins to paint the Skies;
And now the City Emets leave their Hive,
And rouzing Hinds to chearful Labour drive;
High Cliffs and Rocks are pleasing Objects now,
And Nature smiles upon the Mountains brow;
The joyful Birds salute the Sun's Approach,
The Sun too laughs, and mounts his gaudy Coach,
While from his Car the dropping Gems distil,
And all the Earth, and all the Heav'n does smile.
But *Charles*, still wrapt in Shades, like Night appears,
His Sighs the Vapours, and the Dews his Tears.
Yet, O Just Power, with Pity, O behold
The Wretch, whose fault is in your Book inroll'd,
Behold these Streams, with which his Soul aspires
To slake your Wrath, and quench your angry Fires

*Enter* Genius.

*Gen.* Thy *Genius*, lo, from his sweet Bed of Rest,
Adorn'd with Jassamin, and with Roses drest,
The Pow'r Divine has rais'd to stop thy Fate;
A true Repentance never comes too late.
So soon as born, she made her self a Shroud,
The weeping Mantle of a Fleecy Cloud,
And swift as Thought her Airy Journy took,
Her hand Heav'ns Azure Gate with trembling strook;
The Stars did with amazement on her look;
She told thy Story in so sad a Tone,
The Angels start from Bliss, and gave a Groan.
But *Charles* beware, oh dally not with Heav'n,
For after this no Pardon shall be giv'n. [*Exit.*

*Enter* Queen Mother, *Cardinal of* Lorain, Anjou, Alberto Gondi.

*Card.* The King upon the Earth? O riſe, my Lord.
*Q. M.* He has of late been troubled with ſuch Faintings,
And ſee he bleeds at Mouth.
*King.* Stand from me all.
O, Mother, Mother! whither will you lead me?
Through what a Vault of Monuments, and Sculls,
And dead Men's Bones? And you, my Lord *Lorrain*,
Muſt I ſtill journey through this Vale of Death,
And never reach the Paradiſe you promis'd?
I muſt not let the Maſſacre go forward.
I'm warn'd from Heav'n, I ſwear I think from Heav'n.
*Q. M.* Some Scar-crow of a Dream: So far from Sin,
Or ought that's damnable, is our Deſign;
That my Lord Cardinal will tell you, Sir,
'Tis meritorious; and whene'er we ſtrike,
The Church ſhall bleſs it, as a Blow from Heav'n.
*Card.* Therefore, my Lord, I wiſh you to ſuſpect
Whatever thwarts you in your holy Purpoſe;
However veil'd, tho' in an Angel's form,
Conclude it the Suggeſtion of the Devil.
*Q. M.* So; now, I hope, theſe Qualms are at an end,
And we may cloſe purſue the main Intention
Suppoſe the Admiral kill'd; on this, the *Hugonots*
Fall on the Houſe of *Guiſe*; the City riſes
And cuts 'em all to pieces: Now imagine,
Which I am apt to think, the Hereticks
Are more diſcreet, and only ſue for Juſtice,
Without a Tumult, ſhall the buſineſs ſtand?
*Car.* No. If we find they do not run to Uproar,
(Our only hope to colour o'er their Ruin)
Proceed to inſtant Slaughter; or they'll find
Some means for flight, and kindle up the War
More dreadfully than ever.
*Anj.* Is't determin'd
That, with the reſt, the Princes too ſhall bleed?
*Q. M.* My Judgment is moſt poſitive in this:
Let not one Soul of all be left alive;
For 'tis ridiculous, in ſuch extreams,

I'th' midst of Slaughter, Ruin, Blood, and Death,
To think of ever being prais'd for Mercy
Nor can a Mean be us'd, the Duke of *Guise*
Meddles not in it, if a Man escape:
And says, in such a desperate Purge of Humours,
If any Relick of the great Distemper
Be left behind, it runs to a Relapse
More dangerous than before.

*King* As I remember,
Madam, it has been oft your Oracle,
In these late Civil Wars, to avoid a Battel;
That Limbs, tho' ne'er so foul, should not be lopt
Without the utmost, last Necessity,
Because the Body feels too great defect,
Sharp Pains, and almost irrecoverable Weakness:
And will you now cut the great Arteries,
The Princes of the Blood? Most horrid Thought!

*Q M.* Compose your self, *Navarre* and *Conde* live.
Come, come, you must put off this Melancholy,
'Twill breed Suspicion, Sir, let me intreat you
To go upon the Instant straight to Tennis,
While *Morvele* does his business

*King* O my Heart!
If you would have me fixt, you must not leave me,
You must talk out to my distracted Soul,
Lest Conscience drown the Voice of Policy

[*Exeunt all but* Cardinal

*Card* This 'tis to have a Conscience. — Here comes [one

*Enter* Guise

Sear'd as my self, of my own Family.
Is he dispatch'd!

*Gui* Not yet, but *Morvele* waits him,
His Fuzee cock'd, and planted at the Window:
All, all is fixed.

*Card* What, your *Marguerite*
Said she was sick, and would not bed the Prince
Last night?

*Gui* I know not that, but here I stay
To take her as she passes to the Gardens.
How fares the King?

*Card.* A little bound in Conscience:

He

He pukes at Dreams; and as I hear of late,
Spits Blood ——
*Gui.* A fit, a fit, my Lord, o'th' Mother:
I told you so. But see, the furious Princess?
Away. I'll clap my Prow upon the Storm;
And, if a Wrack must follow, let it come.
*Enter* Marguerite.
*Mar.* Ha! Villain! Traitor! Devil! Hence, be gone;
Or I must get into my Grave to hide me.
I've sworn, I've sworn to fly thee like a Fury,
And I am damn'd if e'er I see thee more.
*Gui.* I will obey you. And indeed the Fates
Of these sad Souls that must to day be dol'd
Require my haste. I beg you but to hear me:
Grant me but this, by Hell, and Hell's worst Horrors,
And all the Murders of this bloody day,
You ne'er shall see me more.
*Mar.* What can'st thou say?
For see, I know not how, thou'st charm'd my Rage.
*Gui.* Know then, the Lives of every *Hugonot*
This moment now are sentenc'd to the Grave,
A Massacre of all.
*Mar.* A Massacre!
*Gui.* Madam, I've done. But hark! a Gun went off!
My leaping Heart cries out, It is the Admiral.
The Marriage of *Navarre* was for this end
Design'd, to bring the Princes to the Court:
And, on so great an Enterprise, the King
Compell'd me to the tearing of the Contract,
Or threatned the destruction of my House,
And which was worse, your Death before my Eyes.
What, hoa! *Morvele*! He pass'd the Anti-chamber.
*Enter* Morvele.
Permit me to consult him. Ha! speak out;
Say, is the Admiral ———
*Mor.* Not dead, my Lord.
I think I saw some of his Fingers fly,
And part of his left Arm: I'm sure I hit him.
*Gui.* Here, take this Key; fly to my Closet, haste;
Thou art pursu'd: Farewell.
*Mor.* I'm gone, my Lord. [*Exit.*

*Gui* 'Twas in this manner just, my noble Father
Was [illegible]ted from the Fame of all the World
By such another Villain, and my Soul
Leaps with Revenge, that this proud Admiral
Shou'd, like an Eagle, in his utmost flight
Be topled from the Clouds of all his Glory.
Madam, farewel: I hope you will excuse
What I, enforc'd, did act: I love you still;
And, on this sad Affair, in which perhaps
Your *Guise* may perish, it would warm my Heart
To hear you do not hate me

*Marg* Death and Horror!
Infamy, Vengeance, Murder, Massacre!

*Gui* Now by the Life and Heart of our design
'Tis well dissembled, stood thy Lord in view,
I thus wou'd charge thee, bear thee in my Arms
From the proud hurry of a clashing World,
To *Mahomet*'s Paradise, to Beds of Pleasure,
Where we shall spin the Silken Joys for ever,
Without a break, lengthning the twinkling Moment
To an Eternity of Deathless Pleasure.

*Marg.* Touch me not for thy Life, thou Traitor! Murderer!
Ravisher! Oh thou titled Villain!
In Purple dipt to give a gloss to Mischief!
Follow the bloody bark of thy Ambition,
And never see me more———

*Gui* It cannot be,
Unless you chain me, drag me in Sunless Caves:
You are my Earthly Goodness, all my hope
Of Comfort here. nor wish I more hereafter.

*Marg* Hold, hold, Prophaner, thou hast dishonour'd me,
But this is little to the Crimes that follow,
Thou hast betray'd me, after all my Vows,
To marry one I hate, for thy Ambition
Mak'st me the Cause of this most horrid Vengeance,
At which the Earth shall sicken, Saints be sad,
And none but Furies like your self———

*Gui* Did not your Mother form the whole Design?

*Marg* Whoever form'd or helpt in such contriving,
Hell and Damnation waste 'em; but for thee,
Sear'd as thou art, with Cruelty, Revenge,

I pity thee, O *Guise* ! because I lov'd thee,
And beg thee view those Fiends that gape to seize thee:
Allow at least a possibility,
An unknown Country, after you are dead,
As well as there was one e'er you were born
*Gui* Admit me then once more to share your Breast,
To taste those Secrets from those lovely Lips,
And I in time may be a Proselite.
*Marg* Here look your last ! for from the time I leave you,
Ne'er hope to see lost *Marguerite* more.
*Gui.* I am a Rebel, and have sworn to see you:
By all our former Dearness, and I will
By Heav'n · I will, in spite of your resolve,
I'll gaze upon you till these Crystals run.
*Marg.* You have broke my Heart a thousand several [ways,
And now against my Will this Parting melts me.
*Gui.* Speak not of parting; by those Eyes I beg,
Nor melting Hearts, the Blood runs down from mine.
*Marg.* For all the wrongs you have done me, my Dishonour,
For all your Delays, your Slights, your thousand Oaths,
Your most considerate Pride in falling out,
That I might Court you to be Friends again——
*Gui.* Stop yet · and oh eternal Love shall Crown thee.
*Marg.* For all my Midnight Groans——
*Gui.* Hold, *Marguerite*
*Marg* My Tears, my Watchings,
The bleeding tokens of the fondest Love——
*Gui* Take this, and strike it to my Heart;
But speak your Griefs no more. [*Offers a Dagger.*
*Marg.* By all I've said,
I beg you, Sir, to spare my Husband's Life.
*Gui* What, *Marguerite*? ha! *Navarre* again?
This was too much.
*Marg* Save him, if possible,
And so farewel, thou Ruin of my Glory·
Farewel, thou strong Seducer of my Youth.
Yet I will Eye thee hungerly at last:
Nay, take this Sigh to that thus splits my Heart,
My Husband's Life is all that I implore,
To save *Navarre*, and never see me more. [*Exit.*
*Gui.* She's gone, for ever gone: why, let her go.

Henceforth pronounce all Woman-kind thy Foe;
Or if thy feeble Soul to Love return,
Do not, like *Anthony*, for Life-time burn:
But as a Lion, eager of his Prey,
Compell'd by Thirst, turns from his purpos'd way,
And in some Silver Fountain slakes his Rage,
Then runs more fiercely on his Foes t'engage,
So having quench'd thy Fires with Beauties Charms,
Forget the Pleasures, and rush to Arms [*Exit.*

*Enter* King, Q Mother, Anjou, Lorrain, Alb Gondi.

*King* Command that all the City-Gates be shut,
Except but two, for bringing in Provisions,
And these my Lord of *Rhetz*, see strictly Guarded,
Lest that the Murderer escape.

*Q. M.* You bear it bravely!
Now to the wounded Admiral: be there
As you are now, seem soft and pitiful,
Fond him with Tears, cry out with your Impatience
To be reveng'd upon the Murderer.

*King* You that are made of Artifice instruct me. [*Ex.*

## SCENE II.

*The Admiral Dressing, with all the* Hugonots *about him*

*Adm* A Finger and an Arm? what all this Noise
About the shattering of a Limb? Away.
And in a Cause so great, so glorious too?
Nay, let 'em burn the other to the Shoulder,
Or let that Badger Queen grind every Bone
Betwixt her Teeth, and grin to hear 'em crack.

*Cav* Let's instantly resolve to bear him forth.

*Adm* No: with this mangled Flesh held to Heav'n,
This horrid mash of Blood, and Bone, and Marrow,
Upon my Knees I beg the Power Divine
T'establish thus the Protestant Religion,
To plant it [illegible] the Blood of lost *Coligni*,
If that, al[illegible] may satisfie their Fury.

*Cav.* Take Heart, Sir; hope one Day for full Revenge.

*Enter* Antramont.

*Ant* 'Tis well, my Lord! 'tis well, my *Cato*! well!
You call'd this *Paris Utica* at first
The Stars of Great Men have a Cast Divine,

And

And when they mould with second Thought, the Spirit,
The Air, the Life, the Golden Vapour's gone.
*Langoiran!* O *Langoiran!*

*Adm.* Fate, my *Martia*,
There is a Providence that over-rules:
Therefore submit, haste, for thy Life, away,
I beg thee fly, my *Martia*, to *Geneva*
My little ones shall, with *Teligny*, follow.

*Ant* What, Sir, is't possible!
Is a Plank in this great Vessel rived?
Is't necessary that a Wreck should follow?

*Adm* O, *Antramont*, there is no going forth;
If the King be not in th' Assassination,
Fear not, I shall have Justice: If he be,
Farewel for ever, I ll ne'er see thee more.

*Ant* You shall, you shall why bust you not away?
There are at least ten thousand, your Adherents,
Will clear your Passage to *Chastillon*.
Why do you drag then, when your Fate cries on?

*Adm* Once more I say, my Fate is in the King;
Therefore away: If things go right, you come
To me again, if not, there's one preserv'd
T'embalm my Bowels, O my *Antramont*,
I mean my Babes, that thus have force to thaw me.
That Power, whose most unsearchable Decree
Thus dooms our parting, give thee strength to bear it,
To bear my Death; perhaps thou'lt hear it shortly:
Yet thou shalt hear nothing unworthy me,
Nothing that's faint and flagging at the Goal,
But my last Gasp like my first start of Glory.

*Ant* What, leave thee, *Gaspar*, e'er I kiss thy Wound?
O, let me touch the Batt'ry of his Arm!
Forgive me; thus far I will be a *Roman*:
There's Virtue here, in this most Sacred Relict,
I swear I think there is, to save a Soul.

*Adm.* Be gone, I say; I cannot bear thy Kindness:
Force her away, and bear her to St. *Germain*

*Ant* I go For thee, this Prayer I leave behind me:
Whene'er thou dy'st, the Arm of Angels waft thee
To those smooth Joys that have no gritty Moments.
For her that brought thee to this barbarous end,

The

The Whips of Conscience drive her to Despair;
Conscience! Sh' has none: why then the stings of Pleasure,
Sores and Diseases, Disappointments plague her;
May all her Life be one continu'd Torment,
And that more Racking than a Mother's Labour:
In meeting Death, may her least trouble be
As great, as now my Parting is with thee [*Exit*

*Enter* Alberto Gondi

*Alb.* My Lord, his Majesty, the Queen his Mother,
Approach, to mourn your Chance, and give you Justice.

*Enter* King, Queen, Anjou, Lorrain.

*King* My Lord, I come to pour the Balm of Tears
Into your Wound; I come to threaten Death
To that bold Villain who durst act this Outrage:
And by my Soul I swear, my Father shall
Have such Revenge, as if a King were kill'd.

*Adm.* I thank your Majesty, and humbly crave
Your leave, Sir, to retire home to *Chastillon*,
Where, from these tumultuous *Parisians*,
I may, my Lord, recover this Misfortune.

*Q. M.* What, take a Journey, Sir, in this Condition?
Your Death must follow: But, alas, I fear,
I fear the Truth, with Tears I must avow it,
My Lord, you dare not trust the King and me

*Adm* O, do not tax me with the least Suspicion:
I must believe the Royal Majesty;
But all my fear is for my dear Companions,
And these lov'd Princes, whom the Heav'ns defend.

*King* Therefore my Brother streight shall draw the
Within the City, while for present Safety [Guards
I order Monsieur *Cosen's* Company
To keep your Quarters from all fear of Tumult
O, Father, Father, do not wound my Soul
By a Distrust unworthy of us both.

*Q. M.* Ah, my Lord Admiral, can you imagine
That we are past all fear, or hope of Mercy,
That there's no Conscience, no regard of Vows,
No Grace, no Reverence, fear of Heav'n, nor Hell,
Nor common Care of Fame, ev'n in this World?

*King* To Bed, to Bed; let me intreat you rest.

*Q. M.* Nay, you shall go, my Lord, supported thus

Betwixt your Bosom-Friends Believe me, Sir,
This is not feign'd; there are not two alive
That love you more, than those that now sustain you.
*Adm.* Is't possible? Why, if it were dissembled,
The very Counterfeit of such a Friendship
Were worth a dying for. Alas, my Lord!
O, Madam! Why, why must this Trouble be!
But lead me, lead your poor old Admiral,
Blind with his Tears, and faint with his Blood:
If I do well again, I'll thank you, Sir,
I'll thank you in the Field; O, grant it, Heav'n,
That I may end where no Assassins are,
And fall a Victim in the glorious War. [*Exeunt.*

## SCENE III.

*Enter* Guise, Aumale, Elbeuf, Angolesme, *with* Parisians.

*Gui* Look you, my Lords, this is the Royal Order;
The Dukes of *Nevers* and *Monpensier*
Must wait to guard the Person of the King,
With all the Royal Regiment in Arms:
Haste, for the Day begins to wear apace.
*An El.* We obey. [*Exeunt ambo.*
*Gui* President, *Charton*, Provost *de Merchand*,
The Head of the *Parisians.*
*Prov* Here, my Lord.
*Gui.* Provide two thousand Men compleatly arm'd;
Let each particular Man, on his left Arm
Wear a Shirt-sleeve, and a white Cross in's Hat,
That, upon notice given, all may be ready
To execute his Majesty's Commands:
The *Eschevins* of every several Ward
See in just Order and precisely set,
That upon ringing the Palace-Bell,
Lights may be put directly on the instant
In every Window all throughout the Town.
*Prov.* It shall be done. [*Exit.*
*Gui* My Lord, Grand Prior,
With what Commanders we can raise, be ready
To take the Admiral's Life. But see the Queen!

Enter

*Enter* Queen Mother, Cardinal, Anjou.

*Q. M.* Come, come, my Lords, let's lose no longer [time,
The *Hugonots* proceed not to a Tumult,
But only vent their Fury in high Words;
Therefore away My Lord of *Guise*, your Father
Looks from the Clouds, and cries, Revenge, Revenge.
I think 'twere better too, while you kill the Admiral,
The King's Grand Provost should pursue his Wife.

*Gui* The old gray Sire, the Dam, and little Babes,
I'll take 'em all together in the Nest,
And pash 'em till they Sprawl. You and the Cardinal
Haste to the *Louvre*, when the Gates are shut,
Call the chief *Hugonots* down, and cut their Throats.
My Lord, the Duke of *Anjou*, to your Care
The King commits the City: So Farewell·
There wants no more but ringing of the Bell.

[*Exeunt severally*

## SCENE *The City.*

*Lights in the Windows The President marches his Men over the Stage. The Bell of the Palace rings out*

*Enter* Admiral *in his Night-Gown.*

*Adm* The Palace Bell rings out, loud Cries of Murder,
Guns fir'd, and groans of dying Men below;
The King has giv'n his Warrant for my last;
His Vows, his Oaths, and Altar-Obligations
Are lost: the Wax of all those sacred Bonds
Runs at the Queen's Revenge, the Fire that melts 'em.
They are no more: The Admiral's no more.

*Enter* Cavagnes *bleeding.*

*Cav.* My Lord, God calls us; Death is in the Court:
Fate, in the shape of *Guise*, all over Blood.
I saw your Son-in-Law *Teligny* die,
*Roura*, the Son of Baron *de Atrets*,
With Colonel *Montaumar*, Gallant *Guercby*,
Wrapping his Cloak about his Arm, fought on
Till he was all one Wound, and so expir'd:
But hark, they come'

Adm

*Adm.* Why, let 'em, let 'em come;
We shall ere long, my Friend, be worth their Envy:
To die thus for Religion, O, *Cavagnes*,
It puts the Soul in everlasting Tune,
And sounds already in the Ears of Angels!
And, O, what Cause had ever such Foundation!
I tell thee that the Root shall reach the Center,
Spread to the Poles, and with her Top touch Heav'n.
But see, they come: Stand fixt, and look on Death
With such Contempt, so masterly an Eye,
As if he were thy Slave

*Enter* Besme, Sartabons, *four Soldiers.*

*Besm.* See where he stands! ha, Slaves, what makes you pause? [him.
*1 Sold.* Kill him your self, for my part I'll not touch
*2 Sold.* Nor I: For my part I am sorry for what is done [already.
*Adm.* Cowards indeed! thus to be terrified
Ev'n with the shadow of the Admiral.
*Besm.* It goes against me, yet I must obey:
Sheath all your Daggers in the Traitor's Breast
*Adm.* Young Man, thou oughtest to reverence these gray Hairs,
But I command thee, do as thou art order'd,
Thou'lt cut but little from the Line of Life. [Children.
*Besm.* Die then, die both: Now for his Wife and
[*Stabs both, and Exeunt.*
*Adm.* Heard'st thou, *Cavagnes*? said they not my Children?
*Cav.* I know not what you say; the stroak of Death
Has stunn'd my sense of Hearing.
*Adm.* Yet let's crawl
With all our Wounds into each others Arms,
And Hand in Hand go Martyr'd thus to Heav'n.
*Cav.* I am gone, farewel. [*Dies.*
*Adm.* Why dost thou shudder thus,
And gasp upon my Bosom? 'Twas his last;
My Soul so likes her House, she's loth to part;
But, O what Builder can repair the Ruins?
The Lights are choak'd, the Windows are dam'd up,
The main Beams crack, and the Foundation sinks;
Besides, the Lordly Owner warns me forth:

I

I come, great Master of the World and me,
And, O! Revenge, revenge thy Peoples Blood.
A hundred thousand Sou's for Justice call;
Let not the guiltless without Vengeance fall. [*Dies.*

*Enter the Duke of* Guise *and Souldiers.*

*Gui* So, fling him down, down with him to the Court,
Expose his Carcass to the Peoples Mercy,
Drag him away, and hurl him from the Window:
See all his Bastards strangled on the Spot,
There's Orders for't. The *Hostel de Chastillon*
Be raz'd for ever, his Posterity
Be made incapable of bearing Office,
Or being Noble; burn his Statue, haste·
There's a Commission granted for the deed,
Nay, kill, as if 'twere Sport to see 'em bleed. [*Exeunt.*

## SCENA ULTIMA. *The* Louvre.

*Queen Mother, Cardinal, Duke of* Anjou, *Colonel* D'O.

*Q. M.* Here Colonel, bring forth your Prisoners,
And let me see these Leaders of the Faction.

*The Scene draws, showing the Commanders standing with their hands ty'd behind 'em betwixt the Souldiers in a rank. The Count de* Rochfaucalt, *Marquis de* Renel, Piles, Pluvialt, Pardillan, *and* Lavardin.

Give the Word, Colonel.

*D'O.* Fire on 'em all. [*Shoot.*

[*The Scene draws, and shews the Admiral's Body burning.*

*Gui.* I saw the Master Villain dragg'd along
To Execution, by the common People,
Who from the Shoulders tore the mangled Head,
Cut off his Hands, and at *Mountfaucon* hung him,
Half burning, by one Leg upon the Gallows.

*Enter King, Princes, and* Alberto Gondi

*King.* O horror! horror! O thou cruel *Guise*!
O Mother! Brother! and thou Murd'ring Priest!
Dost thou not blush to sail in Seas of Ruin,
To hang the Flag of a Damn'd Pyrat forth,
Yet call thy bloody Bark the Christian Church?

Or,

Or, tell me, Canst thou lay the Furies here,
Pale *Hugonots* that haunt me up and down
Through Chambers, into Closets, Beds, and Couches?
Or dar'st thou shield me, when the Admiral's Ghost
Claps to my Heart the Dagger of my Word!
*Q. M.* Why are you thus?
*King* The Angel's Words are true,
And *Charles* is near his End. O Mother! Mother!
Hear my last Words, and take my dying Counsel,
Stop the vast Murder that you have begun;
For know, all Churches by Decree and Doctrine,
Kings by their Sword and Balance of their Justice,
All Learning, Christian, Moral, and Prophane,
Shall by the virtue of their Mercury Rod
For ever damn to Hell those curs'd designs
That with Religion's Face to Ruin tend,
And go by Heav'n to reach the blackest end. [*Ex. Omnes.*

---

# EPILOGUE.

By Mr. *Powel.*

*HOW wise are they, that can with Patience bear,*
*And just Reflections moderately hear,*
*Unmov'd by Passion, as unsway'd by Fear?*
*To them we Dedicate this Play to Night,*
*That having long been Banish'd from the Light,*
*Hush'd and Imprison'd close, as in the Tow'r,*
*Half press'd to Death by a Dispensing Pow'r;*
*To take a lawful Tryal for each Fact,*
*Is just come out by th'* Habeas Corpus *Act*
Rome's *Friends, no doubt, suppos'd there might be shown*
*Just such an Entertainment of their own,*
*The Plot, the Protestants, the Stage, the Town.*
*But no such fear our* Hugonots *allarm'd.*
*True* English *Hearts are allways better Arm'd.*
*For if the Valiant in a little Town,*
*Batter'd and Starving, their brave Cause durst own;*

*If*

# EPILOGUE.

If Peaſants ſcorning Death, can Guard our Walls,
And the mild Prieſthood turn to Generals,
Britains ſtand firm, and in ſhort time you'll ſee,
Your own and Neighbouring Realms ſerene and free,
Clear'd from the choaking Fogs of Popery.
No Maſſacres, nor Revolutions fear;
Affairs are ſtrangely alter'd ſince laſt Year,
Infallibility himſelf does run,
The Garden's weeded, and the Moles are gone.
Not Gold to Lawyers, to th' Ambitious Power,
Not luſty Switzer to a luſtful Whore,
To Gameſters Luck, to Beauty length of Days,
Nor to a wrinkled wither'd Widow Praiſe,
Can give ſuch Joy, as to behold once more
An Engliſh Army on the Gallick Shore
That this will be, the Poets Propheſie;
The Poets all were Prophets formerly
T inſpire 'em then, give ours to Night his due,
His Tale is ſomewhat bloody, but 'tis true.
A Tragick Truth ſhown to an honeſt end,
And can the Good or Wiſe of neither Sect offend.
Fancy and Stile, far as the reſt excel,
In our Deliv'rance-Year, let no Tongue tell,
Poets the only curſt on whom no Manna fell.
Plead that they may by Cæſar's Influence breath,
And mix a Lawrel with his Oaken Wreath.
Then ſhall his Glory flouriſh to the height,
Then every Pen ſhall Panegyrick write
This, this was he, who bleſt by Sacred Pow'r,
To England its Religion did reſtore,
So firm, that Rome cou'd never hurt it more

FINIS.

Lightning Source UK Ltd.
Milton Keynes UK
UKOW012332150512

192643UK00006BD/19/P